Moguls and Iron Men

The Story of the

First Transcontinental

Railroad

by James McCague

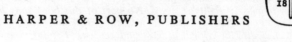

HARPER & ROW, PUBLISHERS

NEW YORK, EVANSTON, AND LONDON

Moguls and Iron Men

To the memory of
Rogers Terrill,
my agent, mentor and, above all,
good friend

CONTENTS

Part Three

The Racing Iron; a Scrambling of Titans

Part Four

The Golden Spike; and Afterward

Epilogue

Recriminations; Scandal; the Public Betrayed?

MAPS

There are sixteen pages of illustrations following page 148.

ACKNOWLEDGMENTS

I am sure that no researcher into times past ever proceeded very far without coming to feel a deep sense of gratitude for libraries, and for those knowledgeable and often dedicated people who serve history so well by keeping alive the records of the men—great and humble, heroes and scamps—who made it.

For this chronicle of the Great Pacific Railroad special thanks are due the directors and staffs of the Library of Congress and the National Archives, Washington, D.C.; the New York City Public Library; the Newberry Library in Chicago; the Union Pacific Historical Museum, Omaha; the Nebraska State Historical Society; the California Historical Society; the Utah State Historical Society; the Bancroft Library of the University of California at Berkeley; and the Stanford Collection, the Stanford Libraries, Leland Stanford University.

Edwin C. Shafer, Director of Public Relations, the Union Pacific Railroad Company, and J. G. Shea, General Public Relations Manager of the Southern Pacific Company, graciously furnished much valuable material on the early beginnings of their organizations. I am indebted also to Howell-North Books, Berkeley, California, for permission to quote from their reprint of *A History of Sacramento County, California;* and to the University of Nebraska Press at Lincoln for permission to quote some of the observations of pioneer James H. Kyner from *End of Track*. Not to be overlooked, either, is the excellent work done by my two student researchers, Thomas Havens and Everett N. Dahl, Jr.

Finally, my compliments and thanks to a whole, long-dead generation of journalists whose earnest pens immortalized the flavor of roaring times and epic strivings the likes of which America will never see again.

PART ONE

The Dreamers; the Doers;
the Congress; and Mr. Lincoln

CHAPTER 1

WASHINGTON, 1860

He was a visionary, undoubtedly a fanatic, and so single-minded that many people back in California had called him crazy, though no one would notice that amid the greater madness running riot in Washington that winter of 1859 and '60. His name was Theodore Dehone Judah. He was a civil engineer, a builder of railroads, and the business which brought him to the nation's capital was the Great Pacific Railroad, the mighty transcontinental to link the Atlantic seaboard with the Pacific littoral. It was an old dream that had begun within two years after the first steam-powered train in America lumbered down channel-iron rails behind an upright-boilered monster called the *Best Friend of Charleston*. Nearly thirty years had passed since then, and many men had given up their lives and their substances to the dream, as Theodore Judah now was giving his.

For years he had preached both the need and the feasibility of a transcontinental railroad, almost always as a prophet without honor, though no man ever had better credentials. A native New Englander, trained as a civil engineer by two years at New York State's Rensselaer Polytechnic Institute, he had gone to work as a surveyor's assistant on the Schenectady and Troy Railroad at thirteen years of age. He had risen in the profession with unusual swiftness: worked as an associate engineer on the famed Erie Canal, helped survey and build various railroads in New York and New England. In 1854 he had gone out to California to survey and supervise construction of the Sacramento Valley Railroad, a twenty-one-mile short line from Sacramento to the placer mining town of Folsom. He was only twenty-seven then, but already possessed of so impressive a reputation that Governor Horatio Seymour of New York had personally recommended him for the position.

Not a rail had been laid anywhere on the Pacific Coast at the time, nor a locomotive whistle ever been heard. Judah had pushed the pioneering

Sacramento Valley to completion in '55, and stayed on to promote the Great Pacific Railroad. Somewhere along the line the idea had taken root in his imagination, and was never to let go for the rest of his life. In the four years that followed he had had a hand in many ambitious little railroad surveys that started out with scant cash and high hopes from San Francisco or Sacramento to the California hinterlands. He had seen them all as opening links in the mighty transcontinental chain. But none of them had amounted to anything. Crazy Judah: the name, applied in derision by hard-headed businessmen bored with listening to him, had stuck.

But other dreamers had rallied around him. Now he was in Washington as the accredited agent of the Pacific Railroad Convention of San Francisco, created by act of the California legislature with delegates from every city and county in the state for the express purpose of settling on a plan for the construction of a transcontinental railroad and urging it upon the Congress of the United States with the official backing of the people of California.

As an accomplishment, however, the Convention sounded more impressive than it actually was. Others had been doing that sort of thing for a long time. Another civil engineer, John Plumbe, had called the first such meeting to order in Dubuque, Iowa, as far back as 1838. A whole host of similar state conventions had sent their agents to Washington during the years that followed. A wealthy New York merchant named Asa Whitney had spent a fortune promoting a series of transcontinental railroad plans in the decade after 1840, and achieved only bitter frustration as a result. Regularly since '52 Pacific Railroad bills had been introduced in Congress, proposing to grant lands and subsidies, even to appropriate outright sums as large as ninety million dollars for construction. None of them had passed, and without Congressional help no one had progressed very far toward the transcontinental goal.

This fall of '59, the great Mississippi River was bridged by only a single railroad in all its sprawling length. The Chicago and Rock Island had accomplished that, between Rock Island, Illinois, and Davenport, Iowa, in '53. But after two disastrous collisions with the bridge piers, steamboat operators had sued to force the span's removal as a public nuisance. Lower courts in Iowa had ruled in their favor, despite the best efforts of a shrewd railroad attorney from Illinois by the name of Abraham Lincoln, and now an appeal was pending in the United States Supreme Court. Meanwhile, the discouraged Rock Island had pushed its railhead only a short way beyond Davenport. A little farther south the Hannibal and St. Joseph Railroad had built westward from the Mississippi to the east bank of the Missouri River. And out of St. Louis two organizations, both calling themselves Pacific Railroad companies, had been struggling across Missouri for several years, and making only slow, sporadic work of it.[1]* No other rails had as yet been laid beyond the Mississippi.

The past, then, had not been very productive. As for the present and the future, Judah was an intelligent, well-informed man, whatever else people said of him. He could hardly have installed himself and his wife in their boarding-house on Fourteenth Street near the Potomac flats before he realized that the portents in Washington held out scant hope of success.

It would be an election year, 1860. And, as usual, the nation found itself racked on the slavery issue, that recurrent illness which had been flaring up ever more virulently since the '40's.

Congress convened in the waning days of 1859, less than a week after the hanging of John Brown of Osawatomie. Already Abolitionists were hailing the old man as a martyr, while Southerners refused to be convinced that the incident at Harpers Ferry had not been the opening gambit in a Northern plot to incite widespread slave rebellion. The Democratic Party threatened to split between moderates and extremist Southerners; if that happened and the upstart, slavery-hating, nigger-loving Republicans won the White House as a result, Southern hotheads predicted that a tidal wave of secession would sweep the cotton states. Sentiment for disunion thrived openly in Washington, few Southern Congressmen bothering to hide their Secesh sympathies; even Cabinet members were involved in backstairs plots or rumors of plots against their government. Aging, ailing General Winfield Scott, Mexican War hero and foremost soldier in the nation, had been called to the capital out of semi-retirement, and as his first piece of advice to President Buchanan had recommended strengthening the Southern forts against the possibility of surprise attack.

It had not been done, however, and would not be. Secretary of War John B. Floyd was an ardent states' rights Virginian and James Buchanan himself, at sixty-nine, was an old and tired man, worn out by the fierce factionalism that raged about him. Nominated by the Democrats and elected as a compromise candidate acceptable to both Southern slavery men and Northern free-soilers, he had ended as men who try to please both sides commonly do: trusted and liked by neither. Because he had spoken out against secession, Southern extremists were accusing him of treachery. But because his strict, legalistic mind could not sanction the prevention of secession by force, uncompromising Northerners hinted that he was guilty of something close to treason. Now, frustrated and disillusioned, he was riding out the remainder of his term, anxious only to preserve the status quo till the prickly problem could be handed along to his successor.

* Superior numbers refer to a section of notes beginning on page 367.

The historian Henry Adams, then a young man of twenty-two, was in town that winter. "An education in treason," he called it, and remarked on "the singular spectacle of a government trying to destroy itself."[2]

In such a murky, storm-roiled atmosphere, few Congressmen were likely to concern themselves with the tedious details of a Pacific Railroad Act. But Theodore Judah was an optimist with the tough-minded kind of dedication to which obstacles hardly mattered. And he was not without influential allies.

On the steamer out of San Francisco for the Isthmus of Panama he had made the acquaintance of John C. Burch, newly elected to the House of Representatives from California, and General Joseph Lane, Senator from the new state of Oregon. It had been a particularly lucky circumstance, for the Isthmian trip was a long, tedious one and a good object lesson in itself on the need for a faster way between West and East. By Pacific Mail steamer from San Francisco down the coasts of Lower California and Central America to Panama City was a fourteen-day run. The land crossing of the Isthmus was short and even pleasant, thanks to a railroad built in 1855 by American shipping interests—it was always a railroad when shippers thought in terms of faster, surer transport; Judah, undoubtedly, did not neglect to make the point —but Aspinwall, the terminal port on the Caribbean, was a steamy, fever-ridden hole.[3] And from there the traveler had still to endure a long sea voyage to Havana, Cuba, and thence northward up the Atlantic to New York. The whole trip ran to five or six weeks even in the best of weather, no small slice out of a busy man's year. The Pacific Mail steamers, side-wheelers rigged with full spreads of sail for auxiliary power, like practically all seagoing steamships of the period, were generally large and well-found vessels, ably officered by men with U.S. Naval training and providing a high degree of passenger comfort. But the Atlantic was a fractious, ill-behaved ocean, and the passage had its perils. The *Central America* had foundered in a Cape Hatteras gale in '57, taking 424 people and some two million dollars in California gold to the bottom; a memorable disaster that had helped to spur agitation for the Pacific Railroad at the time, and still was far from forgotten.

Yet this Isthmian passage was the best there was. Other steamship lines provided service on the route and there was another land crossing farther north, through Nicaragua, but it was longer and there was no railroad.

Clipper ships still plied around Cape Horn between San Francisco and New York or Boston, but that route was seventeen thousand miles long, and old "Cape Stiff" was notorious for storm, fog and contrary winds. In '53 the *Northern Light* had made the run from San Francisco to Boston in seventy-six days and six hours, and the following year Donald McKay's famed *Flying Cloud* had hung up a New York–San Francisco mark of eighty-nine days, eight hours. But these were record runs by flash packets. The normal time was a hundred days or more—frequently much more. And now the great days of the clipper ship were about over, anyway. Steam was taking over on the seas and economic considerations made cargo capacity more important than mere speed. Nowadays the newer Cape Horners tended to be less fine-lined in design, and their owners had to content themselves, more and more, with ladings of low-cost freight and third-class passengers who could afford nothing better.

For confirmed landlubbers, of course, there were the sturdy Concord stages of the Butterfield Overland Mail Company. The service was operated on a twice-a-week schedule each way between San Francisco and Tipton, in central Missouri, over a route that dipped far southward through Texas, New Mexico Territory and southern California. The elapsed time was a fairly reliable twenty-four days. But it was a rough and comfortless ride. The traveler sweltered in gritty desert heat, shivered in mountain cold and snow, fretted over the always-present danger of raids by Kiowa, Comanche or Apache war parties. Food and accommodations at the lonely little way stations en route were strictly primitive, and space for the passengers' personal baggage was limited. Hardy souls in a hurry and traveling light found the service adequate, but scarcely more than that.

What all this boiled down to was the fact that there existed no really fast, wholly satisfactory way across the vast breadth of the United States. In that lay the true crux of the case for the Pacific Railroad. And Theodore Judah, never one to shun opportunity when it came knocking, must have pleaded the case well.

He won John Burch completely. By the time they debarked at New York, the California Congressman-elect had promised to help in the drafting of a transcontinental railroad bill, and to introduce it on the floor of the House. And in Washington, Judah knew, were other supporters, men whose interest in the Pacific Railroad was sincere and of long standing. Senator William Gwin of California was one. Representative Samuel R. Curtis of Iowa was a long-time backer, and had been named in '58 to the chairmanship of the House Select Committee on the Pacific Railroad, a body appointed for the specific purpose of studying the subject and reporting out a bill. Assuredly, Curtis would be a strong captain for the cause. There were other hard-core supporters.

And there were the many—the very great many—who gave lip service to the project. Over the years, public sentiment in favor of a transcontinental rail line had grown to such a pitch that candidates for elective offices long ago had adopted the policy of endorsing the idea in principle, in much the same manner as indifferent church members declared their opposition to sin. Their votes, though, on any given measure, were apt to be swayed by party politics, selfish local interests back home, any of a dozen other extraneous considerations. Of this, too, Judah was aware.

For all his rugged optimism he saw the difficulties clearly. He had been in Washington before, in the fall of '56. He had stated the problem then. "It [the Pacific Railroad] cannot be done until the route is defined," he had written in a pamphlet published at his own expense early in '57, "and if defined the opposing interest is strong enough to defeat it."[4]

The trouble was, as it always had been, the all-engulfing slavery issue that touched and twisted every Congressional debate. The overriding controversy was not at that time whether the slave should be freed or remain in bondage, but rather the extension of free-soil versus slave territory. If the Pacific Railroad's eastern terminus should be placed in the South, then it followed that the new lands it opened to settlement would be pre-empted, in the main, by men of proslavery convictions. By the same logic a railroad originating in the North would mean new free-soil territories. In time territories would become states—the thing had lately been demonstrated in poor, bleeding Kansas—and new states meant control of Congress and domination of the national government. It was as starkly simple as that, and political leaders on both sides understood it perfectly.

Angry Southerners had seen Kansas snatched from their camp at the last moment. "Stolen by free-soil emigration!" they cried, and were in no mood to invite further reverses by voting for any transcontinental rail line with its roots outside of what was being spoken of already as a "Southern Confederacy." Abolitionists and business interests in the North—where Pacific Railroad sentiment was strongest, by and large—were no less adamant. In such a situation it was not conceivable that either side could yield.

It soon became apparent to Judah that the deadlock was even more bitter now than it had been in '56. But he had come to do a job, and he meant to try. He became a familiar figure in Washington during those portentous early months of 1860, and most of the people who met him were impressed.

Surviving photographs show a handsome, impeccably groomed young man (he was then thirty-four) of medium height, with dark, curly hair and a thick, dark beard trimmed somewhat more neatly than many in that era. The expression caught by the old wet-plate cameras suggests a subtle air of persistence, even of quiet doggedness. He does not look like a man who would give up easily, and he was not. The fanatic was not very evident behind so engaging a façade. But he was there.

Crazy Judah or not, this was a man with charm and magnetism. He knew how to meet people, and he could talk.

"His knowledge of his subject was so thorough," his new friend, Burch, wrote of him afterward, "his manners so gentle and insinuating, his conversation on the subject [of the Pacific Railroad] so entertaining, that few resisted his appeals."[5]

He managed an appointment with President Buchanan himself, and outlined his ideas to that courtly, gracious gentleman. No doubt the interview was pleasant, for the President had gone on record early in his administration with an endorsement of a railroad to the Pacific, calling it a necessary and vital tie to bind the Western seaboard to the Union. There was no active help to be had at the Executive Mansion now, though; James Buchanan wanted no part of anything controversial.

An introduction to the influential John A. Logan of Illinois, chairman of the House subcommittee on incidental expenses, proved more fruitful. Logan liked Judah, and was happy to exert the pressure necessary to have a room in the unfinished Capitol turned over to him. Here—there was a bit of the showman in Judah, too—he set up a public exhibition and called it the Pacific Railroad Museum. To supplement the maps, pictures and samples of natural wonders he had brought from California, he raided government archives and the Library of Congress for anything and everything in the way of exhibits that conceivably might dramatize the subject of iron rails spanning the continent. The place was an instant success. For weeks Congressmen, government clerks and department heads, fellow engineers, journalists, railroad enthusiasts, promoters, cranks and plain citizens on the grand tour flocked in to satisfy their respective curiosities and to listen for a spell to the intense young zealot who talked more convincingly than any medicine show professor, and mustered platoons of facts, figures and professional know-how to buttress his every statement.

He was gratified by this sign of the widespread interest in the Pacific Railroad.

His energy and determination spilled over in all directions. When activities in Washington permitted, or perhaps when the endless dickering for influential help at Willard's bar or the crowded dining rooms of Brown's or the Kirkwood or the National palled, he found the time and the funds to carry his message as far afield as New York City and Chicago. He made a point of bringing himself up to date on every new development in his own field of railroad engineering and construction. He became very interested in the Baltimore and Ohio, first railroad to cross the Appalachian Mountains; the solutions to problems its builders had met and mastered there would prove useful when the time came for his own railroad to challenge the Rockies and the Sierra Nevada.

In between trips and long days at the Capitol, the lamp burned late in the rooms on Fourteenth Street while he pored over plans and mapped strategy with this or that ally in the cause.

And none of it—the feverish activity and the hard work; the Pacific Railroad Museum; the loyal friends—came to anything. The transcontinental railroad was a very small straw in the gale blowing up along the Potomac that winter and spring of 1860.

In February Jefferson Davis arose in the Senate to state the only terms on which the South would consent to remain in the Union. No Northerner could find them acceptable. In both houses of Congress factional strife erupted in furious exchanges of bad temper. Insults and challenges to duels were flung across the aisles. Some members, the fire-eaters or the merely fearful, took to carrying loaded pistols to their desks. Legislation of all kinds bogged down and sank out of sight, hopelessly mired in the morass of cross purposes and vituperation. Summer's approach brought Washington's famed heat and mugginess to frazzle tempers even more. Thus the Congress bickered its dismal way toward adjournment. The House bill on which Judah and Burch had labored died in committee. Gwin of California had managed to introduce a compromise railroad bill in the Senate; it was passed over until the next session.

There was no reason for supposing its fate would be any better then.

And so it ended. Resignedly Judah closed his Pacific Railroad Museum, made out his report to the San Francisco Convention and packed his bags. Almost a year of his time had been spent on the Convention's mission, and a great deal more of his own money than he could afford. Yet the expense account he submitted contained just two items:

For printing bill and circular in New York $20.00
For printing bill and circular in Washington 20.00
Total .... $40.00[6]

Industrious, capable, resourceful; these were words various people who knew him had used in describing Theodore Judah. Some had added other, less complimentary ones: humorless, opinionated. There was another friends and enemies alike could have agreed on:

Selfless.

He had made two trips to Washington now, suffered two failures. But he was not yet ready to concede defeat. Away from the demoralizing atmosphere of "a government trying," in young Henry Adams' words, "to destroy itself," the long view—the epic outline of the Great Pacific Railroad—could come clear again. No doubt he was glad to be leaving Washington. But he knew he would be back.

More facts were needed, he told Anna, his wife. Maps, actual profiles, dollars-and-cents cost figures—all the hard, concrete answers needed to convince even men of no vision. He would get them. New arguments would have to be devised and put forward. He would do that, too.

Anna had been with him everywhere, ever since their marriage long before, when he had been a rising young civil engineer with a growing reputation in the fascinating young business of railroad building. They might have settled down to a life of staid success in the serene and well-ordered East. But it had not worked out that way. When her husband had dropped everything and gone out to California in '54 to accept the flattering offer from the backers of the little Sacramento Valley, Anna had swallowed her doubts and gone along without protest. He had told her once, in bantering affection, that she "always seemed to have the right pair of gaiters on" to keep up with him. The remark, and much else of the man's thoughts and feelings during the long struggle to make the Pacific Railroad a reality, were recorded in the letters in which, years later, she recalled their life together.[7]

"Oh how we used to talk it over and over on the steamer enroute to California in July," she wrote of that voyage home.

MR. JUDAH'S RAILROAD

The series of government explorations authorized in an amendment by Senators Salmon P. Chase of Ohio and William Gwin of California to the Army Appropriations Act of 1853, and popularly known as the Pacific Railroad Surveys, had laid out no fewer than five possible routes that might be followed by railroads between the Mississippi River and the Pacific, and each soon had its ardent clique of supporters.

The most northerly, called in fact the Northern Route, followed the forty-seventh and forty-ninth parallels of north latitude from St. Paul, Minnesota, across the plains of the upper Missouri River Valley and through the Rocky Mountains to Seattle in Washington Territory. The Central Route ran along the forty-first and forty-second parallels up the Platte Valley and then through Utah and Nevada Territories by way of Great Salt Lake into northern California and down to San Francisco. A third route, christened the Buffalo Trail by Senator Thomas Hart Benton of Missouri, its principal champion, proceeded by way of the thirty-eighth and thirty-ninth parallels over the Great Plains and through Colorado Territory; and numbers four and five, the Southern Routes, took the thirty-fifth and thirty-second parallels, respectively, into southern California and thence by various ways to San Francisco.

While such a multiplicity of choices could only intensify the already irreconcilable sectional rivalries in Congress, the actual explorations were carried out ably and with comparative thoroughness under the direction of then Secretary of War Jefferson Davis. Taken in the aggregate they comprised the most ambitious scientific examination of the vast and almost unknown lands beyond the Mississippi yet undertaken. The reports, published in 1857 in a set of eleven impressive quarto volumes, included maps, elevations, lithographs and engravings illustrating geographic features of the regions traversed in great detail, and a wealth of additional information covering everything from bird, animal and plant life to mineral deposits, soil fertility or the lack of it and prevailing weather conditions. The Army engineers had added even their estimates of probable railroad construction costs, ranging from a high of $140,871,000 for the Northern Route to a low of $68,000,000 for the extreme southern—a disparity which had led to some subsequent murmurs in the North that Jeff Davis was playing politics with the reports.

The glaring lack in the whole project, however, had been promptly spotted and pointed out by Theodore Judah. No qualified railroad engineer had accompanied any of the expeditions in the field, and the so-called surveys were not really surveys at all, but only reconnaissances which made no serious efforts to fix specific and practicable rights of way. The several Army groups engaged in the work had suffered difficulties and in some cases extreme hardships—one party being massacred by hostile Indians at Sevier Lake, Nevada—and large sections of all the routes were covered only sketchily. Congressman Burch, undoubtedly reflecting Judah's opinion, was openly scornful of the reports. Nevertheless, they represented the kind of basic endeavor that had had to be done, and like everything else pertaining to the Pacific Railroad they had engaged the young engineer's careful attention.

Of the five routes, the Central had a number of advantages tending to give it somewhat more appeal to the public mind than any of the others. Starting out along the Platte River as it did, it was traversing a region through which trails already had been beaten out by the early Mormons, and by the great waves of emigrants heading for Oregon and California all through the '40's and '50's.

The Northern Route, starting in Minnesota—still largely a thinly settled wilderness—attracted only limited local backing. The Buffalo Trail, according to Army engineers, was the least practicable of all. The route along the thirty-fifth parallel did, indeed, follow the storied old Santa Fe Trail for much of the way, but this main thoroughfare to the Southwest had been of early interest chiefly to traders and mountain men seeking commerce with the Mexicans and the Indian tribes of the region; comparatively few emigrants bound through to the Pacific used it as yet. And the southernmost route was handicapped by the fact that the South as a whole was neither so deeply interested in a transcontinental railroad nor so generally railroad-conscious as the more industrialized North.

In addition, as Judah probably had learned in Washington, Pacific Railroad sentiment was especially active in Iowa. It was no accident that Samuel Curtis of that state occupied the chair of the House Select Committee on the Pacific Railroad. There were good and logical reasons. Chicago already was beginning to look like the coming railroad center of the Midwest; most of the little lines that had reached out to the east bank of the Mississippi had done so through Illinois, just across the river from the Hawkeye State. And at Iowa's western boundary the town of Council Bluffs, on the Missouri River, had long been prominent as a main outfitting center and jumping-off place for emigrant trains outbound to the promised lands. Railroad promoters, notably two partners named Henry Farnum and Dr. Thomas C. Durant, had been thinking in terms of surveys from the Mississippi to Council Bluffs as early as 1852, and in '53, the same year the Pacific Railroad Surveys were authorized, the pair had dispatched a young engineer by the name of Grenville M. Dodge to look into the prospects for extending a line westward into Nebraska Territory.

Their company, the Mississippi and Missouri, projected as an extension of the Chicago and Rock Island Railroad, eventually had faltered to a halt amid hard times and short finances, but not before they, like Judah and others before them, had been bitten by the transcontinental bug. As a sort of investment in the future they kept young Dodge at work on his assignment, and even sent him far out past the western reaches of Nebraska. In time, partly as a result of his own explorations and partly from interviews with Mormon scouts, mountain men, fur traders and wagon masters, Dodge mapped out and made up an itinerary for a travel route all the way through to Utah, California and Oregon. It seems to have been a very thorough and painstaking job, complete with suggestions as to the best campsites, water holes and the availability of wood and game along the way. And because supplying the emigrant traffic had grown to be a lucrative business and there was keen rivalry for control of the routes—Kansas City, Fort Leavenworth and St. Joseph, Missouri, all competing hard for the lion's share of it—businessmen at Council Bluffs had published Dodge's itinerary and circulated it widely.

All of this helped to lend the Central Route an air of practicability, of essential familiarity.

Even more to the point, as Judah saw it, the Central Route entered northern and not southern California, and thus matched his own convictions regarding the best western approach for a transcontinental rail line. The Pacific Railroad Convention of San Francisco had placed itself on record as favoring this route—for whatever that was worth—and all of his late efforts in Washington had been bent in that direction. There was, in fact, a kind of reverse advantage, as Judah no doubt perceived, in promoting the railroad's construction from the West. In spite of the Northern Route's projected end at Seattle, there could be no serious argument over the location of a western terminal. The nod had to go to San Francisco, hands down.

Since the days of '49, no other city on the Pacific littoral compared with it in size, vigor or favorable situation. As the port of entry for the gold-hungry hordes swarming around Cape Horn and over the Isthmus, it had swelled from a village of some eight hundred-odd to a seething metropolis of several hundreds of thousands almost literally overnight. And from that initial impetus San Francisco continued to grow and flourish like the green bay tree, spreading from the waterfront up its steep hills in tiers and clots of jostling frame buildings. Five times it had burned to the ground and five times sprung phoenix-like from the ashes, each time bigger and brawnier than the last.

The old, wild days of vigilante justice were past now, but not too long past; the last great outbreak of lawlessness had been put down as recently as '51. San Francisco still was a lusty, full-blooded youth of a city, famed in all the seaports of the world for its Barbary Coast along Pacific Street, and the raffish, robust sin that prospered there. But growth had brought solid commercial attainments and sober financial responsibility, too. The city had its first-generation millionaires and its capitalists and mercantile and shipping magnates in busy offices along the board sidewalks of Market and Montgomery streets. Darius Ogden Mills and William Ralston soon would launch their Bank of California, and it would grow to be a power in the state. The tall windjammers that beat around Cape Horn from the Eastern seaboard frequently sailed from San Francisco for China or East Indian ports and back again before heading out the Golden Gate for the ultimate voyage home. There was a thriving trade between the city and the Sandwich Islands and the western ports of South and Central America.

And with the Pacific Railroad to provide a fast, sure overland route to the Atlantic, all the tea and spices, the silks and ivory and jade of the Orient would pour in over the Embarcadero and on to the American East and the marts of Europe. This was the old dream of the first men who had advocated a transcontinental railroad, an extension of the ancient drive for a short route to the Indies that had sent out the ships of Christopher Columbus and the Cabots, Jacques Cartier and Martin Frobisher and Hendrik Hudson. . . .

The prospect was enough to ignite a less volatile imagination than Theodore Judah's.

Apparently he had decided on his next course of action by the time he and Anna arrived back in California. Theory and enthusiasm were not enough; he had found that out in Washington. No; he would have to locate and map an actual, workable railroad route up the Sacramento River Valley and over the Sierra Nevada Mountains. Only then, with the thing proved possible and practical, could the necessary financial backing for a Pacific Railroad be enlisted. It was a staggeringly ambitious project for a lone man to undertake, but he plunged into it with his customary vigor and assurance, leaving patient

Anna to spend the rest of the summer with friends in San Francisco and Sacramento.

As it turned out, he was tied up in the mountains a long time, mapping, surveying, using a barometer to determine elevations, covering an impressive amount of rough terrain in his search for that feasible passage which, stubbornly, he felt sure was there.

Building a railroad to the Sierra foothills involved no great problems. That had been done already, with the Sacramento Valley, and he had had a leading hand in it. Afterward, others had built little short-line railroads as well—the California Central, the Folsom and Lincoln—and there had been many surveys. Judah had worked on some of them also, familiarizing himself with the country and proving to his own satisfaction that any number of routes existed. Beyond the foothills, though, the mountains stood like snow-mantled titans; a very different proposition altogether.

The Sierra Nevadas were a high and precipitous range sprawled for more than four hundred miles across eastern California and only a little over a hundred inland from the shores of the Pacific, a gigantic wall shutting in the coastal regions. Many of the peaks rose above the fourteen-thousand-foot mark; even the passes hung from five to seven thousand and more above sea level. The Baltimore and Ohio Railroad, which Judah had so admired during his stay in the East, had had a much less formidable obstacle to surmount in the older, more eroded Appalachians. Moreover, thrusting up so abruptly into the skies, the Sierra Range formed a barrier to the prevailing winds off the Pacific, forcing them to dump their moisture in prodigious quantities of rain and snow on the western slopes. Great forests grew there, reaching far up toward the passes, and at the higher levels snow fell from early fall to late spring in accumulations of thirty feet and more. Their very name, the Sierra Nevadas, meant "the snowy mountains."

John C. Frémont, the Pathfinder, had encountered brutal hardships in getting his party over the Sierras on the Army expedition in '43, even with the famous Kit Carson as guide. Later the emigrants and the forty-niners had come through the main passes and established rude roads, and more recently the discovery of the Comstock Lode and the consequent silver boom in Nevada Territory had created a heavy freight and stage traffic eastward. So the barrier was not impassable.

But the flanged iron wheel rolling on iron rails needed far more room on curves and a longer, steadier gradient than multiple horse teams pulling Concord stages or freight wagons. For a railroad there were, and are, only two feasible ways through mountain country. It can follow the watercourses or it can take the ridges between them. On first examination, neither looked very promising in the High Sierras. The sharply rising slopes and the huge volume of rain and melting snows made of the rivers brawling torrents that had carved out deep, narrow and tortuous canyons offering no foothold for road-bed or rails. The ridges were steeply pitched, rugged and cut up by tangles of plunging ravines. No California railroad company had attempted such a route. It was assumed to be impossible, and no one but Judah had thought very seriously of trying.

Before the summer was over he began to understand why.

He looked into the possibilities of a line through Georgetown and Eldorado County. He traveled up through Henness Pass at the headwaters of the Yuba River. The figures he recorded in his notebook were discouraging. Then a Dr. Daniel Strong, proprietor of a drugstore in Dutch Flat, high up in the foothills in Placer County, some seventy miles northeast of Sacramento, got in touch with him and suggested he try the old Emigrant Trail through Donner Pass. Dutch Flat was a small and unimportant community, no more dis-tinguished than dozens of others that had begun as forty-niner camps, boomed feverishly to have their days as busy mining towns, then leveled off and slipped into slow decline as the gold deposits began to play out. The Emigrant Trail still existed as a road up through the mountains and down into Nevada, though not a main-traveled one any more.

Dr. Strong, no engineer, could offer little evidence in support of his sug-gestion. It might turn out to be only a wild-goose chase. But Judah was hardly in a position to scorn any fresh lead, and so as autumn began he was off on one more reconnaissance, this time with the willing druggist as guide and assistant.

Some of the earliest emigrants had made their way into California by this route. The Donner Party had been snowbound and suffered disaster here in '46, starvation forcing the survivors finally to cannibalism, to give the pass its name and an aura of grimness forever afterward. An early blizzard very nearly trapped Judah and Strong also. October had come by the time they struggled back to Dutch Flat. There, in Dr. Strong's store, Judah checked his data, and then rechecked it with a growing surge of excitement.

What the figures sketched out in his trained engineer's mind was a long, climbing spur that rose north of the upper American River and ran in a virtually unbroken line, like a massive flying buttress, clear to the summit approaches.

He had found his railroad route over the Sierras, he told the druggist.

Dr. Strong was not a railroad enthusiast. He had taken no active part in previous agitation for the Pacific Railroad and apparently, till now, had known Judah only by reputation. His original motive in contacting the engineer seems to have been a desire to help secure for his town a share in the rich traffic with the Nevada Washoe and he may even have been thinking, at first, in terms of another and better wagon road. But he was no more able than others had been to resist Judah's infectious fervor. The two men became good friends, and remained so from their first meeting.

Now, Daniel Strong found a clean sheet of paper and spread it out on his counter. And, so the story goes, Judah then and there drew up the *Articles of Association of the Central Pacific Railroad of California,* selecting that corporate title for its obvious tie-in with the Central Route. He and Strong were the first to sign for stock.

Under California law it was necessary that capital stock amounting to a thousand dollars per mile of railroad be subscribed before incorporation could take place, and it plainly was going to take many times that to put rails over the Sierras. But large sums of money never had daunted Theodore Judah. He had once estimated that the Great Pacific Railroad would cost $200,000 for surveys alone, plus another $75,000 per mile for two thousand miles of construction, and had stated his opinion, also, that private enterprise could finance the whole job without benefit of government subsidies.[1] Though he had changed his mind about the subsidies since then, that was for the present beside the point. He had his railroad now, if only on paper.

For the next few days the paper was circulated in Dutch Flat and a few neighboring towns, and enough local people of means were interested to bring total subscriptions to $46,500. (The job was made easier by the fact that only 10 percent had to be paid down upon signing.) Judah rolled up his *Articles of Association* and took the next stage for San Francisco, sure that the city would give him all the backing he needed in short order.

Presently Dr. Strong had a letter from him, repeating that assurance. He had, wrote Judah, gotten "one of the richest concerns in California into it."

Just what he meant, whom he had talked to and what they said, he seems never to have explained. Hints of an oddly secretive streak, a quality almost conspiratorial, show up in the man's character occasionally. Perhaps the representative of his "rich concern" had sworn him to silence, though it seems much more likely that his own aggressive optimism had led him to assume too much. For there is evidence, throughout his career, that Judah was prone to misjudge the California businessman of his time.

The great majority of the state's rank-and-file citizens were disillusioned gold-seekers who had come out in '49 or the years shortly afterward. Many of them had had no intention of settling permanently in California and now felt themselves stranded far from home and old friends. These were the people who ardently favored the Pacific Railroad, or indeed any other project that promised an easier, cheaper means of travel between California and the distant East. These too were the people, in the main, who had flocked as delegates to the San Francisco Convention, of recent memory. But they were not, by and large, people who controlled the dollars necessary to build the railroad Judah had in mind. The successful capitalist, on the other hand, tended to the local and the limited in his outlook. There still was a feeling abroad in the state that any enterprise not connected with the digging of precious metal out of the ground was not worth bothering with. And besides, realizing their isolation from the great Eastern trade and financial centers, businessmen in general were disposed to look for fast turnover and a quick profit when they invested. Long-range schemes, no matter how grandiose, seldom interested them.

And Judah, the visionary, almost certainly touted his new Central Pacific as the first link in the mighty transcontinental railroad that was nothing but a dream as yet. He had sung that song before, too many times. He was "Crazy Judah," the man nobody listened to.

Whatever the circumstances, if any promises actually were made by San Franciscans in high places, they were not kept. Whatever Theodore Judah had counted on, his hopes were blasted in a final meeting on Montgomery Street. Anna had waited up for him in their room at the Russ House. Later she recalled that he came back to her in bitter disappointment, predicting furiously that "not two years will go over the heads of these gentlemen but they will give up all they hope to have from their present enterprises to have what they put away tonight!"[2]

The Judahs left for Sacramento at once.

Interest in the railroad does not appear to have been very spontaneous there either. A meeting was held at the St. Charles Hotel, with only mildly encouraging results. A second one followed, much smaller this time, in a room above the establishment of Huntington, Hopkins and Company, hardware dealers, on K Street. Only a dozen persons attended, including Judah himself.

Dr. Strong was present, down from Dutch Flat for the occasion, accompanied by a B. F. Leete, a surveyor who had worked with Judah. There was another pair of railroad promoters, brothers by the name of Robinson, who had no connection with the Central Pacific; a Mr. Lucius Booth; James Bailey, a local jeweler and friend of Judah's; a Cornelius Cole, who would one day go to the U.S. Senate but was not then greatly prominent; a hulking, genial bear of a man in the drygoods business named Charles Crocker; the two hardware merchants from downstairs, Collis P. Huntington and Mark Hopkins; and finally—the group's closest approach to a man of affairs—a big, pompous, slow-spoken wholesale grocer by the name of Leland Stanford, who had done some dabbling in state politics and was even then seeking the Republican nomination for the governorship of California.

No one present saw any historic significance in the meeting and accounts of it are only fragmentary, from recollections put down in writing long afterward.

Judah unrolled his maps, spread out his sheets of figures and spoke, no doubt with his usual eloquence, outlining his proposed route from Sacramento through Dutch Flat and on over the Sierras, dwelling on the benefits to be gained with the fervent conviction that always marked his statements about the Great Pacific Railroad. But tonight there was a difference.

Perhaps his experience with the arrogant entrepreneurs of San Francisco had taught him shrewdness. Or perhaps Dr. Strong or James Bailey led him aside for a common-sense word or two of advice before the meeting. At any rate, he had little to say, according to those who listened and told the story later, of the continent-spanning aspects of his railroad. There was no panegyric on the glory, the patriotic acclaim and the rich future awaiting the men big enough and far-seeing enough to do the job. Instead, Judah dwelt almost exclusively on the local scene and the profit motive. He stressed the great commercial possibilities inherent in the Nevada Washoe, a bonanza that threatened to eclipse California itself in the wildest days of '49. He spoke of the hordes of silver-seekers already pouring through Sacramento on their way to the Comstock, and of the hordes still to come. He pictured the vast caravans of foodstuffs, supplies, mining equipment needed to sustain them—all of it at prices for which only the high sky was the limit. Every ounce, he pointed out, had to be transported northward and eastward across the Sierra Nevadas to the diggings, and it spelled wealth and influence untold for the men who commanded the best route and the fastest carriers.

The gentlemen of Sacramento here assembled, he declared solemnly, could do that. The Central Pacific Railroad would be the instrument.

The gentlemen were impressed, at least to a degree. The statements about the Washoe and its riches, no matter how extravagantly Judah may have couched them, were true. Probably there was not a man in the audience who was not far more impressed than Judah was by the Nevada silver boom. The firm of Huntington and Hopkins already had turned tidy profits on mining gear sold to the avid prospectors. Every man present had seen erstwhile sane and responsible citizens suddenly drop everything to join the stampede. They all had heard the tales that drifted back, of strike after fabulous strike along the canyons down the eastern Sierra slopes and on out over the high plains of Nevada Territory. They all knew that some of the mining companies out there were paying dividends at rates approaching a million dollars a month.

So they listened, and when Judah had finished every man of them save one subscribed for Central Pacific stock, some for as many as fifty shares each.

The lone exception was Collis Potter Huntington, the hardware man from downstairs. But he lingered for a last few words with Judah, and ended by suggesting that the engineer call on him later for another talk on the subject, this one in private.

"A hard and cheery old man with no more soul than a shark," the San Francisco journalist, Arthur McEwen, wrote of Collis Huntington many years later, long after he had become a millionaire many times over. He was not a great Midas in 1860; nor was he an old man, but a tough and vigorous one of thirty-nine. He already possessed the sharklike proclivities, though, as well as the flinty sagacity of the native New England Yankee. Born in Harwinton, Connecticut, of the traditional poor but respectable parents, he had been successively a grocery clerk, peddler and small storekeeper ever since early boyhood. In '49 he had sailed for the Isthmus of Panama with a stateroom full of trade goods, largely whiskey and other spirits, it was later said, representing the savings of his short lifetime. He had disposed of his stock at a profit in Aspinwall, invested the proceeds in a small schooner and another cargo of goods and spent some months trading up and down the Central American coast. By the time he was ready to book passage for San Francisco—after walking the twenty-four miles across the Isthmus rather than pay a stagecoach fare he considered excessive—he had more than doubled his original investment. No ordinary forty-niner, he was wont to say in later years that the single day he had wasted in panning for gold on the banks of the Sacramento River was one of the few youthful follies he sincerely regretted. Plainly, this was no man to go chasing after will-o'-the-wisps.

He was given to keeping his own counsel and shunning publicity, and few of his Sacramento associates really knew him well. Yet he had a certain reputation for eccentricity, and appears to have enjoyed it; there was a dour sort of vanity in him. He himself used to recall that he had been known far and wide for a ridiculous old hat he wore, its broad brim sagging to his shoulders on both sides. In his earlier years in California he had been a buyer and seller of anything and everything, operating out of a huge tent-store and managing to do very well with goods on which other merchants had given up. And he had a sour sense of humor all his own. A story was told of how the madam of a notorious bawdyhouse in Sacramento had once offered to take a sizable stock of flour off his hands. He named a price, outrageously high. She balked indignantly. But she had her large brood of "girls" to feed, and so the dickering went on at some length. In the end she had to accept his price. Then Huntington, a man of uncompromising religious convictions, blandly refused to deliver the flour. He could not, he informed the madam gravely, take the responsibility of ordering any employee of his to enter a whorehouse.

Perhaps such stories hid much of the driving, implacable urge to success that lurked behind the ordinary, tight-fisted, Yankee-trader exterior of the man. It is unlikely that Judah was able to size him up very well. He had little choice, in any case. He called at the Huntington and Hopkins establishment the very next evening.

Huntington had thought the matter over and was ready with a proposition. He was interested in the railroad, he said, to the extent of underwriting a working survey of Judah's route, and would undertake to bring together six backers to share the cost.

"I did not expect to do it myself altogether," he remembered somewhat modestly in later life.[3]

To Judah the offer must have sounded heaven-sent. His failure at San Francisco had cut the projected length of his railroad to 115 miles, the distance from Sacramento to the California-Nevada border, and thus cut the legal minimum in stock subscriptions to $115,000. And the subscriptions at last night's meeting had brought the total sum to that figure, on paper. But 10 percent of it was not very much cash, and even that was in many cases not immediately forthcoming. Both he and Dr. Strong, for example, had pledged themselves to amounts beyond their means—considerably beyond, in his own case. Hence the actual financing of his working survey with no strings attached —no visible ones, at least—loomed as a tremendous stride forward.

Again Judah found Anna waiting up for him, this time at Sacramento's Vernon House, as she had waited at the Russ in San Francisco, and before that on Fourteenth Street in Washington. Again she was to record her personal reaction to the good news in a letter written long afterward.

"It's about time someone else helped," she recalled saying, perhaps with some tartness.[4]

Collis Huntington's six included, besides himself, his partner Mark Hopkins, the grocer-politician Leland Stanford, Charles Crocker, Lucius Booth and James Bailey. All had attended the meeting over the store. All were local businessmen, successful and respected by their contemporaries; and four of the six—Huntington, Hopkins, Stanford and Crocker—were of considerably more than average financial stature, for Sacramento in the 1860's. In after years there came to be a general public impression that all four had been small and obscure merchants made wealthy, unexpectedly and not altogether deservedly, by their lucky railroad speculation. None of them ever took pains to correct the impression, but it was quite false. Though the dramatic atmosphere of recent California gold strikes and the current Nevada bonanzas tended to keep humdrum mercantile success out of the limelight, there is abundant evidence to show that both Huntington and Leland Stanford were millionaires at the time, or very close to it, and that both Hopkins and Crocker were somewhat more than comfortably well-to-do.

What Huntington said to the others in enlisting their participation he never revealed, nor did any of them. But his reputation for making all sorts of speculations pay off handsomely was well known in Sacramento. No doubt he, and they, went into the Central Pacific on much that basis. The investment required of each man did not appear to be back-breaking, and if the chances for success looked a little remote, the glittering trade with Nevada's Washoe was a prize well worth the gamble.

Nowhere is there a hint that any one of the six visualized himself as founding father of a transcontinental railroad.

Unquestionably, there was a certain amount of behind-the-scenes maneuvering by the six as a bloc. Their original subscriptions for stock were trifling; between them they held less than a thousand shares of the 85,000 ultimately sold. But they were united and they were in on the ground floor. When the Central Pacific Railroad Company was formally incorporated on June 28, 1861, Leland Stanford was elected president, Huntington vice-president, Bailey secretary and Hopkins treasurer. Crocker and Booth were named to the board of directors, as were Dr. Strong and Theodore Judah. And Judah was of course appointed chief engineer.

The survey went forward immediately, from the levee of the Sacramento River right through the city, across the flats of the American River and up the valley to Dutch Flat in the foothills. So rapidly did it move, in fact, that the first crew had to wait at Dutch Flat while advancing summer melted the snow from the Sierra slopes above. Judah outdid himself that summer. With determined thoroughness he investigated two other routes his new associates considered promising: one up the Yuba River and through the North Fork of Yuba Pass; the other by way of Oroville up the Middle Fork of the Feather River across Sierra Valley and through Beckwourth Pass. Neither, he judged, matched his own route through Dutch Flat and Donner Pass, thence down the Truckee River into Nevada Territory. He pushed that line forward with energy unabated, noting with satisfaction that it was some 184 miles shorter than the roundabout way through northern California originally suggested by Army engineers for the Central Route.[5]

There would be difficulties, he acknowledged: gorges down which spates of snow water thundered each spring; tunnels and cuts to be hacked and blasted out of solid granite on the summit approaches; the well-known Sierra snows each winter. Against the snow, he conceded, some means of keeping the railroad open during the worst months would have to be devised. But he was confident that it could be done. His reports pointed out that most of the con-

struction at the higher altitudes would be sidehill grade, and predicted opti-
mistically that the worst of the snow would slide off and thus eliminate the
need for excessive plowing.

No contemporary ever had questioned Theodore Judah's competence, and
no modern engineer has challenged the skill with which he ran his line. No
deep canyons had to be crossed, he stated in another of the reports he kept
flowing back to headquarters at Sacramento. Maximum grades, he specified,
would not exceed one hundred feet of rise to the mile, safely within the limits
of efficient railroad operation, while reaching a top elevation, in the Pass, of
6,690 feet. "The longest tunnel will not exceed 2,350 feet."

Most of this would be borne out, or substantially so. The man knew his
business.

He knew his associates in Sacramento, too, having learned that lesson well.
Always, his reports hammered away at the rich goal. "[The line] commands
and will perform the entire business of Nevada Territory, Washoe, and the
silver mineral region," he wrote. "It will also command the business of the
newly discovered Humboldt mineral district, Pyramid Lake, Esmeralda, and
Mono mineral districts." These were names to conjure with; Nevada was
blooming with precious metals; there seemed no end to the bonanza. Everywhere he looked, Judah saw fresh treasures. He foresaw the railroad making
it possible to transport low-grade ore, scorned by the richer mining companies,
to more efficient smelters for additional profits. He considered the great forests
on lands bordering his route, calculated the board feet of lumber there, and
predicted additional millions of dollars cascading into the pockets of the foresighted stockholders from that source.

And, of course, the transcontinental railroad continued to obsess him. It
never could be kept from his thoughts for long.

"The line over the mountains," he wrote in still another report, "completes
the first western link of the Pacific Railroad, overcoming its greatest difficulties."

"*Completes?*" "*Overcoming?*" This was a survey he was reporting; not a
single foot of roadbed had been so much as graded yet. And now there began
to loom the ominous possibility that not a single foot would be graded, for in
spite of Judah's feverish activity things were not going well. Stock subscriptions dwindled and payment was slow in coming. Neither the patience nor the
open-handedness of the six was boundless. The California public, that had
seen many a little railroad company launched with high hopes and loud fanfare only to come to nothing in the end, began to express doubts that the
Central Pacific ever would be built.

The uneasy directors demanded a cost estimate from their chief engineer.

In his answer, dated at Sacramento on the first of October, 1861, he set a figure of $12,380,000 for construction to the state line. Characteristically, he added figures for extensions to other points as distant as Great Salt Lake—as though any of his colleagues on the board would find even twelve million palatable.

Characteristically also, he again stressed the magnitude of government assistance to be expected. In that first private interview with Huntington he seems to have promised—somewhat rashly even for him—that Congress could not long delay a Pacific Railroad Act, complete with land grants and generous subsidies.

It was high time, the directors decided now, for some of that assistance to take tangible form. They passed a resolution:

> Resolved, that Mr. T. D. Judah, the Chief Engineer of this Company, proceed to Washington on the steamer on the 11th Oct. inst. as the accredited agent of the Central Pacific Railroad Company of California, for the purpose of procuring appropriations of land and U.S. Bonds from the Government, to aid in the construction of this road.

That was dated October 9. Judah had just two days to gather his data and pack his gear. Once again Anna had the right pair of gaiters on and would go with him.

They sailed from San Francisco precisely six months and twenty-eight days after Fort Sumter had been surrendered.

CHAPTER 3

"WE HAVE DRAWN THE ELEPHANT"

Civil war had seemed a long way off and not quite believable, in California. In New York City, though, where the Judahs parted for a while—Anna going off on a long deferred visit to her family in Massachusetts—the streets were alive with bands, placards and the hoarse come-ons of volunteer regiment recruiters. "On to Richmond!" was the war cry trumpeted from every corner by Mr. Horace Greeley's *Tribune,* and as Judah's train pounded southward out of Baltimore the countryside grew patched with the tents of vast encampments. In Washington, Henry Adams' "rude colony camped in the forest, with unfinished Greek temples for workrooms and sloughs for roads," Judah found crowds, restlessness and confusion beyond anything he had expected.

He noted physical changes also. One, in particular, must have seemed significant to his engineer's eye. The Long Bridge across the Potomac to the Alexandria road was under heavy repair and would carry rails now, extended down Maryland Avenue from the Baltimore and Ohio tracks. Apparently someone in authority realized that the gods of this war would smile on the army with the best railroad transport.

Perhaps he took that as a good omen.

The danger of invasion, once thought imminent, had subsided. Old General Winfield Scott was gone and George McClellan commanded all the armies of the Union. But before that happened Congress had learned at Bull Run in July—some of its members at first hand—that hostilities were going to be neither short nor easy; and the Union defeat at Ball's Bluff had lately driven the lesson home anew. Now McClellan was busy drilling the Army of the Potomac to a spit-and-polish glitter, while Congress rumbled with demands that he get on with the war.

It was a new Congress, the Thirty-Seventh, that convened for its second session on December 2, 1861. The old Secessionist bombast was stilled at last, for Secession was a fact now, the Southern champions gone home to their own Confederacy. The slavery issue was being fought out on a far bigger battleground than the Capitol these days, and as one result the Congress no longer was locked in the old, unbreakable stalemate over routes to be followed by transcontinental rails. In the present session, strangely businesslike and even staid after all the dramatics Judah recalled from his last visit, the old argument advancing the Pacific Railroad as a chain of iron binding the Pacific littoral to the Union took on a hard new validity. More, a nation at war needed gold and silver, and those rails could become a channel along which the specie of California and Nevada Territory would flow eastward into the hard-pressed treasury.

Already that talking point had been perceived by others. It was no longer simply the Pacific Railroad; now they were calling it the *Union* Pacific. Well, Judah would not quibble over a name. In the still unfinished Capitol he noticed that an artist worked away on a giant mural over the Hall of Representatives staircase. Its title: "Westward the Course of Empire Takes Its Way." Another good omen, perhaps.

He reopened his Pacific Railroad Museum, added to its exhibits some water colors of Donner Pass painted by Anna on a visit during the previous summer, and went to work.

On the steamer from San Francisco he again had met and made an ally of a newly elected Congressman, this time Aaron Sargent of California. Like John Burch before him, Sargent had promised to introduce a bill in the House. But this time the efforts of others in Judah's absence had begun to bear fruit. The House's Select Committee on the Pacific Railroad had finally permitted its chairman, Samuel Curtis, to report out a bill in the Thirty-Fifth Congress (it was this bill, incidentally, which first named the railroad the Union Pacific), and substantially the same measure had been approved by the House in the Thirty-Sixth Congress. Newly inaugurated President Abraham Lincoln had endorsed it as a military measure, but in the disorganization following the first outbreaks of actual secession the Senate had allowed the bill to be buried. Now Samuel Curtis was no longer in Washington, having gone off to fight the war as a colonel of Iowa volunteers. But another Iowan, Senator James Harlan, had taken over sponsorship of the bill, and promptly introduced it in the upper house of this Thirty-Seventh Congress.

All of which was not to say that Judah found his work already done for him. There remained the very thorny problem of getting action out of a body still preoccupied with a hundred different urgencies.

The defection of the Southerners had left radical Republicans, many of them ardently Abolitionist, in charge of every important committee in both House and Senate. Bent above all else on punishing the rebellious Confederacy, these men had scant time or sympathy for any matter not deemed directly pertinent to that objective. Legislative schedules were crammed with measures stamped emergency, and all the nagging minutiae of a government stumbling very close to chaos competed for the rank-and-file Congressman's attention. In the Capitol basement, Ohio's bellicose Ben Wade and his Joint Committee on the Conduct of the War made life miserable for anyone suspected even remotely of softness toward the slaveholding South. Over all, there was a widely held public conviction that things were not going well, and a blue funk of uncertainty and disgust enveloped Washington as the winter turned the corner into '62 in an incessant dismalness of rain. President Lincoln's earlier endorsement of the Union Pacific bill was hardly likely to be helpful now, for almost everyone was disenchanted with him, his person subject to bitter ridicule, his administration contemptuously tagged "do-nothing." And the threat of war with England hung darkly over all the nation's other woes, ever since the seizure in November of the Confederate envoys Mason and Slidell from the British mail steamer *Trent*.

In such a turgid brew the Theodore Judah who had journeyed to Washington in '56, or even the San Francisco Convention's accredited agent of '59, might have sunk without a ripple. This winter, though, Judah was no neophyte. He thought he knew how things were done in Washington, and he began by seeking out an acquaintance who could get him the favorable attention of Senator Harlan. The old, persuasive eloquence and enthusiasm did not fail him. The Senator, very much impressed, took steps to have Judah appointed secretary of the subcommittee named to consider the Union Pacific bill.

Here was progress of the kind most meaningful in Capitol politics. Now Judah had a voice in the hearings, his finest opportunity yet to push his own ideas and the interests of the Central Pacific.

In the House Aaron Sargent proved even better than his word. He introduced the Union Pacific bill there, obtaining the floor during debate on a totally unrelated matter to do it—a breach of parliamentary etiquette especially brash in a freshman Congressman, but it worked. The House named the inevitable subcommittee to study the bill, with Sargent as its chairman, according to custom. He promptly appointed Judah clerk of that subcommittee.

From that point on, things moved. In due course the bill went into the Select House Committee and Judah, no doubt with Sargent's help, was named clerk of that body also. In the Senate James Harlan was able finally to bring the measure to the floor.

Judah had kept his board of directors back at Sacramento informed of developments as a matter of course, and at some point during this period it appears that Collis Huntington joined him in Washington. Huntington's part in the subsequent promotion of the bill is obscure, though it could scarcely have been very great. For all his business acumen and whatever slight influence he might have been able to bring to bear on California's elected representatives, the Central Pacific vice-president was a total stranger to the national capital and its ways, and Judah undoubtedly continued to spearhead the main effort. But the fact that Huntington was there at all is significant. It suggests that the Central Pacific must already have begun to mean more to him than a mere speculative sideline, and that his sharp trader's mind had grasped some of the possibilities inherent in federal legislation for a transcontinental railroad.

Debates were prolonged while winter gave way to spring and spring to early summer. Partisan politics were by no means dead, despite the war, and for a while the old sectional rivalry over a terminal location raged almost with the old violence. St. Louis interests were determined that their city should surpass Chicago as the mid-continent rail center of the nation, and in the House Missouri and Kansas mustered formidable strength behind a provision designating the 102nd meridian of longitude west from Greenwich as the Union Pacific's eastern commencement point, with the Leavenworth, Pawnee and Western Company of Kansas empowered to build westward to a connection there. The L. P. and W., as yet a paper railroad only, without grade, rails or even a completed survey, was also authorized to establish a junction at Kansas City with the Pacific Railroad Company of Missouri, which already had progressed some two hundred miles of the way westward out of St. Louis, and had its railhead at Sedalia. But St. Joseph, Missouri, determined to hold its share in the great westward movement, managed to make its voice heard too; as a result the already completed Hannibal and St. Joseph Railroad, running across the northern part of the state from the Mississippi to the Missouri River, was given the right to build onward to its own junction with this combine.[1]

All this summed up to an ingenious and workable, if somewhat lengthy and confusing, patchwork of a route. It suffered, however, from a fatal handicap at each end. On the west the 102nd meridian was a shadowy line not clearly on one side or the other of the equally shadowy boundary between Nebraska and Colorado Territories, and thus immediately raised a threat of future complications involving states' rights. And on the east Missouri was a border state, only precariously in the Union camp, with the military situation there in turmoil and Secessionist elements still angry and active.

Senators balked at accepting the House bill, till the hard-working Harlan engineered a compromise substituting the one hundredth meridian—safely within Nebraska Territory—for the possibly controversial 102nd, and granting the Union Pacific permission, along with the Leavenworth, Pawnee and Western Company, to build eastward to the Missouri River, but on a line considerably farther north and comfortably remote from the possibility of Confederate conquest. Since the facts of geography gave the Union Pacific the shorter distance by more than a hundred miles (the course of the Missouri veering steadily westward above Kansas City) Harlan's compromise had the effect, or so it was assumed, of disposing of St. Louis' ambitions effectively yet diplomatically. So, slowly, a workable bill was hammered out.

The final Senate vote was twenty-five in favor, five opposed. The date was June 20, 1862.

On June 24 the House approved, 104 to 21.

President Lincoln signed the bill into law on the first of July, and over the wires of the Pacific Telegraph to Sacramento went Judah's victory message, exultant and at the same time a little cryptic:

"We have drawn the elephant. Now let us see if we can harness him up."[2]

Curiously, nothing was ever recorded to indicate that Judah worked with, or even was acquainted with, any of his opposite numbers on the Union Pacific side of the great effort. Central Pacific historians tend to give him all the credit for getting the job done in Washington, with scarcely a hint that anyone else was involved. Yet both Dr. Durant and Henry Farnum, the two promoters of the Mississippi and Missouri Railroad in the '50's, made trips to Washington to support Samuel Curtis' original Union Pacific bill, and were active backers throughout the long campaign in Congress. The circumstances would seem to have made some sort of liaison between them and Judah very likely; if so, however, none of the three ever mentioned it. Union Pacific contemporaries unanimously ignored Judah in their later writings on the subject, and gave the main credit for the Pacific Railroad Act of 1862 to Samuel Curtis, who was not even a member of Congress at the time of its passage, though his early labors, like James Harlan's later ones, certainly were vital to its eventual success. Perhaps the implicit rivalry between the two companies was obvious to both from the very start; some of the provisions of the Act suggest this strongly. So any cooperation between the two in the interests of getting the Act passed—like their later cooperation in getting it amended—would be uneasy at best, and the less said about it the better from both points of view.

After it was all over, chairman James A. Campbell of the Select House Committee and Aaron Sargent of the House subcommittee signed a testimonial to Judah, citing his services to both bodies and praising, in particular, the accurate and detailed information he had furnished. Thirty-three other House members and seventeen Senators also signed. Such a document was not a common procedure in Congress; plainly, Theodore Judah's ability and personality had made a deep impression.

The text of the Act as finally signed by President Lincoln makes little mention of the Central Pacific. But that is no more than normal, since it was a California company already in being and subject to the terms of the Act only by its own choice, whereas the Union Pacific had to be created *in toto* by the Act itself.

The Union Pacific Company was to be composed of 158 persons, all listed by name—and most of them very eminent names, too, in business and political circles. There were William B. Ogden, first Mayor of Chicago and a railroad man of some note; Territorial Governor John Evans of Colorado; the stalwart Iowan Samuel R. Curtis, now a brigadier general and hero of the recent Union victory at Pea Ridge, Arkansas. Louis McLane, head of the new Wells Fargo and Company express merger, was named; also Hartwell Carver, an original promoter of the railroad sleeping car. A few seemed strange choices: Ben Holladay, for example, rough and ready president of the famous Overland Stage Company which stood to be put out of business by a successful Pacific railroad. Somewhat strangely, too, both Collis P. Huntington and Theodore Judah of the Central Pacific were included, possibly another tribute to Judah's part in the Act's passage.

Five commissioners representing the federal government were also named. The group, collectively titled the Board of Commissioners of the Union Pacific Railroad and Telegraph Company, was instructed to open books for the subscription of stock as soon as possible. When two thousand shares were subscribed and cash to the extent of 10 percent of their value paid in, the Act directed the commissioners to call a meeting of stockholders for the purpose of electing a board of thirteen directors. Two more directors, not stockholders, would then be appointed by the government. As soon as the board was named, direction of the company would be turned over to the stockholders.

Par value of the stock shares was set at one thousand dollars each, capitalization of the company to be $100,000,000.

The company was authorized to "lay out, locate, construct, furnish, maintain and enjoy a continuous railroad and telegraph, with appurtenances, from a point on the one hundredth meridian of longitude west from Greenwich, between the south margin of the Republican River and the north margin of the valley of the Platte River in the territory of Nebraska to the western boundary of Nevada Territory," the actual point to be selected by the President of the United States following surveys. Here the road was to meet the Central Pacific Railroad. Rights of way four hundred feet wide over public lands were granted, with additional ground as needed for operating facilities such as depots, yards and roundhouses.[3]

Public lands amounting to five alternate sections per mile on each side of the right of way were granted, mineral rights to be withheld by the government though existing timber could be used in construction.

Government bonds in denominations of a thousand dollars were to be issued to the company as a loan payable in thirty years and bearing 6 percent interest. Sixteen such bonds were to be issued per mile, except for "three hundred miles of said road most mountainous and difficult of construction, to wit, one hundred and fifty miles westerly from the eastern base of the Rocky Mountains and one hundred and fifty miles eastwardly from the western base of the Sierra Nevada Mountains, said points to be fixed by the President of the United States." For these three hundred miles the number of bonds per mile was to be trebled, and for the country between the 150-mile sections, the number was to be doubled.

The government loan, in other words, would amount to $16,000 per mile in level country, $48,000 per mile through the Rockies and the Sierra Nevadas, and $32,000 per mile between the two ranges. The bonds were to constitute a first mortgage on the railroad and telegraph company. But, the Act also provided, no bonds would be issued nor any land grants made till the first forty miles of railroad had been built and accepted by the government commissioners.

The exigencies of putting together a bill that would satisfy or at least placate the many local interests represented in Congress showed up most markedly, of course, in the provisions having to do with the railroad's location. In the Platte Valley the one hundredth meridian of longitude is nearly 250 miles west of the Missouri River and more than 500 west of the Mississippi, an odd place for a transcontinental railroad to begin. It was left to the President to specify the exact spot on the Missouri to which the Union Pacific might build by the conditions of Senator Harlan's compromise. In actual practice this would be the starting point of the road, and construction would be governed by the same terms applied to the sections from the one hundredth meridian westward. These terms applied also to the Leavenworth, Pawnee and Western Company. And as a further complication, the Union Pacific was obligated to build an Iowa branch which ultimately became known as the Sioux City and Pacific. As a result of all this the Act permitted and even encouraged at least two separate routes between the one hundredth meridian and the Mississippi, though it was clearly the intention of a majority in Congress to favor the Union Pacific. In fact, an immediate flurry of trans-continental railroad promotion in Iowa, Missouri and Kansas followed the Act's passage.

The Union Pacific was empowered to enter California provided the Central Pacific failed to build to the state line. Conversely, however, the Central Pacific was authorized to build eastward all the way to the Missouri River, if neces-sary, on the same terms granted its rival, "until said roads shall meet and connect and the whole line of said railroad and branches and telegraph is completed."

Construction was to be finished and the railroad ready for use by July 1, 1867, or all work done by that date was forfeited to the federal government. A deadline for acceptance of the terms of the Act was set. Track gauge, by no means uniform in the United States in '62, was left to the discretion of the President. Grades and curvatures were not to exceed those of the Baltimore and Ohio, Theodore Judah's old model of what a good railroad should be. The Act specified a number of other construction standards but, in general, con-tented itself with the blanket requirement that the road should be "a first class railroad" in every respect.

And there, in substance, was Judah's elephant.

It was not perfect, and many of its beneficiaries seem to have begun think-ing in terms of needed revisions almost at once. Nor was the news of the Act's passage greeted with wholly unanimous rejoicing; there were still men of influence in the Union who regarded the whole concept of a transconti-nental railroad as harebrained and impractical. William Tecumseh Sherman, whose brother John participated in the debates as a Congressman from Ohio (and voted for the bill), was one. He had written John in '59, warning that such a project never would earn enough to pay the interest on its cost, and was reported to have exclaimed, when he heard that Lincoln had signed the Act of '62, "What, a railroad to the Pacific? I should hate to buy a ticket on it for my grandchildren!"

But the big hurdle had been jumped, all the same. The dream had its chance, now, to become reality. The Union Pacific men lost no time in scheduling a meeting of the new board of commissioners in Bryan Hall in Chicago on September 2. Judah resigned from his three Congressional com-mittees and hurried with Collis Huntington to New York to order railroad supplies before boarding the steamer for Panama and California.

CHAPTER 4

THE NATURE OF THE BEAST

Elephant was an apt word for Judah to have chosen in his triumphal message. In the vernacular of a day when Phineas T. Barnum had the credulous agape over nature's more exotic marvels, and few Americans ever had seen the beast in the flesh, "elephant" conveyed a special kind of meaning. It connoted bigness, a certain strangeness—even, in some usages, a hint of the ominous. Thus combat-wise veterans would grin and tell green recruits on their way forward to Civil War battle fronts that they were "going up to see the elephant," or going up "to look the elephant in the eye."

In a sense, the men who so eagerly had sought the right to build a transcontinental railroad were like those green recruits. Probably not a one of them, Theodore Judah included, understood the full magnitude of the enterprise. It was simply too vast for that, too far-reaching and complicated in its ramifications, involved with too many unknown factors. Young Grenville Dodge—in the Union Army now and unavailable—may have had a better grasp of it than anyone else. He had been over some of the terrain and appreciated some of the difficulties and practical problems: the varied obstacles, some large, some small, but massive when combined in a single whole. Even Dodge knew much of the Far Western country only by hearsay.

In sheer mileage alone the task was gargantuan. Previous railroad construction in the United States had been of the short-line variety, reaching out from city to city by easy stages in the densely populated East, the established South and the new Northwest: Ohio, Indiana, Michigan, Illinois, Wisconsin and Minnesota, which we know today as the Midwest. But from the Missouri River to the Pacific was roughly two thousand miles (no one knew the actual figure till the route could be surveyed fully), and at least a third of them were unexplored miles, or virtually so, in spite of the so-called Pacific Railroad Surveys of '53. Kansas was the sole Union state extending west of the

Missouri, California and Oregon the only ones on the Pacific Coast. In between lay the vast Territories of Dakotah, Washington, Nebraska, Colorado,
Utah, Nevada and New Mexico, many of their boundary lines still only hazily
defined, their natural resources unexamined and scarcely guessed at.

There were exceptions, of course, a couple of them spectacular. In Colorado,
gold strikes had put "Pike's Peak or Bust" into the national vocabulary in
the '50's, and in '59 the diggings along Cherry Creek had set Denver City to
burgeoning and created a rude metropolis where whiskered, unwashed roughnecks could become rich men overnight—a lucky few of them did—and all the
appurtenances of wealth, luxury and booming business were packed in by
mule and wagon train till Denver, in its gaudier aspects at least, bid fair to
rival the urban centers of the East. The same thing was happening on the
Nevada Comstock, with Sun Mountain shaking to the shudder and roar of
stamping mills and smelter furnaces, and Virginia City boasting its Gould and
Curry, Ophir, Savage and Yellow Jacket mines; its uninhibited newspaper,
the *Territorial Enterprise,* with a star reporter who called himself "Josh" and
had not yet hit on the pseudonym of Mark Twain; its celebrated courtesan,
Julia Bulette by name, who took the air in a lacquered barouche with a
heraldic crest (four aces and a lion couchant) blazoned on each door; and a
new opera house that frequently rocked to exuberant applause for such stars
of the day as Lotta Crabtree, Edwin Booth and Adah Isaacs Menken.

And around Great Salt Lake in Utah Territory the Mormons, ruled by
Brigham Young with an authority more absolute than any elected official's
in the nation, had built a community of a very different sort: an austere and
well-ordered agrarian settlement that was little known or appreciated by the
outside world.

But these were isolated specks, tiny motes of civilization surrounded by
the vast and barren unknown.

From the Missouri River to the eastern face of the Rocky Mountains, the
land was thought of as the Great American Desert, and in fact was so designated on maps even in the early '60's. Major Stephen Long, who led an Army
expedition to the headwaters of the Platte in 1819 had reported that "It is a
region destined . . . to be the abode of perpetual desolation," and this impression still was general among Americans east of the Mississippi. It was
not entirely a misapprehension. The region was one of sparse rainfall, treeless
except along its infrequent watercourses, subject to months-long droughts,
cyclonic winds, savage electrical storms and plagues of devouring grasshoppers
in summer and killing blizzards in the winter. Yet limitless herds of buffalo
grazed there, in their heyday perhaps as many as fifty million head; in this
year of '62 white hide hunters had not yet made any significant inroads.

Strangely, it had occurred to almost no one that where the buffalo could live in such numbers cattle and other domestic livestock also might thrive.

Once the Rockies and the Sierra Nevadas were breached, the one from the east, the other from the west, the land between was desert in literal truth, most of it, gritty, stony earth and sagebrush and alkali.

Since the '40's, westbound travelers with their heads full of the rich promise of Oregon and California had seen nothing worth stopping for in these monotonous plains and inhospitable mountains. They had carried on, and left only the deepening tracks beaten out by their going. The first westward-faring Mormons had broken a trail from Council Bluffs up the Platte Valley and along the North Fork of the Platte, through Fort Laramie and the South Pass of the Rockies and thence down to Great Salt Lake. The main Oregon Trail, also known as the Overland, left Independence, Missouri, and followed the old Santa Fe Trail through part of Kansas before veering northward to strike the Platte at Fort Kearney. Then, joining a more recent alternate route out of Council Bluffs, it too ran along the Platte and North Platte rivers through Fort Laramie and the South Pass. From there it struck out to the northwest, where the Army had established Forts Hall and Boise in the Snake River country of what is now Idaho. Its final stages then took it through the Blue Mountains into the Columbia River Valley.

At Fort Hall the California Trail diverged southwestward and crossed Nevada Territory and the Sierra Nevadas into the gold fields and, ultimately, Sacramento and San Francisco. It entered California by a variety of routes, one of them Donner Pass which Theodore Judah had selected for the Central Pacific's passage.

The Colorado gold strikes and the development of Kansas as a state had opened up a comparatively new trail out of Kansas City along the Kansas and Smoky Hill Rivers into Colorado Territory and then northward to Denver City.

Oldest of all the routes westward was the Santa Fe Trail, first opened to travel in 1821. It began at Independence, Missouri, and ran southwestward across Kansas and New Mexico Territory to Santa Fe. There it made a connection with the old Spanish Trail, which looped far to the northward into Utah Territory, then southwestward again to enter southern California. But now parts of this route, and practically all of the Butterfield Overland Mail route, which lay even farther south, were cut off by the hostile Confederacy.

All of these trails had been opened, originally, by Army explorers, traders or the restless, half-savage mountain men, following old Indian trails which, in turn, followed paths trodden out by migrating buffalo since times beyond the memory of man. The great westward emigrant treks and the growth of trade with the Southwest had developed them into well-mapped and firmly established travel routes—and, incidentally, left most of them marked by the graves of those who had sickened and died along the way, and the bleached bones of their draft animals. By the '60's the wagon trains plying them were generally well organized and led by capable, experienced professionals. The transporting of freight to the scattered Army forts, the trading posts and the mining centers had grown into a big and profitable business. In such jumping-off centers as Independence, Leavenworth and Council Bluffs, mountains of merchandise and acres of wagons piled up, awaiting the start of the western haul each spring. By '58, Russell, Majors and Waddell, largest of the freighting outfits, employed 4,000 men and owned 3,500 wagons and 40,000 oxen, which were safer than horses or even mules because the Indians despised them and so were less tempted to attack the trains using them. This firm was based at Leavenworth. And in Omaha, just across the Missouri River from Council Bluffs, Megeath and Company was selling goods at a rate of two thousand dollars per day in season, mostly to westbound Mormon converts.

But this was transient traffic. Its very volume gave proof of how little the land itself supplied. Along all the great trails, road ranches or depots had been established at convenient intervals, and around a few of them settlements had grown up. But they existed only by serving the travelers. They did little to develop the land or put down roots, and raised few crops save a little hay sold on contract to the freighters or the Army's cavalry units. The adventurer or the unwary traveler who wandered only a few miles off the beaten track was liable to find himself in a vast, unbroken wilderness as unknown, almost, as darkest Africa.

The frontiersmen and mountain men who had ventured west earlier in the century still hunted and trapped over the Great Plains and throughout the Rockies, and the best of them—men like Kit Carson and Jim Bridger—gave invaluable service as guides and advisers for the Army and the emigrant groups. As a class, though, they were solitary, restless men, explorers only incidentally and settlers not at all. And they were already a dying breed.

The true settler, the homesteader, had not yet made an appearance anywhere on the scene. This same year of '62 Abraham Lincoln signed the first Homestead Act in U.S. history, entitling a man to a quarter section, 160 acres, of free government land provided he lived on it and made certain nominal improvements.[1] But the first man to take advantage of the Act, one Daniel Freeman, a Union soldier home on leave, would not file his claim (near the present Beatrice, Nebraska) until early in '63. And the real hordes of hopeful sodbusters would not move out onto the plains till much later; *after* the Pacific Railroad had opened up the country, not before.

Meanwhile, the very real demand for faster communications with the Pacific

Coast led to the launching of Russell, Majors and Waddell's famous Pony Express in 1860, carrying tissue-paper mail between St. Joseph and Sacramento in the astounding time of less than eleven days. For all its glamour, though, it proved a commercial failure within eighteen months. With the outbreak of the War Between the States the bulk of through passenger traffic and government mail was shifted from the Butterfield route to the new Overland Stage, traveling the Oregon and California Trails on a schedule of seventeen days each way. The Overland Telegraph, a loose federation of independent companies which strung their wires along the same route, was a going concern by '61. But already it was proving something less than adequate, its wires frequently down, its facilities overtaxed by the growing demand for war news in the Far West.

And all these enterprises existed, by and large, only on sufferance by the Plains Indians.

Primarily, in the huge area bounded (very roughly) by the Mississippi River on the east, the Canadian border on the north, the Rocky Mountains on the west, and including most of Kansas on the south, the Indian population was dominated by the mighty Sioux Nations and the fewer but equally warlike Cheyennes. Nominally, of course, the Army patrolled the area and exercised control. But the Army was spread very thin at best, and now mobilization in the East was draining off most of its experienced officers and veteran troops. In reality its influence could not and did not extend very far from the few forts that had been flung out along the main-traveled routes. Fortunately the Indian had been friendly in the past, on the whole, and efforts were made to keep him that way through government treaties. It was an uneasy peace, however. The growing volume of white travel through the region inevitably carried with it the seeds of trouble; there had been clashes in the past and were bound to be more. The Army long had recognized the potential danger in a situation it referred to, somewhat vaguely, as "the Indian problem."

Cultured Easterners, their concepts still shaped largely by Mr. Longfellow's Hiawatha and James Fenimore Cooper's chivalrous Mohican Chief, were not generally aware of this. The works of Henry David Thoreau extolling the simple, primitive life, and George Catlin's popular paintings of trans-Mississippi Indian life had tended to romanticize the red man in the public mind. But the hard-bitten men on the frontier understood perfectly that the "noble savage" became "that skulking, murderous redskin" the moment he stood in the way of the white man's notion of progress. They accepted the fact and kept their powder dry. The Pacific Railroad would have to do the same.

Despite all the traffic that flowed across its face, then, this was a bitter, empty land. It held no help, but many complications, for the railroad builders.

In the first flush of enthusiasm over passage of the Act of '62, much of this was overlooked or simply not realized. There was a general expectation by all concerned that the people of the United States would rush to subscribe for shares in the great enterprise and pour out the money necessary for the work, now that the government had pointed the way. It seemed only logical, for the nation had been in the throes of intermittent railroad fever ever since the late '30's. By this year of 1862 the United States was crisscrossed by more than thirty thousand miles of track, most of it—and by far the best of it—connecting the towns and cities of the Union states. All of the important urban centers east of the Mississippi, both north and south, enjoyed through rail links with one another, though differing track gauges among the several railroads made it necessary for both passengers and freight shipments to change cars frequently. West of the Mississippi, Iowa and Missouri were still the only states with any rail mileages worth mentioning, and the Missouri River still had been reached at only one point, St. Joseph, and crossed not at all. But the enabling Act, as its terms made clear, was expected to send those rails leaping ahead.

From the technological standpoint, American railroading was ready for its great transcontinental thrust. Thirty years of development had brought the steam locomotive a long way from the first cumbersome little teakettles with their grasshopper beams and inside cylinders, and evolved a simple, basic design which would remain essentially unchanged for the balance of the long steam era. The value of a nonrigid frame with drivers mounted in sprung journal boxes to compensate for uneven track and roadbed was well understood. The center-pivoted and equalized leading truck to impart stability on curves had been in use for many years. So had the counterweighted driver, which smoothed out the alternate thrust and pound of drive rods pushing against offset crankpins, and thus improved riding qualities while at the same time reducing wear and tear on both rail and engine.

The 4-4-0 type of locomotive,[2] also called the "eight-wheeler" and the "American"—a four-wheeled leading truck followed by two connected drivers on each side—had been patented in 1836 and was now the standard engine for road service, both passenger and freight. The advantage of additional pairs of drivers in achieving better distribution of a locomotive's weight on the rails was recognized, however. The "ten-wheeler" was coming into wide use as a freight hauler, and big engines with as many as eight drivers had been built for special assignments on heavy grades.

The steam whistle, the bell, the pilot or cowcatcher to brush obstructions off the tracks, and the kerosene or whale-oil headlight for night operation were all standard locomotive fittings. The latter, though, was not always supplied by the builder; sometimes it was not even owned by the railroad company, but by the individual engineer.

To turn out these locomotives there were, by the '60's, a score or more of builders, practically all of them concentrated in the industrial East, and particularly in New England. Many were small shops which sprang up or went out of business with fluctuations in demand, and many of the larger firms built locomotives only as sidelines to the manufacture of other types of machinery. Among the leaders in both volume and excellence of design and construction were the Rogers Locomotive Works and Danforth, Cooke and Company of Paterson, New Jersey; Schenectady Locomotive Works of Schenectady, New York; Taunton Locomotive Works of Taunton, Massachusetts; Hinkley Locomotive Works of Boston; and Baldwin Locomotive Works of Philadelphia.

The first engines imported from England had been coal-burners, and coal still was the preferred fuel, being recognized as the most efficient in terms of steam produced per pound of weight burned. But as the lines pushed west from the Atlantic seaboard, coal was not always readily available. Wood, though, usually was cheap and plentiful, and so the wood-burner had come into extensive use in America.

Along with the development of the locomotive, speeds had climbed, sometimes fantastically high. In 1848 the *Antelope*, an English-built engine on the Boston and Maine Railroad, had reeled off the first mile-a-minute run in American history, between Boston and Lawrence, Massachusetts. For its time it was an amazing, an unbelievable, feat; it had been doubted by medical men that the human body could survive while traveling at such a speed. But the very next year an American-built greyhound with a single pair of eighty-four-inch drivers, the *Lightning* of the Utica and Schenectady, had hauled eight passenger cars a distance of sixteen miles in just thirteen minutes. Achievements like these were isolated and far above the norm, of course. But they showed what could be done; by the '60's, railroad schedules were approaching levels of speed and reliability that were quite respectable.

In many of its auxiliary aspects, railroad operation had kept pace with the speeding locomotive. In some others it lagged. The telegraph was in general use for dispatching trains and controlling their movements on the larger, heavy-traffic lines. Signal systems were developing, though still far from standardized. The T-shaped rail, first designed by Robert Stevens, president and chief engineer of the Camden and Amboy Railroad in 1830, was accepted as standard by all modern roads, though many miles of older types still survived on less progressive ones. Wrought iron was the standard material, and the ironworks and rolling mills of Johnstown, Scranton, Danville and Allentown, Pennsylvania, made these cities the chief rail manufacturing centers. The Bessemer process for making steel was known, and it was recognized that steel rails were superior, but facilities for producing them were limited. Hence both Central Pacific and Union Pacific would be laid with wrought iron for their entire lengths.

Cars, both passenger and freight, had been developed to more or less uniform design standards also, and rode on sprung and center-pivoted trucks not fundamentally different from those in use today.

With all this, railroading remained a rough and hazardous business, widely accused of a shocking disregard for public life and limb. In an era of fierce competition and practically no government control, railroad managements did, unquestionably, tend to be irresponsible and selfish. But much of the trouble stemmed, too, from the fact that the weights of locomotives and rolling stock and the potential for high speeds simply had outstripped the capabilities of the braking equipment in use. Trains were controlled only by individually operated hand brakes on locomotives and cars, and a long freight or a passenger train running at even moderate speed took a long distance in which to stop, even if the crews were as alert as they were supposed to be. Coupling was accomplished by a primitive system of iron links and pins. These too were hand-operated; the trainman had to stand between the cars while he guided each link into its socket and dropped the pin to hold it. As a result men were crushed to death or brutally maimed, and few car hands stayed long in the game without the stumps of one or more missing fingers as badges of their seniority. On most railroads, safety rules were either nonexistent or flagrantly ignored.

The calculation of stresses on bridges and trestles often was imperfectly understood by the men responsible for their construction and upkeep. And with the increasing use of regular schedules, often competitive, came a growing compulsion on engineers and conductors to make the time regardless of possible consequences. The end result of all this was a distressing outbreak of collisions, derailments and other accidents during the decade of the '50's, and the combination of frail wooden passenger cars and individual stoves for heating turned many of them into frightful holocausts.

The press of the nation reacted in a great, indignant diatribe of protest. Typical, though somewhat more restrained than many, was an article in an 1858 issue of *Harper's Weekly*: "The railroads are insatiable. Boilers are bursting all over the country—railroad bridges are breaking and rails snapping —human life is sadly and foolishly squandered. . . ."

It was too true. Yet such criticism, while it eventually helped to force improvements and badly needed reforms, did little or nothing to stay the typically American, hell-for-leather enthusiasm for railroading as a way of life, or the rush to ride the cars. The truth was that the brash young nation was in the process of wading into the Industrial Revolution—a little gingerly, not yet quite aware of it, perhaps—and the lumbering locomotive engine with its beastlike panting and its brimstone dragon's breath was the most thrilling tangible manifestation of the new age.

The War Between the States would bring a fuller understanding of many things. Not least among them was the hard fact that a nation's heavy industry and its smoke-belching factories were the new measures of its greatness. The hotspurs of the Confederacy did not realize that yet. Neither did the men out on the frontier, nor the common man anywhere. The public, as usual, was preoccupied with its own varied individual concerns. Amid the bellow and fury of war, the Pacific Railroad was one more job to be got on with, simply that and nothing more.

CHAPTER 5

FOUR STRONG MEN

The Central Pacific was riding high. The election of 1860 had swept its president, Leland Stanford, into the state house as California's first Republican Governor, and the transcontinental railroad was among the strong issues tipping the scales in his favor.[1] The same public sentiment that had created the old Pacific Railroad Convention of San Francisco and sent Theodore Judah to Washington as its agent seemed, at last, to have accomplished something concrete. It was reasonable to expect that sentiment to rally behind the Central Pacific now. Judah, arriving home with the Act of '62 in his pocket, so to speak, found himself suddenly the man of the hour.

What he thought of that, after all the years of frustration and ridicule, is not recorded. With characteristic energy he plunged into the railroad's work. In October he submitted his first report since his return, urging that surveys be pushed beyond the Nevada line immediately and that plans be set up for construction as far eastward as Salt Lake.

His associates were not ready to go quite that far, though anxious enough to begin capitalizing on the new Act. Not surprisingly, the new situation appears to have taken them a little off balance. When Judah had left for Washington, the Central Pacific Company was no more than a speculative sideline to everyone but himself. Now, all at once, it was potentially the biggest thing in each man's life. To two of the associates in particular, that called for some hard thinking.

Collis P. Huntington, looking at the matter with the same shrewd and dour objectivity he directed at every business deal, indulged in no pointless enthusiasm. He saw the prospective rewards but he also perceived, more clearly than any of the others, that the federal government, by making the thing possible, had laid down a hard challenge. With forty miles of railroad to be built before the government came into it, he and his associates were still very much on their own. All of the problems remained; of these the need for financing was the greatest, and it would not be solved by fatuous optimism or the small devisings of small men. If they went ahead with it. '. . . But the *if* was rhetorical. They were committed. In all his lifetime Collis Huntington never had backed away from opportunity, and would not begin now.

Charles Crocker, the drygoods merchant, seems to have seen the thing differently. To him it was opportunity pure and simple. Something of a contradictory character was Charley Crocker. He was a gregarious, outgoing type of person, but domineering to a fault. Many of his contemporaries considered him boastful, loud and utterly tactless. He seemed an unlikely sort to be in the ribbon and yardgoods business, a huge man, some 240 pounds in weight, red-faced, big-fisted and bull-necked. He looked more like a blacksmith, and had been one, long ago in Indiana. And before that, a poor boy in a poor New York State family, he had grown used to working hard for a bare, hardscrabble living. The drygoods business had been good to him. At forty-one he was, at last, a successful and prosperous man, had served a term in the state legislature, enjoyed a solid standing in Sacramento.

What he began to think of, nevertheless, was putting it all aside to plunge, whole-hog-or-none, into the building of the railroad. It took a certain courage, or perhaps foolhardiness is a better word. "I grew up as a sort of leader," he declared long afterward. "I had always been the one to swim a river and carry a rope across." He was also, he said of himself, "always trying to turn a dollar into a dollar and five cents."[2]

Perhaps he was only tired of the drygoods business.

He must have thought matters over carefully. Certainly, in the light of later events, he consulted his associates and received assurance of their cooperation in what he proposed to do. Quietly he began to turn his assets into working capital and presently, without any great fanfare, had set himself up as C. Crocker and Company, railroad construction contractors.

All this while the Central Pacific continued to ride a wave of public enthusiasm. Sacramento granted the company a right of way into the city along the American River levee, and in addition deeded over a forty-acre tract between I Street and the river—a gesture of civic generosity somewhat tinctured by economy, for the whole area was low and swampy, known variously as The Slough, China Slough, or Sutter's Lake, and of somewhat questionable value.[3]

The company filed its formal acceptance of the terms of the Act with the United States Department of the Interior on the first of November, 1862, and on December 27 C. Crocker and Company was awarded the contract for grading, masonry, bridges and track for the first eighteen miles out of Sacramento. The board, however, was not unanimous in the decision. Theodore

Judah opposed the contract and apparently was supported by Dr. Strong and James Bailey. But Crocker forthrightly offered to resign from the board once the contract was his, thus avoiding any appearance of unethical practice. Whether or not that had been the basis of Judah's objection is not entirely clear; in all likelihood Crocker's inexperience in railroad construction work was also a factor. At any rate, this first rift among the company's directorate seems to have passed without any overt ill will, and Crocker's resignation was accepted. He immediately divided his eighteen miles into one-mile sections for subletting to other contractors. In a flurry of initial activity the board of directors also commissioned the designing of a large and impressive depot to be put up on I Street. When the finished plans were submitted, Collis Huntington promptly vetoed the idea.

"Fine for by and by," he is supposed to have said, "but for the present . . ." And he proceeded to sketch—in chalk on the iron door of his office stove, according to legend—the outline of a small, plain board-and-batten shack. That would do, he said, till something better was justified.

He was close-fisted, no doubt of it. But he was a realist, too. It was not long before his colleagues became aware that the signs were not all favorable.

Stock subscriptions failed to take the expected upward spurt. Six hundred new shares were sold, and that was all. Of more ominous implication still, only ten of them were sold in San Francisco—and to a total of exactly two buyers—though an all-day subscription drive was put on there. The federal government's backing, implicit in the Act of '62, was not accepted as a guarantee of success; not with that government engaged in a war of survival and fighting, as it often seemed, with its back to the wall. Telegraphic dispatches from the war fronts were subject to agonizing delays and were seldom complete even when they arrived. Battles and campaigns that were reported with comparative promptness and clarity in the East could be glimpsed in California only by fragments and snatches, as through the wrong end of a telescope, darkly clouded, frequently contradictory, heavy with portents of Union disaster. Federal currency declined in value. The times seemed to counsel caution.

Besides, wealthy capitalists in San Francisco were putting their money into Comstock mining shares and getting back returns of 24 percent, as regularly as clockwork. What could a still hypothetical Pacific Railroad offer to beat that?

Yet without San Francisco money local financing on the necessary scale was impossible.

There was the state of California, of course. Its voters had approved a transcontinental railroad in principle, and it long had been customary for states to encourage the development of railroads and similar works of public utility by granting subsidies to their builders. California had contributed $100,000 to the

Overland Telegraph and should be even more generous with the Central Pacific, an enterprise, as the Sacramento *Daily Union* pointed out editorially, of value "greater, beyond calculation, than any conferred by the telegraph." Leland Stanford would see to it. Seldom indeed was a railroad fortunate enough to have its president in the state house, with all the prestige, power and patronage of the governor's office at his command.

Legislation, however, would take time. And Collis Potter Huntington, seeing the problem in its gigantic whole, believing in no miracles and expecting none, foresaw very clearly that the kind of help needed would have to come from the big money marts of the East. He put the thought to his colleagues on the board, was nominated as the man to do the job, and began to make his preparations for a trip to New York.

Problems aside, the new year of '63 opened with high promise. On January 7 an advertisement appeared in the Sacramento *Daily Union*:

Inauguration of Central Pacific Railroad

THE PRESIDENT, DIRECTORS AND STOCKHOLDERS of the CENTRAL PACIFIC RAILROAD COMPANY extend a general invitation to all persons favorable to the work to be present at the Inauguration of the Great Enterprise.

On Thursday, January Eighth at 11 o'clock A.M. at the corner of K and Front Streets.

JAMES BAILEY
Secretary

And on the following day there was another:

Central Pacific Railroad

Proposals will be received by the undersigned at their office, 56 K Street, until the FIFTEENTH INSTANT, at 12 M, for the construction of the AMERICAN RIVER BRIDGE AND TRESTLING, being section 4 of the Central Pacific Railroad of California. Plans and specifications, schedules of timber and iron work, etc., can be seen at the office.

C. CROCKER AND CO.

The eighth was bright and clear. As the lead story on the *Daily Union*'s front page of January 9 described it, "The skies smiled yesterday upon a ceremony of vast significance to Sacramento, California and the Union."

A large crowd gathered for the event, around a stand erected near the levee a short way above K Street, its ends adorned with large American flags. Bundles of hay had been distributed to give comparatively dry footing, and though, as the *Union* account pointed out, the choice of scene was not favorable to the presence of the gentler sex, the balconies opposite, on Front Street above K, were "adorned with a fair delegation." The writer added that "The great preponderance of pantaloons was a disagreeable necessity of the situation," for it had rained earlier.

From a balcony of the American Exchange Hotel, the Sacramento Union Brass Band filled the air with martial music, and two flag-draped wagons, drawn by horses also decked out in red, white and blue, stood ready with earth to be shoveled out for the railroad embankment. One bore a banner emblazoned with the legend, "MAY THE BOND BE ETERNAL," above a design of clasped hands spanning the continent.

Charles Crocker, acting as master of ceremonies, introduced Leland Stanford, who delivered a brief and not very inspired address in which he compared the railroad with the Erie Canal in importance, and promised that progress would be swift. The benediction by a Rev. J. A. Benton followed—a lengthy one, lasting about as long as Stanford's speech—and then Crocker sprang forward and announced ringingly that "The Governor of California will now shovel the first earth for the Great Pacific Railroad!"

The crowd shouted and clapped while the wagons were driven smartly up and the Governor, "with a zeal and athletic vigor that showed his heart was in the work and his muscles in the right place," deposited a single shovelful of earth on the embankment.

Crocker called for a rousing nine cheers and the onlookers gave them with gusto. The band struck up another tune. Then Stanford, reverting to his other role as railroad president, retired to the platform, and there followed an almost interminable series of speeches by no fewer than eight dignitaries, including state senators, assemblymen, clergymen and leading citizens of Sacramento. Collis Huntington was not among them. Legend quotes him, somewhat crustily, to the effect that he saw the troubles ahead far too plainly to take any pleasure in windy ceremony. The *Union's* account makes no mention of Judah either, though he must have been present for so personally gratifying an occasion.

In conclusion, Crocker again stepped forward. "Now then," he declared, "the talk is through and now the labor commences." He went on to say that "A pile driver is now, while I am talking, driving piles for the foundations of the bridge across the American River," and finished, to further thunders of applause: "It is going right on, gentlemen, I assure you."

Slowly the crowd dispersed to the final strains of the brass band. The western end of the Pacific Railroad was under way, while the Union Pacific had made no more than a bare start as yet, and was still months away from any ground-breaking.

Crocker kept his word. The work did go right on, in spite of the difficulties which began to crop up almost at once. The American was a capricious and unruly river. Tailings from hydraulic mining operations upstream filled its bed and aggravated a natural tendency toward flooding. More than once in the past, Sacramento itself had been inundated. As a result, the first several miles of grade along the levee and out into the riverside flats required unusually heavy fill protected by expensive riprapping. The piles for the bridge of which Crocker had spoken so exuberantly had to be driven down through twenty feet of tailings before they reached solid footing. The truth was that Charley Crocker was no railroad construction man, being totally new at the business, so that he had to assimilate one costly lesson after another as he went along. The costs annoyed Huntington. He considered them higher than they should have been, and more than once during the early weeks before leaving for the East he autocratically ordered all construction stopped, and kept it at a standstill until his stubborn doubts were explained away.

The situation distressed Theodore Judah, who had had his reservations about C. Crocker and Company to begin with. He worried about the quality of the work being done. Even more disturbing was his growing suspicion that the company was not Crocker's alone but a joint arrangement between Crocker, Huntington, Hopkins and Stanford, devised as a cynical plan to milk the railroad of the rich pickings promised by government subsidies. There may or there may not have been grounds for suspicion. But it soon became obvious that Crocker's resignation from the board of directors had been a resignation in name only, for he remained as influential as ever in Central Pacific affairs. And it began to be equally obvious that the four—the Associates, they called themselves, and later the public would know them as the Big Four—were emerging as the dominant clique in Central Pacific affairs.

Their personalities and their individual abilities meshed and complemented one another to a singular degree. Huntington was the tacit leader: the financier, planner and policy-maker. Crocker had the physical drive, the energy and the fierce willingness to grapple with concrete problems. Stanford, a pompous, ponderous man in manner and in thought, in many ways inclined to be a heavy-handed bumbler, was nevertheless an instinctive politician, imbued with dogged persistence and a quality of sturdy, single-minded faith in whatever he turned his hand to.[4] In sum, here was the ideal spokesman and legislative fixer.

These three were all big men, of imposing physical appearance and in the primes of their lives, Stanford thirty-nine to Huntington's forty-two and Crocker's forty-one. Mark Hopkins, though older (he was fifty) and a frail, retiring man, was a meticulous office manager and keeper of accounts. Cautious and conservative, he functioned as a valuable foil and counterbalance to the other three. "Uncle Mark," they called him affectionately, and his partner, Huntington, said of him that "I never thought anything finished till Hopkins had seen it."[5]

There were striking similarities in the origins and backgrounds of the four. Both Crocker and Stanford had been born in Troy, New York, though there is no indication that they had known each other as boys there. Crocker had been a saloonkeeper's son, Stanford an innkeeper's. Crocker had emigrated to Indiana with his family, worked as farm hand, sawmill laborer, blacksmith and ironmonger; eventually moved on to California, arriving there in 1850. Stanford had studied law, practiced without conspicuous success in New York State and Wisconsin and finally headed for California in '52. With his brother, Philip, he had gone into the grocery business in Sacramento, struck it moderately rich in a small gold mining speculation, returned to New York for another go at the legal profession in '54 and come back to California for good the following year. Mark Hopkins, a Michigan man, had traveled west via the Oregon and California Trails as an original forty-niner. Restless ambition and poor pickings at home had spurred them all; yet each had achieved his ultimate success not as a gold-seeker but as a prosaic merchant. There was an additional bond in the fact that by backgrounds and natural inclinations all four had been drawn into the new Republican Party in California and participated with varying degrees of activity in its early affairs there.

These were four men, then, widely though their characters differed as individuals, who were cast in the same essential mold; who thought and reacted alike; and who would almost inevitably gravitate together in juxtaposition to the aggressive and enthusiastic dreamer, Judah. And so they did.

Not one of the four was in any sense a railroad man. Every one of them, on the other hand, could claim to be a good and experienced businessman, which Theodore Judah, in all honesty, could not. Judah's position was a somewhat anomalous one. The Central Pacific Railroad was his brainchild, and his alone. He had done all the early, thankless crusading, the first arduous survey work, the long and difficult campaigning in Washington. Yet officially he was only its chief engineer, a hired hand subject to orders. Had he been content with that status there might have been no friction; throughout the subsequent years of construction the Associates never once interfered with the technical judgments of their engineering staff. But regarding the Central Pacific Railroad as his own personal project as he did—and with ample justification—Judah began to find himself more and more often at odds with the powerful four.

But the railroad was being built, that was the main thing. And the work continued to move ahead. On April 27 the *Daily Union* was able to announce that grading was complete from the American River to "Section 11," with all culverts and bridges in and a seven-mile stretch ready for ties and rails.

An ad in the *Union* on May 21 probably signaled a victory for Judah, for it announced to all contractors that sealed bids would be received until the first of June for grading, masonry and bridges on "the remaining portion of the first Division of the Central Pacific Railroad of California, from the line of the

California Central Railroad in Placer County . . . to Clipper Gap, a distance of about thirty miles." The notice was signed by Leland Stanford as president and Theodore Judah as chief engineer.

Governor Stanford, too, was making headway. As early as April 23 the *Union* had editorialized in favor of a bill "which obviates all constitutional objections and which, if passed, will furnish state aid that, with the private and County subscriptions, will insure the great undertaking." The same issue of the paper quoted a correspondent in Nevada advocating that territory's subsidy of ten thousand dollars per mile to the Central Pacific, "providing it is not permitted to run here, there and everywhere over the state to collect larger amounts."[6]

The California bill, also granting ten thousand dollars per mile, was passed by the legislature on April 25. Sacramento County voted to exchange $300,000 worth of its bonds for Central Pacific stock. Placer County, her neighbor to the north, did likewise. But the Sacramento Valley Railroad, through its superintendent, J. P. Robinson, at once filed a complaint in court asking that Placer's board of commissioners be restrained from delivering the bonds. There was a bitter taste of irony in that; the directors of Judah's old railroad had at first offered their property for sale to the Central Pacific as part of the transcontinental right of way, and been refused on Judah's recommendation that it was run-down and overcapitalized.

But other counties, San Francisco among them, were going ahead with plans for elections on similar bond issues.

Throughout that spring and summer, sandwiched in among long, obscure, rumor-ridden reports from Eastern battle fronts—Vicksburg, Chancellorsville, the slow and ponderous shiftings of armies that became Gettysburg—the columns of the *Union* bristled with hints of developing controversy over the Central Pacific. Letters from readers signing themselves with such pseudonyms as "A Constituent," or "Progress," or "R.R." (apparently for Rail Road) protested the growing activities of "individuals, capitalists, companies and corporations" who were fighting the railroad "directly or indirectly with the determination to destroy it." Quite plainly, it seems, the majority of the public, the little citizen, the man in the street, wanted the Pacific Railroad as emphatically as ever. But the very tenor of the defenses grew ominous with implications of powerful enemies rallying against it.

San Francisco was the focal point of opposition. A little belatedly—for the original reaction to the passage of the Act of '62 had been as joyous there as everywhere else—the city awoke to the possibility of a transcontinental railroad controlled by Sacramento. What might have been only the normal rivalry between California's two leading cities was quickly fanned to something hotter by business interests with specific axes to grind.

AP 1

CENTRAL PACIFIC SURVEY, 1863

● INHABITED TOWNS
○ FUTURE TOWNS OR STATIONS
- - - - ADVANCE SURVEY OF ROUTE

H. Scott

0   25   50   75 Miles

The Wells Fargo Express Company, a power in both California and Nevada, did not relish the thought of competition from a railroad over the Sierras, notwithstanding the fact that its president, Louis McLane, was a Union Pacific commissioner. Ben Holladay, proprietor of the Overland Stage Company, now riding high with government mail and transportation contracts amounting to some $1,800,000 annually, was another who had no trouble in perceiving on which side his bread was buttered, though he too was a U.P. commissioner. The California Stage Company and its allied lines recognized the railroad as a dangerous potential rival; so did the Pacific Mail Steamship Company, committed to the Isthmian route between East and West, and the California Steam Navigation Company, which plied San Francisco Bay and the Sacramento River. The Overland Telegraph, whose Pacific companies controlled all wire service between California and Salt Lake City, was understandably reluctant to let a rival telegraph line intrude on a comfortable monopoly. Even the Sitka Ice Company, whose business was shipping and selling ice from Alaskan glaciers, managed by some logic of its own to conceive of the Central Pacific as a competitor.

This was opposition with an important vested interest to protect, and no scruples about how it was done. Among them, the firms involved controlled the San Francisco press almost absolutely, and soon every newspaper in the city save one was printing derogatory editorials on the Central Pacific. More insidious and hence harder to combat were the whispering campaigns and swiftly circulated innuendo. It was peculiarly easy to start that sort of thing in a city like San Francisco, a city still blatantly corrupt, still a melting pot permeated by a wide-open frontier naïveté. The bosses of the Barbary Coast were available to arrange any kind of mischief for a price, with armies of idlers, hangers-on and petty criminals to do the work. In short order every public place, saloon, dive, drawing room and parlor house from Pacific Street to Russian Hill was agog with gossip of the scandalous "Dutch Flat Humbug" and "Dutch Flat Swindle," the railroad that had no intention of crossing the Sierras but was bent only on peddling its fraudulent stock and bleeding the public treasury. The stories spread, as scandal will, into all walks of life in San Francisco, and even farther.

There was a network of small, independent stage and freight lines operating throughout northern California (Sacramento County alone had nine, running no fewer than seventeen routes). All told, they employed some ten thousand men. But every railroad from the original Sacramento Valley on had shut some of them down, thrown men out of work; and the Central Pacific looked like the worst threat yet. Small wonder that these people seized on the "Dutch Flat Humbug" and helped to spread it. The town of Placerville, sitting astride the main Overland Stage road to Virginia City and growing fat on the proceeds, rose up in civic indignation at the thought of that precious traffic being diverted to Dutch Flat. Here, too, the charges of fraud and swindle fell on fertile soil, were repeated, amplified and passed on with gusto.

Yet in San Francisco itself, on the day of the election on the proposal to subscribe a million dollars in bonds for Central Pacific stock, the *Daily Alta California,* leading paper in the city, conceded editorially that the proposition probably would be approved.

"Opposition," the *Alta* noted, "was quiet, but few working around the polls against the measure."

To which, next day, the Sacramento *Union* retorted acidly:

The opposition was very quiet indeed. They had active strikers in every Ward, and paid them to the tune of six thousand dollars, with a promise that they should have a much larger sum provided the Pacific Railroad proposition was defeated. Another quiet operation was getting out thousands and thousands of circulars, full of misstatements and falsehoods, and distributing them, in the dark, broadcast over the city, even to thrusting them obtrusively into nearly every man's domicile.

The voters approved the measure and the *Alta* did not reply to the *Union*'s riposte. But an anonymous pamphlet was distributed shortly afterward, with a purported eyewitness account that told of Philip Stanford, brother of the Governor, driving up to the polling place in a buggy with a bag of gold pieces beside him, standing up and strewing them about him with both hands while calling on the crowd to vote for the Central Pacific Railroad.

There may have been some truth in the tale, though if so an anonymous pamphlet would seem to be a poor way to tell it. Quite obviously the controversy already had reached the bare-knuckle stage on both sides.

In July Judah's report to the board of directors stated that six thousand tons of rails had been purchased and would be delivered in monthly lots of five hundred tons, along with spikes, wrought-iron chairs and the necessary quantities of frogs, switches and other appurtenances to lay sixty miles of track. Contracts had been signed for six locomotives, six first-class passenger cars, a pair of baggage cars, fifteen boxcars and twenty-five flatcars. The American River bridge was approaching completion and most of the first eighteen-mile section of roadbed was ready for the rails.

It was a good report, on the surface. In the East Collis Huntington worked like a titan against heavy odds. But things were not so satisfactory as they appeared. Just to place the orders, get them accepted and entered on the books of hard-pressed suppliers taxed his determination and tough persuasive powers to the utmost. Rails and rolling stock were materials of war, subject to seizure under federal priorities and not really safe for the Central Pacific till they were aboard ship and on the way—not really safe even then, with Confederate commerce raiders at sea and raising havoc with Union shipping.

The war forced prices up and up. That first lot of rails cost $115 a ton on the wharves at Boston, as against an average price, in '61, of only $55 per ton. Spikes and fastenings were proportionately high. And there was no recourse; the Act of '62 specified patriotically that all iron had to be of American manufacture. Locomotive No. 1, a small tank engine of seventeen tons with a single pair of drive wheels (named the *C. P. Huntington,* incidentally), cost $13,688, with freight by way of Cape Horn to San Francisco accounting for $2,282. Before the war $10,000 would have been a high price to pay for a much larger locomotive. And the future promised higher prices still. Freight rates continued to rise steadily, and insurance premiums kept pace.

How to pay became a pinching problem, with company funds limited and steadily growing more so. And Huntington, absent from the East since '49, could not possibly have been prepared for the situation he found in New York. The nation's greatest city was torn apart by Civil War passions, racked by strife and dissension; yet at the same time it bubbled in a ferment of business opportunity, easy money and frenzied speculation brought on by wartime conditions.

Boss William Marcy Tweed and his Tammany Tiger ruled the city politically. Since it was a Democratic organization drawing its main strength from poverty-ridden Irish immigrants packed into some of the shabbiest slum districts in the world, antiwar feeling flourished there. Earlier, in fact, there had been a strong movement for secession and the setting up of New York as a free city. The outbreak of war had put a stop to that, but Copperhead sentiment still was rampant, and growing bolder as Union reverses in the field promised a long, hard war. The federal Enrollment and Conscription Act—the draft— was especially unpopular, with its provision enabling wealthy men to buy immunity by hiring substitutes. This, the restless Irish poor were reminded by Tweed, by New York State's Democratic Governor Horatio Seymour and others, was rank discrimination, condemning the common man to "Mr. Lincoln's charnelhouse," as Seymour shouted in one rabble-rousing speech. This sort of incendiary talk culminated in the Draft Riots of July, when mobs routed the police, pillaged, burned and murdered at will, brought all normal life in the city to a standstill for six days and were quelled at last only by the arrival of a detachment sent up from the Army of the Potomac.

It is probable that Huntington was in New York while the Draft Riots were in progress. If so, he did not remark upon them. A Republican himself, and an uncompromising free-soiler all his life, he was also a man of single-minded purpose. He had come to New York to get money for the Central Pacific Railroad, and did not propose to be distracted by anything, including politics or the nation's woes.

He found the way thorny.

Wall Street, the stock exchange and the whole financial life of New York were dominated by a crew of piratically rugged individualists whose like the nation had not seen before, and possibly never would again. Old Commodore Cornelius Vanderbilt, then in his sixty-eighth year, considered to be the wealthiest man in the United States with a personal fortune of eleven million dollars, was engaged in procuring ships to help the government maintain its blockade of Confederate ports—and in the process wringing additional millions out of old and rotted hulks, or so his enemies claimed. Daniel Drew, the unscrupulous old ex-drover, dripping with piety and homespun foxiness—"Uncle Dan'l," they called him, and "The Great Bear"—was a power on Wall Street and a feared manipulator of railroad securities. Another was Jay Gould, then only twenty-seven but already a master at slippery finance.

It was not by chance that railroads attracted the attention of such men. The great Eastern trunk lines still were building and expanding, spurred tremendously by the war's demands for freight and troop transport and by the swelling inflation of the national economy that went along with war. Henry Clews, a contemporary broker, social lion and informal historian of Wall Street, summed up the procedure for posterity (he was writing specifically of Gould, but it applied generally):

... To buy up two or more bad roads, put them together, give the united roads a new name, call it a good, prosperous line, with immense prospects . . . get a great number of people to believe all this, then make large issues of bonds, for further improving and enhancing the . . . property . . . Then to sell at a profit . . .[7]

But Collis Huntington wanted no dealings with such as these. He was as shrewd as they, and playing lamb to anyone's wolf was no part of his plan.

Then where would he turn?

New York had no lack of banks, and capitalists in plenty. August Belmont and Company was a glittering financial institution, allied with Europe's great House of Rothschild. There was the influential Bank of Commerce headed by Charles H. Russell; the Phoenix; the Manhattan. Junius Morgan and his young Harvard-trained son, Pierpont, headed the New York branch of the international banking firm of George Peabody and Company. There was Moses Taylor, wealthy New York merchant and founder of the City Bank of New York. These were among the leaders, men of social prominence and financial stability, whose words had the power to make or break.

Huntington was not without his connections in the great, alien city. As a California businessman he had had friendly dealings with Moses Taylor and

William E. Dodge, another wealthy merchant and capitalist. He was personally acquainted with Commodore C. K. Garrison, now an Eastern shipping magnate and philanthropist but once a popular mayor of San Francisco, and his son William. He knew, too, the uses of audacity and the bold approach. And he was a striking figure of a man, over six feet tall and austerely handsome, with a flowing, dark beard and hair not yet thinned by the baldness about which he would be inordinately sensitive in later life. With impressive arrogance, considering his circumstances, he offered his Central Pacific securities for sale in blocks of not less than $1,500,000, with no discounting of par value; no speculators need apply.

But if there was no dearth of capital in New York, there were unbounded opportunities for every investment dollar as well. Again, it was the war that had turned old values topsy-turvy. The Union armies were like the many heads of a hungry monster, gulping every commodity imaginable. Uniforms, guns, munitions, machines, foodstuffs, blankets, medicines, beasts of burden, wagons, transport—name it and the government needed it. Supply it—shoddy, sleazy, broken down, condemned as unfit for human consumption; it made no difference—the government would jump to pay the asking price. There was profit even in adversity. Long-headed investors, many with their own private sources of information in Washington and with the Army commands, were putting their money into gold. Each reversal for Union arms—and there were many in that year of '63—debased the value of federal currency and drove gold quotations higher. Even conservative businessmen with an eye to the future could see opportunity unlimited, and without looking too hard for it.

In western Pennsylvania the ironworks along the Monongahela and Allegheny rivers labored full shifts, night and day, and still barely kept up with the insatiable appetite of war. Andrew Carnegie, a young Scotsman presently employed by the Pennsylvania Railroad, already was meditating on the implications that situation conjured up, and pondering the possibilities of a future empire built of iron and steel. Oil had been discovered in Pennsylvania in '59, and out in Cleveland, Ohio, a sober-sided young merchant named John D. Rockefeller was thinking in similar terms on the profits inherent in a growing petroleum industry.

In fact, the times were wrenching and writhing in the accelerated birth pangs of industrial America, and the financial colossi of an upcoming era were even then ripening toward maturity. Collis P. Huntington would be one of them. But in the early summer of '63, in New York, he was a very small frog in a very large and turgid puddle. His Central Pacific Railroad got scant consideration among the host of nearer, surer gambles.

The bankers on whom he called told him bluntly that he had nothing to offer them. His company's securities were valueless till some part of the rail-road was built and operating. Government bonds not yet earned or delivered were not negotiable either, they pointed out.

It was true, and of course he knew it. But all such advice failed to reckon with the deep, stubborn resources of the man; his vast patience, sweet reason, crusty common sense; and always, at bottom, the tough, hard-bitten tenacity of one who put his hand to a task and simply would not quit.

In notes for an autobiography many years later, he told of visiting Boston and "other cities" which he did not name.[8] "I spent months in trying to induce capitalists to enter the company, but they thought it a great risk and would not take the chances." He told of meeting "a person" with whom he had had extensive business relations, and recorded their conversation:

"Going into this great enterprise, I suppose?" the person remarked. "It is all well enough, but California is a long way off."

"Well," said Huntington, "I suppose you don't want to sell goods?"

The person hedged. "I didn't want to say that exactly."

"I suppose you are kind of afraid to say it," Huntington retorted.

"Well," the other man repeated, "California is a great ways off."

"Yes," replied Huntington pointedly, "the trouble is it is further around Cape Horn than it is across the country."

It is a logical guess that the "person" here was William E. Dodge, for it was he who eventually did agree, with a few others, to take $250,000 worth of Central Pacific bonds at 7 percent, provided Huntington personally guaranteed the interest for ten years.

"I will guarantee it," Huntington said he told them, "because if the Central Pacific ever stops short of completion C. P. Huntington will be so badly broken you will never spend any time picking him up."

Back to California went Collis Huntington by rail and Overland Stage, an arduous, bone-racking trip, but he had no time to waste on the longer, more comfortable Isthmian passage. Calling a meeting of the board of directors he laid the unvarnished facts before them: if the Central Pacific was to be built, they would have to bear the burden. A history of Sacramento County published in 1880 quotes him as declaring flatly that "Huntington and Hopkins can, out of their own means, pay five hundred men during a year; how many can each of you keep on the line?"

Dr. Daniel Strong seems to have taken the hint, for he resigned from the board shortly afterward. James Bailey soon followed him. Both were men of limited means, unable to stay in the enterprise in the face of such an ultimatum. Both were friends and supporters of Theodore Judah, who now stood alone in his differences with the Associates.

His situation had not improved with the passage of time. Its precise nature never was spelled out in detail, the matter being kept confidential to the end. But in addition to his reservations about C. Crocker and Company, Judah was apparently disturbed, more and more, by the Associates' repeated refusals to authorize the surveys into Nevada he had kept urging.

The trouble drew rapidly to a head. Even before Dr. Strong's resignation from the board, Judah's letters to him that spring and summer had begun to tell of bitter clashes.

In May he described a stormy session at which "I freed my mind, so much so that I looked for instant decapitation. My hands are tied," he wrote, and complained of secret conferences to which he was not invited.

The breach widened, at last beyond any hope of a reconciliation. Huntington's ultimatum on his return from New York had been, of course, aimed at Judah as well as the other board members. But Judah's personal means were even less than those of Strong and Bailey. Now Mark Hopkins, as company treasurer, pressed him for payment of the large balance owing on his subscription for Central Pacific stock. He countered with the claim that the board had agreed to accept his services as chief engineer in lieu of payment, probably a valid one in view of his reputation for almost childlike honesty. But the Associates denied that such an agreement ever had been made.

All this remained a well-kept secret within the company. No hint of it appears, for example, in the pages of the Sacramento *Daily Union,* which, as September drew to a close, broke out in a generous smattering of good tidings.

On the twenty-second the big square-rigged Cape Horner *Herald of the Morning* arrived in San Francisco Bay with the first shipment of Central Pacific iron: one hundred tons of rails, a locomotive and tender and various smaller items. This was not the first shipment dispatched, the story took pains to point out; that had left Boston on the ship *C. S. Grant* three weeks ahead of the *Herald,* "and is expected daily." The reporter went on to express the fervent hope that the *Grant* had not fallen in with "the Confederate pirates *Florida* or *Alabama.*"[9]

The same issue carried the news that the bridge over the American River was now "ready for raising," and anticipated the laying of the first eighteen miles of track at an early date. There was also a brief telegraphic dispatch from the East to the effect that the first rails for the Kansas section of the Pacific Railroad had been received. However, the *Union*'s readers were reassured, it was stated that the roadbed there was not ready, and so it appeared that the honor of laying the first rail on the Great Pacific Railroad would go to California.

The Kansas section referred to was actually Samuel Hallet and Company, a brand-new organization set up with the backing of important business interests in Philadelphia and St. Louis to take advantage of the rights granted the old Leavenworth, Pawnee and Western Company by the Act of '62. Hallet, an able and energetic young Philadelphian, called his projected railroad the Union Central Pacific and issued a prospectus boldly stating his intention to build out along the Smoky Hill Trail all the way to Denver City. Since such a railroad would in effect constitute the eastern section of the transcontinental, it was apparent that the St. Louis interests were still a long way from conceding defeat. Of the Union Pacific proper there was little news. It appeared to be running a poor third in the race.

On September 30, the *Union* reported that those first rails brought in by the *Herald of the Morning* had reached Sacramento. And the paper now had the additional information that as many as three other ships had sailed ahead of the *Herald,* with rail shipments totaling three thousand tons. They were expected at San Francisco "hourly." The same article concluded with the happy announcement that the California Supreme Court had approved all state and county bond issues pertaining to the Central Pacific Railroad. But, it was predicted with some asperity (and with complete accuracy, as events proved), San Francisco never would pay up until sued.

There was some mild bad news, too. In view of Congress' recent action in passing a bill that set four feet, eight and one-half inches as the track gauge of the transcontinental railroad, the *Union* noted, the Central Pacific would lay a three-rail track in order that cars of the California Central and the Folsom and Lincoln Railroads, both of five-foot gauge, could be used interchangeably. This action of Congress was something of a defeat for the Central Pacific, inasmuch as it overruled an earlier decision by President Lincoln—made under strong pressure from a special California delegation—in favor of the five-foot gauge.[10]

But the good news and the bad alike came too late to be of interest to Theodore Judah. He had broken, finally and irrevocably, with the Associates.

It seems clear that he was forced out in a last bitter showdown. The details were never confirmed, the secrecy which surrounded the affair never officially breached, but the settlement apparently involved a cash payment of $100,000 for Judah's Central Pacific stock, plus some kind of an option permitting him to buy out the interests of his adversaries under certain conditions. None of the Associates ever admitted the option feature, but Anna Judah later insisted that her husband did, in fact, have that right, and that, moreover, he already had gone far toward obtaining the necessary financial backing from "certain gentlemen in New York and Boston."[11]

Judah himself inferred as much in a last angry, secretive, yet oddly half-triumphant letter to Dr. Strong, written just before he sailed from San Francisco in early October.

> If they [the Associates] treat me well, they may expect a similar treatment at my hands [he wrote in part]. If not, I am able to play my hand.
> If I succeed in inducing the parties I expect to see to return with me to California, I shall likely return the latter part of December.

Obviously, from this, he anticipated that events would move quickly. The length of time required by the round-trip journey would have made any protracted stay in the East impossible, on the schedule he was setting for himself. He did not identify the "parties," nor did Anna, though apparently there were broad enough hints, at the time, to nourish speculation that they were representatives of the powerful Vanderbilt interests in New York. The notion is not necessarily farfetched. The Commodore was very conscious of the commercial possibilities involved in connections with the Pacific Coast, having been a leader in establishing shipping lines via the Isthmus of Panama since the earliest gold-rush days. His interest in railroads was of more recent vintage, but he was even then committing himself to it with the aggressive vigor he applied to everything he touched. Under the urging of so persuasive an advocate as Theodore Judah, he might well have been willing to take a hand in the transcontinental railroad, with or without the acquiescence of the Associates. He was never the man to back away from a knockdown fight; what might have happened then offers some fascinating food for speculation.

But Judah saw no one in New York.

He was carried from the steamer on a stretcher, hopelessly ill of yellow fever contracted during the Panama crossing. On November 2 he died.

Tragic in itself, his death marked the end of the first phase in the long history of Pacific railroad promotion. The thirty-year dream had been brought to reality, or to the beginnings of reality. More than any other one man, Theodore Judah had been responsible for that. The concept of the Central Pacific as the transcontinental railroad's western link was his exclusively, and it was this concept which shaped his whole attitude. It was necessary, of course, that the undertaking eventually earn its way; a competent and experienced engineer, Theodore Judah was not so completely the dreamer as to ignore that fact. But to a man of his vision and whole-souled dedication to the great ideal, the profit motive was secondary.

It was not so with the Associates. If Judah had devoted the best years of his life to the dream, they were in the process of gambling everything they owned on its practical accomplishment. The difference in points of view was fundamental and irreconcilable. And from the day the Central Pacific was incorporated as a business enterprise it was the Associates, the businessmen, who held the upper hand. Undoubtedly, in the final showdown, they were ruthless. Yet it seems clear that, whatever the specific nature of the controversy, Judah might have compromised but refused to do so.

The settlement by the Associates enabled him to leave Anna well taken care of in a material way. She returned to her old home in Massachusetts and there lived out her life in peaceful obscurity, returning to California on occasional visits as the years passed, making it clear to her few intimates that she thought her husband had been shabbily treated but indulging in no public recriminations. Anna Judah was a lady.

The wry fact is that Judah was not missed on the Central Pacific. His assistant, a young man named Samuel S. Montague, was promoted to the post of chief engineer. At their first meeting after the news of Judah's death reached Sacramento, the board passed a perfunctory resolution of sympathy for the widow and turned back to more urgent matters. The twin problems of short money and rising costs had been solved only temporarily by Huntington's trip to New York. Soon he went jolting eastward aboard the Overland Stage to take up the battle again. Out on the right of way Charley Crocker was plagued by labor shortages. The innuendoes of fraud and swindle continued to circulate, growing louder and more believable with repetition.

Meanwhile, on October 5 the Sacramento *Union* had printed another Eastern telegraphic dispatch, this one stating that the required minimum of two million dollars in Union Pacific stock finally had been subscribed, and that a stockholders' meeting was called for October 29 in New York.

CHAPTER 6

CHICAGO, '62

The meeting of the Union Pacific commissioners at Chicago's Bryan Hall in September of '62 had been well attended, loudly vocal and enthusiastically reported by the local press. About half the 158 commissioners, representing a score of states and territories, responded to Chairman Samuel Curtis' opening roll call; a highly satisfactory turnout, considering the troubled times. In addition, an impressive number of eminent railroad capitalists and engineers from Eastern centers had come to watch and consider and compare notes. The Chicago Board of Trade gave them all a hearty ceremonial welcome, and the commissioners buckled down to the business at hand with an encouraging show of alacrity and industry.

William B. Ogden of Chicago was elected the Union Pacific's first president. An excellent choice; he had been his city's first mayor, a leading spirit in organizing its first railroad, the Chicago and Galena Union; and was even then busy with plans for consolidating that and various other Illinois and Iowa short lines into the Chicago and Northwestern, to drive westward to the Missouri River for a connection with the Union Pacific. His election was a clear recognition of Chicago's established dominance as a Western rail center. It was recognition, too, of the fact that participation by Chicago railroad interests was considered essential to the Union Pacific's success.

The young city had mushroomed to a population of 125,000, and still flourished at a galloping rate. It sprawled unattractively over noisome swamplands at the confluence of the Chicago River and Lake Michigan; its plank sidewalks stood as much as ten feet or more above streets that were miry canyons, and many of its largest downtown buildings were already being jacked up bodily to keep them above mud level. One of the pioneers in the process was a young man named George Pullman, who had taken a contract to lift the Tremont House Hotel literally by its boot straps while he dreamed of designs for a railroad sleeping car. Chicago slums equaled those of any Eastern metropolis for wretched conditions, disease and rampant vice and crime. But its waterfront was the natural western terminal for cargo schooners from every port on the Great Lakes, and warehouses, grain elevators, cattle loading pens and lumberyards crowded shoulder to shoulder along the Chicago River. Most important of all, the city was only thirty-six hours from New York by rail—the Michigan Southern, Michigan Central and Pittsburgh, Fort Wayne and Chicago all affording connections—and other lines had been pushing out to west, north and south for a decade and more. A brawling roughneck of a town, Chicago; its red-hot rivalry with St. Louis was natural and inevitable, and a link-up between it and the Pacific Railroad seemed nothing short of manifest destiny.

Henry V. Poor, member of a family long active in Eastern railroading and editor of the influential *Railroad Journal,* was elected U.P. secretary. Thomas Olcutt of Albany, New York, was named treasurer, thus completing a slate of officers to fulfill the terms of the Act of '62. An Iowan, Peter A. Dey, was appointed chief engineer. Here was another sound choice, for Dey had served both the Chicago and Rock Island and the Mississippi and Missouri Railroads as chief engineer, had supervised the early explorations by young Grenville Dodge out into the Platte Valley and was a man deeply committed to the concept of a railroad to the Pacific. Before the meeting adjourned he was instructed to go ahead with additional examinations of the Platte Valley terrain, and it was determined that Union Pacific stock should be placed on sale in every large city in the Union without delay.

All this constituted a flying start, or seemed to. Yet behind the enthusiastic sessions and the glowing newspaper reports of them, there seems to have been a curious apathy, a frank recognition of the many problems in the way. As quoted in the Chicago *Tribune,* President Ogden's first speech following his election declared the enabling Act unsatisfactory in many of its provisions, and mentioned changes necessary "before capitalists will be glad to take hold of it." A Nebraska commissioner by the name of Monell found it necessary to take the floor and deny the long-standing concept of his territory as the Great American Desert. It was a myth, he charged, perpetrated by the Southern Confederacy and its spokesman, Jefferson Davis; the very vehemence of Mr. Monell's remarks, also quoted in the *Tribune,* suggests that he was on the defensive, and realized it.

And then, of course, there was the war. Here in Chicago the war seemed very real and altogether too close. A Union offensive in the West had shown signs of stumbling and stalling as '62 wore along. Confederate General Kirby Smith, having turned the Union flank through Cumberland Gap, occupied

Lexington, Kentucky, on September 2, the same day the Chicago meeting convened. Now all of eastern Kentucky was in Secessionist hands, both Louisville and Cincinnati threatened, with southern Indiana and Ohio wide-open to cavalry raids if not worse. All sorts of rumors of Copperhead plots circulated, and were widely believed. And on the eastern front McClellan's vaunted Peninsular campaign against Richmond had collapsed. The Confederacy had scored another smashing victory at Second Bull Run at the end of August. Even as the Chicago meeting drew to a close, Robert E. Lee had seized the initiative and was crossing the Potomac in an invasion of Union territory.

Amid so grim a spate of war news, the Union Pacific's Chicago headlines could not seem really important. And nothing in the day-to-day outlook was very conducive to the building of investors' morale.

When the stock went on sale, Union Pacific officials, like their opposite numbers in California, speedily discovered that the anticipated public rush to buy shares simply did not materialize. Many of the commissioners themselves signed for modest amounts, apparently for appearances' sake in most cases, rather than in any firm expectation of profit. A few prosperous and public-spirited citizens subscribed. But in general the nation's leading bankers and capitalists were supremely uninterested.

All the negative reasoning so soon to confront Collis Huntington held as true for the Union Pacific as for the Central. There were other factors which made the U.P. an even poorer risk. The California road at least offered the prospect of traffic originating in its own Sacramento Valley, and could promise a potential plum in the rich business of the Nevada Comstock. But in heading westward from the banks of the Missouri, the Union Pacific would be striking out into an empty and desolate wilderness in which land was regarded as utterly worthless. Hence the land-grant features of the Act of '62 held little appeal. And in spite of the great migration to the Pacific littoral which had been going on for a long time, and notwithstanding the Colorado gold strikes and the Nevada silver boom, the dominant banking and investment houses of the East tended to be self-centered, preoccupied with business closer at hand. Few of them had any appreciation as yet of the immense profit potentials inherent in the transportation of goods and people between the Mississippi River and the burgeoning societies of California, Oregon and Great Salt Lake. As far as the American businessman was concerned the only possible commercial value of a transcontinental railroad lay in its promise of a short route to the teeming trade ports of the Orient. Even William Ogden had dwelt heavily on that aspect in his Bryan Hall acceptance speech. But the Union Pacific, which seemed destined to start nowhere in particular and end at some indeterminate point in the desert, did not appear likely to fulfill such a promise.

Quite as dubious, to the eye of the prospective investor, were the geographical compromises written into the enabling Act. They threw the race wide-open from the Missouri to the one hundredth meridian; St. Louis was not about to yield by default, and the opening moves in the organization of Samuel Hallet and Company were of course common knowledge among wide-awake Eastern financiers. As they saw it, the Union Pacific could conceivably be out of that race even before it began.

Within a very few months it was apparent that the Union Pacific Railroad and Telegraph Company had small chance of being financed by private enterprise, not without some drastic action by Congress and some very special inducements to the men who controlled the money markets.

William Ogden already had called for the legislative amendments. And in that same speech he had declared also that "Speculation is as fatal to it [the Union Pacific] as Secession is to the Union." In saying that he had only been giving voice to the general conservative viewpoint. Yet in the situation as it existed by early '63 the Union Pacific *was,* in fact, nothing but a gigantic speculation, and no one but a confirmed speculator could be expected to touch it. This truth has been strangely overlooked by historians and commentators in the years since the 1860's, but at the time it was obvious enough to conservative financiers. And the speculator who stepped into the vacuum they declined to fill was Dr. Thomas Clark Durant; native of Massachusetts, a graduate of Albany, New York, Medical College, who had forsaken medicine early in life to join the New York firm of Durant, Lathrop and Company for a plunge into the alien world of railroad promotion. He had done well in it, was then forty-two years old and already a notable financial success. And he had had his eye fixed on the Union Pacific from the very beginning.

There probably was nothing secret about that, though if Durant took any part in the Chicago sessions, even from behind the scenes, there is no record of it. But his interest in the Pacific Railroad was genuine and of long standing, his background as an entrepreneur of Western railroads impressive. He had been active in the promotion and construction of the Michigan Southern, first railroad into Chicago from the East, and had been a prime mover in the formation of the Chicago and Rock Island, and later of the little Mississippi and Missouri. He and his partner in the latter venture, Henry Farnum of Illinois, had been the employers of Peter A. Dey and Grenville Dodge in the original survey across Iowa to Council Bluffs and the subsequent reconnaissances into the Platte Valley. They both had lobbied in Washington for a Pacific Railroad bill during the same period. Farnum was present in Chicago as a Union Pacific commissioner, but the two men were no longer close associates at this time. An unsavory little hint of scandal hovered about Durant's name in connection with that, it being alleged that certain private speculations of his with company funds had contributed to the stoppage of work on the Mississippi and Missouri during the business recession of '53, and seriously impaired Farnum's financial standing as well. No formal charges, though, ever had grown out of the affair.

Even to his contemporaries on New York's Wall Street Thomas Durant was something of an enigmatic figure; one of those men who come to the surface occasionally in any era; apparently well known to their colleagues and associates but, conversely, not really known at all; men with no intimates, yet possessed of wide and influential contacts; men, in short, who can get things done, though the world at large might never know quite how, or fully understand their motives. Throughout his life the Durant personality seems to have baffled most of those who had dealings with him. He was an educated man, cultured and worldly, but quick-tempered, secretive and frequently guilty of insufferable arrogance. His dress and physical appearance tended toward the flamboyant, more suggestive of the Shakespearean actor, say, than the sober financier. He was a lover of luxury, a reckless spender known in New York social circles for the lavish elegance in which he lived and entertained. Yet he was personally abstemious. Few of his associates ever fully trusted him, it appears. Fewer still remained in his own good graces for long.[1]

This was the man who now proposed to set the Union Pacific on the road to reality.

Quietly Thomas Durant began to contact Eastern capitalists of his acquaintance. Many of them, perhaps most, already had declined to subscribe for U.P. stock. But Durant had a new proposition. He was willing, he told them, to advance the cash to cover the necessary 10 percent payment of any shares taken in their names. He would then leave it to their own discretion: they could reimburse him, pay the balance and take the stock at some later date, if and when the Act of '62 was amended favorably; or they could simply wash their hands of the whole matter if they continued to regard Union Pacific as a poor investment. In the latter case, Durant would assume the ownership of all stock involved in the deal.

It was a strange arrangement, but there was nothing openly wrong about it. Deceptions much more sinister were tolerated, if not wholly condoned, by the dog-eat-dog ethics of Wall Street in the 1860's. The Union Pacific Railroad was, after all, a work urgently desired by the federal government itself. Putting one's name on the subscription list was a gesture of patriotism if nothing more. No one was being cheated, certainly; the nominal investor could not lose, since Durant was advancing all the money and taking all the risks. Contained in the proposition also was the small but tempting prospect of something for nothing. Quite clearly, Thomas Durant had taken the measure of these staunch conservatives much more accurately than they had taken his.

At any rate, he sold his proposition to a sufficient number of them to serve his purpose. When by the fall of '63 the required minimum of stock had been subscribed as demanded by the Act, it was largely due to these efforts by Durant. And to do it he had had to put up only a relatively small amount of cash.[2]

He was gambling, of course. It was an incredibly farfetched gamble, founded on an extraordinarily hardy vision of the possibilities. For he was betting not only that the Union Pacific Railroad *could* be built, and at a profit—which hardly anyone else believed—but also that these front men of his would in the end decide not to take over their shares under any circumstances (which is precisely what happened in the majority of cases). The entire manipulation had its overtones of illegality, for among its various restrictive clauses the Act of '62 specifically limited the amount of stock which could be owned by any individual. But as long as the shares were held in various names, and until those names finally declined to accept them, the letter of the law, if not its spirit, remained unbroken. In effect, Durant was acting simply as an entirely legitimate agent.

What really mattered, though, was that he now had virtually full control of a formidable block of U.P. stock, and thus had placed himself in position to wield a potent influence at the upcoming stockholders' meeting in which the practical shape of the Union Pacific Railroad and Telegraph Company would be hammered out.

CHAPTER 7

A GROUND-BREAKING ON THE MISSOURI

Back in the spring of '63 in Corinth, Mississippi, which had been a Union bastion for almost a year, following the bloody, fumbling victory at Shiloh, Grenville M. Dodge was handed orders to report to Washington as quickly as he could get there.

Young Dodge had traveled a long road since the day in '51 when he had first landed in Chicago, a stocky, muscular lad out of Danvers, Massachusetts, just twenty years old and a callow graduate in civil engineering from Norwich University come west to seek his fortune. He had soon gone to work as a survey lineman for the Illinois Central Railroad, later moved on to a job with Mr. Peter Dey on the Chicago and Rock Island, then followed Dey when the chief went with the Mississippi and Missouri. The two had hit it off well and made a good team. By late '53 they had completed the M. and M. survey to the east bank of the Missouri at Council Bluffs, and the young assistant engineer was satisfied that he had found his life's work. By that time, too, he had fallen in love with a Peru, Illinois, girl named Anne Brown, and he married her the following spring. Now he had put roots down in this new trans-Mississippi West; Council Bluffs would be his permanent home. The railroad years in Illinois and Iowa had begun to make of him a confirmed Pacific Railroad disciple, too, in his own fashion as dedicated as Theodore Judah was soon to become, half a continent away.

Dodge had first crossed the Missouri River by flatboat in the fall of '53. A marauding Pawnee brave had very nearly made off with his horse during that first lone venture into the Platte Valley. Later a band of friendly Omahas had moved into his party's camp, made themselves at home and eaten it completely out of provisions. These were his first experiences with the plains Indians who would one day loom large in his career, and they were not pleasant ones. But as he explored farther and farther westward for Farnum and Durant the conviction had grown in him that this was the way the Pacific Railroad would have to go.

Then the war had come and the young engineer-explorer, still barely out of his twenties, had turned to soldiering as an Iowa volunteer. He had risen fast in the Army, finding his natural forte as a repair officer in charge of railroads torn up in the ebb and flow of the Western campaigns. He had been wounded at Pea Ridge, Arkansas; had begun to attract the favorable attention of Ulysses S. Grant as the skirmishes and maneuverings slowly hardened into a Union offensive after Shiloh. This spring of '63 he was a brigadier general, and commanded the military district of Corinth.

But the orders, giving no reason for his being called to the capital, struck him as ominous. He thought he knew the reason.

Just recently he had armed a detachment of Negroes and assigned them to duty as guards over the camps of contrabands—runaway slaves—who had flocked into the Union lines in such numbers that they were becoming a military nuisance. The action had been taken on his own initiative. He considered it necessary and even humane, since white troopers resented the duty fiercely and were not above expressing themselves by firing on their contraband charges with little or no provocation. But the arming of Negroes was a highly radical move at that stage of the war, the kind of thing that aroused Southerners to cries of atrocity and military superiors to stuffy disapproval. By his own account, Dodge expected nothing less than a stiff reprimand.[1]

Arriving at Washington, however, he found that he was scheduled for a private conference with President Abraham Lincoln himself. And at the Executive Mansion Lincoln wasted no time in coming to the point.

Did Dodge, he asked, recall that they had met once before?

The general did. It was in Council Bluffs, in '59. He had still, at the time, been in the employ of Farnum and Durant, and had just returned from one of his Platte Valley reconnaissances. Relaxing after dinner on the front porch of the Pacific House he had been approached by a tall, gangling stranger who introduced himself as Abe Lincoln, an Illinois attorney in Council Bluffs on personal business. Sitting there looking out over the broad, muddy sweep of the Missouri River, the two had talked for a long time. Dodge recalled that Mr. Lincoln had shown himself to be intensely interested in the subject of a railroad to the Pacific Ocean, and in all phases of westward expansion. And the Illinois man had proved so adroit and subtle a questioner that, "When the long conversation was ended, I realized that most of the things I had been holding as secrets for my employers in the East, had been given to him without reserve.

"He shelled my woods," Dodge added ruefully in the idiom of the day.[2]

Now, seated in his study in the Executive Mansion, Mr. Lincoln made it plain that none of that early interest had abated. He had summoned Dodge to Washington, he explained, because the Pacific Railroad Act of 1862 gave him the responsibility of naming the point on the Missouri River from which the Union Pacific was authorized to build out to the one hundredth meridian. Remembering their little talk of four years before, he wanted Dodge's advice on the location of that eastern terminal.

Dodge, of course, recommended Council Bluffs.

Again their conversation lasted a long time. The President listened attentively as Dodge went over the nature of the difficulties to be overcome, and expressed his personal opinion that the job was too big for any manner of private enterprise, and should be undertaken only by the federal government itself.

No, Lincoln demurred, the government could not do that, encumbered as it was with the overbearing burden of civil war. But he impressed upon the general that the government *was* ready to do everything in its power to help, and gave his word that any changes in the Act of '62 deemed necessary by the men assuming responsibility for the railroad would be made.

For a Chief Executive in Abraham Lincoln's difficult position in the spring of '63, this was a very large promise indeed. Oppressed as he was by a hundred and one problems relating to the conduct of the war, plagued by dissident elements both inside and outside of his administration and subject to every kind of carping criticism by press and political factions, the President must have had a very deep and abiding conviction of the Pacific Railroad's value to the Union. Otherwise he would hardly have bothered to call Dodge in from the field on so relatively minor a question as the spot for the Union Pacific's starting point.

In retrospect the entire incident suggests that Lincoln had a deeper motive. Remembering the conversation in '59 as he did, he almost certainly knew in advance what Grenville Dodge's advice would be. Besides, two of the Union Pacific commissioners, T. J. Carter and Springer Harbaugh, already had been assigned to investigate the regions both north and south of the confluence of the Platte and Missouri rivers, and their preliminary reports had favored Council Bluffs also. There is evidence, too, that Dr. Durant had found the time to come down to Washington and urge the Bluffs' advantages on the President. With all this background, it seems much more probable that Lincoln had had his ear to the ground all along, that he knew the Union Pacific officers temporarily elected the previous September were growing discouraged with the slow pace of progress since then, and that he chose Grenville Dodge as the medium through whom to impart his assurances: the "word to the wise" that all would be well.

Dodge, in any event, did not return immediately to his command in Corinth. Instead, he was granted leave to go to New York and meet with Union Pacific officials there. Apparently Lincoln did not directly suggest this; Dodge's own later recollection was that he himself asked the President if he might do so, and Lincoln assented.[3] Both were intelligent men; the message was clearly understood, whatever the manner in which it was couched. And of course it was vastly heartening to the men of the Union Pacific.

Grenville Dodge left no specific details on his activities in New York. The Union Pacific organization scarcely existed as yet, save in name, and it is likely that all talks were informal. Apparently the general conferred with both Henry Poor and Thomas Olcutt, and it may be assumed that William Ogden, in Chicago, was informed of President Lincoln's beneficent attitude. But there were talks with Dr. Durant, too. Durant, of course, already had embarked on his plan for gaining entry into the company; there are indications in plenty that he also had kept in more or less close touch with Ogden, Poor and Olcutt ever since the Chicago meeting. The evidence, then, strongly implies that the doctor's intention to inject himself into Union Pacific affairs was known and accepted, at least tacitly, by the others.

Presently Dodge left New York to spend the balance of his furlough at home in Council Bluffs before returning to Corinth and the further campaigns of the Army of the West. The weeks of late spring and summer passed; fall came; and on October 29 the first Union Pacific stockholders' meeting duly convened in New York City. In the interim, Robert E. Lee's first invasion of the Union had ended in the great defeat at Gettysburg, and Vicksburg on the Mississippi River had fallen to Ulysses S. Grant. Things were looking a little better for the Union, the tide of war inexorably turning.

It was understood that the election held by the commissioners at Chicago had been temporary only, pending the creation of a sufficient number of stockholders to take over company management. The first order of business in New York, therefore, was the election of a board of directors and a permanent group of officers. And of the latter, Henry Poor was the sole survivor of the three named at Chicago, being re-elected secretary. General John A. Dix of Massachusetts and New York emerged as the new president in Ogden's place; John J. Cisco replaced Olcutt as treasurer; and Thomas Durant was elected vice-president. Again, however, it was a good and able executive slate. Dix's railroad experience included the presidencies of both the Chicago and Rock Island and the Mississippi and Missouri (both, be it noted, roads in which Thomas Durant too had been heavily interested). In addition, Dix was a statesman of considerable stature, having served with distinction in a number of government posts, culminating in a Cabinet position under President Buchanan. John Cisco, a successful New York banker, was also Assistant Treasurer of the United States, hence was another figure of national prominence.

In practice, however, General Dix could be no more than a figurehead president for the duration of the war, since he was the commanding officer of the VII Corps of the Union Army in the field. Henry Poor seems never to have taken a very aggressive role in the direction of the company, and Cisco, like Dix, was kept busy with governmental duties. Thus Durant immediately became, and remained, the man in active charge of company operations as well as its business manager and financial agent.

So fortuitous a development inevitably led to speculation, then and afterward, that the scheming Durant had rigged the elections of both Dix and Cisco for his own benefit. Logical though it seems, the suspicion is little more than conjecture. At the time, there were no important objections from other stockholders. Except for their commitments to the federal government, both men were eminently qualified. Moreover, the matter of Congressional revision of the Act of '62 was recognized as of primary importance, and both Dix and Cisco were men known and respected in Washington.

A year of experience in the promotion of stock sales had pinpointed the specific shortcomings of the Act, and emphasized their gravity. By setting the stock issue at 100,000 shares with a par value of one thousand dollars each, the Act severely limited participation by small investors. The provision making the government subsidy loans in the form of first mortgage bonds meant that any company bonds issued had to be second mortgages, with little or no appeal to private lenders. The requirement that forty miles of railroad had to be completed before any bonds could be released at all loomed as a more formidable hurdle the longer it was contemplated. The 1867 completion date was obviously out of the question. And over and above all the other complaints there was beginning to be a universal conviction that the total of government help was inadequate; that the issuance of federal bonds only after the work was done was altogether too hampering a condition; and that the restrictions on the payment of these bonds needed to be eased, else the company could never succeed in convincing private capitalists of its prospects.

The organization of a strong and active lobby at the Capitol, then, was a first consideration. Durant had had experience in that sort of thing. He would see to it.

On October 30, second day of the meeting, Peter Dey submitted his report on the past year's examination of the Platte Valley route. As expected, he reconfirmed the general impression that it was entirely feasible. Before adjourning, the new board of directors boldly ordered him to go ahead with surveys of a line all the way to the Wasatch Mountains on the eastern edge of Utah Territory.

The Union Pacific was a going concern at last.

Meanwhile, cash brought in by stock subscriptions amounted to a woefully meager working capital. Here, too, Durant, the experienced railroad promoter, had a solution in mind, and it was somewhat more sophisticated than Collis Huntington's first financing efforts in his Central Pacific's behalf.

Because the building of a railroad usually entailed costs on a scale exceptionally large for the business structure of the period, the formation of constructing companies as agencies for doing the work without incurring too crushing a liability for personal losses was a common procedure. Operating as an independent contractor, paid by the railroad company but with the railroad's own backers participating, the constructing company offered the opportunity to gain profits commensurate with the risks involved whether the railroad itself eventually succeeded or failed. While it was generally recognized that such an arrangement could lead to shady practices or even outright dishonesty in the juggling of costs and profits, the device was accepted as necessary, and not widely condemned. Few railroads, or large public works of any kind, were built in any other way during the '50's and '60's.

C. Crocker and Company, in fact, appears to have been an effort along this line for the Central Pacific. But C. Crocker and Company was altogether too rudimentary and amateur a device to provide for the financial needs Durant foresaw for the Union Pacific.

Casting about for the sort of organization he envisioned, the doctor soon began to look with sharpening interest at the Pennsylvania Fiscal Agency. This was a concern incorporated under the laws of that state in 1859 as (to quote from its charter) "an agency for the purchase and sale of railroad bonds and other securities, and to aid in like manner contractors and manufacturers." The Pennsylvania Fiscal Agency had not done very well, however, and Durant reckoned it might be available. He commissioned one George Francis Train, a Boston man known along Wall Street and in newspaper and society circles as an odd and flamboyant mixture of speculator, dilettante financier, writer, orator and *bon vivant,* to act as his confidential agent in negotiating for its purchase.

At the same time he began to line up a group of partners. Included was Sidney Dillon, a native New Yorker and self-made railroad executive of some prominence in the East, though not at that time a Union Pacific stockholder. Included too was a Colonel Henry S. McComb, New York financier and a U.P. director. Among other U.P. stockholders who came in were Cornelius Bushnell, wealthy Connecticut manufacturer (and a prime mover, incidentally, in the building of the Union ironclad *Monitor*), and a New York merchant named C.A. Lambard.

Thus, quietly and in a somewhat devious atmosphere, the seeds of future complications were planted.

For the present, there were gratifying signs of progress as 1863 came to an end. In Washington on November 17 President Lincoln issued his first order on the railroad's eastern terminus:

> I, Abraham Lincoln, President of the United States, do hereby fix so much of the western boundary of the State of Iowa as lies between the north and south boundaries of the United States township within which the city of Omaha is situated as the point from which the line of railroad and telegraph in that section mentioned shall be constructed.

Since Omaha lay directly across the Missouri from Council Bluffs, the President obviously was following through on the good intentions he had expressed to Grenville Dodge. But the company felt that the wording was indefinite, so Lincoln obligingly issued another order on March 7 the next year, designating "such first named point on the western boundary of the state of Iowa east of and opposite to the east line of Section 10, in Township 15, south of Range 13, east of the sixth principal meridian in the Territory of Nebraska."

Despite its insistence on detail, the company did not think it necessary to wait, and ground was broken in Omaha on December 2. Dr. Durant came out from New York for the ceremony, debonair in dress and manner as always, though he does not appear to have taken a very prominent role, and permitted his agent, George Francis Train, to deliver the principal oration of the day. Train, already embarked on extensive purchases of town lots in expectation of a railroad boom, waxed flowery and enthusiastic, forecasting completion of the road within five years. His audience, mostly frontier merchants and freighters, small settlers and a sprinkling of traders, plainsmen and buffalo hunters, probably snickered in their beards at that, for no one seems to have shared such vaunting optimism.

Territorial Governor Alvin Saunders of Nebraska was present to turn the first shovelful of earth, and congratulatory telegrams were received from Governors Yates of Illinois and Stanford of California, from Mormon President Brigham Young of Utah and from the mayors of Chicago and Denver City. The latter, anticipating that his town would be on the Union Pacific main line as a matter of course, pledged the wealth of the Colorado gold fields to the great undertaking. Abraham Lincoln also telegraphed his good wishes through his secretary, John Hay.

All in all the affair, as reported locally, did not differ markedly from the Central Pacific's ground-breaking almost a year earlier, though it seems to have been carried out with less polish and on an altogether more modest scale. Omaha was no Sacramento, after all. It was, in fact, a rude frontier town squatting on the bluffs above the muddy Missouri; a thriving one though, nine years old, lustily sure of its own destiny and already boasting a mercantile business in excess of two thousand dollars a day.

Perhaps the most important thing about the little ceremony was a significant omission. At its conclusion there was no one to step forward as Charley Crocker had done at Sacramento and inform the onlookers that work was even then in progress and that "It is going right on, gentlemen, I assure you." Work was not in progress, and was destined to go nowhere for quite a while.

That first shovelful of earth turned by Governor Saunders was virtually the last for almost a year. Much later in the U.P.'s history, Sidney Dillon would consult company records and state that the ceremony and the modest celebration which followed had drained the treasury dry.

The preceding July a disgruntled former employee had ambushed Samuel Hallet in Wyandotte, Kansas, and murdered him with a bullet in the back. The Kansas enterprise faltered to a stop while its backers groped through the throes of reorganization. So for the time being the threat from that quarter faded. That was something.

All the same, it had not been a very auspicious beginning for the Union Pacific.

CHAPTER 8

TROUBLES AND A TURNING POINT

Aaron Sargent, the same who had been so stalwart a friend to Theodore Judah in the House of Representatives that winter of '61 and '62, visited the White House as the new year of 1864 began. With him he brought one more problem and another decision to urge on the badgered President.

The Supreme Court of California was on record to the effect that the foot-hills of the Sierra Nevada Mountains began at a distance of thirty-one miles northeast of Sacramento. The point had been established in an early case not concerning the Central Pacific or any other railroad, and was not regarded as open to argument. Theodore Judah's original survey was in substantial agree-ment, fixing the point at Barmore, thirty-two miles out. On the face of it, no question existed. But the Act of '62 put the burden of decision on the Presi-dent's shoulders, and with a whopping difference in government subsidy bonds involved—$48,000 per mile as against $16,000—a moot point could be manu-factured, and had been.

Sargent exhibited a map purporting to show that the reddish soil of the Sierra slopes and the black soil of the valley met at Arcade Creek, just seven miles from Sacramento. He also submitted (or it was later claimed that he submitted) verifying letters from Joseph D. Whitney, California state geologist; J. F. Houghton, state surveyor-general; and Edward Fitzgerald Beale, United States surveyor-general for California. Sargent himself was no longer a member of Congress, his term having expired in '63, but he still was a loyal friend to the Pacific Railroad and a man of proven nerve and audacity.

Abraham Lincoln may have been aware of the California Supreme Court decision and the details of Judah's survey. More likely he was not; the President had far weightier matters on his mind just then than the question of precisely where a mountain range did or did not begin three thousand miles away. And he too was a friend of the Pacific Railroad. Popular legend has him remarking ruefully that he knew he was being had. All the same, he decreed on January 12, 1864, that "The point where the line of the Central Pacific Railroad crosses Arcade Creek in the Sacramento Valley is hereby fixed as the western base of the Sierra Nevada Mountains."

"Here you see," Sargent is said to have remarked with obvious smugness, "my pertinacity and Abraham's faith removed mountains."

The story has been dismissed by some historians as a whole-cloth fabrication, partly on the grounds that contemporary accounts of the coup refer to Sargent as "Senator," which he never was. However, some kind of very tricky manipulation must have been necessary to get so glaringly favorable a decision out of the White House, even granting Lincoln's preoccupation with more vital wartime matters.

Whatever the truth of it, the new year began with the Central Pacific able to look forward to collecting the top government subsidy for construction of over twenty-four miles of terrain that was at worst no more than gently rolling. The railroad's enemies pounced on the incident as one more instance of the Associates' chicanery in matters of finance. Central Pacific apologists argued in rebuttal that the Presidential decree had the effect merely of moving the entire 150-mile top-bonus section westward, thus costing the government nothing extra in the long run (they neglected to point out, however, that even this resulted in twenty-four miles paid for at $32,000 per mile instead of the correct minimum of $16,000).

More to the point, to the Associates, was the fact that the extra bonds would come due early—and their needs were pressing.

Aside from this initial windfall, 1864 did not start on an encouraging note. The first rail had been laid on the preceding October 26, and by the sixth of November that first locomotive brought around the Horn by the *Herald of the Morning* had been assembled and a head of steam raised in her boiler. But the *Union,* in reporting the event, had to explain that "The engine could not be set in motion because it has not yet been placed on the track. On Monday morning it is expected to go to work hauling iron over the track." This locomotive was a handsome eight-wheeler from Norris and Company, Philadelphia, and was promptly christened the *Governor Stanford.* She broke down on her maiden trip, disappointing a large delegation of civic personages who had been promised the first ride. But, the *Union* reported, repairs were completed by eight that evening and the *Stanford* "made a number of trips as far as 16th Street, crowded with cheering passengers." The date was November 10, and two miles of track had been laid at the time.

By the first of the year that had lengthened to eighteen miles, reaching Junction, the present Roseville, where the Central Pacific survey line crossed the older California Central Railroad. The board, its collective backbone stiffened by Collis Huntington's brass-tacks report from New York, had decided to build on to Newcastle, thirteen miles farther. Again Charley Crocker had bid for the contract, though he claimed that the $200,000 in assets with which he had launched C. Crocker and Company was all used up and his personal credit was beginning to be strained as well.

He got a contract for only two miles, considered to be the most difficult two. Other contractors raised such loud protests of favoritism that the directors felt it necessary to parcel out the other eleven among them. But this, it developed, was not a very satisfactory solution, with the scarcity of labor putting everybody in a bind. The labor situation always had been bad in California, where the population still was small in terms of the state's area, and the mines and the San Francisco docks offered steady work at good wages. Now it was worse than ever, the war drawing off able-bodied volunteers and—far more serious— the Nevada Washoe luring others away as the silver boom, like a chain reaction, went on exploding in ever more fabulous strikes. Hundreds of workers hired out on the Central Pacific solely for the free transportation to railhead, then either kept right on going without ever touching shovel or pick handle or worked only long enough to earn stage fare over the Sierras to Nevada. The contractors took to bidding against each other for the few who were willing to stick, with the result that wages were soon soaring. Even so the pace of the work lagged, with strikes and threats of strikes all along the line.

Charley Crocker, not a man to be bullied by his own help and take it lying down, hit on the idea of importing Irish immigrant laborers from New York and Boston, where the slums teemed with them and they were despised by most Americans, regarded as fit for only the most menial and degrading of jobs. He did so, bringing them around Cape Horn by sailing ship for the sake of cheapness. They were a raw and unskilled lot, most of them, ignorant, illiterate, but rawboned, willing and strong as dray horses. They took to the work of grading and track-laying with that curious affinity the Irishman has always had for railroading in America. But they were wild, undisciplined, hard-drinking fellows, too. They did not all stick, and before long even the rawest of the ones who did began to grow wise to the labor situation, and to the uses of the strike and the slowdown.

But Crocker fared better than his rival contractors. Eventually most of them had to quit, and the bulk of the grading and track work to Newcastle fell to C. Crocker and Company after all, by default.

Yet the work continued to go slowly. There was little system to it. For all his tremendous energy and drive, Crocker still was far from expert; he made no bones about admitting that he "could not have measured a cut if my life depended on it."[1]

Trouble piled up on other fronts. The chorus of opposition to the railroad never slackened, the charges of swindle and humbug circulating more freely then ever, the opposition press now including almost every newspaper in northern California except the faithful Sacramento *Daily Union* and the Dutch Flat *Enquirer*. Early in '63 the Associates had decided on the expedient of putting in a wagon road between the main Virginia City-Placerville highway and Dutch Flat, where it ultimately would connect with the oncoming rails. As a device for diverting some of the Washoe traffic to the railroad as early as possible, the plan made good business sense. But it was denounced as proof positive that the Central Pacific Company had no slightest intention of laying track over the Sierras; that it never had seriously planned on a connection with the transcontinental railroad; that all the charges of fraud were, in short, true.

Now, in the bitterness that increased as 1864 ripened into summer, not even Theodore Judah was permitted to rest in peace. Another railroad across the Sierras was being discussed: the San Francisco and Washoe, to run from Placerville to Carson, California, on the Nevada border, and later to be extended to Virginia City. It still was in the talking stage, but it had an organization and some powerful backing (Charles E. McLane, a brother of the head of Wells Fargo and Company, was its president) and had a survey in progress. Its chief engineer, one Francis A. Bishop, issued a public statement charging that Judah had known his own projected route through Donner Pass to be impracticable, and had been glad to get out, taking a bribe of $100,000 from the Central Pacific Associates as the price of his silence.

The accusation contained just enough of the seeds of truth to lend it the air of authenticity. Judah was in his grave and could not speak out; Anna, embittered and heartbroken, was in faraway Massachusetts; a harassed and indignant Leland Stanford could only issue fuming denials.

The whole sorry Donnybrook spilled over into the new state of Nevada, where the legislators now began to have second thoughts on the proposal to grant subsidies to the Central Pacific. Impressed by the San Francisco and Washoe's claims, they turned instead to a bill that would put ten million dollars in state bonds at the disposal of the first railroad to connect Nevada with the navigable waters of California. Leland Stanford fought back, hurrying by stage to Carson City for a personal plea that the bonds be turned over to the Central Pacific, as the only company with a bona fide claim to them. The best he could get was the tabling of the proposal while a special committee was appointed to examine the prospects of the rival railroads.

All this went on in addition to the ever-present problems of supply and finance. Ties, timber and masonry were the only materials available in California; everything else had to be shipped out from the East via Cape Horn or the Isthmus. Collis Huntington kept it coming, but at prices and freight rates that were back-breaking. The first lot of ten locomotives cost a total of $191,000. Wrought-iron spikes which had averaged two and a half cents a pound in prewar days now ran to six and a half. Bar iron was $110 a ton, bricks thirty dollars a thousand. Telegraph insulators, needed by the thousands, cost thirty cents each. Owing to difficulties in getting deliveries, plus the length of time spent in transit, it was necessary to anticipate needs and place orders as much as a full year in advance; else the work would have bogged down in frequent, costly halts.

The wherewithal to pay continued elusive, for both Crocker in California and Huntington in the East. On the Pacific Coast gold was the only acceptable medium of exchange, and could be had only at premiums of $1.32 to $1.50 or more. The buying power of federal currency fluctuated erratically as the war dragged on. It never was higher than eighty cents on the dollar, and once fell so low that three dollars in greenbacks bought only one dollar in gold. Central Pacific stock was practically unsalable in California and nearly so in the East, in spite of Collis Huntington's best efforts.

"When I entered the railroad company my credit stood very high in New York," he said later, "but capitalists there felt I was placing myself in a critical position."[2] That had been the case in '63; it still was the case in '64. The good credit rating was all he had. He made it do. The details are unclear; there are only his own recollections, put down on paper many years afterward, to go on. But the dogged, persuasive persistence of the man comes through. William E. Dodge granted additional loans, secured as before by Huntington's personal guarantee and the pledging of Huntington and Hopkins paper. Apparently he had power of attorney from the other Associates, and was able to pledge paper of the Stanford firm also.

"I never paid over seven per cent per annum interest," he declared with the rugged pride of the hard bargainer, "while the Union Pacific paid two per cent per month and seven per cent annually besides."[3]

The money came; not easily, but it came.

Many of the California state and county bonds were held up in legal entanglements, notwithstanding the Supreme Court's endorsement of the laws under which they had been voted. San Francisco newspapers continued to hint that those laws had been bought by wholesale bribery and corruption. At times the hints grew very broad indeed. In an editorial studiously avoiding any mention of the Central Pacific Company by name, referring to it only as "Dutch Flat," the *Alta California* returned to the theme that summer:

It was by a shower of gold that it gained admission to our brazen tower—the citadel of the common sense of our people. . . . When the twenty-dollar gold pieces fell thick and heavy, men standing around the polls, not conspicuous before that time for breadth of ideas upon the subject of internal improvements, all at once became railroad men of the most pertinacious and irrepressible sort.

This obvious reference to the anonymous report of Philip Stanford's activities at the polls the previous year was beating a dead horse perhaps, but it was also building an unsavory reputation the company would be a long time living down.

Yet the building of the railroad was not all gloom and grimness. The Central Pacific did what it could to make friends, sometimes with an engaging simplicity. On March 20 the *Union* had printed an account of an excursion to a newly opened granite quarry twenty-two miles out of Sacramento for members of the California legislature and their families and friends. The train consisted of two passenger coaches, each crowded to capacity with sixty riders, and seven flatcars fitted with plank seats. "The locomotive 'Governor Stanford' led the van, gay with star-spangled banners and other devices," declared the *Union* exuberantly, "and on the platform car next behind rode the Union Brass Band, with ten melodious and harmonious instruments of sound."

No one thought of noting the time made, the story went on, but everyone "was pleased with the smooth and steady motion of the train, which showed how well the new track had been laid." The writer let himself go in a bucolic paean as he described the rest of the day. He told of the children, "of whom there were enough for a small regiment," scampering about, wild with delight, while anxious parents warned of poison oak. Matrons and maidens "wandered off among great trees and rocky knolls, according to their 'own sweet will'; while grave legislators and solid men generally gathered around the quarry in groups, conversing learnedly and geologically."

On a more practical note the *Union* also noted that the railroad was able to deliver granite from this quarry to Sacramento for only a dollar a ton, an early sample of the business benefits forthcoming.

Continuing, the reporter told how the band, ensconced beneath a shade tree, "uttered such notes that several of the ladies began to talk seriously about a 'dance on the green.' " But in true picnic fashion sudden thunderheads gathered on the horizon and the locomotive began to whistle urgently, "cutting off a debate, and the motion 'all aboard' was carried without a division."

So it appears that there were lighter moments amid the turmoil and the problems.

Charley Crocker plodded ahead with construction, and the Central Pacific began to look and act like a railroad that was in business to stay. On Wednesday, the first of June, the Sacramento *Union* noted that "the morning train on the Pacific Railroad started out yesterday with one hundred and thirty-two passengers, and a large mail destined for the northern and eastern parts of the state." At the rate track was being laid, the paper added, "it is expected that trains will go on to Newcastle by Friday, or at the latest, Saturday."

On June 10 a small advertisement in the *Union* announced three Central Pacific trains daily each way between Sacramento and Newcastle, running on regular schedules.

It seemed the *Alta California* would have the final word after all, though, for on July 24 it reported:

We are informed that there are now no men employed in grading the Central Pacific Railroad beyond Newcastle, the present terminus, and what few have been at work of late (some fifteen or twenty) were sent a few days ago, to work on the Dutch Flat Wagon Road. . . . The fact is, that institution has got a large-sized elephant on its hands and he is growing larger every day and consequently wants more fodder.

It must have been at about this time, as Leland Stanford confessed later, that the Central Pacific treasury was totally bare for a period of some seventeen days. Things are not always what they seem, however, and these were to be among the last words of triumph the San Francisco press would be able to say on the subject. More fodder for the elephant was on the way. The *Alta California* itself, in fact, had—perhaps unconsciously—conceded its own defeat on the preceding day, July 23, in an angry editorial that began: "In the Congress which has just adjourned San Francisco was shamefully betrayed in the matter of the Pacific Railroad. . . ."

It referred to the Act of 1864 amending the Pacific Railroad Act of 1862, passed by both houses in June and signed by Abraham Lincoln on July 2. By its terms the promise made by the President to Grenville Dodge more than a year earlier was fulfilled, and generously.

Dr. Durant's Union Pacific lobby had labored with shrewdness and skill in Capitol cloakrooms and council chambers. The effort was all-out, and it marked the beginning of the great power of "The Railroad Lobby" and the emergence of a body of "Railroad Congressmen" that would eventually become a national scandal. Yet in '64 the effort was open and comparatively aboveboard. It did not need to be otherwise, for President Lincoln's personal influence and, above all, the overmastering tide of wartime urgency made the task easy.

Collis P. Huntington had thrown his weight into the balance, too, going down from New York to Washington to plunge into the game of Capitol influence with all the astuteness and hard-driving vigor he possessed. He had, as he afterward testified before a Congressional investigating committee, paid some eleven thousand dollars in cold cash to a pair of Capitol habitués named James Stewart and Alexander Henry for "enlightening him in the ways of

Washington."[4] It was one of the few times in his life he failed to get his money's worth, apparently, for the amending act that finally emerged from Congress was a Union Pacific measure all the way, and did not entirely please him.

The Act was generous to both companies, however. Not a single one of the arguments in favor of revising the Act of '62 had been overlooked. There was little organized opposition in either House or Senate, though a few isolated voices were raised in protest against the high-handed methods by which the bill was pushed through. The *Congressional Globe* recorded complaints that the draft finally approved was not the one submitted during committee hearings, but a substitute rushed to the floor without preliminary discussion and with no official teller present to verify the yea and nay votes. But it was wartime; as James G. Blaine, highly respected member of the House from Maine, said later: "The terrible struggle to retain the Southern States in the Union had persuaded the Administration and the Government that no pains should be spared and no expenditure stinted to insure the connection which might quicken the sympathy and more directly combine the interests of the Atlantic and Pacific Coasts."

Two provisions of the new Act promised immediate financial relief for the hard-pressed companies:

First, the railroads were authorized to issue their own bonds in amounts equal to the government bonds, both to be released on the completion of twenty instead of forty miles of road. Company bonds were to be first mortgages on the properties, thus automatically downgrading the government issues to second mortgages. Second, the Act of '62 was amended to permit the government bonds of $32,000 and $48,000 per mile between the eastern base of the Rockies and the western base of the Sierra Nevadas to be released in amounts of up to two-thirds of the total *in advance* as soon as any twenty miles of such roadbed had been prepared for the rails.

Though this provision was not to apply to the Union Pacific west of Great Salt Lake on more than three hundred miles beyond the fully completed and continuous track, it meant that both companies could, in effect, borrow on their prospects rather than their accomplishments. There are indications that Congress intended this as an emergency measure. In practice, however, the grades of both railroads usually were mortgaged to the limit as soon as the Act went into effect.

Of special importance to the Union Pacific was another provision changing its capitalization from 100,000 shares at a thousand dollars each to the more flexible structure of one million shares at one hundred dollars each.

Union Pacific spokesmen had pointed out that the land grants authorized in the original Act were of more apparent than actual value, since most of the land would in fact be worthless until the railroads were finished and the land developed. Congress agreed to the justice of this claim by doubling the grants to ten sections per mile within twenty miles on either side of the track, or a total of 12,800 acres per mile. The Central Pacific benefited to the same extent, for the Act, of course, did not differentiate between the two companies.

Rights of way were cut from two hundred to one hundred feet on both sides of the tracks, but private property could be condemned for the purpose, a feature neglected in the earlier Act. In addition, any coal and iron deposits found would belong to the companies, though other mineral rights still were withheld.

The Act of '62 had obligated both companies to apply all charges for transportation and telegraphic services to the federal government as credits on the government loans. This was eased now, at the Union Pacific's behest, so that only half of such charges were required to be so applied. It was an important concession, since government business was expected to make up the great bulk of U.P. traffic. The Union Pacific's slowness in getting started was recognized also, in an extension of the time limit for completion of its first hundred-mile section by a full year.

But on this point, at least, Huntington must have managed to make his influence felt, for the Central Pacific was granted a specific four years to reach the California state line.

He suffered a grievous defeat, however, in still another provision which empowered the Central Pacific to build only 150 miles eastward from that line. The Act of '62 had set no limit on his company's expansion to the east. It was this setback, undoubtedly, that caused his outspoken discontent with the new Act, though he reacted in his typical fighter's arrogance: "I said to Mr. Union Pacific, when I saw it, I would take that out as soon as I wanted it out."[5]

The remark is a plain indication that the campaign in Congress must have been attended throughout by a running skirmish for advantage between Huntington and Durant, even though both were, of necessity, united in their desire to see the Act of '62 amended. Both were strong men, implacable in determination, equally able though there was a vast gulf of difference between their two characters and their ways of driving toward the goal. Collis P. Huntington was blunt and forthright, yet endlessly patient when he had to be, hiding an infinite capacity for cold calculation beneath an outer crust of tough Yankee granite. Thomas Clark Durant was volatile, extravagant; an extremely devious and complicated man, but within, like Huntington, a powerhouse of keenness and energy. This Washington battleground was their first head-on clash, and Huntington came off second best. But it was due to circumstances, his own inexperience, primarily; and that would not remain a constant factor.

Never for a moment from this time on was either man, or either company, to lose sight of the fact that they were not partners but rivals.

But in July, 1864, in spite of Huntington's ruffled feathers, both sides could view the situation with more satisfaction than either had felt before. The President's signature on the amending Act marked an end to the first phase in the building of the Great Pacific Railroad. That December, standing before a joint session of Congress to deliver his annual message, Abraham Lincoln was able to declare, in part:

"The great enterprise of connecting the Atlantic with the Pacific States by railway and telegraph has been entered upon with a vigor that gives assurance of success, notwithstanding the embarrassments arising from the prevailing high prices of materials and labor. The route of the main line of the road has been definitely located for one hundred miles westward from the initial point at Omaha City, Nebraska, and a preliminary location of the Pacific Railroad of California has been made from Sacramento, eastward to the great bend of Truckee River, in Nevada."

Considering the state of the nation this climactic Civil War year end, the President undoubtedly was reaching for all the encouraging statements he could make. Like most political documents his message was guilty of a certain amount of exaggeration. It was true that Thomas Durant had filed a map with the Department of the Interior in October, and in November Lincoln himself had approved the first hundred miles of the Union Pacific's route. And the Central Pacific's Associates were, at last, pushing the surveys into Nevada, which Theodore Judah had urged so fruitlessly. Nevertheless it took a very sturdy faith as well as a politician's optimism to speak of "assurance of success." The voices of the small minority who had protested the generosity of the amending Act were not stilled, and would not be. In the President's audience that day were thoughtful men who realized it.

James Harlan was one. The Senator from Iowa, sponsor of the original Act of '62 and beyond question a friend of the transcontinental railroad, had voted for this Act of '64, though he had his doubts about allowing the companies to issue bonds on their grades in advance of railhead. He had pointed out on the floor of the Senate that the provision might encourage them in irresponsible fiscal practices.

James G. Blaine was another. Said he cautiously, "A more careful circumspection might perhaps have secured the work with less expenditure."

And Representative John Sherman of Ohio observed that, "If the Act had been delayed until after the War, when the securities of the United States rapidly advanced in value, it could not have passed in the form it did."

But the last two statements came some while afterward, when they could claim only the wisdom of hindsight.

In July of 1864 such sentiments bothered Collis Huntington and Dr. Durant and their respective colleagues not a whit.

PART TWO

*The Snow-Capped Mountains
and the Lone Prairie*

CHAPTER 9

THE MONEY MEN

Dr. Durant had his victory, but the fruits of it were a long while in ripening. For the rest of the year, and well into '65, the Union Pacific failed to act very much like a railroad that was going anywhere.

Grading out of Omaha did not get under way until late summer following passage of the Act of '64. By fall only about two hundred men, a few teams of horses and oxen and a pair of "excavating machines" were at work. The latter are referred to in an occasional report, though their nature remains unknown; they could not, in any case, have been "machines" in any modern sense of the word, and the whole force appears to have accomplished little beyond running the company some $300,000 in debt. The work was scarcely begun before it faltered to a standstill in a heated dispute over location of the right of way.

Chief Engineer Peter Dey had run his line due west for thirteen miles from Omaha to the Elkhorn River. Colonel Silas Seymour of New York, engaged as consulting engineer to the company by Dr. Durant, recommended a change which would increase the distance by nine miles, claiming that Dey's line entailed grades of sixty-six to eighty feet to the mile, a figure he viewed as objectionable. Dey answered with objections of his own. Seymour's line, he pointed out, eliminated these grades only from the Omaha summit westward, leaving three miles of equally heavy grade from the Missouri River bottoms to the bluff on which the town stood. And in addition, the Seymour changes would result in an eighty-foot eastbound grade on the other side of Elkhorn summit, thus adding materially to construction costs while making no real difference in feasible train tonnages.

The controversy was a purely technical one, but it seems that the town of Omaha got into it somehow, and after much argument and many exchanges of reports it was agreed to submit the whole question to the board of government commissioners, who would in any event have to pass on the acceptability of the railroad as finally built.[1] The commissioners took a long time in their deliberations. Eventually they ruled in favor of the Seymour line, but with the proviso that the grades to which Dey objected should be reduced by large amounts of cutting and filling. It never was done. The grades were allowed to stand, and in the end, for reasons not explained, the commissioners accepted the section without further comment.

But all this was a later development. Durant, refusing to wait for the decision, took it upon himself to order that grading should go ahead on Seymour's line. It was not only arbitrary and high-handed; it was a direct rebuff for Dey, whose reputation for honesty and ability made it all the more humiliating.[2] And while the chief engineer still nursed his injured feelings, an even more serious controversy boiled up.

In August Durant awarded the Union Pacific's first construction contract to a man named Hubert M. Hoxie for a hundred miles westward out of Omaha at a rate of fifty thousand dollars per mile, payment to be made in company securities. Hoxie, a onetime minor politician and court house hanger-on in Des Moines, probably had met Durant during the early negotiations for the Mississippi and Missouri Railroad's Iowa charter. He was at this time in charge of the Union Pacific's ferry service across the Missouri between Council Bluffs and Omaha, not a very important or demanding position, in view of the small amounts of material then coming through. But, much more disturbing, there was no evidence to show that he had either an organization to do the work, any funds or financial backing of any kind, or even a shred of experience as a railroad builder. In short, the inference could clearly be drawn that he was acting as a front for someone else. Too, Dey was appalled at the figure quoted. His own estimate of costs for the same section was thirty thousand dollars per mile. Very properly, he at once questioned the wisdom of the contract.

Again he was rebuffed. The contract stood, and in fact Hoxie presently applied for an extension, in a letter dated October 4 at New York City:

To the President and Executive
Committee of the Union Pacific
Railroad Company:

On condition that your railroad company will extend my contract from its present length of 100 miles, so as to embrace all that portion of the road between Omaha and the 100th meridian of longitude, I will subscribe, or cause to be subscribed for, $500,000 of the stock of your company.

H. M. HOXIE
by H. C. CRANE, *attorney*

And this letter was promptly endorsed: "The above proposition is hereby accepted for and on behalf of the Union Pacific Railroad Company."

The endorsement was signed by John A. Dix, C. S. Bushnell and George T. M. Davis, as a special committee, and dated October 3, 1864.

Three days later Hoxie assigned the extended contract to Durant and his associates: McComb, Bushnell, Lambard and an H. S. Gray, another Union Pacific stockholder, who between them had managed to raise a million dollars for construction.

Now, aside from the fact that Hoxie's letter was dated at New York and signed not in person but by an attorney, and overlooking the added fact that Hoxie was totally lacking the means of making good his offer to subscribe for a half-million dollars in stock, the date of the endorsement—*one day before the date of the letter itself*—leaves no doubt that the entire transaction had been arranged beforehand, with Hoxie only a docile cat's-paw.

Actually, he and Durant had come to an understanding at the time the original contract was awarded. The real beneficiary was the old Pennsylvania Fiscal Agency, or what remained of it, now in a considerably altered form. Durant and his syndicate had been successful in purchasing the Agency's charter in March. Changes in its organizational structure had been made so as to insure control through a New York office, while still retaining the rights granted by its Pennsylvania charter, and the corporate name changed to the Credit Mobilier of America, after a similar French company organized in 1852 which was still in operation on the European scene. The name was said to have been suggested by George Francis Train, Durant's confidential agent in the purchase and now a stockholder in the venture. (If so, Train's brainstorm was an unfortunate one, for the French Credit Mobilier was destined for liquidation in '67 amid sensational charges of fraud and corruption.)

Shortly after taking over from Hoxie, Durant and his associates turned the contract over to the Credit Mobilier of America, fearing, they said, that the individual risks were too great. The stratagem was then complete; the Credit Mobilier was in control.

As the constructing company for the railroad in line with established custom there was not necessarily anything wrong with it per se. But the devious and even furtive manner in which the end had been attained was hardly the kind of thing to inspire confidence. Moreover, the Credit Mobilier had proceeded at once to buy up all outstanding Union Pacific stock shares, amounting to a total of some $2,180,000, but of which sum only 10 percent, or $218,000, had been paid down. The stock was acquired easily and cheaply, simply by repaying this 10 percent to the original investors, most of whom were highly dubious about its value anyway. Then, when the Act of '64 canceled the early shares and replaced them with equal amounts in hundred-dollar certificates, the controlling stockholders in both Credit Mobilier and Union Pacific became identical and the two companies, for all practical purposes, were one. Legally, however, the Credit Mobilier remained a separate entity removed from any of the Union Pacific's responsibilities; it could, at the will of Dr. Durant and his associates, become a parasite preying on the railroad's treasury.

Peter Dey probably knew little or nothing of all this background. But no doubt his guesses came close enough to the mark, and when no action was taken on his objections to the Hoxie contract, his position became untenable. For a while he hung on and tried to make the best of it, but a chief engineer without authority is no chief engineer at all. In January of '65 he gave up, his letter of resignation to President Dix remarking wistfully that he was aware he was leaving "the best position in my profession the country has offered to any man."

In the shabby treatment he had received there is something of a parallel with Theodore Judah's from the Central Pacific. Dey, though, was more fortunate than Judah. After leaving the Union Pacific he continued as a respected and successful engineer, and ended his career many years later as the senior member of the State Railway Commission of Iowa.

Durant lost no time in offering the vacated post to Grenville Dodge, undoubtedly the man he would have preferred in it from the beginning. But Dodge, having served with distinction in the battle before Atlanta and taken a near-fatal wound in the head there, was now a major general. After recovering from his wound he had been transferred to the command of troops on the Great Plains, where the Army, just now, had its hands more than full.

The long-recognized "Indian problem" had erupted into a full-scale war in '64, stirred up by Indian resentment over the increasing tide of emigration along the new Smoky Hill Trail to the Colorado gold fields and the growing slaughter of the buffalo by white hunters, many of them draft evaders and bounty jumpers who had fled west to escape the long arm of the government. Some hunters had been ambushed, some emigrants killed, and the year had ended with the bloody massacre—men, women and children—of a camp of peaceful Cheyennes on Sand Creek in Colorado Territory by a militia force under the fanatical, half-mad Colonel John Chivington. It was a miserably inexcusable piece of butchery, worse than anything the Indians themselves had been guilty of. And in retaliation, this January, the Sioux Nations and many of their Cheyenne allies were raiding savagely from northern Kansas all along the Overland Trail, burning road ranches and threatening to drive even the troops into their isolated forts.

Not surprisingly, therefore, it was the judgment of Dodge's superiors in the

War Department that he could not be spared, and he had no choice but to decline the offer. Quite possibly there was an understanding that he might be available later, however, for Silas Seymour took over the supervision of survey and construction work out of Omaha on a temporary basis and the position of chief engineer remained unfilled.

Under the aegis of the Credit Mobilier the grade advanced westward somewhat more energetically than before, with survey parties flung far out ahead in spite of the danger from hostile Indians, which now was great. Still, things seemed to go slowly. At least one Eastern observer found himself decidedly unimpressed with what he saw.

That was Samuel S. Bowles, editor of the Springfield, Massachusetts, *Republican,* who crossed the plains in May as a member of the retinue accompanying House of Representatives Speaker Schuyler Colfax of Illinois on a junket to the Pacific Coast. Colfax was a popular public figure, regarded in some quarters as future Presidential timber, and his party rolled across the West in high style. Ben Holladay provided a special coach on his Overland Stage and a personal agent to see to the travelers' comfort. A detachment of U.S. Cavalry rode along as escort, and in addition to Bowles the trip was covered by Albert D. Richardson, a special correspondent for Horace Greeley's New York *Tribune.* The Union Pacific, of course, was examined with an interested and critical eye en route.

Bowles was disappointed with the slow progress being made. Building a railroad across the plains, he observed, was mere "baby work." He went on to say, in one of his dispatches to the *Republican,* that "Three hundred men will grade it as fast as the iron can be laid," and concluded that it was a shame this whole section of the railroad was not already completed and in operation. As the party proceeded westward he remained unimpressed, noting that the stage horses ascended the storied South Pass on the Oregon Trail at an easy trot. "From here to Salt Lake, over the Rocky Mountains," he told his readers at home, "there are apparently no greater obstacles to be overcome than your Western Road from Springfield to Albany, the Erie and the Pennsylvania Central, have triumphantly and profitably surmounted." Reaching Salt Lake City, the editor further noted that he saw no sign of Union Pacific activity there except one small party of engineers who "seemed to have lost their bearings."

All this was an unfortunate reaction for the Union Pacific. Opinionated and superficial in his judgments Bowles undoubtedly was. But he was also a longtime advocate of the transcontinental railroad, and one of the few men in the East who appreciated the magnitude of its commercial possibilities. The previous year he had gone on record with an estimate that the wagon traffic across the Great Plains carried an annual volume of some forty million pounds of goods, at a total cost sufficient to provide the railroad with a revenue of $48,000 per mile. And the Springfield *Republican* was a widely read and influential newspaper, to make the poor publicity all the worse.

It was a big country out here beyond the Missouri, however, and Samuel Bowles did not see it all by a great deal.

This same spring the Army fought an indecisive campaign against the militant Sioux along the Powder River in the Dakotah Wyoming, and at its conclusion Major General Grenville Dodge led his command homeward through the northern spurs of the Black Hills.[3] It was largely unexplored territory, and the general, probably still influenced by the experience of his early railroad reconnaissances, adopted the daily routine of leaving his main body of troops to take a small squad along the Black Hills summits, mapping the terrain as he went and keeping an eye out for feasible approaches from the eastward plains. It was a risky practice. The Sioux, far from cowed, were ranging all through this country, and he knew it. Nevertheless he continued his informal exploration down Chug Water Creek to its confluence with the Lodgepole without interference. There, with a handful of troopers and a couple of scouts, he struck out and worked southward from Cheyenne Pass around the headwaters of Crow Creek.

And just about then it became apparent that a sizable force of Crow warriors had slipped in to cut him off.

"I knew it meant trouble for us," he wrote later in a considerable understatement.[4]

Dismounting his detachment and putting the horses in charge of a pair of troopers with instructions to stay out of sight on the west side of the long ridge between Crow Creek and Lone Tree Creek, the general held the crest with the balance of his men, working cautiously ahead and sending up smoke signals for his main cavalry force. It was a ticklish, nerve-tearing business, the braves, stripped and painted for war, bursting up the slope at intervals in quick, yelling little sorties, held off only by good shooting and the superior range of the cavalry carbines. But the afternoon wore slowly along toward dusk, and Dodge's signals went unseen by the main column. About four o'clock the Indians' tactics became clear; they began to gain ground, reaching forward in an unmistakable move to occupy the crest of the ridge ahead and cut the hard-pressed detachment off.

The adventure ended happily, the cavalry finally perceiving the smoke signals at almost the last moment and advancing to scatter the Crows. As an incident in the Army's Indian campaigns of the period it was no more significant than scores of other isolated, unsung little skirmishes. But when it was over one of the scouts, laughing, reminded the general of a remark he had made while it was going on: "If we save our scalps, I believe we have found a railroad line over the mountains."

Dodge did not remember having said it, but it was true he had noticed that the ridge on which they had been beleaguered seemed an extraordinarily fine approach from the valley up through the Black Hills summit. And as the reunited command proceeded, he became more than ever convinced that the ridge could be followed within the gradients specified in the Union Pacific's charter, and with a comparatively small amount of work.

He mapped the spot, marking its location by a lone tree on the bank of the creek by that name and by a steep butte that rose above Crow Creek, with a deep depression where granite and sedimentary formations joined, and filed it away in his head for future reference. Very clearly, to judge by this incident, Grenville Dodge had lost none of his consuming interest in the transcontinental railroad. And it appears equally clear that he foresaw his own future as tied up sooner or later with the Union Pacific.

For the time being, though, he was very much occupied with Army duties, and the Union Pacific had its own problems, pressing if prosaic.

The Credit Mobilier as yet had not come fully to grips with its undertaking. There was still, apparently, a lack of understanding of the project's magnitude, or perhaps a lingering unwillingness by Dr. Durant and his associates to commit themselves to the all-out effort necessary. And there still was an over-all opinion that the railroad's importance stemmed from its role as an instrument of government policy—a tangible tie between East and West —with its potential as a common carrier distinctly secondary. Thus the only important source of profits would lie in the construction effort itself. To do Durant justice, it is probable that this opinion, which he shared, had been a strong motive for his formation of the Credit Mobilier. But the profits, if he had expected any at this early stage, were not materializing. The agency had no income except through the resale of Union Pacific stocks and bonds with which it was paid for its construction work. And the market for these remained poor throughout 1865, the war's end notwithstanding.

To keep the work going the Credit Mobilier was being forced to sink more and more of its own capital funds into construction under the erstwhile Hoxie contract. It was an unbusinesslike practice, which could not go on indefinitely. The agency's total capitalization, originally $2,500,000, had been increased to $3,500,000—still little enough in view of the job it was trying to do.

The Union Pacific was beset by the same high prices and labor shortages which plagued the Central Pacific, and faced obstacles in the way of supply only a little less difficult than those of the Central. Omaha lay on the frontier side of the Missouri River, a barren wilderness by comparison with the Central Pacific's terminus at Sacramento. In all Nebraska Territory the white population barely exceeded 35,000, providing no finished industry of any kind. Local building materials were limited to cottonwood timber and scanty deposits of limestone. Even the hay crops raised by the few homesteaders were usually contracted for in advance by the Army, the freight outfits or the Overland Stage. Two railroads, the Rock Island and the Cedar Rapids and Missouri (later a part of the Chicago and Northwestern), now were building across Iowa toward Council Bluffs, but neither railhead was nearer than 150 miles.

A bridge over the Missouri between Council Bluffs and Omaha was ardently desired by all concerned. Action was held up, though, by disputes over the best location and how the costs were to be shared. There was the river itself, of course, offering transportation by steam packet from railroad connections at St. Joseph or St. Louis, and this proved a godsend. But the Missouri was treacherous and strewn with snags and sand bars, navigable for only about three months of the year, what with winter's ice, spring floods and summer's low water. The company had proposed to build its own cars at its shops in Omaha, and did in fact do so later on. But locomotives, rails and other finished appurtenances were as expensive and as hard to get for the Union Pacific as for the Central, with freight charges lower only because of the shorter distance involved.

Although the first rail was laid at Omaha on July 10, serious track-laying did not get under way until September, partly due to continuing repercussions of the Dey-Seymour argument over line location. The goal had been set at sixty miles for the year. It became obvious that it was not going to be reached.

All this constituted an irksome burden of discouragement and a poor omen for the future, but it was not necessarily fatal. Along with it and in spite of it there was a great bustle of activity and some concrete signs of accomplishment. A machine shop and a roundhouse were going up in Omaha, both of good, solid brick construction. A seventy-ton stationary steam engine for the shop was on its way by sledge and ox teams from the Cedar Rapids and Missouri railhead before the year ended. The first locomotives were on the roster, shipped up by steamboat from St. Joseph. Portable sawmills were at work in the river bottoms, sawing out thousands of ties, cords of fuel wood and lumber for bridges and cars.

The cottonwood proved poor tie material; its spike-holding qualities were unsatisfactory and it was badly susceptible to rot. A cumbersome treatment plant was erected to burnetize[5] it: a long iron cylinder into which ties were run in loads of 250 at a time, the doors then bolted shut and the air exhausted by a steam-driven pump. The vacuum opened the pores in the wood and drew out the moisture and chloride of zinc solution was then forced in under pressure. It was a costly process and not entirely successful, since the spike-

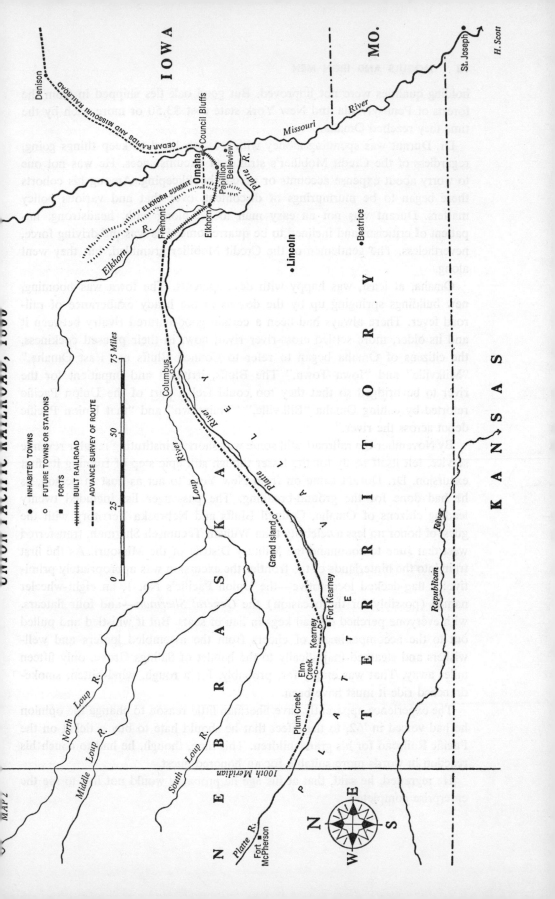

UNION PACIFIC RAILROAD, 1866

MAP 2

INHABITED TOWNS ●
FUTURE TOWNS OR STATIONS ○
FORTS ■
BUILT RAILROAD +++++++
ADVANCE SURVEY OF ROUTE ━ ━ ━

0   25   50   75 Miles

IOWA

MO.

NEBRASKA TERRITORY

KANSAS

Denison

CEDAR RAPIDS AND MISSOURI RAILROAD

Council Bluffs

Missouri River

Omaha

ELKHORN SUMMIT

Papillion

Belleview

Platte R.

Fremont

Elkhorn

Elkhorn R.

Lincoln

Beatrice

St. Joseph

H. Scott

Columbus

Platte River

Loup River

Grand Island

Fort Kearney

Elm Creek

Plum Creek

North Loup R.

Middle Loup R.

South Loup R.

Platte R.

Fort McPherson

100th Meridian

Republican River

N E W S

holding qualities were not improved. But good oak ties shipped in from the forests of Pennsylvania and New York state cost $3.50 or more each by the time they reached Omaha.

Dr. Durant was spending money with a lavish hand to keep things going, regardless of the Credit Mobilier's straitened circumstances. He was not one to worry about expense accounts or precise bookkeeping. Among his cohorts there began to be murmurings of discontent, over that and various policy matters. Durant was not an easy man to get along with, headstrong, impatient of criticism and inclined to be quarrelsome. His was the driving force, nevertheless. The gentlemen of the Credit Mobilier grumbled, but they went along.

Omaha, at least, was happy with developments. The town was booming, new buildings springing up by the dozens in the heady exuberance of railroad fever. There always had been a certain good-natured rivalry between it and its older, more settled cross-river rival; now, in their pleased cockiness, the citizens of Omaha began to refer to Council Bluffs as "East Omaha," "Milkville" and "Iowa Town." The Bluffs, irritated and impatient for the river to be bridged so that they too could feel a part of the Union Pacific retorted by calling Omaha "Bilkville," "Traintown" and "that Union Pacific depot across the river."

By November the railroad, still some way short of instituting regular revenue service, felt itself ready for the lesser though still epic step of running its first excursion. Dr. Durant came on from New York to act as host in person, as he had done for the ground-breaking. The passenger list included twenty leading citizens of Omaha, Council Bluffs and Nebraska Territory with the guest of honor no less a celebrity than William Tecumseh Sherman, transferred west that June to command the Military District of the Missouri. As the first train into the hinterlands of the frontier the excursion was appropriately primitive: a flag-decked locomotive—the Union Pacific's No. 1, an eight-wheeler named (possibly for the occasion) the *General Sherman*—and four flatcars, with everyone perched on nail kegs in lieu of seats. But it whistled and pulled out to the accompaniment of cheers from the assembled loafers and well-wishers and steamed majestically to the hamlet of Salings Grove, only fifteen miles away. That was amply far, probably, for a rough, wind-bitten, smoke-drenched ride it must have been.

The experience apparently gave Sherman little reason to change the opinion he had voiced in '62, to the effect that he should hate to buy a ticket on the Pacific Railroad for his grandchildren. This time, though, he had to couch his reaction in words more suitable for an honored guest.

He regretted, he said, that at his age he probably would not live to see the enterprise completed.

Save for one factor the general might have been speaking more prophetically than he knew. The Credit Mobilier was even then approaching complete deflation, the bulk of its capital buried in the grade that crawled out across the prairie toward the one hundredth meridian.

The factor was once again, and now for the last time, Abraham Lincoln's unflagging determination that the transcontinental railroad be built.

Lincoln was dead now, the shock of his assassination already receding into history. But earlier that year, not long before the tragic evening at Ford's Theater, he had called Oakes Ames, member of the House of Representatives from Massachusetts, to him at the White House. His reasons are not altogether clear. With the Civil War over at last, himself worn out and the bitterly controversial problems of Reconstruction pressing in upon him, he might well have considered the railroad to the Pacific a project that ought to go its own way without additional help. Instead, whatever the background of thinking that went into it, his conclusion had been that the Union Pacific needed a stronger hand at the financial throttle.

"Ames, take hold of this," the President said, as Ames later recalled it, "and if the subsidies provided are not enough to build the road, ask double and you shall have it. That road must be built, and you are the only man to do it; and you take hold of it yourself."[6]

Possibly Ames's recollection was slanted somewhat. Yet the reference to subsidies is strikingly similar to Lincoln's words to Grenville Dodge two years earlier. Then they had smacked of military urgency. But that was past in the spring of '65. Apparently the President, as usual, was thinking far out in front of most of those around him, and saw the Pacific Railroad as an integral part of the broader picture of a nation expanding westward in a mighty postwar resurgence. Significantly, though not very accurately, considering the way later events turned out, he added (Ames again quoting): "By building the road you will become the remembered man of your generation."

He had picked his man shrewdly. Oakes Ames, then in his sixtieth year, had been a member of Congress since 1862, and before that a member of Massachusetts Governor Andrews' cabinet. As a neophyte in the Select House Committee on the Pacific Railroad he had been on hand for the drafting of the original enabling Act, and later of the amending Act of '64, and so was not unfamiliar with the Congress' motives in passing both bills. But far outweighing all that, the Ames Tool and Shovel Company at Easton, Massachusetts, was among the largest and best-managed industrial firms in New England, and Oakes and his brother Oliver were known and respected in all walks of American life as businessmen of the highest caliber. Founded by their father in 1841, the company had flourished and expanded during the various Western gold strikes and the opening of trans-Mississippi settlement.

The Ames Old Colony brand of shovel had the reputation of being acceptable as legal tender everywhere in the Mississippi Valley.[7]

With such a tradition behind him, his own personal fortune besides, and his immense influence in banking and industrial circles—Boston at that time rivaling New York as the financial capital of the nation—it was plain that Oakes Ames could, if he would, bring a great deal of strength to bear on the Union Pacific's problems.

Ames was interested, though he seems to have avoided giving the President a definite answer at the time. Lincoln's request was flattering, of course. And later there were detractors who pointed out that any speed-up of work on the Union Pacific grades must inevitably result in greater sales of Ames shovels and hence greater profits for Ames. He was a businessman; no doubt he took that into account. Undoubtedly, too, others added their pleas to Lincoln's as soon as word got about that he was considering the move. There are indications that Thomas Durant was one who did not welcome the thought of Ames's entering the picture. The "Boston crowd," as he later referred to the Ameses and their group, were not the kind of collaborators with whom the aggressively individualistic New Yorker would have felt at ease under any circumstances. But the indications bulk somewhat larger in the light of subsequent events, probably, than they did at the time. Undoubtedly a majority of the Credit Mobilier's board of directors saw Oakes Ames as a lifesaver, for he commanded money and fresh money was the crying need from everyone's point of view.

He spent some months looking into the situation in his conservative New England way. But this autumn his decision was made. Whether as a patriot or as a hard-headed investor—a little of both, probably; the point was argued long afterward—Oakes Ames came into the Credit Mobilier. Once in, there was nothing halfhearted about his participation. He invested a million dollars of his own money immediately, speedily raised another million and a half from sources close to him and, Oliver concurring, pledged the resources of Ames Tool and Shovel to the rapid completion of the Union Pacific Railroad.

It made a good note on which to close out the year. By the first week of January, 1866, railhead had been pushed into Fremont, Nebraska, forty miles west of Omaha, and the first terminal supply center set up there. The grade was in almost all the way to the one hundredth meridian. Preliminary surveys (rough designations of the route to be followed, though by no means final location lines) had been run under the direction of divisional chief engineers James Evans and Samuel Reed clear to the Humboldt River in Nevada, two hundred miles west of Great Salt Lake.

CHAPTER 10

THE CLIMBING MILES

Charley Crocker was not apologizing to anyone as 1865 ended. It had been a year of mixed troubles and blessings for the Central Pacific and C. Crocker and Company. Progress, viewed in terms of mileage alone, had been less than impressive. On the other hand, boldness, hope and Crocker's own innate, headstrong grit had eased some pressing problems.

From Newcastle the rails had reached out to Auburn, five miles onward, by January of '65. By June they had been pushed forward seven more to Clipper Gap, which put railhead forty-three miles out of Sacramento. In that distance the right of way had climbed eighteen hundred feet of the total seven-thousand-foot ascent to the highest point in Donner Pass, still fifty-eight miles away. None of it had been easy. But construction had grown steadily more difficult out of Auburn, the line looping and twisting on the steepening slopes of the Sierra foothills. For seven of the finished miles the company was entitled to $16,000 each, the basic government subsidy. For all the rest, $48,000 per mile was due. Delivery was slow, however; the first government bond issue, amounting to $1,258,000, did not come through, in fact, until 1866. Meanwhile financing remained rugged and prices skyrocketed.

The second lot of ten locomotives cost $215,000 delivered at San Francisco, up $24,000 over the first lot of ten. All engines came off the ships disassembled and were sent by river steamer to Sacramento, where they were erected and readied for service in the company's shops. Freight charges by way of the Isthmus went as high as $8,100 for a single locomotive. But sometimes, as operations expanded, they were needed in a hurry and had to be sent that way. By sailing ship around Cape Horn was cheaper but slower, and subject to all the hazards of tempest, doldrum and shipwreck. Material in transit usually amounted to a million dollars' worth at any given time now.

Even as the Confederacy weakened and the War Between the States drew on toward an obvious end, federal currency remained sensitive to every Union reversal. The news of Grant's defeat at Cold Harbor in June depressed its buying power to forty cents on the dollar and kited the premium on gold to $2.90. Central Pacific stock skidded to a low of nineteen cents per share at one point, and went begging at that. Bonds—state, county, the company's own or the promise of the federal government's—were exchangeable for working funds at no better than fifty cents on the dollar. Even at that rate California businessmen took them only with reluctance.

There were brighter spots, though. The law providing subsidies of more than two million dollars from the state of California was operative at last. By an additional act put through the legislature in '64, the state undertook to pay the interest on a million and a half dollars' worth of bonds for twenty years. There was a bit of horse-trading involved there, the company in return ceding some valuable lands to the state. More than $600,000 in county bonds finally had been released by the courts also.

And in New York Collis Huntington was making progress. Wall Street men were becoming increasingly aware of him, his dogged persistence like a sort of natural force that could not be ignored forever. Their respect came slowly and grudgingly, but it came. The young investment banking house of Fisk and Hatch began to take a hand in the promotion of Central Pacific securities, and eventually became the company's Eastern agent.[1] William E. Dodge increased his loans till they aggregated $3,250,000; every cent of it, however, guaranteed either by Huntington in person or by notes on Huntington and Hopkins or the other Associates.

"The company had a floating debt of $7,000,000 before they had crossed the Sierra Nevada," Huntington declared many years later. And he added that "The money needed . . . was all borrowed by me."[2]

Among the vice-president's attributes was a very forthright personal ego, so the last statement should perhaps be discounted as a bit of characteristic bragging. Leland Stanford, during the Central Pacific's building period, became indebted to the Bank of California for a total of $1,300,000, and it seems reasonable to assume that some at least of this debt was incurred in behalf of the railroad (though the Governor's political ambitions were always costly too, and might have accounted for much of it).

Regardless, in one way or another, though never easily to be sure, the needed money was obtained. Looking forward to the benefits of the Act of '64, the board of directors voted to carry on. They were through dealing with small contractors though, and no longer sensitive to the howls of favoritism. C. Crocker and Company was given carte blanche to go ahead with construction as far and as fast as possible.

Charley Crocker did. His money grew short and his credit strained. Long afterward he recalled that as "the time when I would have been very glad to take a clean shirt and lose all I had, and quit."[3]

A lesser man might have done just that. Not only did he bear his share of the financial worries and the hue and cry of opponents' attacks that plagued all the Associates, but in addition the full weight of the California labor shortage, a problem still unsolved, fell on his broad back alone. The majority of his grading gangs and track-layers were Irishmen now; good workers, but bringing more of them around Cape Horn or over the Isthmus in the numbers necessary was too costly and time-consuming to be practical.

Crocker had found himself an assistant now, and a good one, recruited from the placer mining operations on the upper American River. James Harvey Strobridge was his name; a native Vermonter in his late thirties, as big a man physically as Crocker himself and an experienced railroad construction man before coming west as a forty-niner. He was a hard man, reputed to have possessed a crackling blue-smoke-and-brimstone vocabulary; an undoubted slavedriver and a tower of strength at Charley Crocker's side. He had been superintendent of construction since early in '64.

But nothing, not slavedriving or hide-scorching eloquence, sweet reason or anything else, was of any use against Irishmen cheerfully convinced of their own indispensability. The slow pace of railhead from Newcastle to Auburn— only five miles in some seven months—had been due in large measure to lack of ready money, but repeated strikes and work stoppages had contributed, too. Various remedies had been discussed and discarded. Mexicans were considered for a while; there were plenty of them in California and more could be brought in easily. But both Crocker and Strobridge felt that they were too slow and indolent for railroad work. Crocker himself had thought seriously of applying to the federal government for five thousand Confederate prisoners of war to be transported west and put to work on the Central Pacific grades under guard. He had, in fact, gone so far as to draft a petition to the War Department. But Lee's surrender at Appomattox early in April put a stop to that.

Then, on a payday later that spring, somewhere above Auburn, he noticed a group of laborers with their heads together in earnest conversation.

"I told Mr. Strobridge there was some little trouble ahead from that," he later testified before the federal Pacific Railway Commission.

He was right. Presently a committee came forward to ask another increase in wages.

Charley Crocker had had a bellyful of that. "I told Mr. Strobridge to go over to Auburn and get some Chinamen and put them to work," he said.

Strobridge refused to take the idea seriously. Chinese, he pointed out, probably averaged little more than a hundred and ten pounds in weight; they made good enough laundrymen, farm hands, flunkies—but railroad laborers? Never! The Irishmen, however, capitulated at once. Here on the Central Pacific they had seemed to have things their own way for a while. But their prior experience as poor immigrants on the Atlantic seaboard had been that of the lowliest among the low, and the mere thought of competitive cheap labor was enough to fill them with a healthy dread. The American Irish as a class, in fact, had tended to be violently pro-Secessionist during the war, not because of any real slavery convictions but simply because the prospects of thousands of freed Negro slaves thrown into the labor market seemed to them a threat to their very existence.

"The Irishmen begged us not to have any Chinamen come, and they resumed work," Crocker recalled with satisfaction.

But that was not the end of it; anyone who thought it was did not know Charley Crocker. It was not his way to relinquish the upper hand once he had gained it. And though his Irishmen were reduced to docility for the time being, manpower still was a problem. The notion of Chinese working the Central Pacific grades clung stubbornly in his head. Strangely observant for such a headlong bull of a man, he had watched Chinese working worn-out gold claims—the only kind they were permitted to work—during his own early fling at mining in the early '50's. Recalling that, he did not share his superintendent's contempt for them.

It was some time, though, before he could get Strobridge to accept the idea. "Finally he took fifty [Chinese] and a while after he took fifty more."

They went to work with an impassive willingness that must have exceeded even Crocker's expectations. They knew nothing about railroad grading, of course. Once shown what was wanted and how to do it, though, their diligence and uncomplaining endurance with pick and shovel and wheelbarrow put the whites to shame. For twenty-six dollars a month to begin with—out of which they supplied their own rations—and later for thirty and finally for thirty-five a month, they came by the carloads from Chinatowns all over northern California. By that fall Crocker had three thousand of them on his payroll. By the end of the year his agents had rounded up virtually every California Chinese willing to come, and were dickering with labor contractors for more to be brought all the way across the Pacific from Canton.

San Franciscans, alert as always for any opportunity to criticize the Central Pacific, viewed the prospect with alarm. Much was made of the invasion of foreign labor. The Chinese's well known addiction to the opium habit was mentioned, as a contaminating influence and a reason why the experiment was doomed to failure. But a reporter for the *Daily Union* watched the first contingent of Cantonese disembark on the levee at Sacramento and wrote: "They were a clear-eyed lot of young men. Opium costs money. They left the soil of their native land poverty-stricken and on the trip over had to forego the luxury of the poppy."

Apparently he was right, for it is not recorded that drug addiction ever was a problem on the Central Pacific. Once turned loose on the grade, in fact, the Chinese settled into the hard, dawn-to-dusk routine with scarcely any adjustment period and remarkably little trouble. Jim Strobridge, apparently, never was able to bring himself to the point of liking them, but he was too good a construction superintendent to let his prejudice interfere with efficiency. He divided the Chinese into work gangs of about thirty, each under the direct supervision of an Irish "riding boss" during working hours. One man was selected from each gang to collect all the wages and buy all the provisions for the group. The Chinese themselves soon carried the organization even further, most gangs hiring an American clerk—a dollar a month per man was the usual rate—to keep wage accounts straight and to see that food costs were distributed fairly. It simplified bookkeeping for C. Crocker and Company and kept the Chinese satisfied.

After deducting his board bill, the average coolie could save up to twenty dollars of his wages each month, unless he gambled it away. For these Orientals proved to be inveterate gamblers almost to a man. Fan-tan was their game and they wagered wildly and frequently argued fiercely over the results. But it was all among themselves. They did not mingle with the whites, settled their own differences and made few demands on their foremen.

There might have been trouble with the Irish, but it never materialized. Fearful and resentful of the coolies at first, referring to them sourly as "niggers" and "Charley Crocker's pets," the Irishmen presently came to realize that, far from displacing them, these slant-eyed, pigtailed little spalpeens actually were the harbingers of a new and eminently better state of affairs.

For all his industry, endurance and willingness the Chinese was, essentially, unskilled labor. The grinding, monotonous, pick-and-shovel toil fell to him, and off the Irishman's back. He was, besides, a handy butt for good, soul-satisfying scorn; a sort of exotic new rube or greenhorn, gabbling to his fellows in high, twittering singsong; feeding on rice, dried cuttlefish, bean sprouts, bamboo shoots, dried seaweed and similar outlandish fodder (all brought in by the company and sold to him as part of the hiring agreement) instead of the Irishman's own good old bully beef, beans, potatoes and bread.

The Irish Paddy had had his share of being looked down on in America. Now, for once, he had someone lower than he and could look down in his turn. He was one of the construction elite, the expert track-layer and iron handler. And he liked it.

In California labor circles, however, it was a very different story. California labor, to be sure, never had evinced much more than a monumental indifference toward work on the Pacific Railroad. All the same, spurred by sudden misgivings for the future and incited by an indignant San Francisco press, leaders began to raise a passionate hullabaloo over this unfair competition by "yellow labor." Working-class people who had been able to shrug off the allegations of "Dutch Flat humbug" now were presented with an issue that seemed bound up directly with their own bread and butter, and all the railroad's old opponents were delighted. Leland Stanford's public statements and reports to stockholders during this period show that the company was stung. For months they were loaded with arguments and apologies aimed at justifying the Central Pacific's Chinese. Without them, Stanford declared over and over again, the company's construction deadline could not be met. It was probably true, but it meant nothing to the agitators. The thing grew swiftly into a *cause célèbre* that lasted a long, long time.

For years to come, the "yellow peril" would stalk California like a chain-clanking, doom-croaking ghost in a haunted house. The Central Pacific's public image would be blackened even more than it was already; its successor, the Southern Pacific, would suffer touchy relations with organized labor far into the twentieth century for its parent's old, alleged sin of having beaten good California citizens to their knees with cheap imported Chinese.

And to the end of his days Charley Crocker's name would be anathema to every soapbox rabble-rouser on the street corners of San Francisco. He had a thick skin; there is no indication that it ever bothered him.

In the summer and fall of '65, certainly, he had no reason to care a tinker's damn. Public opinion was Stanford's problem; let *him* fret over it. For his own part, Charley Crocker had a railroad to build and—at last—the men he needed to do the job. The grade pressed forward with no more interruptions, and the rails came on behind. Eleven miles beyond Clipper Gap lay Illinois Town, the next immediate goal. The land rolled in deeper undulations as the foothills tilted upward. Much cutting and blasting were necessary, and increasing amounts of heavy fill; slow, grubbing work on which the new Chinese cut their eyeteeth and proved their worth.

Railhead arrived at Illinois Town in August.

In August, too, the Schuyler Colfax party rode into California to wind up a triumphal cross-country tour. The Speaker and his attendants had inspected Army posts on the Great Plains, breathed the salubrious air of the scenic Rockies, hobnobbed with Brigham Young at Great Salt Lake, been lionized in Virginia City. California, always flattered by the visits of eminent Easterners, extended itself to do the indicated honors, and the party's stay there was a continuous round of fanfare and entertainment.

Among the experiences to which Mr. Speaker and his retinue were treated, in September, was a special excursion on the Central Pacific from Sacramento to end of track, personally arranged by Leland Stanford and the board of directors. This was the sort of thing to put the ceremony-loving president in his glory, and he made the most of it. Mrs. Stanford and the other directors' wives went along, adding a gracious social flavor to the affair. The newest and best of the company's locomotives and passenger cars were furbished up and assigned to the train, and the finest foods and wines California afforded were served at stops along the line, where crowds gathered to applaud extemporaneous remarks by the distinguished Illinois politico.

From Illinois Town—renamed Colfax in the Speaker's honor—the whole party proceeded by stagecoach and horseback all the way to the summit of the Sierra Nevadas, and thence down through the pass to Donner Lake.

"The rugged mountains looked like stupendous anthills," commented Correspondent Albert Richardson in his *Tribune* story. "They swarmed with Celestials, shovelling, wheeling, carting, drilling and blasting rocks and earth, while their dull, moony eyes stared out from under immense basket hats, like umbrellas." Obviously impressed with the magnitude of operations and fascinated by the Chinese, he went on to tell of the dining camps, where "we saw hundreds sitting on the ground, eating soft-boiled rice with chopsticks as fast as terrestrials could with soup ladles."[4]

The party stayed overnight at a small mountain lodge, the Lake House, on the shore of Donner Lake, and Richardson, now completely carried away, described the scene in dramatic detail:

The carpet was covered with maps, profiles and diagrams, held down at the edges with candlesticks to keep them from rolling up. On their knees were the president, directors and surveyors, creeping from one map to another, and earnestly discussing their magnificent enterprise. The ladies of our excursion were grouped around them silent and intent, assuming liveliest interest in the dry details about tunnels, grades, excavations, "making height" and "getting down." Outside the night wind moaned and shrieked, as if the Mountain Spirit resented this invasion of his ancient domain.

This was heady stuff, well calculated to bring the Great Pacific Railroad to stirring life for his New York readers.

For his part Samuel Bowles expressed great admiration for the "lavish backing" of the Central. He reported that six million dollars in federal and state bonds already had accrued, not a penny of it spent as yet because all the work had been financed through the sale of company stock, the California county subscriptions and the railroad's own operating revenues. Out of this income, Bowles further stated, the company showed a surplus of better than a half-million dollars.

Where he got his information the good editor from Springfield neglected to say. He was a writing man and no financier; evidently his hosts plied him with some very rosy exaggerations and he swallowed them whole. Nevertheless his dispatches, and Richardson's, made excellent publicity for the Central Pacific, for a change. Until then the western end of the transcontinental railroad had been granted only the scantiest of mention in the Eastern press. California was far away and unimportant, and local happenings and war news had monopolized the printed page.

Bowles also gave wide circulation to statements by company officers that they expected to build into Salt Lake City within three years, apparently the first such declaration anyone had seen fit to make.

He had a good word to say for Charley Crocker also, "the engine that drove everything ahead."

All this was in marked contrast to his earlier comments on the Union Pacific.

So the guests departed and the kudos ended. The work had gone on without slackening, all construction from Clipper Gap eastward now officially Crocker's, awarded by resolution of the board of directors in June. Railhead stopped at Colfax for the year while crews moved out on the thirteen-mile grade to Dutch Flat. These were challenging miles, far rougher than anything heretofore encountered, the massive granite escarpment called Cape Horn standing squarely athwart the way just above Colfax. No grade could go through it or over it; the line location markers threaded a precarious path around its towering flank, and there the grading gangs would have to follow. Undaunted, Crocker and Strobridge drove their coolies to it, hacking out arduous pick-and-shovel space while the good fall weather lasted.

On the other side lay a promise of stepped-up operating income, for the Associates' wagon road from Dutch Flat to the main Nevada-Placerville highway was now finished. Critics, however, seized on that as new ammunition and broke out in another bombardment of charges that the Central Pacific would be finished, too, as soon as it reached Dutch Flat and began to siphon off the bonanza traffic. Bishop, the San Francisco and Washoe's chief engineer, repeated his public statement to the effect that the Judah survey line through Donner Pass was impossible as a railroad route. He had completed his own road's survey and cost estimates early in the year and could prove his point, he claimed, by facts and figures gleaned from a personal examination of the

Sierras. Other reputable engineers in the Bay area agreed, also publicly. While they did not quite use the word "impossible," they estimated that any further progress on Judah's survey above Colfax would cost up to $300,000 a mile. Ruinous, they declared flatly; out of the question!

Leland Stanford issued denials. The board urged Crocker on, promising that the work would be paid for out of their own private means if necessary, heavily mortgaged though those already were.

No doubt they were encouraged by the report of George E. Gray, former chief engineer of the New York Central Railroad, whom Stanford had engaged as consultant in July. It seems very probable that the president was motivated by the desire for some sort of authoritative answer to Bishop's odious statements. Possibly, too, (and even more importantly) he was seeking to stiffen his own and his directors' faltering faith. None of them, after all, were either engineers or railroad men; for all they knew, Judah *might* have been wrong, and his successor, Montague, was a young man, experienced but compartively short on reputation.

However it came about, Gray's report was an unqualified blessing. He gave as his opinion that the Central Pacific's completed section was the equal of any railroad in the United States; praise of a very high order for an ex-dry-goods merchant allied with a pair of hardware dealers and a politician in the grocery business. But there was more. The final location line had deviated from Judah's original survey in two places: one a short stretch above Colfax and the other, and more radical, a whole new approach to the Sierra summit laid out by Lewis Clement, engineer in charge of the second division, from Colfax to the summit. Gray approved of both changes, pointing out that they reduced the total length of grade and track work by nearly a mile, reduced the aggregate length of tunneling necessary by more than five thousand feet, and did all this without increasing the ruling grade. He put the probable savings at $400,000.[5]

For reasons not quite clear this report of Gray's does not appear to have been widely publicized. But as a quiet note of factual optimism amid the general chorus of doom-criers it must have been no less reassuring.

The construction trains' steamy grumblings were followed by the whistle screams of locomotives wheeling revenue cars hard on the heels of the track gangs. Three regular trains a day ran each way between Sacramento and Colfax. Business was good. The company set passenger fares at ten cents a mile, freight rates at fifteen cents a ton-mile, payable in gold only.

Collis Huntington had found time to devote to affairs in Washington this year, too. The Act of '64 was amended to permit the issuance of company bonds on a hundred miles of grade in advance of completed trackage. The powerful Union Pacific lobby had been most instrumental in pushing that through. But Huntington was learning fast; the Central Pacific's own private interests were not neglected. In March Senator John Conness of California had sponsored another amendment sanctioning the railroad's assignment of construction from Sacramento all the way south to San Jose to a subsidiary railroad company called the Western Pacific,[6] with all the benefits conferred by the Acts of '62 and '64. Thus the troublesome little problem of extending the transcontinental to San Francisco, which always had been taken for granted as the desired western terminus, was neatly solved.

October came, with five thousand men and six hundred horse and mule teams delving at the Cape Horn approach. Still the labor force was increased. By December it totaled seven thousand Chinese at thirty dollars per month and 2,500 white men, mostly Irish, at thirty-five plus board. The Chinese's drink was tea. Great barrels of it stood along the grade, constantly replenished by coolies from used powder kegs slung at both ends of long poles on their shoulders. The Paddies hooted in derision and slaked their own thirsts with copius drafts of water or better yet, when there happened to be a town handy and they could sneak out from under the cold eye of Jim Strobridge, with whiskey. The men were housed anywhere and anyhow, in tents, plank shacks, dugouts, and supplied by wagon trains from end of track.

Colfax stood at 2,242 feet above sea level, up five hundred feet from Clipper Gap. The distance from Sacramento was fifty-four miles. There were fifty still to go to the Sierra summit.

Mark Hopkins summed up his accounts at the end of the year and cautiously reported some good news. Central Pacific gross earnings for the twelve months were $405,591.95; net, $282,233.44. Out of that came $150,-000 in interest charges and a sinking fund of $105,000, to leave a profit of $27,233.44. But construction costs for the year amounted to something in excess of three million dollars, bringing the total for construction from Sacramento to more than five and a half million. Total cost of the railroad to date was above six and a half million. Miscellaneous assets included unpledged county bonds, materials and supplies on hand but not yet used, and accounts receivable. Together they summed slightly less than a million dollars.

If the picture fell a good way short of the one Samuel Bowles had painted for the Eastern public, this annual report for 1865 still was quite respectable, all things considered.

CHAPTER 11

HIGHBALL ON THE PLAINS

Early in January of '66 Colonel Silas Seymour sat down in his Omaha office to answer a letter from a minor functionary in the U.S. Department of the Interior. Just how, the fellow wanted to know, did the Union Pacific define the term "first class railroad," as specified in the original Act of Congress of '62? It appears that the Pacific Railroad did not advance westward without a certain amount of bureaucratic heckling.

With some asperity Seymour stated the self-evident truth that a first-class railroad was one fitted in every respect to handle its prospective traffic. Furthermore, he wrote, it would seem that five government directors and three government commissioners, fortified with the government's own written specifications covering grades, track gauge, degrees of curvature and general quality standards, ought to constitute an ample safeguard against any temptation the company might feel to cheat. Being something of a pedant, however, and having taken pen in hand, the colonel then went on to state a few specifics. First, with regard to motive power:

A first-class railroad should be equipped with locomotives of twenty-eight to thirty tons in weight; drivers five feet in diameter; cylinders sixteen inches in bore and twenty-four in stroke. (To digress a moment for the sake of comparison, the Union Pacific's own 4000-class engines of seventy-five years later, the famous "Big Boys," usually conceded to be the largest steam locomotives ever built, weighed over 604 tons, rolled on sixty-eight-inch drivers, had four cylinders twenty-three and three-quarters inches in bore and thirty-two in stroke and carried twenty-eight tons of fuel, a weight equal to one of Seymour's locomotives in its entirety.)

Rails, the engineer continued, should weigh not less than fifty pounds per linear yard, more wherever steeper grades and heavier engines required. For fastenings at rail joints he recommended either fishplates or wrought-iron chairs. The latter was the older and less satisfactory device but was more readily obtainable; hence he advised its use on the Union Pacific as a means of expediting construction. Ties should be eight feet long, six inches wide and at least eight thick; roadbed of adequate width and built of the best material in local supply; drainage ditches to conform to roadbed and the nature of the country traversed.

All of this was simply a summation of recognized railroad standards, with which the gentleman at Washington could not quarrel. And Seymour closed on the testy note that, so much being established, everyone concerned might more profitably occupy himself with "the vigorous prosecution and speedy completion of the road" than with any further exchanges of lengthy and pointless letters.

Perhaps unconsciously, he was expressing the new spirit abroad on the Union Pacific. There was a general stirring of vitality among all departments of the enterprise, a regrouping of forces to meet the challenge of the new year just beginning. There was nothing haphazard in this; it was simply effect following cause. The coming of Oakes Ames and his money had been the first catalyst. The second seemed quite unremarkable at the time.

This February a pair of brothers by the name of Casement—John Stevens and Daniel T., of Ohio[1]—put in a bid as track-laying contractors. They submitted it to the Union Pacific Company direct, though the Credit Mobilier then had sole responsibility for all construction to the one hundredth meridian. But Thomas Durant accepted it in his official capacity as vice-president of the railroad, a good example of the single and inseparable identity the two organizations already had achieved. It appears from the records that the Casements' bid was routine and that Durant engaged them more or less on a trial basis, little realizing what a prize package he was buying.

Ramrod of the team was John S., more familiarly General Jack, for he had served throughout the War Between the States and been breveted a brigadier for merit on the battlefield at Franklin. He was a thoroughgoing railroad track boss, thirty-seven years old and experienced in the work since boyhood; so much his credentials showed. For the rest, he appeared a bit of a gamecock, only five feet and four inches tall. But he spoke with a blunt economy of words and a quiet self-assurance, and the full red beard he wore hinted at a fiery fighter and disciplinarian behind the stocky façade. There was, at first, less to be said of brother Dan, an altogether quieter and more ordinary seeming fellow on the surface. But he was the ideal man to backstop General Jack, an organizer and logistics expert unmatched anywhere—as events would prove.

The events took shape, though not immediately, for work still was suspended while winter held on. But spring came, and with it a third decisive change in the vital chemistry of the Union Pacific enterprise. In April the advance survey parties moved out into the field, grading crews and track gangs following as the frozen earth softened in the thaw. And from Washington, the office of the War Department, came electrifying news: Major General Grenville M. Dodge was granted indefinite leave from the Army and freed to accept Dr. Durant's offer of more than a year's standing.

There was a touch of irony in the fact that the superior officer who had to approve the leave was that confirmed skeptic, William Tecumseh Sherman. But Sherman was facing up to a changed set of circumstances this spring. The Indian wars of '64 had not been settled. All through '65 hostilities had flared up and subsided only to flare up anew. Treaties based on solemn government pledges to respect tribal lands and rights had been made and promptly broken by ill-advised or overzealous officers, or by aggressive frontier civilians who refused to be regimented by any official dicta from far-off Washington. Independent young braves had not always respected the peaceful counsels of their elder chiefs either. The rights and wrongs of the situation aside, the thing simply boiled down to an inevitable collision between two cultures that were irreconcilable, the one old and primitive, the other new and dynamic. Sherman, for one, was beginning to grasp this, and to accept its correlative fact that what he had on his hands was nothing short of total war, to the point of extermination if necessary.

As the general commanding the Military District of the Missouri, he was the man responsible for the pacification of formidable guerrilla armies scattered the length and breadth of the Great Plains. It was a large order and a largely thankless job, and Uncle Billy, who understood the importance of railroad transport in modern war, perceived very clearly that the Union Pacific could be an invaluable adjunct to the military, regardless of his private opinion on its ultimate peacetime prospects.

He let Dodge go with sincere regret, nonetheless, a measure of the high regard he held for him as man and as soldier. Possibly some strings were pulled in Washington by Durant and the Union Pacific lobby, now strongly reinforced by Oakes Ames's membership in Congress. Ulysses S. Grant, commanding general of the Army, also approved the move, apparently with reluctance equaling Sherman's, but unwilling to stand in the way of the Pacific Railroad's progress.

Hurrying to Omaha, Dodge took up his duties as chief engineer on the first of May.

For him this was the final step to the peak of a career toward which he had set his face since early youth. For the company it meant completion of the virile organization it needed. Dodge's reputation as a railroad man, and a protagonist of the Pacific Railroad in particular, was widely known. In '64, following passage of the amending Act, President Lincoln had been urged from several quarters to appoint him a Union Pacific commissioner. Probably nothing but the pressures of war had prevented his doing so. This same reputation now enabled Dodge to take command of the railroad's engineering staff with scarcely a ripple of the professional jealousy and skeptical reception he might otherwise have encountered. And because of the war-enforced interruption of his career, he came to the job not as an original applicant but as the one man urgently needed and wanted; a position of strength that would prove no mean asset in complications that came later. He came, moreover, matured and fortified as a leader by the years of Army command.

The measure of how badly Durant wanted him for the Union Pacific is recorded in the salary he received: ten thousand dollars per year, a magnificent stipend for an engineer in the 1860's. As an additional inducement Durant threw in a block of one hundred shares of Credit Mobilier stock. These were placed in Mrs. Dodge's name, probably at the general's own insistence.

He was a young man still, thirty-five this spring.

He found things in Omaha very much on the move. The town still was growing, spreading in boom-time newness along its bluff above the wide Missouri. In its streets was the bustle of business enterprise. In its spanking-new residential districts the imposing brick and frame mansions of prosperous bankers and merchants were going up, self-consciously ornate with spacious porches, galleries and cupolas and white-painted scrollwork gingerbread. A whole new working-class suburb known as Train Town clustered about the Union Pacific roundhouse, shops and yards. Supplies brought upriver from St. Joseph or ferried over from Council Bluffs stood in stacks on the levee. Rails, ties, coal, all sorts of railroad material waited in huge dumps along the tracks for outbound trains to railhead. And amid all this newness, the old remained also; it was a time of metamorphosis in progress. Omaha's floating population still included emigrant families impatient to head out on the westward wagon haul; grizzled freighters discussed the Indian troubles while they waited for ladings; traders and buyers from Bates of St. Louis and the American Fur Company bargained over the going price for buffalo robes; there was even an occasional buckskinned roughneck in off the prairie for a taste of high life in the city. The old frontier town still was here, a modern metropolis rising from it and around it. Uniforms were much in evidence: the advance guard of demobilized veterans from the armies of the Republic, at loose ends and hungry for opportunity in these piping times of peace.

Omaha, facing the future with blatant confidence, would never be the same again. Directly and indirectly, the railroad was responsible.

Most encouraging to Dodge were the assistants he found ready to work with him: men like Samuel B. Reed and James Evans, both divisional chief engineers, the former soon to be named superintendent of construction. Among the lower echelons were Percy Browne, Marshall Hurd, L. L. Hills, F. C. Hodges and others. These were young men all, capable and ambitious, a hardcore engineering staff already wrapped up in their jobs and beginning to manifest an eager *esprit de corps* in their attitude toward the work ahead.

Data gathered in the surveys of the preceding year had been gone over, checked and evaluated during the winter. As a result, a roughly plotted line with definite figures on levels and distances all the way through to Great Salt Lake was about ready for final consideration, though much of it ran through territory still virtually unexplored and left weighty decisions on location still to be made. The most pressing one of all, Dodge realized at once, concerned the transit of the Rocky Mountains, where three alternatives posed a bristling array of advantages and disadvantages. It appeared that he had come on the scene just in time to shoulder the responsibility of recommending a choice between them.

Almost from the outset it had been assumed that the railroad's main line would be built through Denver City in Colorado Territory. The Union Pacific directorate ardently desired this—the thriving city and its nearby gold fields were obvious reasons—and the citizens and the local government in Denver were anxiously awaiting the arrival of railhead. The projected route lay along the South Fork of the Platte River, feasible enough as far as Denver. But it entailed a long southward swing to the city, and a consequent turn northward through the high range of the Rockies, thence to Great Salt Lake by way of the Yampa, White and Uinta River valleys. The extra mileage would be costly and the mountain passes were high and rugged, though Denver partisans insisted they were passable. Survey parties were out on a final examination of this route even as Dodge arrived in Omaha.

Farther north, and firmly entrenched in the public mind as the natural way west, ran the old Oregon Trail. A railroad route in this direction would follow the North Platte Valley by way of Fort Laramie and the famous South Pass, but would then have to swing back to the southward to reach Salt Lake via the Big Sandy and the Black Fork rivers. This was the route used by the Overland Stage, and, as Editor Samuel Bowles (no engineer, to be sure) had remarked in '65, it offered no visible obstacles to a railroad right of way.

Till Dodge's advent as chief engineer, these two had seemed the only logical choices. Midway between them lay the Black Hills, only a spur of the main Rocky Mountain chain and flanked both north and south by higher, more massive ranges, but themselves so steep and tortuous that they seemed to forbid any railroad grade on the face of it. Yet this would be the most direct route by far, if only a way could be found. And still vivid in Dodge's memory were his skirmish with the Crows there a year ago, and his impressions of the long ridge climbing between Crow and Lone Tree creeks to the summit.

In his own words, "As soon as I took charge of the Union Pacific I immediately wired to Mr. James Evans who had charge of that division and who had been working on this mountain range for nearly a year, describing this range to him."[2]

But Evans' examination would take time, and Dodge was not by inclination a desk-bound engineer. Without waiting, he left Omaha for a personal inspection of the route and the work along it from railhead all the way to the eastern face of the Rockies. With him went Consulting Engineer Silas Seymour and Government Commissioner Jesse L. Williams of Indiana, himself a well-known civil engineer. David Van Lennep, company geologist, was a member of the party also, charged with the special mission of prospecting along the way for mineral deposits, stone for building and, above all, coal. It had been decided early that Union Pacific locomotives would ultimately be coal-fired, a decision almost mandatory in this empty, treeless land. (In practice, however, coal would have to be supplemented for a long while to come by cottonwood chunks from the Missouri River bottoms and the infrequent watercourses along the right of way.)

The grade, this spring, was already past the one hundredth meridian and going forward at a satisfactory rate. The rails, powered by the ferocious energy and efficiency of the Casement brothers, had plunged westward out of Fremont. The company still could be in trouble, though. The extension of time granted by the Act of '64 set June 27, this year, as the deadline for completion of the first hundred miles of railroad. Any unforeseen delays now and that date still might not be met.

There would be no delays; not with the Casements on the job.

CHAPTER 12

GENERAL DODGE'S ARMY

Over the thin strand of iron that reached out past Fremont a revolution in railroad building was on the move that spring of 1866. Dan Casement, the headquarters man in charge of ladings and dispatching from the Missouri River levee and the yards at Train Town, helped shape it. General Jack thrust the spearhead westward over the raw earth of the grade, faster than rails ever had been laid before. Suddenly the labor shortage was a thing of the past. Great civilian armies forged through five long years of war had melted overnight. Most went home to families and farms and jobs. For some it was not that easy, and chief among these were the Irish.

If this oft-repeated mention of the Irish seems to say that they constituted the main labor force of the nation in the '60's, the impression is essentially correct. Irishmen had been coming to America since colonial times. They had fled British overlordship, oppression and poverty in always increasing numbers during the early nineteenth century. The potato famine in Ireland in the '50's had spurred the exodus, and they still were coming. As a result, what the Negro slave had been to the agrarian South the unlettered but strong-backed Irishman was, in a very large measure, to the industrial North. He had dug the Erie Canal, put his sweat and his muscle into the grades of the earliest railroads in America. He had been drafted in huge numbers for the Union armies; with his ingrained affinity for the rebel and the underdog he had joined the Confederate armies too, in almost equal numbers. Now he was out again and looking for work: root hog or die. It was no mere happen-so that the Union Pacific grades were dug, and its iron laid, by Irishmen. There were others, of course—native Americans, German immigrants, English adventurers, even a three-hundred-man force of Negro freedmen of whom little is known except that they were said to have made good workers—but first to last, the backbone of the labor crews was Irish.

Some of them were as green as the old sod of their homeland, and some had been railroad veterans before they went to war. To all of them, though, this vast, flat Western land and the railroad crawling out into it were like nothing they had known before. The reverse was equally true; the Great Plains never had seen their like either. Their skills were not the pioneer skills of the frontier. They were neither tillers of the soil nor builders of homes. They would pass on, but their passing would leave its mark on this land forever. And some of them would stay out here, though they did not know it yet.

Most of the best of them went to the Casements, shrewd hirers of railroad help. What they saw, after bumping over the forty-odd miles of track from Omaha and piling off the Union Pacific freight cars in their faded blue or butternut regimentals with their bandanna-bound bundles, was a revelation from the start. They gaped at the four huge house cars standing at end of track, each one a ponderous eighty-five feet long—more than twice the length of a standard railroad boxcar—by eight high and ten wide. These were the nucleus of the camp. One was partitioned off into a ten-by-twelve-foot office, a ten-by-twenty kitchen and a dining room forty-seven feet long. Another was unpartitioned, a dining hall with rough board table and benches running its full length. A third was half dining car and half bunk car. The fourth was given over wholly to bunks, built three tiers high on both sides with an aisle down the middle, and in it stands of U.S. Army rifles ready for instant use.

That did not bother them greatly. They had been told of the Indians. And they were Army veterans almost to a man, schooled in the soldier's creed that made his rifle wife, mother, father and friend all rolled into one. General Jack Casement was pointed out to the new hands: the big boss, and a real wildcat with the hair on. That did not bother them either; they were used to Army discipline.

General Jack knew his business; they were not long in finding that out. Meanwhile, things here at railhead took some getting used to. The place was literally a town on wheels. Cattle grazed on its outskirts, a whole herd of them, five hundred head driven right along with the boarding train. There was a butcher in the crew, assigned a special boxcar for cutting and storing the slaughtered beef. A baker and his helper presided over two more, one filled with a stock of sacked flour. It did not look as though a man would starve out here, at least. The Army had never been this good. A carload of grain for the draft horses and mules was carried. Additional boxcars held various other food stores and building supplies. And the place bustled like any frontier jump-off town, with caravans of wagons rumbling off into the prairie westward with more materials and provisions for the graders out ahead. The air was alive with the clank of locomotive side rods, the grumble of exhausts in diamond stacks and the hiss of steam as trains pulled in from Omaha. Every mile of track laid down required forty carloads of food, tools, iron and what not.

The Casements' gang included engine crews who ate and slept here at railhead. Locomotives pushed the whole cumbersome outfit westward as fast as the rails went down, and that was a mile a day.

The newcomers were skeptical. Lay a mile of track in a day? Who ever heard of such a thing? They did, and without delay. Rudely they were shaken down into the work routine.

The day began at dawn. Breakfast was hearty: beef, beans, potatoes, fresh bread and plenty of strong tea or black coffee. At the work—and no time was wasted in getting to it, for there it was right at the doorstep—each man had his specific job to do. The old hands knew theirs; the new men were assigned to gangs, told what to do by their foremen and expected to pull their weight from the start.

Everything was based on the iron trains from Omaha, loaded there with careful precision under the supervision of Dan Casement. Each car carried rails, ties, spikes and chairs in exactly calculated quantities. The first iron train of the day pulled in close behind the headquarters cars. It was unloaded immediately, the material thrown off onto the right of way alongside the track. Iron train and headquarters cars were then backed into the clear and the first of two small, four-wheeled "lorry cars" was shoved down from end of track. It was loaded, swiftly but with the same precision as each car in the iron train had been, ties, rails, spikes and chairs in carefully related quantities. A horse was hitched to it with a long rope. The teamster—usually a wiry small boy perched on the nag's back; perhaps an ex-drummer boy from some Army regiment or a runaway come west to see the world—yelled and thumped his heels in, and off went horse and lorry car at a gallop. At end of track men jumped in to stop the car. Its wheels were chocked, the horse unhitched. Men seized the ties and spaced them out on the grade ahead, using the burnetized cottonwood mostly, the better, more costly hardwood ties placed only at the center and ends of each rail length.

Now the two rail gangs moved in from right and left. The first pair of men in each gang laid hold of a rail's end and drew it out over a greased roller built into the lorry's front. Other gang members took hold, two by two, as the rails' twenty-eight-foot lengths came clear. Each pair of rails was carried forward, fitted into its chairs right and left, and gauged. The lorry was shoved ahead over the new rails (even, wrote a Chicago *Tribune* correspondent a little later, "ere their clang in falling had ceased to reverberate"), and the process was repeated. Spikers followed close behind, setting the spikes and driving them home. A crew set a final tie in place under the new rail ends. Another tamped in ballast. As soon as the first lorry car was down to its last few rails, these were thrown off and the car itself manhandled off the track to make way for the second, now loaded and ready. Then it was shoved back on, the urchin and his horse hitched up, and back it went to the supply dump.

The whole operation moved forward as fast as a man could walk, until the material from the iron train was exhausted. There usually was another one waiting. The track-layers could take a short breather while it was unloaded and backed clear in its turn. Then the cycle began again.

What the Casements had developed was simply a production-line technique applied to track-laying. Each man had a specific job to do, learned it thoroughly through constant repetition and did it without having to wait upon a foreman's orders or the actions of anyone else.

There was an hour's break for the noon meal—beef, beans, potatoes, bread, tea and coffee as before—which gave a man time for a pipe and a short rest. Then back to work again till the sun slid down to touch the prairie's western rim and long shadows came creeping over the waving grass and put a stop to activity. Then supper, and the gangs were their own men till morning.

Not all the Irishmen found a place with the Casements. The track gang had started out of Fremont this spring with something over a hundred men. By early summer it was two hundred strong, and still growing. But the graders' camps, as far as a hundred miles or more out beyond railhead, employed far greater numbers. So the job-hunters gravitated farther westward, signed on, usually, at Omaha or Fremont and were sent ahead by train and wagon. The graders' daily routine did not differ markedly from the track-layers'. The accommodations were rougher; there were no boarding cars, of course, and the men lived in tents, pitched close together in ordered rows for convenience and protection against Indian attacks. Sometimes a semipermanent plank shed or two would be erected to provide office, kitchen or storage space, if the camp was a big one.

The work itself was simple, practically all pick-and-shovel work: turning up the earth to build a level bed for the rails coming on behind. First expectations had proved out; this prairie country offered few problems and fewer obstacles to railroad construction. The sod and the dirt beneath it yielded easily enough to tools and Irish muscle. Little cutting was necessary, and never to any serious depth. There were few deep sags or stream beds requiring heavy fill. The dawn-to-dusk workday prevailed here also, with the usual hour's break at noon. The meal was brought out from camp by chuck wagon and eaten on the spot. Then it was swing the pick and heave dirt, the very lack of physical hindrance keeping the work going, hour on hour, mile on mile.

It was brutal drudgery, by modern standards. But it was no worse than a laborer's normal lot anywhere in America in the '60's. Eastern factory hands worked hours equally as long, under conditions frequently as dangerous to life and limb—more so in many cases—and usually far less healthful. These men were young, practically every one an Army veteran toughened to outdoor life and hardship. The miserable, mud-slogging campaigns up and down the Mississippi and across the Potomac, through the mountains of Tennessee and Virginia and over the lowlands of Alabama and Georgia, the rough bivouacs of the Peninsula, the Wilderness and all the rest, had killed off the weak and the sickly and rooted out the faint of heart. Here on the Union Pacific the diet was rude and monotonous, but Army rations had been infinitely worse, and not nearly so plentiful or steady.

And the money was good. The Casements and the grading contractors paid up to $2.50 a day as construction drove ahead and the call went out for more and more men. The fact was that most of these Irishmen had never had it so good, and it appears that they knew it. There were no significant strikes or slowdowns.

Saturday was payday, as a rule, the men receiving their weekly stipend in either silver or greenbacks, or both. But there was little uniformity about it. Everyone, the Casements and the grading bosses alike, were subcontractors working for the Credit Mobilier and hence responsible for their own payroll arrangements. The men, however, did not generally understand this, knowing nothing of the Credit Mobilier's involved manipulations and caring less. A large number of them do not seem to have realized that they were employed by contractors, in fact, and simply assumed they were "workin' for the U-Pay Railway." It was a misunderstanding that would lead to a few complications later. Many of the grading contractors were original settlers in Nebraska Territory, who had existed by serving the emigrant trains, the Overland Stage and the Army in one capacity or another, and now turned to and helped build the railroad because that offered a bigger opportunity and fatter profits. Some others were Army veterans come west to better themselves, and differed from their laborers only in the matter of personal ambition. Being small operators, these fought a constant battle to stay solvent and their workers were not always paid regularly. Some of them failed, or decamped if the going became too rough, and the poor Paddies never collected their back wages at all.

There was not, in truth, very much on which a man could spend money out here on the Great Plains.

South of the grade flowed the sluggish Platte River—"a mile wide and an inch deep," the saying went—in its leisurely twistings and turnings sometimes close and sometimes miles distant. Along its far bank ran the Oregon Trail; emigrant wagons and Overland Stage coaches raising their brown dust clouds, and the gaunt poles of the Overland Telegraph in a line reaching westward; now paralleled on the north bank by those of the Union Pacific Telegraph, which marched right along with railhead. But the south bank of the Platte was as remote as a lunar landscape to the toilers on the railroad. Its scattered towns and way stations were not for them.

They were not altogether isolated, though. On the north side of the river lay the old Mormon Trail, and the grade followed it quite closely for much of its length. So a weary workman pausing for a moment, straightening to rest his aching back, might watch wagons creak past, loaded high with ramshackle household effects, on their seat boxes leathery men and their toil-worn women in sunbonnets and Mother Hubbards; more often than not broods of mop-headed youngsters clustered at the tailgates to peer out from under the canvas tops. He might wave or even call out some ribald pleasantry if there happened to be an attractive girl in evidence. The emigrants, for their part, eyed the sweaty railroad roughnecks, the rhythmically swinging picks and shovels, the clanging rails and the grunting locomotives with a kind of awe, perhaps, or with tired impassivity. Whatever the railroad promised, they had not been able to wait for it.

Now and then other travelers would come along: freighting outfits with bull whips cracking; lone men or parties of men in buckskins darkened and glazed with the dirt of years, bearded and unshorn, riding with scabbarded Hawken or Henry rifles or the newer, brass-mounted Winchester yellow-bellies. They were latter-day mountain men and fur trappers, old plains hands, buffalo hunters or traders, out here so long they were more Indian-like than the Indians themselves. They might ride in, share coffee and food around a grading crew's campfire, partake from the whiskey bottle as it went around, maybe spin a yarn or two—always of Indians, or buffalo, or the big country out beyond the Rockies—and in the morning ride out into the unknown from whence they had come. It was a big country; there was room in it for all kinds.

There was more room in it than anything else. It was an empty country, too, or virtually so; taken all together the passers-by were hardly enough to dent the loneliness. Few of the Paddies had anything more than the haziest idea of how far it was to the Pacific or where they really were going or what they would find when they got there. It did not really matter. This was a good job, working on the U-Pay Railway; each day was sufficient unto itself.

Still, the prairie took a great deal of knowing before a man could feel anywhere near at home on it. Nothing in the previous experience of these Irishmen from the East matched it. There was, in fact, nothing quite like it anywnere else on earth except the even vaster and more remote steppes of inner Asia. The most immediately striking thing about it was its very lack of any distinguishing features. Day after day for as far as a man could see in any direction there was not a tree, not a shrub, not a hill; nothing at all to break the unvarying, flat monotony. And yet it was not really flat. It rolled in long, unending swells like some vast, petrified ocean, shallowly gullied and cut up by the spring runoff of melting snow, the gullies quickly parched to dryness as the season moved along, and everything carpeted by the gray-green, bunchy buffalo grass that had been growing and reseeding itself and dying for aeons past, with nothing to break the sod that formed a thick, springy mat over the earth.

Under the all-pervading effect of empty barrenness it had a kind of grim grandeur, even a slowly growing, low-keyed beauty all its own, tinged all summer long by the delicate purple of the pasqueflower, the crimsons and pinks of wild geranium, yellow and lavender prairie smoke and bright red splashes of Mexican poppy. There was grama grass and bluestem in addition to the buffalo grass. It grew knee-deep in places, even man-high in the deeper hollows; a rich green in the lush days of spring, turning tawny brown and yellow as summer wore along and the sun beat down out of the high, blue-white sky.

This was fertile land, though almost nobody knew it yet.

Over such unobstructed vastness the wind had a clean sweep. It blew almost without cessation, the smell of distance and sun and warm grass in it. At times it could pile up lowering masses of thunderheads with incredible suddenness, and blow them away as quickly, or dot the far horizon with the writhing funnels of prairie twisters. But summer weather in '66 was good on the plains; apparently storms hampered the Union Pacific's progress not at all. And the engineers, being practical men, found a use for the wind. At the little fuel and water stops along the right of way they sank wells and powered the pumps with windmills, so that the completed railroad stretching westward took on a small and homely farmyard touch.

The railroaders had heard much of the buffalo, and began to see more as the miles out of Fremont dropped behind. Closer to Omaha and the fringes of civilization the herds had been thinned out and driven off by hunting. Now the big beasts appeared more and more frequently, sometimes in scattered bunches, occasionally in herds of impressive extent. Objects of great interest at first, they soon became so commonplace that little notice was paid them. They were too incredibly stupid and placid to be dangerous under ordinary circumstances, too ugly to elicit much but contempt on close acquaintance. Sometimes they became a nuisance. A herd crossing the track paid not the slightest attention to a locomotive's whistle, and engineers learned in a hurry not to try to run through them; they simply massed in front of the oncoming train, both the dead and the living piling up before the pilot till the engine stalled and stopped. Then the train waited—for hours, maybe—till the herd had passed.

Telegraph crews came to hate the buffalo for a different reason. The thick hump manes shed as warm weather came on, and drove the great beasts to use anything handy as scratching posts. In this treeless land the telegraph poles served admirably, and soon drew them like flies to the honey pot. Poles were uprooted and pushed flat repeatedly, till replacing them grew to be a troublesome chore. For years afterward, all the way across the plains, they remained leaning crazily askew from the pressure of massive bodies milling and crowding in to rub away the universal itch.

Curiously, no serious effort was made on the Union Pacific to live off the country by utilizing the natural supply of buffalo meat, which grew more abundant as railhead moved westward. Down in Kansas, where Samuel Hallet and Company had now been reorganized as the Union Pacific, Eastern Division (a name that would shortly be changed to the Kansas Pacific) and was hustling to make a race of it to the one hundredth meridian, a young plainsman named William Cody presently launched himself on the road to undying fame by contracting to provide buffalo meat for the grading and track-laying crews. But the Union Pacific's contractors, though they occasionally hired a hunter for the same purpose, usually preferred to rely on the beef cattle they drove along with them.

Buffalo got most of the publicity back East, but they were not the only creatures out here. The prairie, so empty at first glance, teemed with other life. The graders and iron gangs began to see herds of antelope; graceful, lightfooted little animals that would lift dainty heads at their approach, stare curiously and then ghost off with white rumps flashing in the sun like heliographs. They passed prairie dog villages, whole acres of closely spaced burrows, each with its mound of excavated earth and its occupant sitting bolt upright like a stocky tent peg, the entire population vanishing into the ground as though on cue, all at the same instant, if a man approached too near. The little prairie wolves called coyotes slunk along on the flanks of the buffalo herds. Big, lanky jackrabbits were almost as prolific and plentiful as the buffalo, and multitudes of grasshoppers sprang up ahead of boots striding through the grass, and whirred away in all directions. Incredulous Irishmen made the acquaintance of the "fool hen," a bird so stupid he could be approached and knocked over with a stick. Known as the partridge or ruffed grouse, he would be a prized game bird to later generations, the foolishness bred out of him by harsh experience.

There were deadlier things on these plains. Now and then a man was rattlesnake-bitten. Folklore to the contrary, the omnipresent nostrum, whiskey, proved a poor cure.

The Great American Desert was a fading myth and, all unknowing, the railroad was helping to explode it. People would come to love this illimitable plain with its sweeping distances and its austere charm. They would be along later, though: cattlemen and homesteaders, sodbusters and their women, and the broods of children they would raise. People who would stay and sink roots into this earth and take the time to look and learn and know it. The railroad builders were not among them. They had a date at the California line.

Aside from the unceasing hard work, they thought it a pretty dull life. The work week was a full six days. Sundays a man could spend in such small personal chores as washing and mending clothes, or in any other way he wished; but there was not much choice. Mail service had advanced westward with the rails, so that those with friends or families back home could read or write letters—those who knew how. Many did not. The Irishmen, Roman Catholics almost to a man, could go off by themselves to count their rosaries and say their Hail Marys in decent reverence if they wanted to, for there was little or no provision made for formal religious observances.

Occasionally, especially at railhead, if someone of importance happened to be out from Omaha, a buffalo hunt would be organized. The riflemen would swarm aboard a locomotive turned over to them for the day and cruise down the track, seldom stopping or disembarking until a herd or perhaps a lone old bull was found within range. Then everyone blazed away from pilot deck, running board, gangway or tender, the engineer hauling down on his whistle cord, the whole party yipping like banshees as the harried brutes galloped along beside the grade and finally went down or veered away to safety.[1]

Reminiscences handed down in later years indicate that fishing in the Platte or its occasional tributary streams was a favorite pastime. The men swam, too; such swims, in fact, afforded the best practical means of getting a bath. There were the inevitable card games, and dice rolled on a blanket. In the brief evenings between supper and bedtime the recent war was an unending topic of conversation. Since many crews included veterans of both Union and Confederacy it was rehashed and fought over and over again, often violently.

And there was whiskey.

Quite early, General Sherman wrote with wry wit to his brother John, the Congressman, predicting that "So large a number of workmen distributed along the line will introduce enough whiskey to kill off all the Indians within three hundred miles of the road." He was wrong about the Indians, for firewater only made the angry red man angrier. But the general knew his Army veterans. The graders, track-layers and engine crews were indeed manly consumers of redeye, rotgut and forty-rod, and the whiskey peddlers were not long in seeking them out. Practically every large construction camp soon had its tent saloon with a plank laid over a pair of kegs for a bar, or sometimes only a wagon with the liquor dispensed straight from a barrel lashed alongside, a tin cup fastened to it by a short length of chain. Few of the contractors objected, realizing full well that whiskey was a potent help in keeping the men satisfied and on the job.

Whiskey had always been the downtrodden Irishman's one great solace and he would not be deprived of it now. The bosses intervened when necessary to keep the drunken brawls from becoming lethal, and the hard work and hot sun of the morning after fried the hangovers out of sweating hides.

Like an army in itself—hard-bitten, sinewy, honed to rawhide resilience, profane, brawling, alcoholic and altogether unstoppable—the work force moved westward. The graders followed the location stakes. General Jack's iron men followed the graders. Stinking-hot locomotives reeking of black smoke and valve oil hauled their cars along behind with the physical wherewithal flowing out from the East. The army simile is not an idle one. A little later on, as public attention began to focus on the spectacle of the transcontinental's building, many newspaper correspondents likened this Union Pacific effort to the march of Sherman's conquering horde across Georgia to the sea in '64.

In a very real sense, in fact, these Union Pacific men *were* an army, with Major General Grenville Dodge at the top and the likes of Brigadier General Jack Casement for corps commanders. Department heads, almost all, had been lieutenants, captains, majors. For foremen there was no lack of tough corporals and sergeants. Recent privates swung the picks and shovels and spike mauls, pulled the throttle and stoked the firebox, rode caboose and car top. Hostile Indians, raiding more fiercely as the year went on, would feel the effects of that. But it ran much deeper, welding the work gangs together with the glue of military training and *élan*. The five-year War Between the States had left in these men a sturdy sense of organization and discipline, and leaders like Dodge and Casement knew how to use it to the fullest.

One final appurtenance of an army in the field might be mentioned—as it was, often, by the men themselves. All the way across the plains and on to the distant finish, there was scratching and swearing and recurrent complaints of cooties in the camps.

CHAPTER 13

MERIDIAN 100

Hitting their steady mile a day, Jack Casement's Paddies reached Columbus, ninety miles out of Omaha, early in June. Or perhaps it would be more accurate to say that Columbus reached railhead; it was something of a dead heat, apparently. The town, which had grown up around an Overland Stage station on the south bank of the Platte, crossed the river en masse to meet the advancing railroad.

Big things were afoot out here, the air crackling with the excitement of boom times. George Francis Train was much in evidence in Nebraska Territory this spring and summer, a loud and ebullient booster for the Union Pacific, the great West, the good life, progress and prosperity. His real estate speculations in Omaha were making him wealthy. Now he was investing heavily in choice sites in the new Columbus, hailing the town as the geographical center of the United States, logical spot for Nebraska's capital, even predicting that it would one day be the national capital.

Railhead did not pause, however, nor Jack Casement wait upon ceremony. West of Columbus the Loup River flowed into the Platte. It was crossed by way of a fifteen-hundred-foot iron bridge, ready and waiting for the rails. The track hurried on, following the graders like a hungry iron serpent. Milepost 100 was set up comfortably ahead of the June 27 deadline. And still there was no slackening of speed. The one hundredth meridian lay 247 miles west of Omaha. Dr. Thomas Durant was determined that the railroad should be there by fall, and General Jack had no objection. His work force was increasing steadily, settling to the rhythms of the job, and so were the grading crews out in front. Bridge gangs worked from five to twenty miles ahead of railhead, under orders not to delay the track-layers.

One hundred fifty-three and a fraction miles out of Omaha, the first division point was established at the tiny German settlement of Grand Island. Nothing had been there before; like Columbus, the town moved bodily across the Platte to greet the oncoming track men. By August end of track was thirty-seven miles farther west and even with old Fort Kearney, of long-standing importance as a stage and emigrant station on the Oregon Trail. Again there was a mass hegira across the Platte, and Kearney became a Union Pacific town. For the Overland Stage this summer the handwriting was on the wall in large and glaring letters: its day was drawing to a close. Omaha lay 191 miles to the rear. The supply line was lengthening, but the mile-a-day pace had been maintained, and would be. Revenue service, both freight and passenger, was in effect between Omaha and Kearney. The construction contractors and the Army had top priority and practically monopolized the traffic; it is significant that the first timetables were issued under the authority of Construction Superintendent Samuel Reed. Small shipments of purely commercial freight were squeezed in only where there was room, and paying passengers had to find seats atop flatcar loads or in cabooses. Nevertheless, the Union Pacific was beginning to function as a common carrier at last.

West of Kearney, however, Indian troubles began in grim earnest. They were no new or sudden thing. Since '64, survey parties had been subjected to harassment, and often driven in off their jobs. And once the first few miles out of Omaha had been covered, graders and track gangs had never been able to be sure that some wandering party of wild young braves would not swoop down out of nowhere, stampede cattle and work stock and even take a white scalp or two if the chances looked good. Heretofore it had been more nuisance than serious hazard. But now the railroad was thrusting deep into the range of the vast Republican buffalo herd (named for the Republican River which winds through southern Nebraska and northern Kansas) which constituted the main commissary for the tribes of the central Great Plains.

The controversy arising from the white man's killing and wilding the buffalo, making the red man's hunt more difficult, had always been at the bottom of the Indian trouble. Without the great herds, the Indians' way of life could not survive, and they knew it. And the wisest of the chiefs understood very well that this new "fire road" forging up the Platte would bring in its wake depredations greater than any that had gone before. Between Sioux and Cheyenne and the Union Pacific it had to be war; there was no other way.

The Army stood ready to give its protection, such as it was. General Sherman, Grenville Dodge's good friend and old corps commander, issued orders to deny no request of the railroad. Generals Phil Sheridan, fiery leader of Union cavalry during the war, W. C. Augur, George Crook and others all commanded troops on the plains this summer, and all knew and respected Dodge. "There was nothing we could ask them for that they did not give," he wrote later, "even when regulations did not authorize it, and it took a large stretch of authority to satisfy our demands."[1]

The Army, though, had been trying for a long while to pacify the hostiles, without conspicuous success. And the Union Pacific took a great deal of protecting, with graders now working as far as two hundred miles in advance of the track-layers, and survey and location crews strung out even farther ahead. The cavalry, undermanned at best, had to spread itself terribly thin. As the classic remark by veteran Indian fighter George Crook explained, it was difficult to surround three Indians with one trooper.

So the railroad men had to defend themselves, in very large measure. And they did not do badly. "Graders and track-layers, tie men and station builders had to sleep under guard," Grenville Dodge wrote, "and have gone to their work with their picks and shovels and their mechanical tools in one hand and the rifle in the other, and they often had to drop one and use the other."[2] Dodge himself, returned from his reconnaissance west this August, was caught in an attack while conducting a group of government commissioners out to inspect the track work beyond Kearney. Without warning a Cheyenne war party fell on a graders' camp within five miles of the guardian cavalry's command post. To a man his party snatched up rifles and helped beat off the attack.

Yet beef cattle and draft stock were run off by the hundreds of head, and here and there men died in an abrupt, cruel instant of surprise, slumping to the ground with bodies torn by arrows or musket slugs as the raiders hit and ran.

Such casualties were relatively few, in the aggregate, and few of the names were remembered for very long. The dead were buried where they fell, usually; right in the grade itself, according to a legend which persisted for long years afterward. The wounded, like the sick or those injured in accidents, received such makeshift comfort as their mates could give. If they were in bad shape and happened to be fortunate enough to be close to a military post, they might hope for the ministrations of an Army surgeon. Failing that, they were sent back on the first train eastbound to the nearest town boasting a doctor—and either made it or did not. Medical care on the U.P. Railroad was as rough and ready as everything else out here on the wild frontier.

This same summer a government peace mission met with Red Cloud, Man Afraid of His Horses, Spotted Tail and other Sioux chiefs at Fort Laramie in the Dakotah Wyoming. Negotiations were long and difficult, and in the end there was no peace treaty.

"You destroyed the buffalo. You lied to us," Red Cloud told the government men bluntly. "And now you will get nothing from us but war."

So things would get worse before they got better.

Meanwhile, Indians or no, the work did not stop or even slow down seriously. Dodge sent orders to graders and track-layers to stand their ground and fight if attacked, never to retreat. And it is not recorded that they ever did. General Jack Casement drove his gangs hard, and harder still as the last of summer wore on. The tough Irish veterans idolized him for it. They said he was only five feet and four inches high, but every bit as wide. Tall tales grew about him. They told of a loaded boxcar that had to be moved, with no locomotive handy at the moment. Men massed behind it and pushed, sweating and straining to no avail. Then General Jack put his shoulder to the end sill and called for a real effort. The car moved, and rolled docilely to where it was wanted.

He could ride the wind itself into the ground, they claimed. Once, coming alone out to railhead, he was almost cut off by an Indian war party. He put spurs to his horse, the savages pounding at his heels, yelping their war cries and winging arrows all around him. Mile after mile the chase continued, but the general galloped into camp at last, the redskins speeding one last volley and wheeling away. Casement slid from his foundered horse. He was bloody from head to foot, and anxious men crowded around to help him.

"Hell," he bellowed, "it's only a nosebleed!" and sent them packing back to their jobs.

Apocryphal, very likely. But it took a man to inspire stories like that.

The Indian trouble had its odd little sidelights at times. It was not all-out war as the white man understood the term. Warriors who raided a graders' camp without mercy one week might ride into another the next to cadge a little food and tobacco and drink a round of coffee, scalding hot with sugar spooned in heavily, the way they liked it. Chief Spotted Tail and sixteen or seventeen Sioux braves rode up to the Casements' headquarters one day late in '66. The track-layers dropped their work and scrambled to arms, but the chief made the peace sign and, a little dubiously, they let him come in. He and his warriors were there, he explained gravely in his guttural English, because they wanted to see how their white brothers did this work on the fire road. Still somewhat guardedly, the whites took them on a tour of the camp. The red men watched with grimly wooden faces while several lengths of rail were laid, and grunted with only slightly quickened interest at the kitchen car with its sides of fresh beef, its potatoes and beans and other foods in plenty. But the dark faces really lighted up and came alive when they were taken into the bunk car and saw the long stands of rifles there. Still they said nothing, however. One version of the story has it that the chief was invited into a locomotive cab and taken for a short ride up and down the track, clapping his hand over his mouth in the Indian sign for amazement at the spewing steam, the blazing firebox, the pound and roll of rods and drivers. When it was over and he was back on terra firma, Old Spot finally got down to business.

The Sioux, he declared, had come for their share of the good things they had seen here, particularly the guns. Many guns they wanted, with plenty of powder and bullets. And if the white men did not give them these things, he added, then he, Spotted Tail, would return with many warriors and take everything.

Jack Casement happened to be absent from the camp at the time, but his boss track-layer, Captain D. B. Clayton, was quite equal to the occasion. He laid a clenched fist gently against the chief's nose and in a few bristling sentences dared him to come ahead and try it.

There was no attack that time.

Meanwhile October had come, and on the fifth day of it end of track had poked its way up to the one hundredth meridian.

It was an epochal occasion, for which Dr. Durant, keeping in close touch from New York, had been waiting with eager impatience. The one hundredth meridian was a great deal more than just milestone 247. Ever since being written into the Act of '62 it had loomed as a combination of goal and jumping-off place; victory over the Leavenworth, Pawnee and Western in the dash from the Missouri[3] and the beginning of the real transcontinental drive to the Pacific. Its attainment meant that the doubters had been wrong. More to the point, it meant the kind of progress that might bolster the lagging confidence of impor-tant Eastern capitalists with money to invest. Money still was needed; it was always needed. And there were personal considerations. Durant so far had enjoyed scant opportunity to display his bent for doing things in the grand manner. The ground-breaking in '63 had gone almost unnoticed by the nation at large. The crude little excursion in '65 had suffered by comparison with the Central Pacific's impressive Sierra trip for the Schuyler Colfax party. This time, Durant wanted his railroad's achievement celebrated by an excursion that would stand unmatched for splendor in all the annals of American railroading.

And so it was.

The Great Pacific Railway Excursion, it was called, and advertised beforehand in New York, Chicago and other centers as "celebrating the attainment of the 100th meridian, at the 247 mile post, in 182 working days, or more than a year ahead of Federal requirements."

Invited guests included President Andrew Johnson and his Cabinet, the ambassador of every important foreign nation then represented in Washington, high officers of both Army and Navy and a veritable *Who's Who* of leading capitalists and railroad executives. The main party, one hundred in number, departed from New York on the evening of October 15 via the New Jersey and

Pennsylvania Central Railroad to Pittsburgh, thence to Chicago by the Pittsburgh, Fort Wayne and Chicago. Here a local contingent joined the group, which then split up. One party proceeded to Omaha over the Chicago and Northwestern and the Cedar Rapids and Missouri to Denison, Iowa, and were taken the rest of the way by stage. The other traveled to St. Joseph, Missouri, via the Chicago, Burlington and Quincy and the Hannibal and St. Joseph Railroads, then boarded the steam packets *Denver* and *Colorado* for the forty-eight-hour run upriver to Omaha.

These latter were the fortunate ones. Both steamers were luxury ships, in a day when riverboat travel achieved the ultimate in high living. The ladies and gentlemen danced to the strains of lilting waltzes played under the mellow Missouri moon, and in the gilt and gingerbread dining salons tables groaned under arrays of rich and exotic foods. Dinner consisted of thirty entrees, including larded antelope, braised bear, saddle of venison, roast mallard, wild turkey, quail on toast, roast grouse and rabbit potpie. These were followed by eighteen pastries and no less than six desserts, with tea, coffee and chocolate; the whole garnished with awe-inspiring decorations: a huge cornucopia done in spun sugar, a sponge candy pyramid, various other fancies worked in nougat and rock candy.

Hubert Hoxie, Dr. Durant's old accomplice, turns up again here. This time, as the Union Pacific's assistant chief of transportation—a promotion possibly earned or at least hastened by his amiability in the contract matter—he was the agent charged with keeping the guests comfortable, happy and royally entertained. A man of ability and many parts, Hoxie. "The Ubiquitous," they had dubbed him by the time the two packets docked at Omaha.

The city greeted the reunited tourists with a gala grand ball and a tour designed to emphasize the phenomenal growth and development of the onetime frontier town—680 new buildings erected this year alone! Some of the delighted excursionists expressed amazement at finding themselves, "after a week's journeying westward from New York, still among people of wealth, refinement and enterprise," the Omaha *Herald* reported indulgently.

But the amazement was premature. The excursion proper was only about to begin, and more marvelous experiences awaited. The *Railway Pioneer,* a special newspaper issued by the company for the occasion, chronicled them all.

At noon on Tuesday, October 23, the guests, now mustering two hundred, boarded their special train. It consisted of nine cars pulled by two of "the Company's powerful locomotives profusely decked with flags and appropriate mottoes." There was a baggage and supply car, then the "mess or cooking car," followed by a small car fitted up as a "refreshment saloon." Then came four brand-new coaches fresh from the company's Omaha car shops, and behind them was the famous "Lincoln car." This alone was an object of considerable interest. It had been built in 1864 at the government's military car shops for the late President's use; it featured thick boiler plate inserted between inner and outer wood sheathing as a protection against assassins' bullets, and an extra-length bed to accommodate Abraham Lincoln's six-foot four-inch frame. But the President, it was said, had used it only on his last, tragic journey from the White House home to Illinois. Later Dr. Durant had purchased it from the government as his own personal car, and later still he had turned it over to the Union Pacific for the entertainment of just such distinguished guests as those who rode it now.

Last in line came Durant's new private car, a palatial creation of George M. Pullman, resplendent with paneling of rare woods, rich hangings and plush and brocade upholstery. For this excursion it was "devoted to members of Congress and others who felt desirous of making a critical examination of the road and the adjacent country."

Though President Johnson and his Cabinet members were among those who had sent their regrets, this was an assemblage of celebrated names, wealth and influence the like of which never had rolled over American rails before. The Senate was represented by Rutherford B. Hayes of Ohio, destined to be President; Benjamin Wade, the great Civil War Abolitionist of Ohio and a current Presidential hopeful; J. W. Patterson of New Hampshire; J. M. Thayer and T. W. Tipton of Nebraska Territory. Monsieur O'Dillon Barrot, secretary of the French legation, was present with his compatriot, the Marquis Chambrun of Paris. So was the English Earl of Arlie. General John Bates of the War Department had come. General Philip St. George Cooke, commander of the Military District of the Platte, had brought his entire staff, all handsome and dashing in full-dress uniform. Chicago was well represented by Joseph Medill, publisher of the powerful *Tribune*; John Crerar, the industrialist; sleeping-car magnate George Pullman; Robert T. Lincoln, son of the late President. Nebraska had sent, in addition to her two Senators, Governor Alvin Saunders, Chief Justice William Kellogg and Luther Kountz, the leading banker of Omaha. These were but a sampling. Noted editors were on hand, or had sent correspondents. George Francis Train was there, accompanied by Mrs. Train and her personal maid, and as usual eloquent with praise for Western development and its prospects.

The Union Pacific delegation was led by Dr. Thomas Durant. John A. Dix was absent, having been appointed U.S. Minister to France at the termination of his military duty (he would finally resign as U.P. president a little later this fall). Company directors present included Edward Cook of Iowa, John Duff and C. A. Lambard of Massachusetts and courtly, white-haired Sidney Dillon of New York. There were several of the government directors and commissioners, among them Iowa's Samuel Curtis, first sponsor of a Union Pacific bill in Congress. General Grenville Dodge and Colonel Silas Seymour; both Casement brothers; the ubiquitous Hoxie and his chief, Webster Snyder; all were kept busy answering questions put by the eager guests.

Also on hand were two official photographers and a pair of bands, the Great Western Light Guard of Chicago and Rosenblatt's Band of St. Joseph. Both of them poured forth music while the famous restaurateur, H. Kinsley, "the Delmonico of Chicago," specially engaged as caterer, served a sumptuous luncheon in the cars as the train chugged onward along the westward path of empire.

As evening spread a golden haze over the prairie, the excursion train pulled into Columbus, where a camp site had been prepared and supper was waiting. It was served and eaten around campfires under a waning moon. And then, for a fitting climax to this first day in the Wild West, a detachment of Major Frank North's Pawnee Scouts staged a frenzied war dance. "And the congregation of lady and gentlemen spectators," the *Railway Pioneer* declared archly, "were only too glad to know that the Indians were entirely friendly." Then at last, bed: hay-filled mattresses, soft buffalo robes and blankets in individual family tents. The excursionists, pleasantly weary and stuffed with rich foods and the wonders they had seen, drifted off to sleep, "lulled by the howling of the distant wolf and the subdued mutterings of the Pawnees."

Everyone turned out at dawn. They had little choice, for Dr. Durant, leaving no emotional stop unpulled, had arranged for a blood-curdling outburst of Pawnee war whoops to greet the new day. Some reassurances were necessary before the ladies and gentlemen were satisfied that they would not be scalped out of hand. But no doubt, over a hearty breakfast ("sumptuous" was the word again), the officers of General Cooke's staff told about the Pawnee Scouts and their picturesque leader, Major North.

An experienced plainsman and one of the most colorful figures on the frontier, he had lived long among the Pawnees, knew their language and their ways and was known to them as the White Chief. So formidable a fighting force had he made of his Scouts that the U.S. Army had enlisted them as regulars. But, as these proper staff officers probably went on to explain tolerantly, the Pawnees made miserable soldiers from a spit-and-polish standpoint. Regulations meant nothing to their savage minds. They were wont to cut the seats from their uniform trousers in defiance of the strictest orders, and in battle, more often than not, discarded trousers altogether in favor of breechclouts and war paint. Being hereditary enemies of the Sioux and

Cheyenne, however, they served as good allies for the white troops. And, the officers conceded, they were among the most effective guardians of this wonderful transcontinental railroad; as the guests would shortly see for themselves.

The train stopped a little way farther on, at the Pawnees' main encampment. Here a sham battle was staged, a mighty spectacle complete with volleys of blank cartridges, blood-chilling Indian yells, clouds of boiling dust and thunder of ponies' hoofs—and in conclusion, the mock Sioux were unhorsed and scalped to a man.

Then onward once again, luncheon and more band music en route. And in the afternoon the train behind its double-headed locomotives rolled majestically up to the climactic one hundredth meridian—and kept right on going. For, as the Union Pacific men explained proudly, the work had not stopped with the achievement of this goal; even as the excursionists converged on Omaha the rails had leaped forward another thirty miles across the plains, and their relentless westward surge was still continuing. The party slept that night in another luxurious camp at milepost 279. Still the track had not ended.

The guests were satisfactorily impressed. Would they never overtake the racing railhead? they asked in awe. Yes, promised Dr. Durant, smiling— tomorrow.

Meanwhile a telegraph office was set up and the many gentlemen of affairs in the party were invited to dispatch messages back home. A printing press was set up also, a special edition of the *Railway Pioneer* run off and distributed. In the morning there was a swim in the Platte River for the hardier gentlemen. After breakfast a meeting was called for nine o'clock in the public square of a newly laid out town site: Camp No. 2, Buffalo County, Nebraska; a mayor was elected, and a town council. This was an impressive object lesson, tangible proof that the railroad was bringing civilization into the wilds, and opportunities for investment along with it. The Credit Foncier had been organized by this time as an agency for the profitable disposal of the Union Pacific's land-grant acreage, with George Francis Train as a guiding genius and chief drumbeater. It never achieved the fame (or the infamy) of its near-namesake, the Credit Mobilier, and in any case had not yet hit its full stride, this year of '66. But its day was coming, and the Great Pacific Railway Excursion helped.

Diversions were planned for the tourists' every waking minute. Following the meeting a buffalo hunt was announced for all who wished to take part— and most did, or at least went along to watch the fun. Hunting the buffalo was an inescapable feature of every trip over the Great Plains, then and for many years afterward. Perhaps this one was not the usual success, however, for the *Railway Pioneer* did not dwell on it. Later in the afternoon came the trip's *pièce de résistance*: a leisurely journey over the final eight miles to railhead. Here everyone alighted from the cars and stood by, entranced, while General Jack Casement's iron gang, in fine fettle for the event, laid eight hundred feet of track in thirty minutes. It was a striking demonstration of the why and the how of the great enterprise's astounding march to the West. And still before the watchers' gaze stretched the grade ahead, as far into the distance as the eye could see. The skeptics, if there were any in the party, found little to say now.

So at last they turned homeward, but not until after a memorable night spent there at railhead. Among the entertainments plotted by their Union Pacific hosts were an hour-long fireworks exhibition, a band concert beneath the stars and a lecture on phrenology, a popular fad of the day, with the distinguished cranium of George Francis Train volunteered as a demonstration piece.

On the return trip there was a stop for picture-taking at the ceremonial arch erected over the right of way at the one hundredth meridian; another to inspect a prairie-dog town twenty-five miles square, one of the wonders of the West at which travelers never tired of marveling, along with the buffalo herds, the Indians and the vast, limitless country itself. And on the last night out there was an ultimate, unexpected treat, another of the storied thrills of life on the plains: a prairie fire roaring and crackling, sending its flames high into the darkened heavens. It had been arranged beforehand, courtesy of Dr. Durant.

From Omaha the grateful guests departed for Chicago, weary, no doubt somewhat sunburned, rumpled and begrimed with lingering traces of prairie dust, but filled with the consciousness of having been present at the creation of an epic and aware as never before of the Union Pacific Railroad. There had been nothing like the Great Excursion of '66 in American railroad history —or for that matter in American history. Dr. Durant was well pleased. The rival Central Pacific, laboriously climbing toward the summit of the Sierras this fall and soon to be engaged tooth and nail in its severest test, had done nothing as spectacular as this.

CHAPTER 14

THE WHEELS ROLL WEST

In Omaha Grenville Dodge got back to serious work, for there was much to do before this most successful year on the Union Pacific was closed out. His report this fall had been a portentous one, and not quite what his board of directors had anticipated.

Three years of preliminary surveys along the route by way of Denver City had failed to reveal any pass short of eleven thousand feet in height through the main range of the Rockies. Snow would be a problem and a considerable amount of slow and costly tunnel work would be necessary, with the mileage lengthened by the swing to the south and then back northward again. The findings on the northerly route via South Pass had not proved promising either. The pass was subject to heavy winter snows also; enough, in the engineers' opinion, to constitute a hindrance to railroad operations. And the South Pass route, too, would add some forty extra miles of main line trackage, with a commensurate increase in costs.

But—and most important of all—the summer's field activities had backed up Dodge's own preference for the more direct middle way over the Black Hills. Divisional Chief Engineer James Evans, acting on his instructions, had found the lone tree and the long ridge rising out of the plain essentially as Dodge had described them. And his line location survey had established the fact that a feasible grade did indeed exist all the way to the Black Hills summit. It entailed a maximum rise of ninety feet to the mile—stiff, but well within practical and legal limitations—with a corresponding drop from the crest westward. Maximum curvature, however, was only six degrees, remarkably easy for a mountain railroad. And as a clinching advantage, Van Lennep, the company geologist, had discovered extensive coal beds close to this projected line during his examination of the terrain with Dodge in the spring.

Dodge had named the summit for his old friend and commander, William

T. Sherman. As soon as he found his own judgment verified by Evans' survey, he submitted his report, recommending the Sherman Summit route without reservations.

It was dated October 15, on the eve of the Great Pacific Railway Excursion. Undoubtedly this delayed consideration of it by the board of directors, though even so their action seems to have been reasonably prompt. The matter was too important to permit any prolonged temporizing. And very probably the excursion gave Dodge an opportunity to press his recommendation in personal talks with Dr. Durant and others. For all that, some directors remained unreconciled to the prospect of losing Denver as a Union Pacific city. In the end the question was referred to the separately appointed government directors, and these, on November 23, decided to approve Dodge's report and the Sherman Summit line.

The announcement of their decision hit Denver with the impact of catastrophe; of double catastrophe, in fact. Earlier in the year Congress had passed legislation releasing the Kansas Pacific from the original requirement that it connect with the U.P. at the one hundredth meridian. Instead, it was given the right to build all the way across Kansas and into Colorado Territory for a terminus at Denver. But as it happened, the bad news from the Union Pacific coincided with a rumor (false, but no one knew it at the time) that the Kansas Pacific was about to go bankrupt and abandon construction.

The double blow was too much to take, and for a while Denver wallowed in the depths of depression. Disgusted businessmen, saloonkeepers and madams shuttered their premises, sold out cheap and headed for greener pastures in what amounted almost to a mass exodus. There was at the time a spirited rivalry between Denver and Golden, center of the Clear Creek mining district, for the prestige and the solid commercial advantages of becoming Colorado's territorial capital; and this snubbing by the Union Pacific sounded like a death knell for Denver's ambitions. But then the reaction set in: anger, a mighty outcry of protest and a determination to do something about it. The inevitable delegation to Washington was named and sent on its way. It was, of course, unsuccessful; the decision it protested had been made, in effect, by the national government itself.

Eventually, righteous indignation took a more constructive course. Territorial Governor John Evans led a movement by Coloradans to build their own railroad linking Denver City with the Union Pacific's main line, and so in the long run neither side lost by the government directors' decision.

Meanwhile, General Jack Casement had not rested. End of track moved on across Nebraska, still hitting its mile-a-day average. The old Hoxie contract had ended by agreement at the one hundredth meridian, and a fierce tempest had blown up inside the Credit Mobilier. High-handed Dr. Durant was out as the agency's president, ousted from its board, too, in a bitter quarrel of which the full details never were told. It seems certain, however, that it stemmed from Durant's resentment of the growing control exercised by Oakes and Oliver Ames, and their disapproval, in return, of some of his business methods. Now Durant was vowing that the Credit Mobilier, his own brain child, had had its last contract from the Union Pacific. He backed up his words, moreover, by awarding the next hundred miles of construction beyond the one hundredth meridian to a man by the name of Boomer. Of the nature of this deal, nothing is known today. Boomer was a Chicagoan, the chief bridge contractor to the Union Pacific, but there is no indication anywhere that he ever put in a foot of U.P. grade or track, or, in fact, that the alleged contract ever existed, save in Durant's mind.

In any event, the Credit Mobilier already had more than fifty of the hundred miles completed at the time, and it went right on in the expectation of a verifying contract from the Union Pacific board, Durant's hostility notwithstanding.

Alert frontier entrepreneurs had begun to follow the construction crews and to eye the direction and progress of the grade with interest. As winter came on, the prairie earth hardening under the first scurrying windrows of snow, there was much speculation as to where the next terminal construction base would be set up. An enterprising pair of brothers, Peniston and Andrew Miller, got the word somehow or simply made an educated guess, and hurried to move their trading post from the tiny settlement of Cold Water into the triangle of land formed by the confluence of the North and South Forks of the Platte. Sure enough, the track-layers came clattering along in due time, the rails crawling over a long wooden bridge across the North Platte River, the Casements' camp on wheels rolling in, bunk cars, cooking and mess cars shunted onto the sidings quickly laid down and spiked in place. Their big warehouse and company store went up. Supply trains steamed in from Omaha to fill them. Grenville Dodge came on in person to lay out a Union Pacific town site.

Another wide-awake businessman named John Burke appeared with a log building knocked down, hauled in by ox teams from Cottonwood Springs and put together again. It became a hotel, a single bleak room with rough bunks built around the walls. An otherwise unsung journalist by the name of Clark pre-empted a boxcar, set up a small printing press in it and cranked out the first issue of the town's first newspaper, the *Pioneer on Wheels*.[1] It was becoming a popular word in Nebraska Territory this fall: "Pioneer," a word given new form and meaning by gangs of tough Irish war veterans and locomotives trailing gray smoke down the prairie wind.

Canvas, raw lumber and cut sod blocks bloomed into homes and places of business along General Dodge's brand-new streets. The population that winter swelled from nothing to more than two thousand. Much of it was railroad: Casement iron-slingers and their pick-and-shovel brethren called in off the frozen grade ahead. But a new element, too, was making its presence felt for the first time along the U.P.'s trail. They came swarming in: drifters, saloonkeepers, gamblers, blacklegs, trollops, all sorts and degrees of shady opportunists sniffing after the railroad's payroll dollars like coyotes with noses for a ripening buffalo kill.

So North Platte was born, and grew.

Railroad construction was officially closed down there on December 11, with end of track twelve miles beyond, at milepost 305. The pace of a mile per working day had been held to the end, in spite of iron deliveries that had sometimes been erratic and the always lengthening supply line.

Back in Omaha, while the blizzards blew in and North Platte caroused, General Dodge sat down with the engineers called off the advance surveys into winter quarters. One of them, young Percy Browne, had had a bad time of it. Still engaged in an examination of the Denver route that summer and fall, he had struggled with his party up through Berthoud Pass, 11,300 feet high in the Colorado Rockies; then northward through Boulder Pass, 11,700 feet; and finally into Argentine Pass, nearly 13,000 and choked by fifteen feet of snow. Such arduous and painstaking trial and error was necessary in territory so nearly unexplored. In Argentine an early storm caught the party. Their horses and pack mules had to be abandoned as they foundered and died. Afoot and half-starved, on the verge of exhaustion, the men fought their way down to the lower levels and finally made their way back to Denver. There they found it had all been for nothing; Dodge's report recommending the Black Hills route already had been dispatched. But it was impossible to keep in close touch with survey parties working in that remote and trackless country.

Now, however, the maps and data were encouraging. Approval of the Sherman Summit passage meant that the through line to Great Salt Lake was complete, though virtually all of the final location work from Sherman westward through the Wasatch Mountains remained to be done. From Omaha the line had five hundred miles in which to climb a gradually ascending rise of five thousand feet, and fifty miles more for the additional climb of two thousand feet to Sherman Summit. Compared with the Central Pacific's problem of overcoming some seven thousand feet of rise through the Sierra Nevadas in only a hundred miles, the Union Pacific had had all the best of the going.

Total cost of the railroad to the one hundredth meridian—construction,

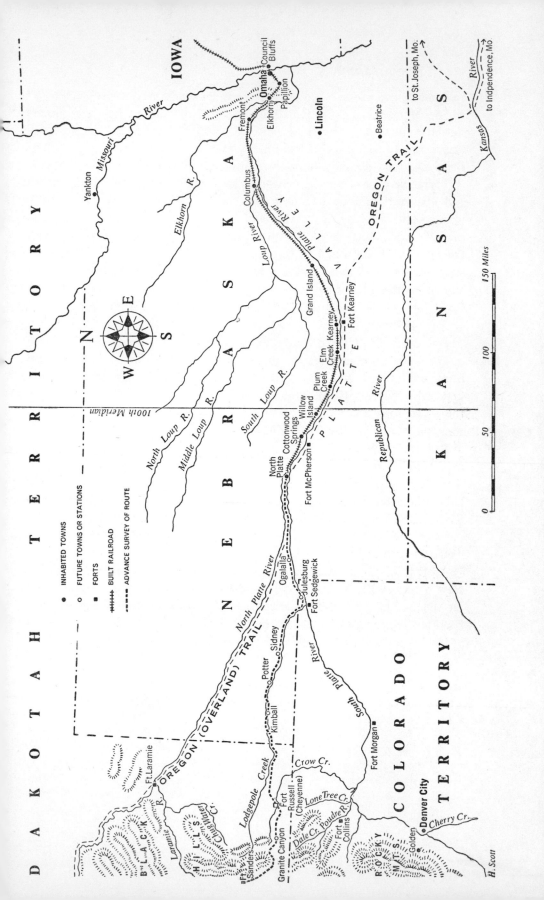

equipment, everything—had run to more than thirteen million dollars. The additional costs to milepost 305 would bring that, probably, to around sixteen million. The Credit Mobilier had supplied practically all of it. But Oakes Ames, having set his hand to the task, showed no inclination to falter. From the East his only instructions were to go ahead.

There were new developments in Omaha, all good. The Cedar Rapids and Missouri Railroad had now built far across Iowa from Denison, and was expected to have its tracks into Council Bluffs by early spring, completing a continuous rail link with Eastern supply centers. It was hoped that the Missouri River would be bridged before next summer's end. Meanwhile, steam packets had been bringing in fresh supplies of iron, fastenings, coal and new locomotives from Rogers, Taunton, Schenectady and other builders. Great rafts of ties had been floated down the Missouri from timber cuttings upriver. All this material stood in long, high-piled supply dumps along the sidings in Train Town, ready for springtime's westward haul.

The engineers considered the picture with sober satisfaction. Boldly Dodge proposed his goal for '67: New Fort Sanders in the Dakotah Wyoming, 288 miles beyond North Platte and across the Black Hills. The record for '66 stood at 265 miles, in itself a fine achievement. Beating it would take some mighty doing. But the engineers agreed.

Political honor had come Grenville Dodge's way this fall. Old friends and neighbors in Council Bluffs had proposed him as the Republican nominee for the U. S. House of Representatives and the ex-soldier vote had rallied solidly behind him. So the new year would see him in Washington as a member of the Fortieth Congress. He was not altogether happy about it, had not sought the nomination, had been far too busy to campaign for the office. Now he would have to find the time, somehow, to fill two jobs.

All that winter the U. P.'s plans were made and assignments drafted. In New York, as the months went by, there was news of the Central Pacific. Dr. Durant had his paid observers in California, and their reports made good reading for a Union Pacific man.

Out there in the high Sierras the Central was in trouble.

CHAPTER 15

CAPE HORN PASSAGE

With the first stirrings of spring in '66, Charley Crocker had hurried his track gangs out of Colfax on the start of the long, curving climb around Cape Horn.

The winter had been a mild one in California. Of the thirteen miles of grade to Dutch Flat, about eight had been put in before the first of the year. Methodically hewing and shoveling, Crocker's coolies had cut their way out around the face of the massive granite promontory as long as the footing lasted. After that they worked in bosun's chairs swung out into thin air from the top of the precipice high above. White miners were brought in to teach them how to sink holes into the sheer rock with hammers and cast-iron hand drills, tamp in gunpowder and cut fuses. In spite of the language barrier the Chinese, with their aptitude for precise imitation, proved ready learners. Swaying on a thin rope's end over dizzy emptiness did not bother them. Neither did the danger inherent in the use of gunpowder; their ancestors, after all, had invented the stuff. They soon caught onto the principle of cutting fuses of varying lengths for each round of charges, so that all would go off in one hugely satisfying cataclysm of sound and destruction, tumbling tons of rock and earth down the precipitous slopes. Great believers in evil spirits and personal devils were these simple Cantonese peasants. The noise, they believed, frightened the imps away much more effectively than the firecrackers of old China, and they used the gunpowder prodigally. More than once, rubble the engineers had counted on for ballast or fill was scattered far and wide by overgenerous charges.

So the narrow shelf for the grade was carved out, section by section, two thousand feet and more above the brawling American River. It was no innovation in railroad construction; twenty years before, the roadbed for the New York and Erie Railroad had been blasted out along the Delaware

143

River cliffs in New York State by the same method. But for Crocker and his coolies it was cut-and-try, and painfully slow work, a far cry from the grade and rails the Union Pacific was pushing out across the flat Nebraska plain this spring.

Yet the engineers, and Charley Crocker, found cause for encouragement. Hard though the work was, slowly as it went, Cape Horn was proving less difficult than they had anticipated. Hewn out of almost solid rock, the road-bed required costly retaining walls in only two places along the entire passage, aggregating a mere three hundred feet.

Now, too, a hard core of tough and knowledgeable leaders was shaping up, men fortified by experience and committed to seeing the job through. H. H. Minkler was boss track-layer. Arthur Brown, in charge of all bridge, trestle and timber work, had been a good man from the beginning. A. L. Bowsher was foreman of the telegraph crew which kept pace with railhead every mile of the way. Samuel Montague, Judah's old understudy, was proving an able and dedicated chief engineer, capably assisted by Lewis M. Clement. Butler Ives, William Eppler and S. M. Buck were other engineers, working far ahead this spring on surveys across Nevada and deep into Utah Territory. There was a spirit of optimism on the board of directors, a conviction that the railroad had begun to conquer its heavy grades and was ready for the final attack on the Sierra summit.

As early as December of 1864, Montague's report had stated that "Present facilities afforded by your road and the connecting stage lines for the accommodation of travel across the mountains are unequalled by any other route.

"Persons traveling by the Central Pacific Railroad and the Dutch Flat and Donner Lake wagon road reach Virginia City in from four to six hours less time than by any other line. Since the California Stage Company placed their coaches upon this line in July last the average time for the trips from Sacramento to Virginia has been but seventeen hours," the chief engineer had added, and described the road as "built in the best possible manner," everywhere wide enough to permit teams to pass each other without difficulty and with "commodious hotels . . . erected along the route."

Montague's remarks were perhaps a little on the rosy side. Placerville thought so, at any rate. The *Mountain Democrat* there had attacked the Sacramento *Daily Union* as a "shoddy organ" for publicizing the report, and complained bitterly that it had "heaped falsehood upon falsehood with regard to the Dutch Flat route."

But now, with every mile the rails advanced toward Dutch Flat, the Central Pacific was gaining ammunition to be fired back at its detractors.

Financially, the company's prospects were improving also. Money still

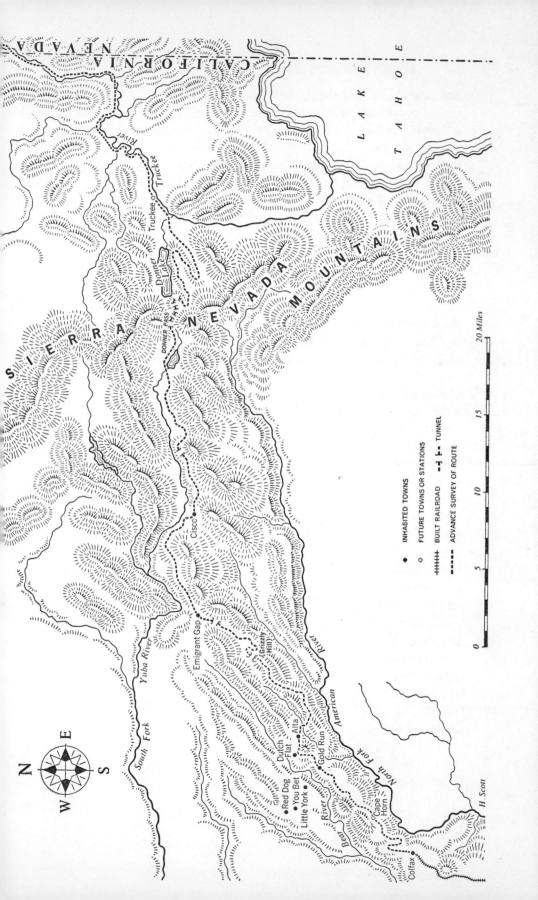

CALIFORNIA NEVADA

LAKE TAHOE

SIERRA NEVADA MOUNTAINS

Truckee or Truckee River

Donner Lake

DONNER PASS HWY.

Cisco

Emigrant Gap

(Grizzly Hill)

Yuba River

South Fork

Red Dog
You Bet
Little York

Dutch Flat
Alta

Gold Run

Bear River

North Fork American River

Cape Horn

Colfax

H. Scott

INHABITED TOWNS
FUTURE TOWNS OR STATIONS
BUILT RAILROAD
TUNNEL
ADVANCE SURVEY OF ROUTE

N E S W

20 Miles
15
10
5
0

was a problem, and would be right to the finish, but Collis Huntington's tireless persistence in New York was continuing to bear fruit. With the nation recovering rapidly from the effects of war, government bonds began to appreciate in value and government currency to stabilize. After a slow start the federal construction bonds were coming through more promptly and Huntington was disposing of them through Fisk and Hatch—and disposing of the company's own securities, too—at rates that were increasingly more gratifying.

Throughout May the blasters and graders clawed their way around Cape Horn, Minkler's track-layers at their heels, the railroad steadily climbing. It was a wet spring, with heavy rains. There was nothing like a mile-a-day pace on the Central Pacific. The terrain was incomparably more rugged than Nebraska's, of course; even allowing for that, though, the skill of Crocker's men still fell a long way short of the Casements' efficient techniques. Basically, the Central's methods remained the old, plodding ones of the past. The Chinese laid ties at a rate of one per man per hour—a figure unimpressive on the face of it, though their sheer numbers, as yet unmatched on the Union Pacific, took up much of the slack.

One by one, gritty little mining towns with old, storied forty-niner names were reached and passed by railhead: Gold Run; Red Dog; You Bet; Little York. The grade went on ahead. The Sierra rampart loomed closer, and with it serious new construction problems that could not be put off. Heavy tunnel work began just above Dutch Flat. Theodore Judah's survey had envisioned eighteen tunnels. Montague's and Clement's relocation of the line had cut the number to fifteen, still a stupendous amount of blasting and digging, which had to be started early if track-laying was to proceed on schedule. Tunnel work already was under way. Crews had been moved up to begin excavating western and eastern headings for the long summit bore in August of '65. The job going more slowly than anticipated, however, the engineers had decided to expedite it by sinking a vertical shaft at the midway point in order to work both ends of each heading.

As this shaft deepened a hoisting engine was deemed necessary; hence the sweaty saga of the "Black Goose."

She was a small Hinkley locomotive purchased for the purpose from the Placerville and Sacramento Valley, a little railroad started as another California rival of the Central Pacific but now bogged down in discouragement after twenty-odd miles. The motive power people put her into the shops at Sacramento and stripped her of various fittings not required for her new role, and in the process someone with the railroader's incurable penchant for nicknames took to calling her the "picked black goose." Thus humbled and shorn, the little engine was turned over to the operating department and towed to railhead, then at Gold Run. That much was easy enough; the troubles were yet to come.

A Southern Pacific pensioner named J. O. Wilder told the story in his old age, many years later. He said he had it straight from one of the protagonists, a Central Pacific bullwhacker remembered for posterity only as Missouri Bill.[1]

At Gold Run the locomotive, her name now shortened to plain "Black Goose," was jacked up, shifted off the rails and subjected to the ultimate indignity of losing her wheels. Then by means of traveling jacks she was moved laboriously—fourteen inches at a time, the jacks then removed by pairs and painstakingly repositioned—to a waiting log truck. The operation was difficult but they accomplished it without mishap; the Goose was biding her time. Firmly bolted and guyed to the truck, a cumbersome vehicle equipped with massive wheels two feet wide in deference to the rainy season which now was laying slick mud over every road and trail, she started her ascent to the Sierra summit behind Missouri Bill's ten yoke of oxen, the whole proceeding supervised by the Central Pacific's chief wagonmaster, L. P. Pratt.

For a while the ponderous equipage rolled along decorously enough, if slowly. But a half-mile east of Dutch Flat the Black Goose began to assert her peculiarly baleful individuality. The occasion was a head-on meeting with a ten-mule rig coming downgrade. The mules took one look at the strange monster, snorted, laid their ears back and stampeded, leaving their wagon a wreck and the Goose's iron hide blistered from what Missouri Bill referred to as "her first cussing."

It was not to be her last. "From that day on," the bullwhacker reported simply, "the Black Goose raised hell on the trail."

Not a horse or mule team encountered her without bolting out of hand. They headed, said Bill, for either the hills or the ravines, whichever looked best to them at the moment, "and they were not particular what they took along with them." He added reminiscently, "I will give the mules credit, however, that before starting they did their best to kick everything loose."

Word of the weird contraption prowling the trails spread through the back country, and local teamsters and mule-skinners did their best to avoid the dreaded Goose. "It was with fear and trembling that those in charge of wagon trains . . . tackled the trails in that vicinity," the bullwhacker continued, as quoted by Mr. Wilder. "Even the stage horses would balk at the sight of her."

Finally Wagonmaster Pratt hit on the idea of blindfolding every horse and mule that had to pass, and supplied Central Pacific teamsters to lead the hooded animals past the locomotive. After that things were a little better, except when an occasional passing driver was too stubborn or too impatient to take the warnings seriously. These invariably suffered, whether their teams were young and skittish or old and spavined.

Grades grew steeper and roads softer as the equipage toiled higher up the mountain. Pratt, nervously respectful of the Goose now, and taking no chances, covered the muddier sections with long stretches of corduroy road. Still the oxen bogged down frequently. Time and time again company freight teams hauling supplies to the tunnel crews higher up had to be stopped and pressed into service to keep the engine moving. At Emigrant Gap the road topped a minor divide and dived into a steep descending grade. Here the Goose's great weight threatened disaster that could have been far worse than any number of stampeded teams. They had to shackle her with heavy log chains and tackles hitched to the trunks of big pine trees along the road; then ease her carefully down the slope as far as the length of the gear permitted; then block the truck wheels, shift the tackles and do it all over again.

Arriving at the town of Heatonville, the Goose "caused great excitement," as Missouri Bill reported laconically. Stripped and wheelless though she was, she still was the only locomotive ever to penetrate the High Sierras, and possibly the first locomotive some of these backwoods folk ever had seen.

From here the going was all upgrade again, the last leg to the summit. It was negotiated with no more untoward incidents, though bridges over the upper and lower outlets of Kids Lake, the Yuba River and Drivers Creek all had to be rebuilt before the Goose could pass. The tunnel foremen had been waiting for her with what patience they could muster. She was jacked off the truck and moved for the final time, to a stout timber platform already prepared at the mouth of the midpoint shaft, now almost ninety feet deep. They bolted her down and hooked her to the hoisting gear, stoked her firebox with wood chunks, raised a head of steam in her boiler and put her to work earning her keep, attended by a pair of engineers named Con Collins and George Gifford.

The trek from Gold Run had taken six weeks, gallons of sweat and no one knows how many bruised bodies and shattered tempers. For Missouri Bill, Wagonmaster Pratt and their fellows it was all in the day's work; nobody had said building a railroad over the Sierra Nevadas was going to be easy!

Crocker's coolies, all this while, had labored forward along the location line, the track-layers in their wake. The rains held on past spring and into early summer. Roads became impassable. The stage from Colfax to Virginia City lay mired in the mud of Gold Run's single street for weeks on end, its sodden passengers forced to choose between laying over or going ahead on horseback. Freight moved only by pack mule. But there was an object

Dutch Flat, in the Sierra foothills, where Theodore Judah first drew up the
Articles of Association of the Central Pacific Railroad of California in 1860.
HOPKINS TRANSPORTATION LIBRARY, STANFORD UNIVERSITY

The *Governor Stanford,* first locomotive on the Central Pacific, is already at work hauling rails a short way out of Sacramento late in 1863.   HOPKINS TRANSPORTATION
LIBRARY, STANFORD UNIVERSITY

Theodore Dehone Judah,
the dreamer who first put the
Pacific Railroad on the road to reality.
BANCROFT LIBRARY,
UNIVERSITY OF CALIFORNIA

Leland Stanford,
wartime Governor of California
and Central Pacific President.
HOPKINS TRANSPORTATION LIBRARY,
STANFORD UNIVERSITY

Collis Potter Huntington, Vice-President.
BANCROFT LIBRARY,
UNIVERSITY OF CALIFORNIA

Charles Crocker,
who built the Central Pacific.
HOPKINS TRANSPORTATION LIBRARY,
STANFORD UNIVERSITY

Mark Hopkins,
Central Pacific Treasurer.
BANCROFT LIBRARY,
UNIVERSITY OF CALIFORNIA

James H. Strobridge,
Central Pacific Construction Superintendent.
CALIFORNIA HISTORICAL SOCIETY

Gold Run, a typical Sierra mining town, with the Central Pacific grade in the foreground, 1866. Virtually every cubic foot of earth and rock dug out of the cuts and put down on the grade was handled by means of two-wheeled carts like those shown.   HOPKINS TRANSPORTATION LIBRARY, STANFORD UNIVERSITY

A Central Pacific mail and passenger train stops in Dixie Cut for the Gold Run station (barely visible at left) while construction work still goes on in background. The year is 1866. HOPKINS TRANSPORTATION LIBRARY, STANFORD UNIVERSITY

The little *C. P. Huntington,* one of the Central's first locomotives, pauses for her picture at Alta, in Placer County. Note the absence of a headlight; many of the Central's engines were not equipped with them during the early construction years. HOPKINS TRANSPORTATION LIBRARY, STANFORD UNIVERSITY

Central Pacific Chinese take a rare breather amid the granite rock formations through which they had to blast and hew the right of way on the approach to Summit Tunnel, 1866. HOPKINS TRANSPORTATION LIBRARY, STANFORD UNIVERSITY

(*Above*) Central Pacific yards at Cisco, California, staging point for the assault on the Sierra Summit in 1866 and '67. Note the store shed and massed wagon transport in the background. The locomotive is the ten-wheeler *Idaho*.   HOPKINS TRANSPORTATION LIBRARY, STANFORD UNIVERSITY

(*Below*) Though things did not look so bad when this photograph was taken at Cisco in the spring of 1867, snowplows like this failed utterly to keep the Central's right of way through Donner Pass open during the brutal winter of 1866-67. Note the three locomotives coupled in behind, and the Chinese coolie in the foreground.   HOPKINS TRANSPORTATION LIBRARY, STANFORD UNIVERSITY

Central Pacific supply wagons shuttling between Cisco and the eastern heading of Summit Tunnel, probably during the spring or summer of 1867. Until the tunnels were completed and the rails laid through, such roads as this afforded the only means of travel over the Sierra Nevada. HOPKINS TRANSPORTATION LIBRARY, STANFORD UNIVERSITY

Carrying precious water across the Forty-Mile Desert to Central Pacific construction workers, this train of primitive tank cars nears the Humboldt Slough in 1868. Such water trains were necessary virtually all the way across Nevada, once the Truckee River was left behind. HOPKINS TRANSPORTATION LIBRARY, STANFORD UNIVERSITY

Though blistering heat and lack of water created hardships, it was this kind of straight and level going across the Nevada desert that first enabled Charley Crocker to make good his boast of "a mile a day in '68." Here, rails have been unloaded and end of track is in the distance ahead. HOPKINS TRANSPORTATION LIBRARY, STANFORD UNIVERSITY

Dr. Thomas C. Durant,
Vice-President, Union Pacific Railroad.
UNION PACIFIC RAILROAD

Grenville M. Dodge,
Union Pacific Chief Engineer.
This picture, however, was made many years
after the completion of the Union Pacific.
UNION PACIFIC RAILROAD

Oakes Ames,
Union Pacific chief financial backer.
UNION PACIFIC RAILROAD

Oliver Ames,
who replaced the figurehead John A. Dix
as U.P. President late in 1866.
UNION PACIFIC RAILROAD

Sidney Dillon,
President of the Credit Mobilier of Amer[
and later of the Union Pacific.
UNION PACIFIC RAILROAD

Samuel B. Reed,
U.P. Superintendent of Construction.
Note the Army uniform trousers; such left-
overs from the recent war were much in evi-
dence among Union Pacific men of all ranks.
UNION PACIFIC RAILROAD

General "Jack" Casement
UNION PACIFIC RAILROAD

Dan Casement, doughty brother of General Jack, is the bearded man standing
in the doorway. This group of U.P. construction men was photographed in the
vicinity of Echo, Utah Territory, early in 1869.   UNION PACIFIC RAILROAD

The Great Pacific Railway Excursion train at the one hundredth meridian, October, 1866. Note the lettered archway, the flag-decked locomotive and the deer antlers mounted on the headlight, a frequent embellishment of which early U.P. engine crews were very fond.

NEBRASKA STATE HISTORICAL SOCIETY

This photograph of Casement tracklayers at work is said to have been made during the Great Excursion to end of track in October, 1866. The inked arrow supposedly identifies Dr. Thomas Durant.

UNION PACIFIC RAILROAD

(*Above*) Omaha levee: Missouri River steamboats unloading U.P. construction materials, 1866 or '67. The *Colorado* was one of the two steamers used in the Great Excursion of '66. NEBRASKA STATE HISTORICAL SOCIETY   (*Below*) U.P. locomotive No. 53, a Norris eight-wheeler, was later wrecked by Cheyenne Indians at Plum Creek, Nebraska. The water pump just behind the smokestack, the reel or windlass mounted on top of the cab and the tender footboards suggest she was being used in construction service when this photograph was taken. UNION PACIFIC RAILROAD

Casement Brothers' construction train in western Nebraska toward the end of 1867.
UNION PACIFIC RAILROAD

The U.P.'s controversial Dale Creek trestle, just west of Sherman Summit. The company claimed it to be the longest and highest railroad bridge of its time.
UNION PACIFIC RAILROAD

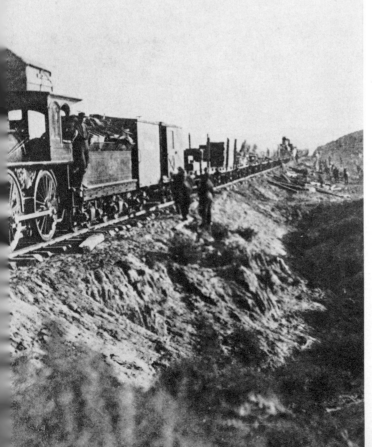

This contemporary drawing of t'
Union Pacific depot at Omaha
1868 is probably somewhat fan
ful. Nevertheless it conveys a go
impression of the polyglot natu
of the U.P.'s early passenge.
Whether the reversed N's on t'
depot sign were the artist's err
or the original sign painter's r
mains an unanswered question.
NEBRASKA STATE HISTORICAL
SOCIETY

Union Pacific iron train unloadi
rails and ties, probably somewhe
in Wyoming Territory, 1868.
UNION PACIFIC RAILROAD

Carmichael's camp, a typical large graders' camp, in the Bitter Creek Valley, Wyoming Territory, in 1868. The U.P. grade can be seen running diagonally across the middle background and going through the deep cut just above camp at left. The camp was supplied by way of the wagon road at right.   UNION PACIFIC RAILROAD

Union Pacific R.R. Views Across the Continent, West from Omaha
A. J. Russell, Artist
No. 94---Supply Trains, Last Siding, C. Peck's Out

End of track near Archer, Wyoming Territory, in 1868. Supply wagons going forward to graders' camps ahead. This was one of Mr. Russell's celebrated "Union Pacific R.R. Views Across the Continent," widely distributed to an eager public as interest in the transcontinental railroad heightened toward the finish.   UNION PACIFIC RAILROAD

Union Pacific's No. 119, soon to taste glory at Promontory Summit, was photographed at Omaha early in 1869.   NEBRASKA STATE HISTORICAL SOCIETY

This work train at Promontory shortly before the golden spike ceremony has been identified as both a Central Pacific and a U.P. train. The locomotive's balloon stack suggests the former. Note the ties unloaded beside the track; the old-fashioned switch stand, left; and the other work train in the right background.   NEBRASKA STATE HISTORICAL SOCIETY

Colonel Savage's classic photograph of the meeting of the rails at Promontory Summit, Utah Territory, on May 10, 1869. The two chief engineers shake hands in front of their respective locomotives: Samuel Montague and *Jupiter* of the Central Pacific, left; Grenville Dodge and No. 119 of the U.P., right.   UNION PACIFIC RAILROAD

Union Pacific poster
announcing the opening
of transcontinental
rail service.
NEBRASKA STATE
HISTORICAL SOCIETY

lesson here for travelers and local citizens alike: the railroad did not stop. The rails were laid and the iron trains lumbered upgrade, staccato panting of double-headed locomotives and clang of spike mauls echoing among the mountain crags.

Railhead reached Dutch Flat on July Fourth.

For the citizens it made a double holiday, all the traditional rites and trappings—waving flags, whiskey toasts, patriotic oratory and fusillades of firearms—given special point and emphasis by the advent of Dutch Flat's own railroad, born right here in Dr. Strong's drugstore nearly six years before. For the Central Pacific, all the public doubts and charges of fraud and humbug made the town a milestone somewhat comparable to the one hundredth meridian achieved by the Union Pacific later this same year.

There was no time taken for rest and self-congratulation, however. The company marked the occasion by running an excursion train to Sacramento and back, and let.it go at that. The same day, Chinese diggers broke through the headings in Grizzly Hill Tunnel, ten miles above Dutch Flat. President Leland Stanford promptly issued an official communiqué proclaiming that the event practically refuted "the slanders which have been heaped upon the company by its enemies in their oft-repeated declaration that Dutch Flat was to be the terminus of the road."

He made his point. The cries of "Dutch Flat Humbug" dwindled and soon were heard no more. But sincere doubters continued to predict stubbornly that the railroad would come to grief amid the impassable snows of the Sierras.

Cisco, a small logging and lumber center fifteen miles away, was the next target; the last town of any consequence on the line to the summit.[2] The grade required huge amounts of cutting and filling now, the country growing progressively rougher with every mile gained. It had been Crocker's and the engineers' original intent to carry the rails over much of this uneven terrain on timber trestles, but they had soon given that up in favor of solid fill. It was the better, more permanent method and probably cheaper, too, with the army of Chinese manpower Crocker had assembled. But it was hard work and grindingly slow, all done with blasting powder, pick and shovel, hand cart, mule cart and human muscle. Excavating machinery, rudimentary at best in that day, had no part in Central Pacific construction. Not even horse-drawn scrapers or levelers seem to have been used to any appreciable extent. The Chinese simply shoveled their carts full of earth and rock blasted out of the cuts, trundled them forward, dumped them at the end of the grade and went back to do the same thing over. Some of the sags and gullies and ravines were fifty feet and more in depth, and correspondingly wide; each cartful of fill amounted to hardly more than an insignificant mote in the abyss. But numbers and unending repetition told. Like a great, sluggish earthen river flowing uphill in contradiction of all natural law, the grade wound and curved on the path laid out by the survey stakes.

From the first, many of the cuts had had to be carved through flintily obstinate rock formations. Gunpowder still was used with too lavish a hand all too often, the engineers frequently exasperated when good fill was blown sky-high and wasted. At such times someone was sure to feel the rough side of Charley Crocker's tongue. He was everywhere along the line, bullying, cajoling, praising, blaming, forcing the men to match his own unflagging energy.

"I used to go up and down that road in my car like a mad bull," he told the historian, Hubert Bancroft, "stopping along the way wherever there was anything amiss and raising Old Nick with the boys who were not up to time."[3]

Jim Strobridge, in direct charge of construction, lived with his job—literally —in the headquarters car at end of track, raising plenty of Old Nick on his own. His wife was with him, keeping house there in the car, and would remain till the end, the only woman to be involved in the transcontinental railroad's building. "The heroine of the Central Pacific," they would be calling her before it was over. She was no softening influence on Jim, however. He drove the men, the Chinese especially, with an iron-handed ruthlessness that accepted no excuses and made no allowances for human frailties. The Chinese, a faceless, inscrutable multitude, took it and did as they were told and left no record of their thoughts. The Irish, always irrepressible, expressed themselves in wry work songs that grew along the grade:

> Early in the morning at seven o'clock
> There were twenty tarriers drilling at the rock.
> And the boss comes around and he says, "Keep still,
> Come down heavy on your cast-iron drill!"

And the chorus would swell out in a jeering lament for the working man's lot:

> Last week a premature blast went off,
> And a mile in the sky went Big Jim Goff.
> Now when next payday come around,
> Jim Goff a dollar short was found.
> He asked the reason; came this reply,
> "You were docked for the time you were up in the sky!"[4]

Contrary to a general impression (shared at the time even on the Union Pacific), Chinese did little of the actual track-laying on the Central. They lugged the ties and set them in place, tamped ballast, pushed the iron cars, distributed spikes and fetched and carried; but the rail handlers themselves, the elite corps who laid the iron, gauged it and spiked it fast, were, like Jack Casement's bully boys on the Union Pacific, almost all Irishmen.

They were good, and got better with the constant practice. But they set no records; this tough Sierra passage was not the place for that. Its sweeping, climbing curves slowed the work. The wrought-iron rails, thirty feet long and fifty-six pounds to the yard, were bent to conform to the engineers' curves by a method crude but effective. Each was laid on its side across a pair of ties placed one at each end, and six or seven men stepped aboard to bend the curve in. A brawny Irishman with a sledge hammer then started at one end and worked his way to the other, each standee stepping off as the hammer crashed down, stepping back on as it went up again, the next man stepping off in his turn. Their weight, holding the springy iron rigid under the blows, did the job. When the hammer man had worked his way down the rail's full length, it was stood on end and gauged, either by the foreman's eye or with a taut cord. A few more licks with the sledge to straighten any kinks and smooth out the curve and the job was done, the rail ready for laying, the next one brought up and positioned for treatment.

Ties were trued in place by butting their ends against a rope strung along the surveyors' right-of-way stakes, the foreman going flat on his belly to sight along each stretch, and using hand signals to indicate where earth was to be tamped in or dug out to bring each tie level with its fellows. It was Central Pacific practice, apparently, to put down ties for a considerable distance ahead of the rails. This was thickly forested country and there was a plentiful supply of them always at hand, all good redwood, pine or cedar. This same abundance of timber made wood the standard Central Pacific fuel.

With the Dutch Flat wagon road connection an accomplished fact, revenue operations expanded rapidly. The company now had an impressive locomotive roster, each engine not only numbered but named, after the traditional fashion of railroading in America. In this the Central differed from the Union Pacific, where names were abandoned quite early in favor of the more prosaic and businesslike system of numbers alone.

The names followed no discernible pattern. Of the first six locomotives in service on the Central Pacific, four bore titles honoring individuals. In addition to the *Governor Stanford* and the *C. P. Huntington* there was a *T. D. Judah*, one of the two smallest engines on the roster (the other, ironically, being the *Huntington*). California Senator John Conness was also honored. Later, two other engines were named for Civil War heroes: the *Phil Sheridan* and the *U. S. Grant*. Others bore the names of towns along the line, notably the *Gold Run*. Appropriately, for a railroad with transcontinental intentions, there was an *Atlantic* and a *Pacific*. Other names were classical in derivation, or merely resounding: *Hercules, Growler, Mars, Hurricane, Diana, Sultana, Leviathan, Tempest, Hector, Terrible, Vulcan, Tamaroo....*

The standard eight-wheelers had been augmented by heavier motive power as the grades steepened. The *Mogul* or 2-6-0 type, a burly freight hauler with three pairs of drivers and a two-wheeled leading truck, first developed in 1864, was widely used on the Central Pacific. A ten-wheeler named the *Auburn*, built by McKay and Aldus Iron Works of East Boston and delivered this year of '66, was among the most powerful locomotives of its day.

A set of rules and regulations published by the company in 1868, and probably in effect at this time also, indicates that the rudiments of modern operating procedures were already taking shape. Westbound trains were given rights to the track over eastbound traffic until they fell twenty-five minutes behind their card time, at which point they lost all rights. Freights were instructed to keep out of the way of passenger trains. Top speeds for the latter were set at twenty-five miles per hour, not to be exceeded except on special order. Freights were limited to ten miles per hour east of the Junction (present-day Roseville) and twelve miles per hour west of there. In case of accidents or unscheduled stops on the main line, conductors were instructed to station men with red flags or lanterns at safe distances in both directions, and in foggy or stormy weather track torpedoes were to be clamped to the rails at least a half-mile away.

Engineers and firemen were ordered not to pile wood on tenders in such a manner that it might fall off. They were further enjoined against throwing wood off while locomotives were in motion; any chunks too large to fit into fireboxes were to be left at stations.

Standard time did not exist in the United States of the '60's.[5] But the clock of a Mr. G. M. Parker, 34 K Street, Sacramento, was designated as the governing timepiece on the Central Pacific. Conductors and engineers were to compare their watches with it daily, "when practicable." Variations of five minutes between watches, however, were considered acceptable.

In '66 and for some years to come, no trains were run after dark above Colfax (contemporary photographs indicate that locomotives used on this section were not always equipped with headlights). Mountain railroading was new in California; the Central Pacific was a pioneer, and crews were learning by experience. Among other things, they developed an early respect for Cape Horn. Even by daylight, rolling downgrade with beetling cliff on one side and yawning space on the other took a special variety of nerve, cold judgment and light-footed nimbleness. Three brakemen, head, swing and parlor, rode the swaying car tops, ready to club the hand brakes down—and pray!—if the hogger in the cab ahead felt his tonnage getting away from him and broke into a flurry of urgent whistle blasts. Mr. Westinghouse's air brake still was a long way in the future.

Every job was a man's job. The clumsy, the weak and the timid did not last long.

Seven miles out of Dutch Flat the rails passed Emigrant Gap, gateway from the old American River trail to the South Fork of the Yuba. The track did not follow the Black Goose's arduous climb and precipitous descent; instead, it dove through a three-hundred-foot tunnel under the divide. It was late November, at this high altitude already winter, before the track-layers worked their way into Cisco.

There they remained for the balance of the year. The fifteen miles from Dutch Flat had consumed only a trifle less than five months. But the time had not been wasted, the road climbing 3,400 feet in the twenty-eight miles from Colfax. On one three-mile stretch the grade had lifted a steady 116 feet to the mile, the maximum permissible under the Act of '62. Construction costs for the year had been heavy: over eight million dollars for the twenty-eight miles, though the figure included, too, an impressive amount of grading, trestles and tunnel work above Cisco. Operating revenues, both gross and net, were approximately double those of '65. But the total cost of the ninety-two miles of completed railroad out of Sacramento had ballooned to the neighborhood of $17,750,000, an astronomical debt for a railroad that still had not quite sold the public on the proposition that it could get where it wanted to go.

Cisco, at an elevation just short of six thousand feet, stood more than a thousand below the highest location stake on the survey line—in exact figures, 1,131 feet still to be climbed, with only fourteen miles in which to do it. And there was no blinking the fact that the slow-starting Union Pacific, now digging in for the winter at North Platte, had spurted far ahead in the race. Charley Crocker would have to hump.

There were compensations, however. The Union Pacific had suffered its defeats on the eastern front, where Collis P. Huntington was rounding out a richly satisfying year. With his board of directors committed to building all the way to Great Salt Lake and his engineers already busy in northern Utah, Huntington had decided that the time had come to go down to Washington and remove that odious 150-mile limitation from the Act of '64.

He did it with astounding ease, and without, he boasted, having to spend a single dollar.

"I talked with every member of Congress," he said, "excepting a few, who were interested in the Union Pacific; or in the Credit Mobilier. The bill passed the Senate with a vote of about thirty-four against eight. In the House Thad

Stevens [of Pennsylvania] took charge of the bill and it went through with a majority of sixty-one."[6]

Most decidedly, Collis Huntington had learned his way around Capitol Hill! For all that, there were some who disapproved strongly of his activities there. Following the House vote, he recalled, he was approached by Congressman Alley of Massachusetts.

Said Mr. Alley, "There must have been great corruption and much money used in passing that bill."

"Well, Mr. Alley, I am surprised to hear you speak in that way of your associates here," Huntington replied suavely, and proceeded with more characteristic bluntness, "I am very much surprised, but I will be frank with you, and tell you that I brought over half a million dollars with the intention of using every dollar of it, if necessary, to pass this bill. I got a large majority of members, that I knew were in favor of it, without the use of one dollar. We still had our means and wanted to get every vote."

Continuing, Huntington told the Congressman that he had gone into the gallery with a pair of opera glasses and examined the face of every man "—and I am a good judge of faces. I saw but one man who, I thought, would sell his vote. And," Huntington concluded crushingly, "you know devilish well I didn't try it on you."

The Union Pacific lobby seems to have been inexplicably negligent while this coup took place. But Dr. Durant and his colleagues were learning, if they had not been aware of it before, that Collis Huntington was no man to be dismissed lightly. Later this fall the lesson was driven home even more pointedly when Huntington engineered the purchase, from under their very noses, of a 66,000-ton consignment of rails which put Union Pacific iron in very short supply for a while. Later he claimed that in doing it he also managed to defeat a movement by the Pennsylvania mill owners to capitalize on the rivalry between the two railroads by raising prices. His own explanation— that he simply pretended Central Pacific work was proceeding so slowly that any large purchases of iron were out of the question for the time being— seems a little too pat to be fully credible. But the 66,000 tons he did buy brought him face to face with another problem: ships to carry them around the Horn. His account of how he got the ships, told as before to the Bancroft historian, David R. Sessions, reveals the Huntington shrewdness in much more detail.[7]

He told of approaching a Mr. E. B. Sutton, a shipping agent. "I said, 'Well, I want to get a good ship, a good steady ship—safe. You can go out and run around and give me a list of what you can find.' "

In a few days Sutton returned with three or four names of available bottoms. "You can have this one for so much and this one for so much."

They bargained, Huntington objecting flatly that the charter rates were too high. "I can't take one of those ships," he declared, and added that he was in no hurry; ships were coming in constantly.

Three times Sutton left and came back again. His list eventually numbered twenty-three ships. While they dickered, Huntington jotted the names down.

"Well," he announced suddenly, "I'll take them."

The agent gaped. "Take them? Take what?"

"I will take those ships if they are a A-number-one."

Sutton protested that it was impossible, that he had thought Huntington wanted only one. "I will have to have three or four of them myself," he pointed out.

"Not those you won't!" Huntington said grimly.

The upshot of it was that he got all twenty-three, enough to carry 45,000 tons of his rails. And he told of Sutton's rueful admission afterward, "Huntington, you would have had to pay ten dollars a ton more, at least, if I had known you wanted all those ships."

The saving amounted to $450,000, Huntington noted, well pleased with himself.

But the Sierra Nevadas still had to be crossed.

The miles above Cisco were brutally inhospitable, cut up by precipitous gorges and heavily timbered ridges. Most of the tunnels were concentrated here; ten of them in the twenty-five-mile section from Cisco over the summit and down to Donner Lake. The tunnel work, though started early, had been carried on only sporadically during the winter of 1865-66. That was a mistake, it was realized later. By midsummer John J. Gillis, the engineer in charge of tunnel operations, had his crews working in twelve-hour shifts around the clock to catch up. This fall he led a force over the divide and down the far slope, measured off the eastern face of tunnel No. 12 by the light of a bonfire and had his men digging before midnight. In spite of such feverish activity many of the tunnels were far from ready, including No. 6, the 1,659-foot bore at the summit. Much of the grade above Cisco was not yet in, the land not cleared either. And now snow was beginning to fly, a plain hint to call it quits for the winter.

Instead, Charley Crocker massed his men on the slopes out of Cisco for an all-out drive.

CHAPTER 16

TIME OF TRIAL

The winter of 1865-66 had been a phenomenally mild one in California. Looking back later, Leland Stanford would express bitter regret that the many lawsuits which held up the Central Pacific's state and county subsidies had slowed construction just long enough to rob Charley Crocker of that good weather for the Sierra crossing. But for its enemies' spite work, Stanford claimed, the railroad might have met the Union Pacific at Laramie in Wyoming Territory, instead of where it did.

As it was, Crocker's luck ran out. The winter of 1866-67 was a tail-twister, the worst in years. Snow fell early and continued late. Storm followed storm; forty-four, all told, before it ended.

Dense stands of timber blocked the location line above Cisco. Axmen and grubbers worked knee-deep in snow, then waist-deep, finally so deep that there was nothing for it but to abandon that part of the work till spring. But while it lasted the right of way had to be cleared to a width of two hundred feet; for twenty of them the trees not merely felled but the stumps grubbed out, too. Where picks, shovels and straining ox teams could not do it, blasting powder was resorted to, as many as several kegs to a charge for some of the bigger stumps. These were California redwoods, many of them giants with boles eight feet in diameter. Engineer Lewis Clement noted in one of his reports that as many as three hundred men labored ten days to clear a single mile.

The labor force totaled ten thousand now, white men and Chinese. Soon half of them were assigned as snow shovelers in a losing battle to keep the ground bare for the grading crews. Crowded into the deep, trenchlike cuts, men and draft animals hampered each other to the point of futility. At last Crocker gave it up, sent some of his graders to the rear and concentrated the rest on tunnel work. All the headings were deep enough now so that the coolies could drill and blast and shovel without hindrance from the snow. Rubble was passed arduously back from hand to hand, hoisted out and disposed of. But snow remained a problem nonetheless. The cuts leading to the tunnel faces deepened and lengthened with each new storm, howling gales drifting them full even as weary men struggled to pitch the snow out. Other passages were excavated to the dumps where the broken rock from the tunnel headings was piled, for it was needed for retaining walls in the canyons. This work, too, was kept up stubbornly throughout the winter, great domes hollowed out under the drifted snow, eerily lit by lantern light and flickering tallow dips while the masons cut and fitted the rock lowered to them through shafts punched down from the surface.

There was a shortage of skilled masons, or perhaps only of white men willing to work under such miserable conditions. The harassed Crocker proposed to train Chinese for the jobs. Strobridge protested; it had never been done before; these pigtails were not masons, everyone knew that. "They built the Great Wall of China, didn't they?" Crocker retorted. The Chinese proved to be good masons.[1]

All the same, it was a grueling battle. And as one gray day followed another it looked more and more like a hopeless one. On February 18 the worst blizzard of the winter swooped down, flinging snow in a blinding curtain from two o'clock that afternoon until ten P.M. on the twenty-second. A five-day interval then while gale winds whipped it into drifts sixty feet deep; then more snow, continuing without interruption till March 2, burying cuts, trails, camps, everything under a total fall of ten feet. Supply trains fought their way up into Cisco with four, five or more locomotives pulling and pushing, behind snowplows bucked through the drifts by as many more. They stalled frequently, nevertheless, and had to be dug out by the tireless coolies and their shovels. From Cisco the forward crews were provisioned by sledge and ox team, armies of snow shovelers going on before. Oxen bogged down, and pack mules were used. Paths shoveled out from bunkhouses became narrow snow tunnels two hundred feet and more in length. Like troglodytes in some ice age come again, tunnel crews and masons crawled underground to and from their work places.

Off duty the men wolfed down heavy meals and crept into bunks and blankets to find respite of a sort from the back-breaking labor. But there was no respite from the ceaseless snow. The camps had been thrown together roughly and hurriedly; it was impossible to seal their log walls against the stuff. Driven by icy Sierra winds, it sifted through every chink and cranny. Clement, the divisional chief engineer, had an office and bedroom as headquarters. He was away sometimes, up and down the line. Each time he returned to the mountains, he reported, "The snow had to be shoveled out of the house before I could get into it." And he added on a note almost of hopelessness that "One had to be on the ground to have any idea of the trouble we had to contend with on account of the snow."

Few who were on the ground did much telling about it, however. No important visitors with journalists in attendance braved the winter and the heights for firsthand inspections this season. Even Charley Crocker, never averse to talking about himself, appears to have been content with a recital of the bare facts when chroniclers approached him in after years.

Yet he was more than ever "the engine that drove everything ahead" this bitter winter. His private railroad car long since forsaken, he floundered on horseback up and down the right of way, his beard often rimed with ice, his broad face crimson with cold. His sorrel mare and great bearskin overcoat became traveling landmarks from Cisco to the summit and beyond; not the meanest coolie doing the most menial job escaped his roaring attention. It became his habit to act as paymaster in person, carrying the funds in a pair of bulging saddlebags; silver coins on one side, gold on the other. Contemporaries marveled at his knack for handling the taciturn Chinese, who feared and obeyed big Jim Strobridge because he was the boss, but seemed to bestow on the bigger boss, Crocker, a very real measure of trust and even affection. The foremen often complained that he was a man who found fault where none existed, but something in his bluff, blustering Western personality reached out and captured an elusive rapport with the little yellow men.

Possibly it was simple honesty. In a day when the Chinese in America was frequently cheated and ill used by his white masters, Charley Crocker had a reputation for treating his labor, white and yellow alike, with scrupulous fairness. The Chinese, in particular, got their odd rations—dried oysters, bamboo sprouts, salted cabbage, abalone and all the rest of it—regularly as promised, and at prices Crocker had quoted verbally in advance, though it must have been difficult to obtain at times and its cost fluctuated.

It was well that morale stayed high, for the winter wore on without letup. The hampering snow was not the worst of the difficulties.

Here at the crest of the Sierras, the tunnels had to be bored through solid granite of a hardness no one had anticipated. It blunted and broke the cast-iron drills and proved almost impervious to gunpowder. Veterans of the construction force were to tell later of charges that exploded out of drill holes as from cannon muzzles, barely scratching the rock. Stolidly the Chinese drillers drove their holes deeper and doubled and redoubled the charges. The results were better, but only a little. Gunpowder was expensive, and had been scarce right from the beginning of construction. The only supply available in California was manufactured by two small mills at Santa Cruz; their entire output combined was never enough to satisfy the Central Pacific's needs, and Collis

Huntington had wrought miracles of persuasive ingenuity to keep eastern gunpowder coming during the war years. Now, though the war was over, the Army and Navy were buying heavily to replenish their arsenals, and this kept the supply short and the price high. Prices went up from an already inflated five dollars per keg to eight and ten and more. It was not unusual for five hundred kegs to be used in a day's work. In one month alone the powder bill totaled $54,000.

No. 6 tunnel, at the summit, proved the severest trial. For months the vertical shaft where the Black Goose labored at her hoisting chore had been pushed downward at a rate of only seven inches a day; not till late in December, '66, was it deep enough for lateral headings to be started. Even then, at both ends and in the middle alike, twenty-seven inches was the best day's progress recorded. The work was hard and wretchedly frustrating; unpleasant and dangerous too, with Chinese jammed into the dim-lit, airless headings till conditions grew so bad no white man would have endured them. Then someone —an itinerant Swedish chemist named Swanson, according to some accounts —sought out Charley Crocker and suggested the use of nitroglycerin. With misgivings, but goaded to desperation by the slow pace of the work, he and Strobridge decided it was worth trying.

A strong element of mystery, and some controversy, surround this use of nitroglycerin on the Central Pacific. The explosive was not precisely new, having been invented by the Italian chemist, Sobrero, in 1846. And it was well known to be far more powerful than gunpowder. But because it could not be detonated readily by methods then in use it never had been accepted as a satisfactory commercial explosive. Somewhat paradoxically, however, it was tricky stuff, unstable and extremely hazardous to handle, and this had given it a highly dubious public reputation. In April of this same year, '66, a shipment of "blasting oil," as it was called, had exploded in the Wells Fargo warehouse at San Francisco, killed a dozen men and caused a notable panic in the streets. The same month, another accidental blast had destroyed the ship *European* at Aspinwall, Panama, with a toll of fifty lives. There was no direct evidence linking either shipment with the Central Pacific, but a widespread suspicion seems to have sprung up locally, to the effect that the Central was in fact guilty of shipping and using nitroglycerin, and it did nothing to enhance the railroad's already tarnished public image.[2]

For this reason, and in simple prudence as well, Charley Crocker shied from any thought of transporting finished nitroglycerin up by rail and trail from the lowlands. Instead the ingredients, glycerin and nitric and sulphuric acids, were hauled in by teams and mixed by one James Howden in a specially prepared log factory near Donner Lake. The white men made no bones about being scared of the mixture, though apparently it was they—a few of the nervier foremen, working under Howden's supervision—who inserted the explosive liquid into the coolies' drill holes. The imperturbable Chinese stopped it, cut and set their fuses as unworriedly as though this were the familiar gunpowder. For safety's sake the charges were generally set off at the beginning of the noon hour or near the end of a shift, when stragglers were fewest.

"Fire in the heading!" the foremen would bawl as they lighted the fuses. "And she's on a short fuse!" they usually added, to hasten the laggards.

All hands would run for shelter, then wait in nervous expectancy. Would she or wouldn't she? She would; the blast shook the mountain, shattered the sullen granite as gunpowder never had, littered the heading floor deep with broken rock.

But there was no earthly way to tell whether every charge in a round had been detonated. The first coolie to slam his pick or shovel into a patch of spilled nitroglycerin was disintegrated with a flash and a roar into fiery nothingness, and most of his fellows in the vicinity along with him.

Strangely, from the Western point of view, such accidents do not seem to have deterred the Chinese very seriously. They were fatalists, and gamblers to the bone in a sense Caucasians simply could not grasp. A man blown to bits had lost his personal wager with the evil spirits, that was all. The living shrugged and worked on, glad to be lucky.

White men, though, had difficulty seeing it that way, Charley Crocker not least among them. No shirker, he himself was badly shaken by one close call. And tough Jim Strobridge lost an eye to a flying granite fragment (though there is no indication that it kept him off the job for long, or ever slowed him up in the future). But Crocker had had enough.

"Bury that damned stuff!" he ordered.

Buried it was. The homemade explosive was used, apparently, only in tunnel No. 6 and, to a lesser extent, in No. 8 on the eastern Sierra slope. The work was finished as it had begun, with plain, dependable black gunpowder.

By a mocking little twist of chance, these bitterly wrought tunnels on the Central Pacific constituted the last major project of their kind in North America to be carried through by manual labor alone. The steam drill, in fact, already had been perfected to the point of practical workability. It was known to Charley Crocker and he could have used it. Why he did not is a question that has never been definitely answered.

Some sources maintain that Collis Huntington did actually purchase a steam drill in the East and had it shipped around Cape Horn. The vice-president was not a man who parted with a dollar very readily, and seldom showed any inclination to meddle in the material construction of the railroad. On the other hand, he was never penny-wise where the Central Pacific's progress was at stake. But, says this account, both Crocker and Strobridge summarily rejected the machine as newfangled and impractical. Another story has it that Crocker himself considered the use of a steam drill, but gave the idea up in view of the delays and difficulties involved in bringing it around the Horn and up through the arduous Sierras to the work sites. The fact remains that the coolies, their gunpowder and a smattering of nitroglycerin got the job done, though at awesome cost.

The winter's vast accumulation of snow changed from a nagging hindrance to a real and brutal hazard as spring came on with its first intermittent thaws. The danger of snowslides had been anticipated. Earlier in the winter great snowbanks massed on the crags above Donner Pass had been blasted away; it was a wise precaution, but gradually rendered ineffectual as the blizzards piled them up again. Now they began to let loose without warning, thousands of tons of snow and earth and rock roaring down in sudden, treacherous disaster. A long trestle above Cisco was ripped loose and demolished. Worse, all along the stretch across the summit and down to Donner Lake men and buildings were crushed, buried and carried far down the mountain slopes.

One bad slide struck in bleak predawn darkness, smashing a log bunkhouse with three subcontractors and sixteen or seventeen white laborers inside. Eventually they were missed, though no one seems to have realized what had happened until late the following afternoon—a fair clue to the groping and confusion that must have existed under the constant scourgings of snow and storm. It was six that evening before the wreckage was located and the men dug out, by lantern light in the chill early dusk. Only three of them were dead, most of the survivors still conscious and not badly injured. Caught in their bunks built against the thick log walls they had been protected from the worst of the slide's crushing force.

Not many were so fortunate. A twenty-man crew of Chinese was caught in the open near the entrance to Donner Peak tunnel, No. 9. This time there were no survivors; probably the winter's worst single killing, though it appears that no one had either the time or the inclination to keep tallies and compile total casualty lists. On the eleven-mile eastern slope to Donner Lake the descending pitch was steeper even than the ascent on the west. Along here slides struck again and again. It was, of course, the Chinese who bore the brunt, overwhelmed, obliterated—gone, usually, till late thaws uncovered their bodies. Afterward, veterans of that terrible winter recalled that most of them still gripped shovels or picks in their frozen hands.

Every body *was* eventually found, however, and interred by the company in special Chinese cemeteries. That, too, was part of Charley Crocker's agreement. Some ten years later the Hip Song Tong carefully exhumed each Chinese's bones, polished them and shipped them back across the Pacific to the homeland in keeping with their belief that only thus could the spirit of the deceased achieve repose in the hereafter. The ghosts of those blown to atoms in the tunnel headings were, presumably, doomed to wander through the high Sierra forever after.

With the slides growing steadily worse, the brute granite still resisting drill, gunpowder and pick in the summit tunnel, Charley Crocker regrouped his forces for a fresh offensive on another front. From New York Collis Huntington had sent disturbing news. Dr. Thomas Durant, encouraged by the reports of his California informants, was passing the word in the East that the Central Pacific was hopelessly trapped in the Sierras. The Union Pacific, he was announcing publicly, intended to build all the way to California's eastern border, and would be there ahead of the Central. The situation was serious; Huntington's moneyed contacts were getting nervous, potential investors shying off. Some tangible refutation of Durant's claims was urgently in order.

By November Crocker had a characteristic counterstroke under way. He mustered his idle graders, loaded them and their tools and supplies aboard sledges, called in his bullwhackers and dispatched a cavalcade up the snow-choked trails from Cisco, over the summit and down the other side to begin putting in a grade along the survey line to Nevada, below the worst of the snow. Then he followed with a more ambitious thrust. This time he sent rails, spikes and fastenings by the same route; enough iron for forty miles of track, all told. And he was not through yet. His dander up, he backed it with three locomotives and forty cars, a monumental effort no one but an aroused Charley Crocker would have had the nerve to try. The whole ponderous aggregation of tonnage had to be dragged by main strength up and over the summit and down again, through snow eighteen feet on the level, where it *was* level, and forty to sixty in the drifts. A road existed, meant for stages and freight wagons, but not in any such weather, and never for such a caravan as this. It proved passable, just barely.

"We hauled locomotives over," Crocker told the Pacific Railway Commission almost twenty years later, and he added, to forestall any misunderstanding, "When I say we, I mean myself." He went on to explain matter-of-factly, "We hauled the locomotives on sleighs, but some of them on logs because we could not get sleighs big enough for some of the engines."

Other than that he scorned the details, but no doubt the job was done, as with the Black Goose, by means of heavy log chains, tackles and multiple ox teams, foot by grudging foot, abetted this time by the omnipotent files of patient coolies. Unlike the little Black Goose, however, these were full-size locomotives and cars, and the going was incomparably rougher. This time, unfortunately, Missouri Bill, if he was still on the job, failed to pass the story on. It may be that nothing like it had been done since Hannibal led his war elephants over the Alps, twenty centuries before.[3]

Now Central Pacific iron could reach out for Nevada and the Great Bend of the Truckee River, leaving the conquest of the Sierras to be completed later. It was a magnificent gamble, for nothing put down here could be construed as a "continuous line" under the Acts of '62 or '64. Not a foot of it was eligible for federal bonds or land grants as long as the Sierra gap remained unclosed. But it was no time for playing safe. Collis Huntington had won the right to go out and meet the Union Pacific as far to the eastward as Charley Crocker could go.

Out on the forks of the Platte Jack Casement's iron men were ready to go again.

CHAPTER 17

WAR PATHS AND SURVEY STAKES

All winter long, railroad supplies piled up at North Platte. The town had twenty permanent buildings before the turn of the year into '67, and uncounted tents, shacks and sod hovels. More went up as spring came on, the clatter of hammers and snarling of saws echoing out over the rivers north and south. The Union Pacific had a brick roundhouse with stalls for forty locomotives, ten of them already occupied. The railroad's water tank and frame depot were hailed proudly as "of beautiful proportions." The original log hotel had been superseded by the new Railroad House, whose proprietor boasted it had cost him eighteen thousand dollars, shipped in knocked-down form all the way from Chicago. He stood to make that back many times over, for the mushroom community at the forks of the Platte was a funnel through which poured everything and everybody bound west this spring. It was choked to overflowing by emigrants and commercial travelers headed for Oregon, California and Great Salt Lake; miners and prospectors for Denver, Clear Creek, the diggings in Nevada and the new gold strikes far up in northwestern Montana Territory.

North Platte was an Overland Stage station and an outfitting center for freight companies outbound on the spring haul. The canvas covers of more than a thousand of their wagons whitened the outskirts of the town. Some eight hundred teamsters, bullwhackers and mule-skinners swaggered in the rutted dirt main street and bellied up to its legion of bars, elbowing space for themselves among well-dressed passengers awaiting seats on the crowded stagecoaches, land speculators loud with the insistence of optimism, the greasy buckskins of buffalo hunters, blue Army blouses and the flannel shirts and broad galluses of unemployed railroad Irishmen drowning their idleness till the bosses should give the word to go.

By May fifteen thousand tons of government freight crammed the Union

Pacific's godowns along the tracks. Mail came in, only five days from New York City.

The town had a vast and intoxicated faith in its own future. "The Paris of Nebraska," it called itself, blithely oblivious of the fact that its population, swelling toward the five-thousand mark, included few serious merchants or businessmen. This was the third of the terminal towns on the U.P.'s westward march from Omaha. Fremont had been the first, then Kearney. But North Platte was the first of the riptailed roarers.

The new year was one of yeasty ferment all over the Great Plains. It was '67, the year the buffalo hunters began to spread westward in an incredible, slaughtering horde, the ranks of experienced old-timers swollen by heedless greenhorns seeking easy money and adventure. There had been a trade in buffalo hides since the earliest times. By '58 Omaha had been one of its leading centers. But in the past the hides had almost all been robes tanned and finished with careful artistry, many of the best by Indian squaws. That was all changed now; the demand from the East doubled and trebled, and not only for the fashionable robes alone. War had boosted the demand for leather. Manufacturers were discovering that the spongy, elastic buffalo hide made excellent belting for factory machinery. Buffalo leather was coming into widespread use for carriage and sleigh upholstery, and wall paneling in the homes of the well-to-do. Now even rough flint hides—skins pegged down on the prairie and dried board-stiff—were articles of commerce, and the railroad pushing out through the ranges made it economically worthwhile to transport them by the carload to tanneries back East. All this did not happen overnight, of course; but '67 marked the beginning of the big years, and the portents were plain.

The unpacified Indian nations watched in growing anger, and vowed again to defend what they considered their own. This would be a bad Indian year.

In the East there was a mighty stir of restlessness. Ex-soldiers found themselves not quite willing to settle down into the dull ruts of peacetime, and not always able to get their prewar jobs back even if they wanted to. Discouraged small farmers in Illinois, Kentucky, Indiana, Ohio and Wisconsin began to heed the siren song of virgin land free for the taking under the federal Homestead Act. Suddenly, it seemed, the nation east of the Mississippi was getting small, splitting at the seams.

So they all came straggling west: the adventurers, the malcontents, the failures; and the honestly ambitious, hard-working poor as well. With them, hard on the heels of those first gamblers, brothel keepers and whiskey drummers who had followed the Casements' iron into North Platte, came a veritable army of con artists, thieves, whores and toughs crowded out of Eastern city slums, a carnivorous horde hungrier than the native prairie grasshoppers. They gravitated to the Union Pacific as naturally as water runs downhill. The railroad was not only the fastest, easiest way west, it was the biggest thing out here. And North Platte was where the pickings were best.

With none of this did the U.P. concern itself, as yet. It had problems in plenty without looking around for more. In January Grenville Dodge, always careful to cultivate the Army's goodwill, wrote to General Sherman at St. Louis and outlined his objectives for the year ahead. Back came a prompt reply:

> I have just read with intense interest your letter of the 14th. Although you wanted me to keep it to myself, I believe you will sanction my sending it to General Grant for his individual perusal, to be returned to me. It is almost a miracle to grasp your proposition to finish to Fort Sanders this year, but you have done so much that I mistrust my own judgement and accept yours.[1]

Plainly the general was doing a smart about-face in his views on the Pacific Railroad. To him at least, the new spirit on the Union Pacific and the drive toward accomplishment were apparent and impressive. And his sending of the letter on to Grant had interesting political implications which Dodge would certainly understand. The star of Ulysses S. Grant was rising high, in government and in public esteem alike, and '68 would be a Presidential election year. The Savior of the Union would be a good man to have in the U.P. camp.

Almost before the frosty earth had thawed enough for clods to be turned by pick and shovel the advance grading outfits were assembled and sent lumbering out of North Platte. Locomotives coupled into the Casements' work train and followed. From milepost 305 the iron began to move ahead once more.

Even earlier, in the first week of March, Dodge had his survey parties out of winter quarters at Omaha. It was a cold spring, however, heavy snows lingering on the ground. The first outbound parties were held in North Platte for six weeks by a succession of late blizzards. Other engineers had wintered in Salt Lake City and had a better start, getting into the field by the first of April. The job laid out for them was a big one: nothing less than locating the final survey stakes for the most rugged sections of the route, over the Black Hills and the high bleakness of the Dakotah Wyoming, then on across desolate desert regions that lay west of the North Platte River and through the Wasatch Mountains to Great Salt Lake.

It was difficult work, professionally exacting, and of vital importance. The original survey of the over-all route had amounted to little except the determination that a feasible through line existed. These field engineers had to locate it, establish the one best line if more than one seemed feasible, and mark it out precisely for the graders who would come along later. The country still was almost unknown, ill-explored, poorly mapped. No one deceived himself on the dangers, known and unknown. Of the former, Indian hostilities might well be worse than anything the graders and track-layers had faced on the prairie up to now. This was an ambitious gulp Dodge was trying to bite off; perhaps too ambitious.

The long-delayed warm weather brought new troubles when it came. Melting snow from those late storms swelled the Platte River and every tiny tributary into flood, and spotted the prairie with great patches of watery morass, washing out grades and turning trackwork to twisted ruin. Harassed Superintendent of Construction Samuel Reed worked night and day, throwing every available laborer into the breaches. Part of the Casements' construction train was dispatched to the rear to repair damage. At Omaha the Missouri boiled in muddy spate far later than usual, into June and even July, holding needed materials stranded on the Council Bluffs side.

There were forebodings of another kind of trouble in the air. Dr. Durant's split with the Credit Mobilier remained unhealed. Of his shadowy contract with Mr. Boomer no more was heard. Another was negotiated with a new man named J. M. S. Williams, providing for a little more than 267 miles of construction westward at a cost of fifty thousand dollars per mile. Williams promptly assigned the contract to the Credit Mobilier. But Durant, himself an old hand at such evolutions, was not taken in as easily as all that. He protested the Williams contract in writing, pointing out that "Part of this work has been done for weeks . . . contracts have been made, and merchandise delivered, for nearly one hundred and fifty miles of road, which the company has paid for, as shown by the books."

Oliver Ames was the Union Pacific president now, put into the job by his brother Oakes and the so-called "Boston crowd" of the Credit Mobilier. But the Ameses were not railroad men; and Durant, now the acknowledged holder of a sizable block of U.P. stock, refused to relinquish his grip on company affairs. So matters stood at an apparent impasse. In reality Durant seems to have been saving face more than anything else. He had sworn that the Credit Mobilier should not have another U.P. contract, and the use of intermediaries like Williams made the vow good, or sufficiently so for appearances' sake. But the doctor was a fox whose devious mind overlooked nothing. His protest against the Williams contract—actually amounting to the grave charge that construction costs were deliberately being duplicated—was made, it appears, primarily to put himself in the clear against a possible day of reckoning. For the present, grade and track moved on, financed as before by the Credit Mobilier in spite of all the contractual confusion.

Such front-office skirmishing created an uneasy situation for Grenville Dodge. Later events make it perfectly clear that he was personally an Ames man, more and more at odds with Durant. The vice-president was not an easy man to like; most of the men out on the line resented him as a crafty, meddling self-seeker.[2] Wisely, though, Dodge concentrated on his own duties as chief engineer and steered shy of open controversy. But he was well aware of what went on, behind the scenes as well as before, and must have realized that a showdown was bound to come. He was aware also that Union Pacific securities continued to sell poorly on the open market despite the progress now being made. Last fall's Great Excursion had fired imaginations and stirred wide public interest, but conservative Eastern financiers remained unconvinced of the railroad's potential. It was still a long way to the Pacific, and west of the one hundredth meridian the road was heading into the worst of the rainless belt. Lands there could be of no possible value, the railroad notwithstanding. So said the doubters, and as usual they were listened to.

But for Grenville Dodge more pressing worries came thick and fast this spring, brought by his old plains adversaries, the Sioux and Cheyenne.

Hostilities burst anew in raids from Montana Territory all the way to the Smoky Hill River in Kansas. War parties cut the new Bozeman Trail to the Montana gold fields, kept wagon trains penned within Army stockades along the Oregon Trail, burned coaches and road ranches on the Overland Stage road, wiped out buffalo hunters who ventured into the Platte and Republican ranges. Down south, Colonel George Armstrong Custer led his spanking-new Seventh Cavalry out of Fort Hays, Kansas, in a grand strategic sweep designed to scythe the offending hostiles from the plains. But Custer, an authentic war hero, was still a long way short of proficiency as an Indian fighter. He marched his regiment with drill-field snap and flying guidons, swinging far west and then northward clear to the Platte River, within sight of the Union Pacific right of way. The enemy simply melted before him and closed in to harass his flanks like angry hornets, never offering a pitched battle. Cholera broke out among the troops. There were desertions. In the end the dashing, dandy Custer left the regiment and hurried home to his wife at Hays. In Washington his War Department superiors called that desertion, too. He got a court-martial out of it, and a year's suspension from command. The Indians had not been hurt.

On the Platte the Second Cavalry and mounted infantry of the 21st, 30th and 36th Regiments marched and countermarched out of Forts Kearney, Sedgewick, Morgan and McPherson. Major Frank North's Pawnee Scouts, who might have been more effective than any of them, were mostly pinned down by guard duty along the lengthening U.P. The upshot: a few lodges burned, a few war parties scattered, but no decisive engagements. The wild horsemen, elusive as smoke, slipped through to hit and run and hit again.

In the Black Hills, in May, a Sioux war party scattered a survey crew working up Dodge's ridge to Sherman Summit and killed its leader, L. L. Hills, assistant to Divisional Chief James Evans. It was the worst raid the railroad had suffered thus far, the party being saved from wholesale massacre only by the courage and resourcefulness of a young axman, J. M. Eddy, who rallied the men and led them in a running fight till the marauders withdrew. But in the course of it the crew was driven far off its job and badly disorganized, eventually wandering into Fort Collins, some fifty miles southwest in Colorado Territory.

Worse than that, the death of Hills, first Union Pacific engineer to fall in the line of duty, was a blow vastly more crippling than the loss of the occasional grader or track hand who had died in the raids of '66. Trained engineers, seasoned to the work and the country, were indispensable, since they alone could carry out the surveys without which neither grade nor rails could advance. If these surveys were allowed to stop now, so would all railroad construction, within a matter of months or even weeks. And there were many engineers, scattered on advance missions far out in the wilderness west of Sherman Summit this spring, who were as vulnerable as Hills had been. The news from Fort Collins suggested that two such parties, especially, might be in real trouble. A reconnaissance group led by Thomas Bates had gone unreported for a long time. And from Fort Sanders, early in June, came a message telling of other difficulties encountered by an advance survey crew in charge of the same Percy Browne who had had such a bad time of it in the mountains beyond Denver the previous fall.

Browne had been among the first engineers out of Omaha in March, fighting his way through the late snows to LaPorte Station on the Overland Stage in Colorado. From there he led his party over the Black Hills by forced marches and reached Sanders in early May. Here he picked up his troop escort, a detachment of G Company of the Second Cavalry, and headed out on his assignment.

It was a critical one. His orders were to run a line 275 miles westward to the Green River in the Dakotah Wyoming, the stretch on which construction work would jump off in '68. To do it he had been provided with a typical advance survey party, consisting of an assistant engineer by the name of Francis Appleton and a full crew of rodmen, chainmen and flagmen. Most of these were graduate civil engineers also, but without field experience. In addition, there were axmen to clear the terrain where necessary and teamsters to handle the considerable train of wagons and pack animals. In all likelihood, too, there was a professional hunter along, for this was the usual practice in regions where wild game might be expected. Except for such game, the party had to carry all of its provisions and supplies with it. Once out of Sanders the men were altogether on their own; no line of communication with the rearward railroad bases, no prospect of contacts with even the remote outposts of civilization for perhaps weeks on end.

Denver lay far to the south, blocked off by the mountain chains whose rigors Browne knew only too well. Also southward, the road ranches of the Overland Stage—themselves isolated and perhaps already wiped out by Indian raids for all Browne knew—offered dubious refuge in case of trouble. Northward, the Oregon Trail and Fort Phil Kearney on the Bozeman lay under siege by Red Cloud's Sioux. To the west there was no real settlement short of Great Salt Lake. Not even the boldest of the buffalo hide men had as yet penetrated this country beyond the Black Hills.

Browne's party mustered, probably, something over forty men, the military escort included.

For the first hundred and fifty miles the survey route ran across the Laramie Plains, a lush and rolling grassland where great herds of buffalo and antelope grazed; an age-old hunting ground the Sioux surely would defend with jealous fury. And in the spring of the year, the tribes' supplies of winter meat depleted and their hunting parties ranging far and wide, it was a doubly dangerous locality for white men to venture into. Browne was well aware of this, and so were the troopers. They took what precautions they could. Every civilian member of the party went armed, and most of them, like the graders and track-layers behind, were Army veterans who would not shun a fight. All in all it was a force strong enough to give a good account of itself in battle. Camp sites were selected with defensive considerations in mind; horses and pack mules were picketed close and the troopers stood sentry-go all night. But working hours ran from sunrise to dusk—both favorite times for Indian forays—and all day long the party, like all survey parties, was innately vulnerable to attack by the very nature of the work it did.

Browne, as the engineer in charge, had to proceed well out in front—the most vulnerable spot of all, even though a few troopers were generally assigned to reconnoiter on ahead. His was the responsibility for determining the over-all line to be followed, working from rough maps prepared by earlier reconnaissances, and for designating reference points in the terrain for the surveyors who came on behind. These, with front and rear flagmen separated by a half-mile or more and rodmen and chainmen strung out between, laid down the actual line of the right of way, recording distances, compass directions and elevations, and putting down stakes to guide the final location crews that would come later, just ahead of the graders. The pack train plodded in the wake of the rear flagman, and the axmen worked along the line of march as needed, clearing away obstructions to give a clear line of sight for the transits.

Such a long and straggling formation was naturally in a poor position to defend itself, and posed a nearly insoluble problem for the small force of cavalrymen. But they did their best, using the accepted escort tactic of keeping to the highest ground available and scanning the plain in all directions, ready to ride hard for any point threatened by attack. It was sketchy protection at best, however. The grass-grown swales and hollows of the prairie afforded cover that even a veteran trooper could overlook, so that the situation was ideal for the quick, sneak onset that was the Indians' forte.

Six days after leaving Fort Sanders, nevertheless, Browne had his party at Rock Creek, fifty-five miles out. It was good progress; he was a tireless leader and a top engineer. But there the inevitable suddenly caught up with him.

Sioux raiders cut off a wood-gathering detail just at dusk, killed a Sergeant Clair of the escort and ran off a team of mules. The rest of the detail managed to fight their way back to camp, and all night soldiers and workers alike lay on their rifles and kept an uneasy watch. With the first gray of dawn the enemy struck again: a flurried drumming of hoofs in the half-dark; quick yelp of war whoops; spatter of musketry and hissing whisper of arrows. This time a youngster named Clark was killed (a nephew, as it happened, of the influential New York newspaperman and political figure, Thurlow Weed, which gave the affair a somewhat inflated prominence in the Eastern press). But the charge was beaten off, and so were others that followed throughout the long day in a series of actions so hot that Corporal Cain and Privates Doyle, Hughes and Lipe were subsequently cited in dispatches by the commander of the Second Cavalry. Toward evening the Indians drew off for good, and Browne led his battered party back toward Fort Sanders.

Word of this attack, telegraphed to Omaha, reached Grenville Dodge shortly after the news of the earlier Hills disaster. It was enough. The chief engineer at once prepared to take the field himself with a relief expedition.

But Percy Browne was not waiting. At Sanders he buried his dead, reorganized his party and sallied out again with a strengthened cavalry escort. Though a young man like most of his colleagues, Browne was already a veteran as service went on the Union Pacific. He had joined the company as a rodman in '64 and worked his way up through the engineering ranks, was fiercely ambitious and devoted to the enterprise.

On this second try luck smiled for a while, and he was able to run his survey line unmolested. The party worked its way across the Laramie Plains, forded the North Platte River and headed into the Red Desert beyond.

This was the first of a number of desert basins that lay west of the Continental Divide. It was a region of bleak red sandstone, wind-tortured mesas, arid earth clumped sparsely with the dun gray-green of sagebrush and crusted with bitter alkali deposits; a blasted land, forbidding and empty-seeming. But along its southern edge the Overland Stage ran, and Sioux war parties long had been accustomed to riding across it to and from their raids southward. Browne may or may not have been aware of this. He had made one previous trip over the Divide and was not unacquainted with the terrain.

But his maps were inaccurate and misleading, and he appears to have become confused because the few scanty watercourses he found ran, not westward as he had expected, but eastward or every which way. What he did not know—what no one knew till a long time afterward—was that all these desert basins were the remnants of prehistoric sea beds with basic topographies quite alien to the mountain slopes in which they were set. Finally, still puzzled, he left his main party to run a line westward from the North Platte as far as possible while he himself took eight troopers and struck on into the desert to reconnoiter. July had come now and time was wasting. His luck was about to turn again, this time irreparably.

On the twenty-third of the month, a hundred miles out in the wasteland, Browne and his eight were jumped by another Sioux war party. They made a race of it to the nearest high ground, dismounted and broke up the first charge with a volley from their carbines. Then from noon till almost dark there ensued a battle in the classic Western pattern, their nine rifles holding off an overwhelmingly stronger force of Sioux (three hundred, the troopers claimed later), who circled in and out of range in lightning little sorties, yelling and firing in the usual Indian attempt to stampede the horses. In this, as dusk came down, they were at length successful. Their final spatter of shots put Percy Browne out of the fight, writhing in the agony of a slug through the stomach.

Night came down and the harassed men held a terse council in the dark. The Indians had retired, reluctant as always to press a night fight, or perhaps satisfied with a booty of nine horses. Browne insisted through the clenched teeth of pain that the troopers leave him and make a run for it, toward the stage road and possible help. Many of the enlisted men in this postwar Army of the plains were characters who left much to be desired: raw, ignorant recruits; toughs from city slums; wanted men using the uniform as a refuge from the law. These were of a better stamp. Refusing to abandon the wounded engineer, they devised a makeshift litter out of carbines and a blanket and carried him by relays as they stumbled southward in a groping, half-hopeless night march through the gritty sagebrush. The nearest Overland Stage station was LaClede, fifteen miles away. They made it, but Percy Browne died before sunrise.

Grenville Dodge, meanwhile, had moved rapidly and was now well on his way west, quite ignorant of this final tragic development of course, and still hoping that he would be in time to mend a bad situation. His expedition was a strong one, organized around a large force of fresh laborers and surveyors to reinforce the harried crews he expected to find along the forward route. But by the time the party got out of Omaha it had grown to somewhat unwieldy proportions, for reasons beyond Dodge's control.

Brevet Major General John A. Rawlins, chief of staff to General Grant, joined at Grant's special request. Rawlins had contracted tuberculosis, and it was his superior's hope that the Western trip would prove beneficial. But the Army was awake to the seriousness of continued Indian hostility, and Rawlins had been given the specific assignment of examining the country and recommending locations for a new string of forts beyond Sanders. It was a mission in which Dodge's cooperation could be of immense future benefit to the Union Pacific, as the chief engineer well knew. Accompanying Rawlins were his own aide-de-camp, Major William McKee Dunn of the 21st Infantry, and a John Corwith of Galena, Illinois, apparently another friend of Grant's. There were other civilian guests in addition, and a party of engineers headed by Jacob Blickensderfer, Jr., a Union Pacific man deputized by President Andrew Johnson to investigate the country and recommend the spot to be designated as the eastern base of the Rocky Mountains, a matter now becoming pertinent as railhead approached the Black Hills and the payment of top government subsidies pended. With Blickensderfer as assistants went Government Director T. J. Carter and Colonel Silas Seymour, as well as the company geologist, Van Lennep. Two companies of the Second Cavalry from Fort McPherson under Captain John Mizner were assigned as escort.

Already, in a little more than two months since the start of construction for '67, Jack Casement's iron gangs had pushed end of track another seventy miles forward, up the valley of Lodgepole Creek between the forks of the Platte. North Platte had shriveled overnight to a rueful little railroad town of three hundred, its vaunted "Paris of Nebraska" dream buried in the debris of boom gone bust. The railroad terminal camp had moved a giant's stride farther on, to raw, raucous Julesburg, which now roared more loudly and lawlessly than North Platte ever had.

Dodge's party arrived in Julesburg late in June, to be greeted by Jack Casement and Construction Superintendent Samuel Reed. After a brief inspection of railhead they moved out on the trail westward, going by easy stages in deference to the state of General Rawlins' health. Somewhere along here young J. M. Eddy joined them, sent on from Fort Collins at Dodge's request. The hero of the Hills affair proved to be a youth barely twenty-one. For all that, he was a veteran of the War Between the States, having enlisted at the age of sixteen in the 13th Illinois Volunteer Infantry and served in Dodge's own XVI Corps. So their meeting was something of a reunion. Out of it came a promotion for the young axman and the start of a railroad career that took him, ultimately, to the general managership of the Southwestern System many years later.

A hundred and forty miles beyond Julesburg, at Crow Creek, the base of the long grade up through the Black Hills, a site for the next division point and terminal town was laid out and named Cheyenne. General C. C. Augur, now commanding the Department of the Platte, led a detachment down from Fort Laramie to pay his respects to Rawlins and to establish a new Army post at the spot, to be named Fort D. A. Russell. Here, the journal of the expedition noted, the Fourth of July was celebrated with a patriotic oration by General Rawlins to the assembled soldiers and railroad graders.

Cheyenne at the time had but one permanent building, a small log cabin owned by a French-Canadian trader. Before the party pulled out, a mixed force of Sioux and Cheyenne attacked a Mormon grading crew working down the slope east of Sherman Summit, killed two men and rode away unscathed, right under the noses of the Army detachments.

Here, for Rawlins and the civilian guests, was a sudden, brutal demonstration of Indian warfare as it was fought out here. They had read and heard much, and the general and his aide were military men accustomed to death and violence; but there was nothing like scalped and bleeding corpses—and an enemy vanished into thin air—to drive the point home. For Grenville Dodge it was a sobering reminder, if he needed one, of what might be happening to his survey parties farther out beyond the Black Hills. Pushing harder now, the inspection-tour aspect of the expedition forgotten, he led his force up over Sherman Summit and down the western slope.

At Fort Sanders the garrison still knew nothing at all of the Thomas Bates party, had had no word from Percy Browne since the fight at Rock Creek a month earlier.

But Browne's survey stakes were easily followed and presently, out in the Red Desert west of the North Platte crossing, Dodge came up with the main Browne party. He found them in hapless straits, their water supply almost gone, most of the horses and pack mules dead, Assistant Engineer Francis Appleton discouraged and at his wit's end, even the cavalry escort exhausted and on the verge of demoralization. And very soon, even as scouts moved out for a further search, Browne's eight troopers reached Sanders from LaClede Station and their grim news was sent on from the fort. It had been a very near thing, and all the more tragic because of it; Percy Browne had died with rescue almost at hand.

But this advance survey could not be allowed to stop, regardless of vain regrets and whatever the cost. Vigorously Dodge took hold and reorganized the party, arranging for fresh mounts and supplies, a new escort from Fort Sanders. "They were in good spirits," his report noted, possibly with more hope than conviction. The men stuck, though, as tough-fibered a crew as most who helped to build the U.P. Francis Appleton, who might have thrown up his job in despair, was promoted and placed in charge with the same assignment Browne had had. His confidence restored, he would stay with the Union Pacific to the end, and do well.

Meanwhile Dodge pushed on, now more anxious than ever for some trace of the Bates party. And presently he found that, too, his scouts riding in to report an unidentified group approaching the column, but so slowly and in such a straggling fashion that they might be another Indian war band maneuvering for an ambush. This was always a possibility which only the foolhardy ignored. And so contact was made with due caution, the delay maddening to the poor devils, who were not Indians at all but white men in desperate condition: crawling on hands and knees, ragged and sun-scorched, with swollen, blackened tongues protruding between parched lips.

Haltingly, Bates croaked out a story of disaster. His party had been without water for three days. A water hole in the desert had proved poisonous, sickening the men. They had abandoned their dying horses and mules and, aware that their maps were untrustworthy, were trying doggedly to reach the North Fork of the Platte by following a compass course due east. But for the meeting with Dodge's column they never would have made it. They had seen no Indians, suffered no attacks. The hostile land itself had beaten them.

They too were sent back to Sanders for rest, medical care and regrouping. And like Appleton and his party, Thomas Bates and his men did not quit either.

Dodge continued westward. Still in the Red Desert, he located the site for another division point and named it Rawlins in the general's honor. There were no more survey parties needing succor. Sioux raiders, if any glimpsed the column, found it too strong to be attacked. The Red Desert and the desolate Bitter Creek region beyond were examined, mapped and left behind. The party made its way at a leisurely pace through the passes of the Wasatch Range, Dodge and his engineers still reconnoitering, and on into Utah Territory to Salt Lake City; then turned in a long northeasterly arc to the Wind River and the Sweetwater country, and at last headed eastward once more, this time by the South Pass route.

The country was a rugged, unspoiled vastness of pine-timbered mountain slopes and bare, wind-tortured badlands, an interesting and beautiful land; a welcome contrast to the monotonous prairie and the desert wastes on the Union Pacific route. Grizzly bears teemed in the wooded country along the Sweetwater, as many as fifty or sixty of the big fellows to be seen on any day's march, and Rawlins and Major Dunn, ardent huntsmen both, longed to try for trophies. As diplomatically as he could, Dodge forbade it. He knew the destructive potential of an aroused grizzly, and was not unmindful of the official embarrassment that could attend a mauling of Ulysses S. Grant's good friend and chief of staff while under the Union Pacific's aegis. All the same, the two crept out of camp one early morning, as foolish as any pair of rank tenderfeet begging for comeuppance. And they very nearly got it. Dodge missed them, aroused Sol Gee, one of the scouts, and followed. They came up just as the two nimrods stumbled onto a bear, fired at close range and broke and ran before the unexpected juggernaut charge. Dodge had to dash in and divert the wounded grizzly's attention, and Sol Gee brought it down with a quick snap shot just in time to save the Union Pacific a chief engineer.

The same Sol Gee got drunk a little later on, when the party stopped briefly at a fur traders' camp. Inadvertently he was left behind, and Major Dunn, perhaps eager to atone for the bear episode, volunteered to backtrack several miles and fetch him. That too might have had serious consequences, for the delay threw the column into near-contact with a strong Sioux war party on the prowl. Several days of edgy hide-and-seek followed, each force endeavoring to entice the other into a situation where it could be taken at a disadvantage. But both were so strong that neither cared to risk a straight-out attack, and in the end they disengaged and went their separate ways.

Thus the expedition returned to Omaha in the fall, and General Rawlins and his aide-de-camp departed for Washington. Apparently the outing did little to improve the general's health, for he died of tuberculosis within two years. He had had the time of his life, however, besides absorbing a valuable object lesson on the West, the nature of the Indian enemy and the magnitude of the Pacific Railroad undertaking. His official report to General Grant included enthusiastic praise for the fortitude and heroism of the railroad men, from the lowliest laborers to the leaders in charge, and had the effect of bolstering the company's already excellent relations with the War Department.

But the trip had been a costly one for Dodge, its pace slowed and its length unreasonably protracted by the obligation to play host. As far as Union Pacific interests were concerned the long detour via the Wind and the Sweetwater had been little more than pure sight-seeing. And on his return Dodge soon discovered that he had been away from the scene of construction much too long.

Out on the grade to Sherman Summit, Colonel Silas Seymour had indulged his penchant for meddling with location lines again. This time, quite gratuitously, he had taken it upon himself to ease James Evans' original grade from ninety feet of rise per mile to eighty. To do so he had introduced a series of curves so sharp that the resulting friction would, in actual train operation, more than offset any advantage gained by the easier gradient. And in addition, to avoid excessive fill as the line climbed up from the plain onto the ridge, Seymour had found it necessary to put in a section of ninety-foot grade of his own—so that his interference boiled down, finally, to a sorry exhibition of engineering theory botched and gone astray in application.

Evans, an able and conscientious man, raged in impotence. Dodge was somewhere to the westward with Rawlins, unavailable for appeal. From New York Dr. Durant backed up his consulting engineer as he had done at Omaha in '64. By the time Dodge arrived on the scene at last and learned what had transpired, work on Seymour's new grade was well under way.

Still fuming, Evans wrote an official report on the whole affair, arguing the superiority of his line over Seymour's with such sound engineering logic that the Union Pacific's government directors not only incorporated it in their own report for the year, but immediately ordered all grading stopped till a team of government commissioners could inspect the terrain in person and render a decision. In the end they upheld Evans, but by the time that had come to pass the onset of winter weather was well along; valuable time had been wasted and a considerable amount of money and effort gone down the drain. Dodge, for his part, was as angry and disturbed as Evans, but powerless to do anything to remedy the situation. He had to content himself with a strong protest in his own report for '67 and let it go at that. But he did not forget, and was not the kind to knuckle under indefinitely.

Silas Seymour's motives remain, to this day, somewhat clouded. Partly, no doubt, they stemmed from honest conviction unfortunately mixed with a tendency to be officious. He appears to have been something of a book engineer, a pedant, though his professional reputation was generally considered excellent. He was widely ridiculed by other Union Pacific engineers, though, for a theory of his which held that parallel timbers laid lengthwise made a better support for rails than the conventional crossties—a type of thinking that was archaic even in the '60's. But many Union Pacific men considered him nothing but a willing toady and cat's-paw to Thomas Durant, and most of them regarded him with contempt. Samuel Reed, writing to his wife about this time, sketched a vividly comic little vignette of the man:

Col. Seymour was outfitted after the following style: First, the horse which he selected and paid a good round price for was, or ought to have been, a twin brother of old 'Knockumstiff.' On the horse he would have placed the saddle, attached to which his carbine in its case securely strapped and buckled to be convenient in case of a sudden Indian attack, also his poncho, bed, etc. in bulk about a barrel, leaving very little room for the Colonel. When he mounted he would hoist his umbrella and leisurely follow in the wake of the escort, or perhaps leading them a few paces. The Pawnee made fun of him from beginning to end.

But not so comically, Reed added in the same letter that "Seymour seems to be determined to delay the work as much as possible. The object apparently is to injure somebody's reputation. General Dodge appears to be the scapegoat."

Samuel Reed wrote a great many letters home from the Union Pacific's construction camps, and many of them tend to reveal him as a chronic worrier and complainer. Nevertheless, he had been a key man in the U.P. organization since the original ground-breaking, and his opinion amounted to considerably more than idle gossip. Quite plainly, the bad blood between Dr. Durant and the Ames faction was beginning to make itself felt out on the right of way. To Durant, incurably prone to quick and violent resentments, it made no difference that Grenville Dodge was the chief engineer he himself had chosen. Now Dodge was gravitating toward the Ames camp; whether he liked it or not, that meant he had to face a feud with Durant.

There was still another complication for Dodge as he made his way back to Omaha this fall. He would have to leave again soon, for Washington and the second session of his Congressional term. It was no time to be absent, but again there was no help for it.

The official objective remained: Fort Sanders by the end of '67. And the year was running downhill toward late fall now, with the race still touch-and-go. By the middle of August General Jack Casement had pushed railhead 430 miles out of Omaha, 125 of them covered in a sustained rush of four months, in spite of a lengthening supply line and iron stranded at Council Bluffs by the flooding Missouri, which got things off to a tardy start. The graders had kept pace with him, a hundred miles ahead. By September, end of track was at milepost 460, about halfway between Julesburg and the new town site called Cheyenne. There was an all-rail link with the East now, for the Cedar Rapids and Missouri had built its track into Council Bluffs at last, in January. All this was on the plus side. But the hoped-for bridge over the Missouri had not been built yet, or even begun.

In September, also, another U.S. Government Peace Commission journeyed to North Platte by special train to sit in one more conclave with the unregenerate Sioux and Cheyenne. This one looked important, with some big names on it: General William T. Sherman in person, General Alfred Terry, Congressman John B. Henderson of Missouri, among others. The long blood-letting on the plains was growing irksome to the public back East and the Army felt its prestige at stake. At Washington the Andrew Johnson administration was showing a growing disposition to distrust the military and put "the Indian problem" into civilian hands. But past disillusionments and the unflagging slaughter of the buffalo herds had left the Indians embittered. Some chiefs came to the peace council; many of the most respected ones stayed away. Still, there was a kind of halfhearted truce on the plains this fall. The men of the Union Pacific Engineering Department thought of Percy Browne, L. L. Hills and other dead men, had their doubts but hoped for the best.

The plainer fellows who ran the trains—engine crews and car hands and lonely telegraphers in their shanties along the line—hoped for the best, too. Fresh in their minds were things that had happened a good deal closer to home this summer. Notably at Plum Creek . . .

CHAPTER 18

"THUNDER ALL ALONG THE SKY"

Early in that spring of '67, as part of the Army's far-flung operations against the hostiles, General Winfield Scott Hancock had marched from Fort Larned out in western Kansas with a cumbersome force that included artillery and even pontoon boats for the river crossings. He had had little better luck than the golden-haired Custer at finding a decisive battlefield, but he did come down hard on a large Cheyenne encampment on the Pawnee Fork of the Arkansas River. The place was deserted, the Indians prudently scattering at his approach. But they had had to abandon their lodges and their meager worldly goods, and these Hancock burned before marching back to Larned with at least a quasi victory to report.

All this was far removed from the Union Pacific Railroad, of course. But as a result of it, broken little bands of Cheyenne drifted northward all summer long, weary from the soldiers' chivvying, feeling homeless, ill-used and resentful. One party of Chief Turkey Foot's young braves crossed the Platte and happened on the U.P. right of way at a shallow, dry stream bed a few miles west of a station named Plum Creek.[1] These Kansas Cheyenne had none of the Sioux's hatred for the "fire road." They never had heard of it, in fact, and their first distant glimpse of the trains was the first sight they ever had had of any railroad. A number of years later one of them, a brave by the name of Porcupine, told the story to George Bird Grinnell, a sympathetic young naturalist and writer sent west by the U.S. Biological Survey on a census of the dwindling buffalo, and thus left a rare first-person account of the railroad's impact on the unsophisticated Indian mind.[2]

For several days, according to Porcupine, the party hung about the vicinity, watching from afar and marveling at the trains, the wolf-howling of the whistles and the strange things in front that "smoked like a white man's pipe, puffing." One Indian advanced a theory that the white men must burn horses to make these things go so fast. Could the Cheyenne, he wondered, do likewise if they burned *their* horses? The others doubted it, but there was a general, awed agreement that the white men's medicine was very strong, very good.

Presently they ventured to approach the right of way, and were struck with fresh amazement by the rails. There was a lively discussion as to their nature. One brave, Red Horse, suggested that they might be an iron trail left behind by the smoke wagons. No, said an older man named Spotted Wolf, this must be a road built for the wagons to travel on. Yes, the others agreed, that seemed more likely.

The discussion continued. Mightily excited as they considered this marvelous new thing, the braves rode up and down the track, blowing occasional blasts on a battered cavalry bugle one of them had acquired, taking cover whenever a train approached. That they could remain unseen all this while speaks significantly of the immense emptiness of the prairie, even so close to the Platte River and in a comparatively settled area. For Plum Creek was just thirty-nine miles west of Kearney, only 230 west of Omaha, and end of track at the time was somewhat more than two hundred miles beyond.

Inevitably, the thought occurred to one of the Cheyenne that the smoke wagons must carry many valuable things. If they could manage to throw one from its track, break it open, now . . . The white soldiers, the yellow legs, had driven them away from their lodges and their hunting grounds, burned everything they had and made them poor; their blankets were ragged, their ponies thin and worn from hard riding. Their own hearts were bad from so much trouble, and they had need of the white men's medicine to become strong again.

With an industry not often shown by Indians they uprooted a tie, bound it across the track and settled down to await developments, building a fire as dusk thickened into full night. The date was August 6, 1867, in its own modest way a historical milestone, for this little band of dispossessed Cheyenne was about to set a shattering precedent in Indian warfare.

What first came along, however, was not one of the smoke wagons but, in Porcupine's words, "a small thing with something on it that moved up and down." The Indians had cut the telegraph line and used the wire to bind the tie to the rails, and this was a handcar with a small crew sent out from Plum Creek to find and repair the break. The men noticed the fire ahead but apparently did not take alarm; or if they did, were given little time to react. Dark figures converged on them from both sides of the track and war whoops split the air. Pumping hard in a last-ditch effort to run past, they hit the tie and were flung sprawling as the handcar careened off into the dry creek. Though armed, they had no chance to fight. Only one man, a William Thompson, managed to scramble up and run, but a mounted Cheyenne—it was the brave, Red Horse—overtook him, shot him through one arm, knocked him flat with a sweep of the rifle butt and sprang to the ground with knife flashing.

In a matter of moments poor Thompson was stabbed through the neck and scalped. It felt, he told a reporter on the Omaha *Herald* afterward, "as if the whole top of my head was taken right off." But he forced himself to lie still, feigning death; his only chance. And it worked. Red Horse vaulted to his pony's back and rode off. Incredibly, then, Thompson saw the dripping scalp fall to the ground and crawled over to seize it, somehow obsessed in his crimson half-daze of pain and terror with the notion that it might be attached to his head again if he should manage to survive.

Emboldened, gripped in the exulting frenzy of first blood, the Cheyenne went to work once more. This time they pried the ends of a pair of rails out of their chairs, bent them up to the vertical and piled more ties into the gap while Thompson watched, flat on his belly in the grass, too dizzy and sick to crawl away, perhaps only half-conscious now and altogether helpless.

Low over the eastern horizon, after a while, the Indians saw a pinpoint of light rising, and then another. They knew nothing of locomotive headlights, and thought at first they were stars. Then, as the rails began to hum with the rumble of something approaching, they mounted and rode eastward to investigate. In fact, two Union Pacific freight trains were coming, one running close behind the other.

Manning the first locomotive were Brookes Bowers, the engineer, known to his mates as "Bully Brookes," and fireman Gregory Henshaw, who bore the mouth-filling nickname "Drummer Boy of the Rappahannock," apparently due to a fancied similarity of his surname and that of a folk hero of the late war. Bowers saw the Cheyenne riders dash into his headlight beam and reached to widen out on the throttle, probably shouting a warning across the swaying cab to Henshaw. It was no new thing for mounted hostiles to chase Union Pacific trains, frequently peppering them with arrows and rifle slugs, and the usual practice was simply to increase speed and outrun them. So, bucketing along the uneven rails at perhaps thirty miles an hour, the eight-wheeler slammed full into the broken track and the tie barrier, jolted off onto the ballast and went wallowing into the shallow creek bed with a crash of rending metal and a great, anguished roar of escaping steam. A pair of brick-loaded flatcars next behind the tender were catapulted over the wreckage, hurling bricks far and wide. The first five or six boxcars lurched off the track, the lead one telescoping against the engine and opening up in a crackle of splinters to spew its lading along the right of way. Almost immediately it blazed up in flame from the riven firebox.

Down on deck at his firebox door, the Drummer Boy of the Rappa-hannock never had a chance. The jackknifing tender pinned him against the boiler backhead and he was burned alive. Hurled bodily through the right-hand cab window, Bully Brookes landed beside the locomotive, rolled over and sat up groggily in the wreckage, both hands clutching at the entrails that spilled out through a long gash in his abdomen.

Back in the caboose, which had not left the rails, conductor William Kin-ney, brakemen Fred Lewis and Charles Ratcliffe and a deadheading fireman whose name was not recorded were shaken but unhurt. Bewildered, not sure what had happened though they had heard war whoops and a ragged burst of rifle fire, they all piled out onto the ground. One look ahead at the sullen flicker from the burning boxcar was enough. Kinney, evidently a railroader all the way, thought first of the freight following, and ordered Lewis back to flag it.[3]

The brakeman demurred. Go back there alone, the whole damn prairie crawling with redskins?

But the freight had to be flagged. Kinney started off at a run himself, his lantern bobbing. Lewis and the deadheading fireman followed.

Ratcliffe, the other brakeman, elected to dive under the caboose. Then, peering out and glimpsing the legs of an approaching Indian, he changed his mind, crawled out the opposite side and bolted after the others, hearing a chill-ing outbreak of shrill yells, like hounds on a scent, as the Cheyenne saw him and took up the pursuit.

The oncoming train was within a mile now, the locomotive's headlight clearly visible, with Kinney, Lewis and the fireman silhouetted in its wash of radiance. But the Indians were close behind; too close. Above the labored gush of his own breathing, Ratcliffe heard the engineer whistling for brakes, and presently the screech of wheels on rails as they were applied. The big bull's-eye headlight loomed above him; against its harsh yellow glare the nerve of his pursuers broke and they veered away. But the hogger would be slamming his Johnson bar around the quadrant and cracking his throttle to back down, Ratcliffe knew. Panic-stricken now lest he be left behind, he lurched on in a staggering run, past the pilot and down alongside the locomotive as it chuffed in reverse motion. He jumped for the gangway step; hands reached to catch his outstretched arms. Gasping and shivering, he was dragged into the cab, safe—but he had had the scare of his life.

At Plum Creek, the operator telegraphed a report of what had happened to Omaha. But the dispatcher there, either misunderstanding or afflicted with a one-track mind, replied by repeating the train orders, and presently added a brusque message to "Get out of the way as soon as possible." With no help to be expected from that quarter, the disgusted crew tramped out, climbed aboard the train and backed out for Elm Creek, eighteen miles farther east.

Plum Creek's tiny population, alerted by this time and convinced that a horde of murdering Indians would be down on them at any moment, went along by spontaneous decision. Only the telegraph operator stuck to his post, stubbornly barricading himself in the depot while he went on pounding out pleas for aid.

But any more raiding just then was very far indeed from the minds of Porcupine and his fellows, who were busily wallowing in the ferocious exuberance of victory, and affluence beyond the greediest Indian's dreams. They scalped poor, injured Bully Brookes and threw his body into the flaming wreckage. They broke open the unburned boxcars, and from each dragged out an abundance of plunder richer than the one before had yielded. The train had been a valuable one: bales of cotton goods; bolts of bright calico; barrels and bags and crates of tools, tobacco, flour, sugar, coffee, trade goods; boots and shoes and store clothes; velvets, ribbons and furbelows for the fancy women up the line at North Platte and Julesberg and the Army ladies at the posts along the way; cases of Army rifles, too, and the bullets to fit them; samplings of all the appurtenances of civilization the Union Pacific was now carrying westward to supply the march of empire. They found a barrel of whiskey, beat its head in and in no time at all were capering in a drunken prairie Saturnalia, snatching brands and flinging them up and down the length of the train till a huge bonfire roared from head end to caboose.

All this Thompson watched, pressed flat in the concealing grass like a nightmare Dante overwhelmed by a foretaste of Inferno. Toward morning he regained his strength and his senses sufficiently to crawl off to a safe distance, and then climb to his feet and walk. Still grimly clinging to his scalp, he staggered down the track fifteen miles to Willow Island, the next station west.

Frustration piled on frustration as the railroad tried to rally its Army guardians. The telegraph wires were down farther west also (whether by another Indian foray or some other mishap is not clear) so there was no help to be had from that direction. Belatedly, officials at Omaha woke up and used the Overland Telegraph to flash the word west. But then it developed that the Army was occupied in other areas, and for the moment embarrassingly helpless. The nearest post was Fort Kearney, but it was in the process of being dismantled, the only troops on hand a token detachment acting as caretakers. Practically all of Fort McPherson's cavalry and mounted infantry were scattered on routine scouting missions. Sedgewick, out on the Overland Trail in Colorado Territory, could do nothing but send for Major North's Pawnees, then on duty somewhere beyond railhead, west of Julesberg. And this took time. Meanwhile the railroad lay helpless as a broken-backed snake, its traffic at a standstill while the Cheyenne—no one had any accurate idea of their strength—gathered themselves to burst out in renewed fury, for all anyone knew.

The Plum Creek people, finding themselves still unmolested when daylight came, finally mustered enough nerve to venture back home. They found the station as they had left it, the embattled telegrapher still punching away at his key and no sign of Indians anywhere. After a while some of the bolder spirits rode out toward the scene of the wreck.

The Cheyenne were still there, happily carousing. Through a telescope the whites watched them riding in drunken circles over the prairie, some decked out in looted feminine finery, with bolts of gay-colored calico tied to their ponies' tails, unrolling to billow in the wind behind them. Too few to attack, the watchers lay and waited, swearing under their breaths, sweeping the horizon for a first sight of the avenging cavalry that did not come. It was late afternoon before the sobering Cheyenne collected the choicest of their spoils and rode off at last, and the white men dared to go up and poke in futile anger at the smoldering wreckage.

Much later a train steamed in from the west and disgorged the Pawnee Scouts, in full battle regalia and eager for a fight, if somewhat tardy. They led their horses down out of boxcars and rode off on the cold trail. They never caught the raiders, though they forced them into a running fight and caused them to abandon most of their plunder. For some while afterward the Army made strenuous inquiries in an effort to identify the culprits. They failed, however; not till Porcupine told his story to George Grinnell were these Cheyenne surely known and their niche secured in the history of the West: the first Indians ever to wreck a railroad train.

Quite a crowd of the curious gathered while the wreck was cleared away, the broken rails replaced and things made ready for the resumption of service. The remains of engineer Bowers and fireman Henshaw were exhumed from the ashes and shipped to Omaha for burial. There was barely enough left of them, the morbid related, to fill a pair of boxes thirty inches long by a foot wide; both boxes together weighed no more than thirty pounds. Others noted with amazement that several brand-new Spencer repeating carbines had been left by the Indians, who usually were avid after firearms above all other of the white man's artifacts. As it turned out, these Spencers were the first repeating rifles the Cheyenne had ever seen. When they handled them and found them breaking at the breech, the braves threw them aside in disgust.

The indestructible Thompson was among the first on the scene, bandaged and still hopeful, carrying his scalp in a bucket of water to keep it from drying out. With the long, dark hair floating, an eyewitness reported, the thing looked like a drowned rat. But Thompson insisted on taking it with him on the first train to Omaha, where a Dr. R. C. Moore thought it might be stitched back in place. The operation was a failure, though, and Thompson returned to his native England shortly thereafter, understandably fed up with the wild American West. He took the scalp with him, but later sent it back as a gift to Dr. Moore, possibly in gratitude for a good try. Moore in turn eventually presented the grisly relic to the Omaha Public Library, where it remained, displayed in a jar of alcohol, for many years.

Thus ended the Plum Creek Massacre, as it came to be known. In Nebraska the incident was not forgotten for a long time. Most disturbingly, to Union Pacific men, it had happened on a section of railroad that had been completed and in regular operation for over a year; a grim reminder that danger existed everywhere on the line, not just at railhead or beyond.

Among those present to report the affair for Eastern readers was a young Welsh-American journalist out here as a correspondent for the *Missouri Democrat* and the New York *Herald*. Ironically, he was on his way to North Platte at the time, to cover the negotiations of the newest Peace Commission. Henry M. Stanley was his name, and he was soon to become far more celebrated for certain activities in Africa than as a chronicler of the American frontier. Yet he saw many things of eye-opening interest as he journeyed on, and reported them faithfully. Of the Peace Commission itself there was not much to say, for it accomplished little. But Julesburg was something else again, and Stanley found Jack Casement's crew at end of track worthy of any newsman's attention.

He breakfasted as a guest in the dining car at railhead and afterward watched the iron gang, Captain Clayton supervising in person for the occasion, lay twenty-five pairs of rails—seven hundred feet of iron—in five minutes. Scribbling in rapid calculation, young Stanley announced that, at the same rate, the gang could put down better than sixteen miles a day.

Well, hardly! There was a difference between hasty statistics and the realities of human endurance, even a Casement Irishman's.

But the Casements' production-line techniques were improving with practice, the roster of their manpower growing. The crew was five hundred strong now. In normal operation—no stunt but the regular workday routine—a pair of rails a minute snaked out over the roller in the lorry car. "Down!" the foreman shouted, and down they went. Ten spikes to a rail, no more, no less. Three blows of a maul to drive each one home; the next two rails lay in the chairs waiting; four hundred rails to a mile, and a mile a day was no longer a record to brag about, not so long as the loaded iron trains kept coming. These gangs could better that, and did, and still their greatest exploits were to come. It was no wonder Union Pacific iron had left North Platte to wither on the vine, and Julesburg now boomed in frenetic brevity.

Incredulously Henry Stanley wrote of stepping off the train there and elbowing his way through jostling crowds to the Julesburg House, where he sat down to a feast "composed of various styles of soups, fricandeaux, vegetables, game in abundance, pies, puddings, raisins, apples, nuts, wine and bread at discretion, for the moderate sum of twelve bits." He confessed to being fooled by the swaggering clientele he saw there, flashing thick gold watches on heavy chains, dressed in modish clothes and gleaming boots of patent leather. These must be important railroad capitalists, he was sure, till inquiry disclosed them as mere ticket agents, conductors, locomotive engineers off duty and the like. They were, he wrote, "the upper ten-dom of sinful Julesburg."[4]

Stanley, no neophyte, had seen North Platte in its high-flying heyday, but this was three times worse (or better, depending on one's point of view). It was the second Julesburg, renamed from the original Canvastown. The first Julesburg had boasted of being the toughest stage station on the Overland Trail, and brought its reputation with it in a migration to the railroad tracks. All the seamier predators from deflated North Platte had followed along in the wake of the iron gangs, and the choicest riffraff from disappointed Denver City trekked over to cut in on boom times come again. Town lots sold for a thousand dollars and up. The streets were lined with stores, warehouses, vice dens and big canvas "dancing saloons" where luxurious foods and potables fresh from Omaha and Chicago were to be had, and shoot-outs and head-peelings erupted almost every night. "The Wickedest City in America," the town dubbed itself; a champion at iniquity and proud of it.

The population soared somewhere around the four-thousand mark but seemed greater, so crowded was it, so blatantly strident. Stanley saw soldiers, gamblers, tame Indians on the take, railroad boomers, land speculators, Mexicans. The prevalent wickedness brought out even the Bible-thumpers, religious evangelists shouting of red-hot hellfire, brimstone and salvation in the moiling, sandy streets. Perhaps they made some converts, though the odds were long. Sin was a lot gaudier.

"The women," wrote Stanley, "are expensive articles, and come in for a large share of the money wasted."

He described them, gliding through the streets in broad daylight in their fancy Black Crook dresses with dainty little derringers slung at their waists, "with which tools they are dangerously expert." But even at so early a date he noted the ascendancy of "western chivalry." It would not, he said, allow these women to be abused by any man they happened to have robbed.

"I verily believe," he concluded,

that there are men here who would murder a fellow creature for five dollars. Nay, there are men who have already done it, and who stalk abroad in daylight unwhipped of justice. Not a day passes but a dead body is found somewhere in the vicinity with pockets rifled of their contents. But the people generally are strangely indifferent.

Fun was fun, but Jack Casement did not remain indifferent. The general was no blue-nosed reformer. He knew his Irish veterans, and had no objection to the good relaxation inherent in raw whiskey, gambling, willing women, stomp-and-gouge fisticuffs and the occasional ripping apart of a saloon or bawdyhouse. But his job was to ram Union Pacific iron westward, and there came a day when the casualties grew too heavy. Too many of his iron-slingers were turning up incapacitated from broken heads or disease on Monday mornings. Too many of them were losing their pay to the nimble-fingered proprietors of the faro, blackjack and rondo-coolo games; too many of those corpses with rifled pockets had been Paddies off the U.P. grades, or trainmen waylaid in the clustered shadows down along the sidings.

There was no civil law in Julesburg, and the Army had its hands full elsewhere. But the place still was a Union Pacific town.

General Jack was fortunate enough to catch Grenville Dodge by telegraph in Salt Lake City, and got the chief engineer's instant approval for handling matters as he saw fit. From his bunk cars at railhead he broke out the rifles that had been used, so far, only on the Indians. With a picked force of tough track-layers he descended on Julesburg, struck with swift military precision on a fine, late-summer evening, and rounded up the worst of the lawless element's kingpins.

Legend has it that he gave them the traditional hour to get out of town. For those lacking horses, he announced crisply, there would be a Union Pacific train leaving for Omaha. They had their choice: be on it or stay and face the consequences. Apparently quite a few opted to stay, possibly deceived by the general's small stature. The dearth of trees in Julesburg was a momentary embarrassment, but U.P. telegraph poles proved adequate in the emergency. Legend (again) says that as many as thirty or more hard cases were strung up on the spot. The Union Pacific, quite understandably, never publicized what amounted to a barefaced mass lynching, and Henry Stanley appears to have left town some while before. Local press reports, if any, did not survive. As it happened, nothing in sinful Julesburg survived for long. Entirely apart from Casement's vigilante justice, the town's day was about done. The railroad already had picked the site staked out by Grenville Dodge that same summer, and named Cheyenne, as its next terminal Gomorrah.

North Platte lived to build a new future on the railroad's shirt-sleeve respectability. Not Julesburg. When winter came, nothing remained but a dump heap by the track, coyotes poking hopefully into rusty refuse, discarded bits of plank and scraps of rotting canvas. The cold wind blew among warped board headstones leaning every which way in a sandy graveyard; the living had all gone elsewhere. There is a Julesburg today; the third town to bear the name and located back on the old Overland Trail where the first one had its beginnings. Julesburg II simply died, and no one mourned.

But the time for that was not quite yet, as the eventful year of '67 proceeded toward its end in a burst of new and altogether different activity. This October another excursion came west to marvel at the country and the Great Pacific Railroad. The Eastern public was arousing to a lively interest in what was going on out here, and tourist trips to end of track would be the order of the day from now on. But this one, called the Editorial Rocky Mountain Excursion, eclipsed them all for sheer fun and frolic. Even the Great Excursion of '66 paled in comparison with the triumphant invasion of a contingent from the nation's Fourth Estate shepherded along the right of way by the ebullient George Francis Train—who also reported the proceedings, as a special correspondent for the Omaha *Weekly Herald,* in some of the most rococo prose ever put to paper.

The party reached Omaha on October 9, its very arrival signaling the improving pace of transportation in America. "New York to Omaha in sixty-four hours, piloting two hundred live editors," wrote Train in his opening salvo. "We left there at 8½ o'clock on Saturday, without change of cars, stopping three hours in Chicago. This is the quickest time on record."

It was only a foretaste of things to come, he added, declaring that "Two years hence one will travel from New York to San Francisco in five days, and thence to Constantinople or to Canton as he pleases. Seven hundred millions of Asiatics will shake hands with three hundred millions of Europeans over the Rocky Mountain gold fields, and America will collect the toll." Here again was the old visualization of the transcontinental railroad as a sort of modern-day Northwest Passage, a short cut between Europe and the riches of Ind and Cathay.

There would be an official address of welcome, a banquet and a ball for the editors that evening, Train went on to say, and they would "leave for the fifty thousand buffalo around Kearney" on the morrow. And he wound up his story with a final exuberant boast on the skyrocketing business opportunities in Omaha, and the merits of thinking big: ". . . if my five thousand city lots bring Farnham street prices, I will realize thirty millions. I shall invite one thousand European and American guests on a six months excursion over the Union Pacific round the world."

In this atmosphere of rampant enthusiasm, the two hundred journalists were launched westward across the plains. At Fremont, Train wrote: "The Colossus of Excursions over the Colossus of Rhoads opened wide its editorial eye as it entered the Colossus of Valleys." The Platte, he meant, and went on to describe the editors' reactions: "They never before had seen so much land to the acre. They say the corn and wheat soil weighs thirty ounces to the pound; so fat if you tickle it with a spade it laughs with potatoes."

Here the party had an opportunity to meet Grenville Dodge and General Rawlins, just then returning eastward from the summer-long swing beyond the Rockies. There was an open-air meeting featured by patriotic speeches by both generals, and a band concert.

At Columbus, a favorite town of Train's and one in which he held large parcels of real estate, the editors were treated to a lively display of rough-and-tumble Western politics in action. There was a heated controversy in progress at the time over the location of the Nebraska state capital; and Train, characteristically, was deeply involved. The Credit Foncier, he wrote, had seen Columbus' future early, and now "the great Editorial Excursion notes its magnificent agricultural surroundings." Their consensus, he reported, was that this must be the future national capital, "when fanaticism sleeps awhile, when party spirit fades away." And he seized the opportunity for a bitter attack on the "speculators" who were urging the selection of "Lincumcity" as Nebraska's capital.

George Francis Train was himself a speculator second to none, of course, and his Credit Foncier was selfishly interested in Columbus. In this case, though, and the Union Pacific's considerable effect notwithstanding, the town was not to live up to the grandiose destiny he claimed for it. Lincoln, the scorned "Lincumcity" over in Lancaster County, became the state capital after all.

But there were all sorts of facets to the Train personality, and all of them ebullient. From Willow Island he wrote more seriously, in a philosophic and inspirational vein:

The New Chicago of the New Northwest is already a giant of enterprise. . . . There is thunder all along the sky from California to Maine. See, the lightning day dawns. The white man will be emancipated as well as the black. There is a rainbow in the sky along the path where tempests trod. 'Twas written by a hand on high. It is the autograph of God. . . . Long may national administration wave.

Draw on me at sight for five elk, ten buffalo, fifteen antelope and one prairie dog. Omaha likes me; I like Omaha. You are my friends and I am yours.

Apparently written in response to an earlier and flattering article about him in the *Herald,* this paean of Train's was not quite so wild as it may sound to modern ears. It mirrored a certain basic truth bound up with the times and the country; bound up, too, with the nature of this mighty railroad building westward toward the Pacific. Floridly though he expressed himself (it was a florid age), this man Train knew whereof he wrote, and he knew his audience. There was a spirit of rough and vital renaissance abroad in Western America, the War Between the States over at last, the promise of benevolent empire and the good life bright in men's minds. This *was* the way people felt out here; the Union Pacific itself was part and parcel of the feeling, and George Francis Train was not a bad spokesman.

Even the reference to "five elk, ten buffalo" and the rest was a kind of extravagant frontier brag on the lavish natural wealth the promoters saw in this new land.

Grand Island received the excursionists with the firing of cannon and a grand turnout of the people. At Kearney, as promised, the buffalo hunts began in earnest. The main party was conducted on a tour of the old fort and thence out to the main range south of the Platte River. But one small group stayed behind and enjoyed a hunt of its own, reported in a dispatch to the *Herald* by someone signing himself only with the initial "S." A locomotive and crew having been furnished by Mr. A. A. Bean, Union Pacific master of transportation, the party jogged along to a large prairie dog village, and had no sooner alighted at its edge than a large buffalo bull was seen in the distance. With some dash and eloquence, S. described what followed:

All hands mounted again and Spencer Smith, the Engineer, put on steam to head the giant off; we succeeded and got within a hundred yards and he crosses the track; he proves to be an immense bull and as he speeds along, about forty shots are fired at him. Mr. Kinsley, the best shot in the train, has evidently struck him as he pauses, and with buffalo obstinacy when wounded, he halts and turns around, when several other shots from the same unerring hand bring him to the ground.

But Indians were spied lurking in a patch of timber bordering the prairie, so everyone remounted the locomotive and "with three cheers for Bean, three for Kinsley, and three for Spencer Smith, the Engineer, we returned to Kearney."

The Mr. Kinsley mentioned was the same "Delmonico of Chicago" who had catered so ably for the Great Excursion of '66. He was present in a like capacity for the junketing editors. John Corbutt, the "premier Photographist of Chicago," was along to take pictures; he too had served the earlier tour. But this one, Train boasted enthusiastically, was "the biggest thing yet."

It was an altogether less formal and more fun-loving group than the august collection of personages that had graced the Great Excursion. Between the lines of the dispatches pouring back to Omaha—all printed verbatim in the *Herald* under a standing column head: "THE EDITORIAL EXCURSION"—one senses that the way was smoothed by the happy lubrication of alcohol. J. C. Stoughton, correspondent for the *New Republic,* a paper widely known as a strong temperance organ, had been christened "Bottle" by unanimous acclaim, and Train reported in an early story that he "has not been 'tight' during the trip; however, he may turn out yet."

Rank-and-file excursion members wore large white lapel badges bearing the legend "Rocky Mountain." Those who served on the executive committee wore red badges. It was not so very different, after all, from many a modern businessmen's convention.

Some distinguished names joined the party at various points along the way. Nebraska's Senator Thayer lent the authority of his presence. Governor Jayne of Wisconsin was out for a look at the Pacific Railroad this October. The British peer, Lord Morley, was on the plains for a buffalo shoot with the Honorable Peter Cooper of New York, publisher of the monthly *National American.* They too spent some time with the excursion.

At North Platte, after another rousing citizens' welcome, there was an editorial powwow with twenty genuine redskins provided for the occasion by Major Patrick, the U.S. Indian agent. Senator Thayer presided and Colonel Smith spoke for the editors, followed by a correspondent identified only as "Shirt Lift" with an oration in praise of President Johnson and a Mr. Bulton, who recited Henry Wadsworth Longfellow's "Excelsior" in what passed for the Indian tongue. "One hundred dollars worth of presents were distributed," wrote Train, "and the Indians only got ten, as usual." Carried away by the spirit of good fellowship, an excursionist who had not uttered a word since leaving Chicago (said Train) arose and astonished everyone by addressing the tribesmen in Indian, "and concluded by dancing the Chinese polka."

Throughout their progress westward the excursionists were in receipt of telegraphic reports from the Union Pacific's Samuel Reed, keeping them abreast of developments at railhead. Each was duly passed on and printed in the *Herald* with Train's dispatches:

"Two miles of track laid at 12 M. today."

"One mile of track laid this morning."

"Four miles and one tenth of track laid today."

These reports indicate strongly that Jack Casement was driving ahead in hard spurts, keeping his daily average high in spite of the fact that interruptions in the flow of iron from Omaha were now causing occasional slack days. The situation is verified in the good-natured message which Train found waiting for him at Alkali, a small station on the line near Julesburg:

"We have no city. Can't make a speech but will give you a bully welcome. Have provided your party with two hundred Government shoes in place of the usual transportation. Am sorry you are not with us today; are laying five miles of track. We can't get material enough to-morrow, but will show your party how it is done."

(*Signed*) J. S. CASEMENT
"End of Track"

They did, and Train told about it, but without his customary hyperbole. The country itself proved a spectacle more impressive than any accomplishment by men, it appears, for his next dispatch, written at railhead, held an uncharacteristic note of something approaching awe:

The Platte Valley is on a rampage today. The Rocky Mountains are clad in snowy white in honor of the great editorial excursion. We have seen Casement and Clayton lay a mile of track in two hours, and two hundred editorial note books have chronicled the fact. We are now setting on rocks in a deep canal [a puzzling word; he may have meant canyon] on the pine bluffs and Corbut is photographing the party, A more picturesque scene could not be taken. Fifty excursionists are standing on the largest rocks—say three hundred feet—along the track, overlooking the excursion train.

But man's works were not insignificant either. The writing of the dispatch was interrupted just at this point by a telegraphic message from Mrs. Train in New York City, saying that she would be in Omaha on the following Saturday. Train included that in his story, too. "New York to the Rocky Mountains in three minutes!"

The big country was shrinking, time and distance being annihilated by the march of science and the iron rail; an awesome thing to contemplate, surely. But George Francis Train was not the type to remain awed for long. Commercial opportunity and the Credit Foncier were matters too close to his heart, too pressing. Rather lightly he dismissed an open-air meeting at end of track with Governor Jayne in the chair and speeches by "Mr. Cowles of the Chicago *Tribune* and Mr. Waterman of the Cleveland *Leader*," and responses by himself acting as proxy for Samuel Reed and General Casement.

The excursion proper turned back for Omaha from here. But a small party went on to Cheyenne, then just thirty-three miles beyond end of track and already a fast-growing town impatient to greet the rails. Evidently there was a further expedition up past Sherman Summit, too, for Train later shepherded the rear guard of the excursion homeward with a splendid new idea buzzing in his brain. He told of it in a ringing promotional panegyric sent on ahead to shout aloud from the columns of the *Weekly Herald* of October 24:

The Credit Foncier of America have selected one thousand acres of hill, valley, bluff and cannon [canyon] around the celebrated Laramie Springs, the purest water of the mountains, for the new Saratoga of America. An American watering place in the Rocky Mountains will be the aristocratic sensation of 1868. When Saratoga and Newport became the Sodom and Gomorrah of America, a change was needed. My long thought of plan is maturing.

The name of this watering place, he said, was Wyoming, situated seven thousand feet above Omaha and a thousand above Cheyenne, only a quarter of a mile from the railroad and "the only place where a train can stop on the steep grade." He spoke of the splendid trout streams and the mountain scenery, and then wound up and let fly with a burst of pure pitchman's poesy:

Sick people are not known here; a few went out to start a graveyard and got well; old men receive their youth; wounds and bruises heal like magic. Your enterprise demands that you should be first informed of this magnificent speculation. . . . Dr. Foster of Clifton Springs Water-Cure, New York, will find correspondents there. Thousands of his invalids will pick out mountain springs, will join the European patient. . . . In a canon near the spring a splendid hotel will be erected for the tourist. . . . The Belmonts, the Vanderbilts, the Durants and Drexells will set the example. The American shooting box in the Rockies will be the great sensation. . . . Many of the wealthiest men of our nation are with me in establishing the Rocky Mountain watering place of Wyoming.

Thus went the opening gun in a rolling barrage of railroad land promotion that would echo and re-echo throughout the Eastern states and on across the Atlantic to the crowded old nations of Europe for the remainder of the nineteenth century and far on into the twentieth. The Pacific Railroad was bringing many things along in its dusty wake; the dream of Utopian profit was running a little too fast perhaps. It was a shimmering magic-lantern fantasy distorted by its very brightness, but the shape of things to come all the same. Sun Valley, Jackson Hole and dude ranches by the score would be delayed a bit, but they would be along. The George Francis Trains had their part, too, in empire's westward march.

So the second remarkable excursion on the great Pacific Railroad passed into history. As with the first one, the Union Pacific had left nothing undone to make it a memorable experience for its guests. Newspapers from as far away as London and Belgium had been represented in the party, but the great majority of the editors were from small-town journals all over Illinois and Indiana, giving the affair a kind of homey, grass-roots touch which the more pretentious junket of '66 had lacked. As a result of it the farmer, the mechanic and laboring man, the small businessman and storekeeper of mid-America would get a fresh and intimate look at the West and the transcontinental railroad building across it such as they never had had before. The effects would be incalculable, but over the long haul quite considerable.

CHAPTER 19

SIERRA SUMMIT

In the eastern Sierra foothills between the grim mountain ramparts and the plain that flattened out toward the Nevada line, the valley of the upper Truckee River was a land of lush green meadows and great forests of ponderosa pine, cathedral-like in their lofty hush and spacious vistas. Pioneers coming west on the California Trail long had found a pleasant oasis here, in which to rest and regain strength between the barren hardship of the Nevada desert and the bitter Sierra haul. The men of the Central Pacific's labor gangs, fresh from battling icy blizzards and near-impossible roads with their three locomotives, forty cars and tons of rails and ironwork, found it a welcome respite also. But '67 had begun now. Time was of the essence, and Charley Crocker gave them precious little rest.

The survey line ran almost due east. The coolie horde turned to on the grade, track-layers right behind them, driving toward Nevada. Then, as spring came on, Crocker hustled the bulk of his Chinese back to the unfinished business in the mountains.

Snowdrifts as deep as sixty feet buried the abandoned grade there. It was impacted too solidly to be bucked by any plow. From below Cisco all the way to the summit, from the summit down to Donner Lake, it had to be shoveled out by hand, each shovelful pitched from man to man through six or seven relays, in places, before it could be dumped clear. The grade, when finally it was uncovered, had settled badly through successive freezes and thaws. Fresh sags had to be filled in, much work done over. The tough granite of Summit Tunnel still broke drills and resisted gunpowder blasts with impassive stubbornness. The Chinese sank their drill holes deeper in spite of the granite's hardness, spaced them more closely, tamped in heavier and heavier powder charges. Slowly but steadily the four headings were chewed out toward their meetings.

Between this operation at the summit and the grading and track work that continued on the eastern slope, 11,000 Chinese, 2,500 whites and 1,000 horse and mule teams labored. Recklessly—for the nearly fruitless Sierra struggle already had devoured money at a gargantuan rate—Crocker went on recruiting more men. The Union Pacific's mile-a-day drive across Nebraska in '66 had been noted in Sacramento; with no joy, certainly, but without any inclination to surrender the Central's own ambitions either.

The company had anticipated Collis Huntington's 1866 success in Congress by pushing out beyond the original surveys south of Great Salt Lake. Some difficulties with the terrain had been encountered in that region and Engineer Butler Ives had been instructed specifically to explore for a possible alternate route to the north of the lake. Now, this spring of '67, another party under Butler Ives was pushing reconnaissances even farther eastward: through Weber and Echo Canyons in the Wasatch Range and on to Fort Bridger on the eastern slope of the Continental Divide. This was territory the Union Pacific regarded as its own, the same through which Grenville Dodge would travel with General Rawlins later in the summer, and other advance surveys of the U.P. had examined it even earlier. So Ives's presence there was a defiant challenge. The rivals were beginning to spar at close range.

Advance surveys and rough maps, though, were not rails. Both companies were bluffing, in effect. The race still was wide-open. But still the stubborn Sierra stood in Charley Crocker's way.

Impatient in his driving determination to show progress, he laid rails from Cisco up to the mouth of the western heading of Summit Tunnel, ordering ties dropped on the bare grade, not bothering to ballast. The construction crews on the upper Truckee were grading and laying rails rapidly now, working both eastward and westward simultaneously. But summer was moving along; soon the best part of '67 would be gone, almost another full year used up in the conquest of the implacable Sierras. And the job was not yet done. A sizable gap on the eastern slope remained without grade or rails. What another winter's snows would do to the track so hastily laid up from Cisco was anybody's guess—and nobody's guess dared be very reassuring after what had gone before.

For the gentlemen of the board of directors there was perhaps a wistful sort of comfort to be taken in the fact that no one in California questioned the legitimacy of the Dutch Flat and Donner Lake route any longer. For almost the first time in its short life, the Central Pacific was winning friends and popular support in its home state. The few who would lose by the railroad's completion—the town of Placerville, the stage and wagon freight operators—still were opposed, but the violence was going out of their efforts.

Resentment stirred up over the importation of Chinese labor lingered among special-interest groups, and those who doubted on general principles remained loudly vocal. But plain Californians in general were heartily in favor of the Pacific Railroad—as they always had been, really, under all the noisy furor of hostility—and now began to grow openly optimistic and even enthusiastic as the road went forward despite all the predictions of its imminent doom.

Years later Collis Huntington answered hecklers who questioned the Associates' motives with the statement that: "California was full of people that wanted to come East, including women and children. That point had its weight with us. It is very well to sneer at that, as people of small minds will; but it had its influence on us, and a very large influence." The words have a certain dubious ring of self-righteousness, perhaps, but the situation of which he spoke was very real.[1]

"We talked railroad, we dreamed railroad, we lived railroad," a pioneer woman who had come west by wagon train remembered long afterward.[2]

Late in June trouble cropped up briefly as the long-suffering Chinese laborers rebelled at last, laid down picks and shovels and brought work in the Sierra tunnels to an abrupt halt. They demanded forty dollars a month wages instead of the thirty they were then getting, and in addition asked for a reduction of the workday to ten hours in the open and eight in the tunnels. There was nothing unreasonable in this. By the company's own policy, tunnel shifts were not supposed to exceed eight hours anyway (though the rule apparently had not been observed very strictly!). But Charley Crocker angrily laid the trouble to paid agitators working for the Union Pacific. Throughout the period of construction, in fact, both companies seem to have been inordinately suspicious of one another, even to the point of adopting various elaborate codes for their telegraphic communications between New York and Sacramento and the two railheads. In this present instance, however, a brief story in the Sacramento *Union* of July 3 hinted at grimmer reasons for the Central Pacific's difficulties.

The Chinese, said the *Union,* "denied the right of the overseers of the company to either whip them or restrain them from leaving the road when they desired to seek other employment."

Regardless, Crocker refused to compromise. He stopped all shipments of the special Chinese provisions, ordered that no more pigs or chickens be butchered for their benefit and issued an ultimatum. The coolies could return to work by a given day with his promise that no punitive measures would be taken against them; otherwise they would be fined the cost of keeping their foremen and draft animals idle for as long as the strike lasted.

Friendless in an alien and hostile land, the Chinese capitulated. Presumably Charley Crocker kept his word, for they never struck again.

There were encouraging developments as summer went on. The shrinking Overland Stage, accepting the inevitable here in the Far West as it had in Nebraska, now operated a regular service between Cisco and Virginia City. Already the railroad had changed the pattern of transportation in northern California and its connections eastward. Even the Associates' Dutch Flat wagon road had fallen into the discard as the rails moved forward. It never paid its costs, and finally was presented as a goodwill gesture to the counties through which it passed. Rail traffic between Sacramento and Cisco was heavy. The company's annual operating receipts would push close to a million and a half dollars by the time the books were closed on '67.

But C. Crocker and Company was through, worn-out and flat on its back. Crocker's own spirit still was willing, the flesh too for that matter; but the company was out of money and its credit was all used up.

Repeated efforts had been made to bring outside capital into the firm, without success. The problem, of course, was not Crocker's alone. Not since '63, at least, had C. Crocker and Company been an actual independent entity, and for months the Associates had been thinking in terms of some new corporate device to bring fresh funds into the project. All the federal government subsidies, the California state and county bonds, the proceeds of the mortgaged grade for a hundred miles ahead of construction, had been spent. But now, with the great hurdle of the Sierra passage nearly surmounted, the time seemed propitious.

Collis Huntington talked matters over with some of his moneyed contacts in New York: the Garrisons, father and son, shipping magnates; wealthy merchant-financiers Moses Taylor and William E. Dodge. He had talked to all of them before, times without number, persistently, persuasively, and only Dodge had helped. Not a man of them had been willing to buy Central Pacific stock, for the reason, among others, that they objected to going into an unlimited partnership. But this time William K. Garrison suggested that if Huntington and his colleagues would organize a new company, by which means investors would know the extent of their liabilities, he thought he could get the Commodore, his father, to go into it.

The upshot was the Contract and Finance Company, organized late in October as a typical construction agency of the period, very much on the same lines as the Union Pacific's Credit Mobilier. As Leland Stanford testified before the Pacific Railway Commission, years later and a little wistfully: "We thought that by forming the Contract and Finance Company and agreeing to give it the stock of the [Central Pacific] company, that company might be able to interest capital. Of course this was practically giving the contractors all the assets of the company, but it was better for us to do that than to fail."

What followed bore a rueful resemblance to the hopeful days of '63, complete even to the disappointments that ensued. Again the mining and shipping wealth of San Francisco was solicited. Leland Stanford spent hours and days closeted with men like W. C. Ralston, Lloyd Tevis, Edward Barron, Michael Reese. Again Darius Ogden Mills, whose Bank of California flourished in wealth and power now, owning or controlling every important mine, smelter and stamping mill in Virginia City on the Comstock, was approached. Strangely, for a financier of his era, Mills was not railroad-minded, and it is one of history's ironies that within a very few years a connection between the Comstock and the Central Pacific's main line, undertaken by one of his Bank of California underlings against his better judgment, would grow into the storied Virginia and Truckee, most fabulous bonanza railroad of them all. This fall of '67 he could see no future in the struggling Central Pacific, and bluntly said so.

In California financial circles, Darius O. Mills was the bellwether. If he would not go in, neither would anyone else. Lloyd Tevis, president of Wells Fargo and Company, stated the prevailing sentiment. The Contract and Finance Company, said he (this too in the form of subsequent testimony before the Pacific Railway Commission), "was liable to great embarrassment and I very much doubted their ability to carry out their contracts."

So opportunity knocked a last time for the nabobs of San Francisco, and went unheeded.

It was not heeded in New York either, though there it was a somewhat nearer thing. The younger Garrison tried hard to make good on his inferred promise to Huntington, and came very close to convincing his father. In the end though, the Commodore, with an old man's crotchety conservatism, decided he did not like the proposition after all; it was too large an undertaking, the times too uncertain.

The result: the Associates were on their own as before. To quit now was unthinkable; they were far too deeply committed for that. Going ahead might mean failure in the end, but it was the better risk. The Associates—now five in number, including Crocker's brother Edwin, who had come in as the Central Pacific's attorney—strained their individual resources somewhat farther and took over the Contract and Finance Company themselves. Where the money came from was a matter of some curiosity among observers at the time, and it remained so. Charley Crocker, for one, had been protesting for quite a while that his credit already was gone. Edwin Crocker, long a successful Sacramento lawyer and politician, was a man of considerable means, and so, of course, was Leland Stanford. The hardware firm of Huntington and Hopkins had grown and prospered steadily throughout the early years of Central Pacific construction; no doubt it was able to stand this fresh strain on its credit. There were doubters all the same, and the doubts would one day grow to become a *cause célèbre*.

But for the present the financing was managed successfully, and the new company obligated itself to build the remainder of the Central Pacific Railroad, from the California line to Great Salt Lake, at a cost of $43,000 per mile in cash and an equal sum in Central stock. The arrangement meant, actually, that the stock did not have to change hands at all and the cash was in effect paid by the Associates to themselves, though of course it had to be raised somehow to begin with.

The affair was entered into with some misgivings, it seems, at least by cautious Mark Hopkins, who telegraphed his partner in New York City, to break the bad news from California and ask how much of the new stock the firm of Huntington and Hopkins ought to take. Huntington's reply was terse and characteristic:

"Take as little as you can and as much as you must."[3]

In the end, it appears, each of the five Associates subscribed for equal shares in the Contract and Finance Company, making it a closed corporation and heightening the similarity to the Union Pacific's Credit Mobilier. Why no effort was made to open the books for public subscriptions, especially in view of the changing popular attitude toward the railroad in California, was never definitely explained. Later, Leland Stanford dismissed questions on that score with the statement that "It would have been of no use." After all the scheming and planning, therefore, nothing was really changed, the outward appearance of the Central Pacific least of all. Charley Crocker remained in charge of construction, and the work went on, unslackened.

In August the Summit Tunnel headings had met at last, though it was the end of November before the job was finished and rails could be laid through to the east end, finally breaching the Sierra crest. A celebration was called for: the inevitable excursion. They had been few and far between on the Central Pacific lately, and this one was not all it might have been, as things turned out.

It began impressively enough. The double-headed locomotives *Idaho* and *Tamaroo* pulled out of the Sacramento depot early on the morning of Saturday, December 7, with ten passenger cars painted in the Central's bright yellow and crowded with various state legislators and officials, the members of a society known as the Sacramento Pioneers, and their collective ladies. There was a flatcar besides, its purpose not specified, and two baggage cars, one fitted out as a temporary diner, the other as a bar. Altogether the guest list ran to more than seven hundred, including the ubiquitous Sacramento *Union* reporter to write the proceedings up in the next issue. He soon found more to write of than had been anticipated.

At Emigrant Gap a jerky start ripped the platform completely off of one of the passenger cars and there was some delay while a new car was substituted. At Summit a thick snow was falling, quite obliterating the expected scenic view of Donner Lake. But the undismayed guests, in a mood for fun, put on an informal snowball fight of their own, "much to the demoralization of high-crowned hats and immaculate shirt fronts," the man from the *Union* commented. Luncheon was served, and afterward several of the male guests ventured on a walk down the grade to inspect the tunnels on the eastern slope. At three in the afternoon the locomotive *Yuba* was backed into Summit Tunnel and coupled up for the return trip to Sacramento. Hardly had the train started, however, than it ground to a stop again, someone having pulled the coupler pin. Then for some fifteen minutes the crowded cars lay stranded in the tunnel, the passengers almost suffocated by smoke and on the verge of panic. Finally the *Yuba* was coupled up again and another start made. This time all went well until a passenger by the name of A. P. Smith raised a cry that his gold watch and chain were missing. Several others voiced the immediate suspicion that the mishap in the tunnel had deliberately been plotted by pickpockets, and in the ensuing search two men were found to have boarded the train, uninvited, at Cisco on the trip up. Smith's watch was not found on either man, but the conductor promptly stopped the train and both suspects were summarily ejected into the snowstorm, miles from any station.

More mishaps followed. At Yuba Pass the fireman, crawling out along the running board to oil the cylinder valves (a regular and necessary part of his duties in those days, and the reason firemen were known as "tallow pots" till the end of the steam locomotive's era), missed his footing and fell off. Fortunately the deep snow along the track saved him from injury, and, the engineer having whistled for brakes, he was eventually able to climb back into the cab. But at Colfax another rough start tore away the front platform of the last car in the train, and there was once again a delay while the damaged car was turned on the turntable so that its sound end could be coupled up. It was late that night before the excursionists finally rolled into Sacramento, utterly weary but on the whole pleased with the day's experiences, wrote the *Union* reporter, "except the ladies, who were much fatigued."

End of track crossed the state line on December 13, and the first Central Pacific construction train steamed into Nevada. It was a victory roughly comparable to the Union Pacific's attainment of the one hundredth meridian more than a year earlier, and it made hollow Dr. Durant's boast of building to the California line. But this occasion was allowed to pass without a celebration.

The grading and track gangs working westward had struggled up the eastern Sierra slope to within about two miles of the summit before snow stopped the work at that end. The record for '67 was some forty-seven miles of track laid down.

It was not yet a continuous railroad, however, for a gap of seven miles remained near Donner Lake. The surveyed line plunged in a steep descent of 116 feet to the mile here, over terrain so broken and cut up that even the work mules could barely keep their footing. This was a potentially serious setback, though Samuel Montague and Colonel Gray, who still served the company as consulting engineer, were sure the line could be shifted slightly and the difficulty overcome. But they calculated that the added cost might be considerable. They were told to go ahead; what other possible decision was there? Meanwhile, freight and passengers were transferred from the summit by stage and wagon, and revenue service was inaugurated over the new rails into Nevada.

But everyone was aware that the winter's first snowfalls heralded fresh troubles. Theodore Judah had predicted that snow would be no problem, that it would slide off harmlessly and leave only a minimum of plowing to be done. But those old reports of Judah's, if anybody remembered them now, were like fond memories of some golden time before reality had intruded on the dream. The snow would not slide off, and no plows known to railroad practice could handle it. Crocker, Strobridge and the engineers had been very concerned with the problem, and there had been much discussion of it by the board this summer. It was hoped that perhaps an answer had been worked out.

Who thought of it first is not certain. Probably no one man; the idea may have been born during the winter of 1866-67, when work in the tunnels had proceeded without serious interruption in spite of the drifted snows above. The solution was simple enough in concept. It might be a mammoth task in the doing, though.

What it amounted to was the construction of snowsheds or galleries: a series of timber tunnels covering the right of way, anchored firmly to the mountain rock itself, built with sharply sloped roofs to shed the crushing weight of slides. Experimental structures already were under way, started during the summer with Arthur Brown, superintendent of bridges and buildings, in charge. Such snowsheds were not precisely a new idea, though nothing like them had so far been tried on any American railroad; not, at least, on anything approaching the scale the Central Pacific was likely to find necessary. The bad snow section comprised about forty miles, and it was conceivable that all of it might have to be covered. The cost? No one could say with any accuracy; a million dollars, perhaps much more. But for Charley

Crocker as '67 ended, iron running eastward was the driving need. Too much time had been lost already. The Union Pacific had come on too fast.

In the summing up, it had been a year of plain, dull drudgery. The Central Pacific had fought no Indian wars, coped with no gaudy terminal-town sin, set no records to match the deeds of General Jack Casement's Irish bullies and fetch the journalists flocking to titillate the folks back home with tales of empire in the making. There had been no buffalo where Crocker's coolies strove; no high Army brass had journeyed westward out of Washington to invest the Central Pacific with an aura of patriotic *hip-hip-hurrah!* The Union Pacific was the Cinderella girl of '67, the Central only a drab slavey.

So much for the year that was past. The future was hardly likely to be worse. All summer, iron and track supplies had poured up from the Sacramento levee and over the Sierra hump. Looking ahead from the Truckee River, Charley Crocker saw the high plain of Nevada stretching to the horizon. Desert country, most of it, rock-ribbed, barren and inhospitable, offering no welcome. But it was blessedly flat, and there would be little snow out there. After the Sierra summit, those were two features infinitely to be appreciated. Casting his thoughts still farther eastward, Crocker set his jaw and wrapped up promise, hope and challenge in a single gruff declaration of intent.

The Central Pacific, he announced publicly, would lay a mile of track every working day in '68.

CHAPTER 20

CHEYENNE

The Union Pacific had one last act to play out before the curtain fell on a most eventful year.

Cheyenne, restless in its awareness of ripening destiny, counted off the first week of November and most of the second while it waited for smoke to bloom on the dusty gray plain eastward and herald the railroad's coming. On the thirteenth the Casements' headquarters train steamed in, preceded by its advance guard of lorry cars, clanking iron and shoulder-swinging track gangs. There was a depot already erected, and an enthusiastic escort of citizens trooped out along the grade and back again, watching in admiration till the grinning Irishmen hammered home the final spikes in the final tie, straightened up and knocked off for the day, exactly 516.4 miles west of Omaha.

The first passenger train from the East arrived the following evening. Aboard it, among others, was Sidney Dillon, president of the Credit Mobilier. He found more than he had expected, probably: a population bumping four thousand, practically all of it milling in high festival spirits around the depot; a city hall and a main thoroughfare, Eddy Street, strung with bunting and brilliantly illuminated with torches and kerosene lamps; and a welcoming committee prepared to do the honors. There was a speakers' stand adorned with a large lighted transparency which bore the mottoes: "THE MAGIC CITY GREETS THE CONTINENTAL RAILWAY"; "HONOR TO WHOM HONOR IS DUE"; and "OLD CASEMENT, WE WELCOME YOU." This last, the Cheyenne *Leader* took pains to point out in its next issue, "if relating to the General's years, is certainly a misrepresentation; but if to the accomplishments of a life time, few men have ever done so much."

One E. Brown, the paper also reported, acted as chairman in the absence of Mayor William Hook, and a Judge Miller presented the resolutions of the welcoming committee, "which were unanimously adopted."

The town, very much a going concern, had its Common Council, civic law of a sort, saloons to the number of at least a hundred, a pair of two-story hotels already building—one of them another joint enterprise of that go-getting prairie Midas, George Francis Train, and an associate named West Point Cozzens—and a brass band to serenade the railroaders. All this on the barren flatland in the bend of Crow Creek where Grenville Dodge had found only a rude trader's cabin just five months before. Raw lumber for building had been freighted up from Denver, and large contingents of that city's madams, gamblers, toughs and legitimate businessmen who had not pulled out earlier for Julesburg had seen the light later and rolled into Cheyenne aboard the Concords of the shrinking Overland Stage. And more kept coming, many representing fleshpots the railroad thought it had left behind.

Scarcely had Dillon and Casement concluded the Union Pacific's formal acknowledgment of the official welcome, some who were present told later, than a long freight pulled in; mostly flatcars loaded high with lumber from knocked-down buildings, furled tents, furnishings and all the other paraphernalia of establishments of business and pleasure hastily disassembled for a move. A brakeman swung down off the slowing cars with an ear-to-ear grin, swept off his hat in a flourish to the crowd that still milled about the depot and announced loudly: "Gentlemen, here's Julesburg!"

Since Cheyenne would be the railroad's winter base and staging center for the Black Hills drive, Casement held his outfit there for a week, putting in switches and sidings while he waited for supplies to accumulate from Omaha. Then, with November two-thirds gone and the year running out fast, he led his rail gangs out for the final sally. Sherman Summit was thirty-two miles away and something over two thousand feet up. Twenty miles farther, over the crest and down the western slope, was Fort Sanders.

They did not make it.

Winter caught them amid the curves and rocky bosses ten miles short of the summit, eight thousand feet above sea level. At that altitude, higher even than Charley Crocker's men had had to carry Central Pacific iron in the Sierras, steely cloud banks rolled down over the sculptured bleakness of the hills and the wind flowed in a scourging, numbing cold that glazed rails with sleet and laid a frozen rime of snow over the grade. Reluctantly the little general surrendered to the elements, pulled his headquarters cars back to Cheyenne and turned his weary Irishmen loose for a winter on the town.

The failure was not of their own making. Delays arising out of the dispute over Silas Seymour's relocation of the survey line, which came to a head during these last weeks of fall, had held up the work, as Grenville Dodge pointed out in a bitterly angry report dispatched to New York on January 1 of the new year.

So '67 ended, after all, on an unfortunate note of frustration and ill will. Actual accomplishments had been impressive: 240 miles of track laid; regular railroad service pushed the full width of the Great Plains; the Black Hills ascent well begun. All this was a long step forward and a worthy year's work under any ordinary circumstances. But now it was tarnished by the stigma of failure. Fort Sanders was the announced goal, and Fort Sanders had not been achieved.

Net earnings from the year's revenue operations aggregated a good round $2,061,000. Much of it had come from the hauling at reduced rates of men and materials for the contractors. Even so, it was estimated that income from purely commercial traffic came to about four times the cost of operations, an encouraging sign of the rapidity with which Nebraska was being settled. In the nation at large there seemed to be a growing appreciation of the potential of this new West. This same year an article in *Harper's Weekly* had predicted that "The demands of trade will call for a second track, to be used exclusively as a freight road, over which an endless line of slowly-moving vans shall continuously pass, leaving the other track for the use of impatient passengers only."

Inflated war and postwar costs were slowly coming back into line also. By the close of '67 the price of rails averaged $97.50 a ton, delivered at Omaha, as compared with a peak figure of $135 a ton. The Union Pacific owned a roster of fifty-three locomotives, nine first-class passenger cars, four second-class passenger cars and more than eight hundred freight cars. The government commissioners, industriously pursuing railhead in the armored Lincoln car, had inspected the completed railroad to within a few miles of Cheyenne and filed their official recommendation for acceptance by the government board.

This was all excellent. To the casual eye, the Union Pacific appeared to be doing better than well. And in New York the impression was heightened by the lavishness of the company's offices, probably the finest in the city, according to admiring visitors, who commented on the classical paintings and statuary and the singing of caged birds which lightened the fusty atmosphere of business. This was Thomas Durant's doing; the vice-president still was the generalissimo in charge, though Oliver Ames occupied the president's chair. But if love of luxury was among Durant's failings, the weakness of self-deception was not. He had at hand the reports of the advance surveys westward from the Black Hills, and reports, too, from his agents in California. This winter, he perceived, was a time for sober stock-taking, for the marshaling of strength and the laying of plans for the last, driving run for the finish.

And in so doing, Charley Crocker's challenge from the banks of the Truckee was not to be underestimated.

PART THREE

The Racing Iron;
a Scrambling of Titans

CHAPTER 21

MOSTLY BRIGHAM YOUNG

The situation as 1868 began was one to put an edge on both companies' efforts. From the Central Pacific railhead at Camp 24, squatting on the California-Nevada border, it was some six hundred miles, in round figures, to the center of the Mormon community on the eastern shore of Great Salt Lake. From Sherman Summit the Union Pacific had roughly five hundred to go. But Charley Crocker, in coming down out of the Sierras and through the winding canyon of the Truckee River, had put the worst of his going behind him. Dodge, the Casements and Samuel Reed, on the other hand, had said good-bye to the long, easy miles across the Nebraska plains. The bulk of their mountain work lay ahead, still complicated by incomplete surveys and hampered by Indian hostility. It seemed a standoff; if mileage favored the Union Pacific, the terrain appeared to be on the Central's side.

Neither publicly nor privately was either company disposed as yet to accept a meeting at Great Salt Lake, or for that matter anywhere else. For every mile gained by the one over the other, $32,000 in government subsidy bonds and a like amount in private company issues comprised a reward worth fighting for, with land-grant acreage of unknown potential value in addition. But over and above that, circumstances gave the thriving agrarian stronghold of the Mormons a strategic significance of which both sides were very acutely aware. As the only large and important settlement on the transcontinental route between the Missouri River and California it was a considerable prize in its own right.

True, there were the Comstock and other mineral lodes in Nevada, a state still seething in the fevered prosperity of mining boom. But if the Central Pacific Associates ever had contemplated stopping short with a railhead at bonanza, as their enemies had claimed so vehemently and even

Theodore Judah had suspected, the time for that was now long past. Bonanza, which inevitably changed sooner or later to borasca, was no real foundation on which to build a transcontinental railroad. The Union Pacific, too, had had its opportunity to digress for the gold of Denver City, and rejected it.

So Great Salt Lake was left as the decisive way station on the Pacific Railroad route. The company which got there first and then struck out beyond to cut the other off would control the trade between East and West, the globe-spanning commerce between Orient and Occident and back again.

There were problems, though. The Mormons—more properly the Latter-day Saints of Jesus Christ, as they called themselves—were not ordinary settlers; and their president, Brigham Young, was no ordinary man. East and West alike, the public at large knew very little about the Latter-day Saints, and understood even less of what they knew. Savage persecution had driven these people into their remote Western isolation to begin with, and left them justifiably suspicious of contact with the rest of the nation for more than two decades afterward.

"Give us ten years of peace and we will ask no odds of the United States," Brigham Young had declared in '47. And by the time the ten years were up the nation had seen him come uncomfortably close to demonstrating that his defiance had real teeth in it. Throughout the '50's the rising tide of westward emigration and the advance of the Army posts which protected it had provided irritants that kept the old hostilities alive. There had been ill will and provocation on both sides: disputes, Gentile outposts burned, men killed. In '57 and '58 outright war with the United States had threatened, the Mormons mobilizing to harass invading Army columns led first by General William S. Harney and then by Colonel Albert Sidney Johnston till a precarious peace was arranged by U.S. Territorial Governor Alfred Cumming. By its terms the Mormons had accepted Cumming's governmental status (though Brigham Young remained the real ruler in Utah) and agreed, grudgingly, to the stationing of permanent Army detachments in the territory.

In the years that followed, inevitably growing contact with the East had broken down the old isolation to a very considerable degree. The Pony Express, the Overland Telegraph and the Overland Stage all had helped. A steady influx of new converts, many of them from England and various European countries, had helped still more. A large percentage of these newcomers were artisans and tradesmen rather than farmers. Their presence forced a slow but inexorable swing away from the old, purely agrarian economy, and this in turn began to generate the need for increasing contact and commerce with the rest of the nation.

Brigham Young, a statesman of real vision, had favored the Pacific Railroad from the beginning. He had been among the original subscribers for Union Pacific stock following passage of the Act of '62, taking five shares. He had telegraphed his good wishes on the occasion of the ground-breaking at Omaha in '63, and was said to have silenced the misgivings of certain Mormon elders with the brusque remark that a religion which could not stand contact with the rest of the world was a religion not worth protecting.

Grenville Dodge had laid the foundation for mutual friendship and respect between Union Pacific men and the Mormon people during his early Western reconnaissances for Farnum and Durant and his subsequent tenure as an Army commander in the West. Construction Superintendent Samuel Reed, a genial and personable man, had been in Salt Lake City many times in the course of preliminary Union Pacific survey work, and he too had made friends and established an atmosphere of marked cordiality.

In all this the Union Pacific held an advantage over its eastward-coming rival. By comparison, the Central—enmeshed in early difficulties in California and Nevada and slow to push its surveys to Great Salt Lake—appears to have been singularly negligent about impressing its identity on the Mormon awareness.

But even for the Union Pacific there were potential pitfalls. In the spring of '67 Colonel Alexander McClure, Republican political leader in Pennsylvania and founding publisher of the Philadelphia *Times,* had made a trip west (he was not overly impressed by his ride over the U.P. rails, incidentally) and reported Brigham Young of two minds about the railroad's coming, his mood wavering between anticipation of the material benefits it would bring and latent doubts about the possibly unfortunate consequences to himself. McClure was an astute political observer, and probably read the signs correctly. "The day the iron horse first sang his song in the valley of Utah," he wrote later, "dated the decline and fall of the Mormon ruler."[1]

Young, a man of iron will and aggressive personal convictions, was one who took careful handling, always. Thus the Pacific Railroad was walking a pretty thin line in Utah Territory. Any misstep could be serious indeed for the company making it. And for the Union Pacific, Grenville Dodge's report in January of 1868, summing up the findings of the preceding year's survey activities, seemed to presage the worst kind of misstep. The projected route around the south end of Great Salt Lake and thence across the desert to Humboldt Wells in Nevada, the chief engineer indicated, was impracticable by reason of the rough terrain. Conversely, a line swinging northward around the lake worked out much more favorably. From an engineering standpoint, only one recommendation was possible.

The trouble was that such a northerly line cut Salt Lake City off the transcontinental route. And Salt Lake City, it had been tacitly accepted by everyone concerned, was an essential point on the line. It was the territorial capital, Utah's largest urban center by far; the center, too, of Mormon sentiment and activity favorable to the railroad. By-passing the city at this late date in favor of Ogden, thirty miles north, would be construed as bad faith. Worse, it certainly would be taken as an intolerable affront by Brigham Young, whose reaction was all too predictable—and not pleasant to contemplate.

In New York City, whither Dodge was summoned for a series of conferences with company officials and department heads as '68 began, there was consternation but no ready solution. Figures were figures; a surveyed line might in some cases be subject to compromise, but apparently not in this instance; not where Grenville Dodge and his rugged engineer's integrity were involved. The U.P. board was reluctant to accept his recommendation but equally afraid not to. Dodge, with the opinion of his entire engineering staff squarely behind him, stood his ground. The question was finally referred to the government directors, just as the earlier contretemps over the Denver City route had been.

The government men backed Dodge, as indeed they had to do, for there was no alternative. The company's map showing the northerly line was duly filed with the Department of the Interior. The matter then was officially beyond compromise, even had compromise been possible.

Understandably, however, it was deemed advisable to withhold the news from Brigham Young as long as possible, pending some indication of what the Central Pacific had in mind. Both companies went to great lengths to avoid revealing their plans and survey lines to one another, but field engineers on both sides had been meeting and mingling with their opposite numbers in and around Salt Lake City for many months past. Ives's and Epler's activities during '67 had been apparent to U.P. observers, so it was no secret that the Central, too, had investigated routes both north and south of the big lake.

The Central Pacific people were slow in filing their map, not doing so till almost the end of January, and it was some undetermined time after that before Union Pacific officials were sure of the route it indicated. When they found out, though, the information came as a vast relief. The Central Pacific engineers were not magicians either; they too had settled for the northerly line.

Still it appears that no one broke the news to Brigham Young for a while. Late in May Samuel Reed negotiated a contract with the Saint himself for grading and tunnel work from the head of Echo Canyon in the Wasatch all the way to Ogden. And before June was a week old, Leland Stanford came hurrying into Salt Lake City by stagecoach, bent on hiring Mormon labor for the Central Pacific's Utah grades. He was a little late to obtain Young's personal services; was received, in fact, with politeness but a marked lack of warmth. But he did manage to retain the Mormon contracting firm of Benson, Farr and West, who agreed to put in a hundred miles of grade from Monument Point westward. The scramble for advantage in Utah Territory was now on for fair, though both railheads were still long distances away. And Brigham Young, it appears, remained in ignorance of both companies' true intentions.

It is difficult to understand how this could have been so. Monument is the northernmost point on Great Salt Lake. Assuming that Young was aware of the Benson, Farr and West contract—as he must have been before events proceeded much farther—its location alone was an unmistakable clue to the line the Central, at least, had elected to take. Yet precisely how and when the unwelcome facts were made known to him is something of a mystery. Both Dodge and Sidney Dillon of the Union Pacific have been credited with telling him the truth at last. It has been theorized also that Leland Stanford was the one, though contriving in some way to convince the angry Mormon leader that the northerly route was the Union Pacific's doing. The notion of such backstairs intrigue is romantically tempting. But Brigham Young was nobody's fool, and a man normally well informed of everything that went on in Mormon Utah. It would seem much more logical to believe that he found out for himself what was afoot, perhaps directly from Washington or perhaps by a little judicious inquiring on his own. The route of the transcontinental railroad could not, after all, have been a very well-kept secret for long.

His reaction was immediate, and as violent as everyone had feared. Salt Lake City boiled over in indignation. Official protests were dispatched to Washington by both the Utah territorial government and the Mormon Church. To no avail, of course; for the Union Pacific it was Denver all over again, but far worse. For Brigham Young was no mere political leader or elected official. Brigham Young *was* Utah and the Mormon Church, a complete despot whom no one crossed with impunity. At his word—literally as awful among his people as any Papal Bull in a devout Catholic land—not a Latter-day Saint in the territory would lift a finger to help the object of his wrath.

He proceeded to hurl that word like a thunderbolt. Or so Grenville Dodge remembered it later: "Then Brigham Young gave his allegiance and aid to the Central Pacific, hoping to bring them around the south end of the lake and force us to connect with them there."[2]

Young's "allegiance and aid" summed to a very potent amount of help indeed. Previously, he had declared himself ready and able to furnish sufficient labor to grade two hundred miles both east and west from Salt Lake City. There were foodstuffs besides: beef and grain and vegetables from the well-kept Mormon farms; draft animals and the fodder to feed them. All this could be poured out as from the mouth of a vast cornucopia in the midst of arid desert, and the builder who got the benefit of it would be helped on his way immeasurably. The rival who did not would find the drive across Utah long, hard and frustrating.

In June or July, hammering home his overt hint to both railroads, Brigham Young preached a fiery sermon to a crowd of the faithful in the great Tabernacle at Salt Lake City, denouncing Grenville Dodge in the bitterest of personal terms and thundering belligerently that no railroad could be built or operated across Utah without the aid and consent of the Mormon people. It was a good and eloquent try, but in reality a last-ditch one. Neither company showed any disposition to budge from its survey line; an embarrassing denouement for the embattled Saint, who found himself thus bereft of *any* Pacific Railroad to support. So in the end he had no choice but to yield as gracefully as he knew how or stamp himself as an outright obstructionist by fighting both railroads.

"Then," as Grenville Dodge put it drily, "President Young returned to his first love, the Union Pacific, and turned all his forces and aid to that road."[3]

A tolerant and forgiving man was Dodge, willing to stretch the truth a little to let bygones be bygones. For that was not quite the way it was. The Mormon chieftain was not a man used to yielding; his surrender was somewhat less than wholehearted, and his grudge against both companies lasted for over a year, at least. But he was too much the statesman to fall into the error of pushing a lost cause, and far too good a businessman to let personal resentment stand in the way of earning an honest dollar. He made no move to break his grading contract with the Union Pacific, and in fact subsequently took on more of the work, till the total of the U.P.'s obligation to him amounted to more than two million dollars. Neither did he place any obstacles in the way of Benson, Farr and West, whose Central Pacific contracts likewise grew in the months that followed.

And he also began to think in terms of a railroad of his own, to make the best of the situation by connecting Salt Lake City with the transcontinental line at Ogden.

Thus the opening gambits for Great Salt Lake ended reasonably well for all hands. In the final accounting, perhaps the Central Pacific came off best, in that it gained a degree of Mormon aid and recognition it might not have had otherwise. To balance that, the Union Pacific, the "first love," might have lost everything, but did not. Call it a draw, then. Utah was wide-open. The race still would go to the swift.

Regarding that race, and backtracking a little in time, there was much to consider and some critical decisions to be made at the Union Pacific's New York conferences during the early weeks of '68. A major handicap lay in the fact that the bloody Indian warfare of the previous year had cut serious gaps in the advance surveys. The line to the Green River for which Percy Browne had given his life remained incomplete, and such other reverses as the Thomas Bates party's near-disaster had left much reconnaissance work undone. But in partial compensation for these failures, the cost of grading and track-laying for the big year of '67 had proved encouragingly less than expected, and Dodge's preliminary cost estimates for construction across the Dakotah Wyoming were heartening also. The Credit Mobilier had paid its first cash dividend in December, arousing new interest among prospective investors; its board of directors, as a result, were in an optimistic frame of mind for the drive westward from the Black Hills.[4]

The Ames faction was beginning to gain the upper hand on the Credit Mobilier board, though Dr. Durant and his partisans were by no means quiescent. The contractual hocus-pocus of the past had boiled down, at last, to a hard and fast agreement whereby Oakes Ames assumed responsibility for 667 miles of construction westward from that old jumping-off place, the one hundredth meridian, at rates varying between $42,000 and $96,000 per mile, depending on the nature of the terrain and the anticipated difficulties to be overcome. It was a very complete and binding contract, much of it, however, covering grade and track already put in (essentially the same situation Dr. Durant had protested earlier), and a vastly bothersome amount of explaining would have to be done on that score one day. But for the present it had the effect of committing Oakes Ames and every penny of his considerable resources solidly and irrevocably to the completion of the railroad across the Wyoming. In round figures the contract totaled $47,000,000, at the time probably the greatest financial undertaking ever assumed by one man in the nation's history. For by the contract's terms and the manner in which it was negotiated, Ames alone was the titan who shouldered the responsibility for taking Union Pacific stock and bonds and converting them into cash to defray the cost of the work— converting them at face value possibly, or even at a huge profit; but also, perhaps, at a staggering loss. Yet he steadfastly gave the word to go ahead at full speed, regardless of the effort necessary.

So the New York meetings adjourned with Grenville Dodge ordered to have the final location line from Fort Sanders to the Green River ready by June 1;

to Ogden on Great Salt Lake by fall; and in addition to have as much as possible of the survey line west of the lake developed by the year's end. The rails were to follow as far and as fast as Casement Brothers could drive their Paddies. It was urgently desirable that railhead be in Ogden by the earliest practicable date.

If the stint planned for '67 had seemed ambitious, this one for '68 was incredibly so. From Sherman Summit it was three hundred miles to the Green River, and from there to Ogden 180 more. Dr. Durant expressed some mild criticism of Dodge and Samuel Reed because the goal for '67 had not been met, quite overlooking the fact that it was his own man, Silas Seymour, who was to blame. Very definitely, relations between Dodge and Durant were worsening now. Oliver Ames and Sidney Dillon, too, were more than ever determined that the doctor must be ousted from his post as Union Pacific vice-president, or his authority curtailed. But that, plainly, was going to take a bit of doing. All in all, the atmosphere on Nassau Street must have been uncomfortably guarded and chilly. Yet there was agreement on the goals desired, and Dodge made no objections to the schedule set for him in the field. Apparently he thought it could be made. Time was all-important and expense be damned. That too was implicit in his orders.

CHAPTER 22

THE TRUCKEE TO THE HUMBOLDT

A party of engineers under General William Jackson Palmer, who had conducted a preliminary exploration into southern California for a proposed extension of the Kansas Pacific Railroad, traveled homeward on the Central Pacific in February. The chronicler of the group, a Dr. William Bell, told of their train's slow climb to Cisco with a pusher engine laboring at the rear end, and exclaimed over the mountain scenery which he called "Alpine in character."

He also told of leaving the warm cars at Cisco and proceeding by Overland Mail Company sledges "with forty feet of snow underneath" to Donner Lake. There the party again had to transfer, this time to conveyances identified as "mud wagons." The mud, Dr. Bell remarked, was two feet deep. His account makes it plain that this winter of 1867-68 the Central Pacific people had learned their lesson, and were wasting neither time nor manpower in any effort to keep the rails passable between Cisco and the Truckee River trackage. It also suggests, though only barely, the difficulty of this mountain crossing. From the passengers' point of view, the Central Pacific had made little progress in a year of hard work.

Somewhat later in the spring the eminent Charles Loring Brace, churchman and pioneer social welfare worker, journeyed over the same route. He too was impressed by the scenery and commented on the "slow and careful" ascent to Cisco. With the authority of an experienced world traveler, he stated that nowhere else on earth was there anything to compare with this Central Pacific endeavor except the Brenner Pass Railroad in the Austrian Tyrol. But he was greatly awed, also, by what he called the "fearful wilderness" between the Sierras and Great Salt Lake, and summed up his observations on the Central Pacific's prospects in the opinion that, "The cost of the road and the great expense of running it will always be an obstacle to cheap freights or low rates."

He added that, "Men experienced in these matters doubt if they [both Central Pacific and Union Pacific, apparently] ever carry freights of importance from one coast to the other, except the lightest and most valuable."[1]

Obviously, then, many intelligent and thoughtful men still doubted the ultimate value of the transcontinental railroad. None of the manifest difficulties seen by Mr. Brace, however, seem to have made him feel that the road would not be completed. That battle at least had slowly but surely been won.

Slow and sure are the words, too, that best describe Charley Crocker's progress as '68 got under way. It was necessary to divert much of his labor force back to the mountains again, just to keep the sledge and mud wagon route open for the passage of supplies and revenue traffic. There was very little evidence for quite a while that he would make good his mile-a-day dictum. The first of May had come before the rails, crawling along the north bank of the Truckee, drew up across the river from a station known as Lake's Crossing, only fifteen miles inside the Nevada state line.

Nestled in the fertile Truckee Valley between the steep slopes of the Sierra foothills and low, rolling hill country away to the eastward and southward, the place had been a favored camping spot for California-bound emigrants since before the gold rush days of '49. The ill-fated Donner Party had helped to manufacture its own downfall in the fall of '46 by tarrying here too long before attempting the Sierras. Since '59, the year of the great Comstock strike, it had been a way station on the stage road to Virginia City, only some twenty-odd miles to the southeast. A man by the name of M. C. Lake had set up a trading post and built a toll bridge over the river in '63; his claim to the land was valid enough so that the Central Pacific had to negotiate with him for a right of way. The place, according to contemporary wags, had a total population of two men, one woman, three pigs and a cow.

Here Charley Crocker established his first Nevada terminal town. There was some argument over a name for it, many practical spirits speaking up for Argenta, in honor of the most important commodity, Comstock silver, the new town was expected to provide in the way of railroad freight. But others among Crocker's employees were old Mexican War comrades of General Jesse Lee Reno, a fairly obscure Union officer from West Virginia who had been killed at South Mountain during the War Between the States. Just why they thought of suggesting a tribute to him at this particular time and place is not clear. But for some reason the name appealed to Crocker. So Reno it was, and still is.

The town was born officially on May 9, a land agent of the Central Pacific moving in to conduct a public auction of company real estate. The coming of the railroad was a big thing for Washoe County, the value of the place as a

Virginia City connection being obvious, and the event touched off an enthusiasm almost comparable to a brand-new mineral stampede. Twenty-four hours before the bidding was scheduled to begin, eager buyers had converged on Reno in such a horde that they swamped the meager accommodations available at the trading post and overflowed into open-air camps all around the town site. Sales of provisions and blankets dropped a small-sized bonanza all his own into the hands of the enterprising Mr. Lake. The first of the railroad lots to go on the block next morning fetched six hundred dollars, and succeeding ones went even higher as the competition warmed up. A total of two hundred was knocked down before the auctioneer rapped his gavel a last time and shut up shop for the day. Within a week thirty new buildings sprang up. Within a month there were a hundred. The Washoe City *Eastern Slope* moved in, changed its name to the *Evening Crescent* and gave the town its first newspaper. Crocker's men did not linger, of course, but Reno refused to wither. Reno was in business to stay.

For the first time, the Central Pacific was tasting the same heady tonic of boom times born at railhead the Union Pacific had savored in its march across Nebraska.

The grade went eastward, still following the Truckee River but still at no breathtaking pace. Again most of the labor force had to be diverted to the rear to tackle the stubborn Sierras. Again thirty-foot accumulations of snow had to be pitched and scraped away by hand before the sixteen miles of track above Cisco could be uncovered and put in shape for the summer's traffic, while Charley Crocker fumed in impatience and from New York the watchful Collis Huntington telegraphed a warning that "Durant has started for the Pacific Ocean."

But on June 15 the final seven-mile gap below Donner Lake was closed by grade and rail. Once more, for the first time in over a year, the Associates had a continuous railroad line. Now government subsidy bonds on completed trackage could be applied for, and mortgages issued on the grade stretching out into Nevada. Supplies could rumble in an uninterrupted flow up from Sacramento, over the hump and down through the Truckee Valley. The experimental snowshed built last year had stood up well during the winter. Hopefully, the board of directors deemed it worthwhile to go ahead with others, and Arthur Brown mobilized axmen, carpenters and every sawmill in the vicinity of Cisco for the monumental job. Now, too, Crocker had his mountain force available again at full muster; ten thousand Chinese to delve with pick and shovel in the Nevada earth, the Irish track-layers beginning to hit full stride behind them.

Early in July the rails forsook the Truckee River and headed out on a

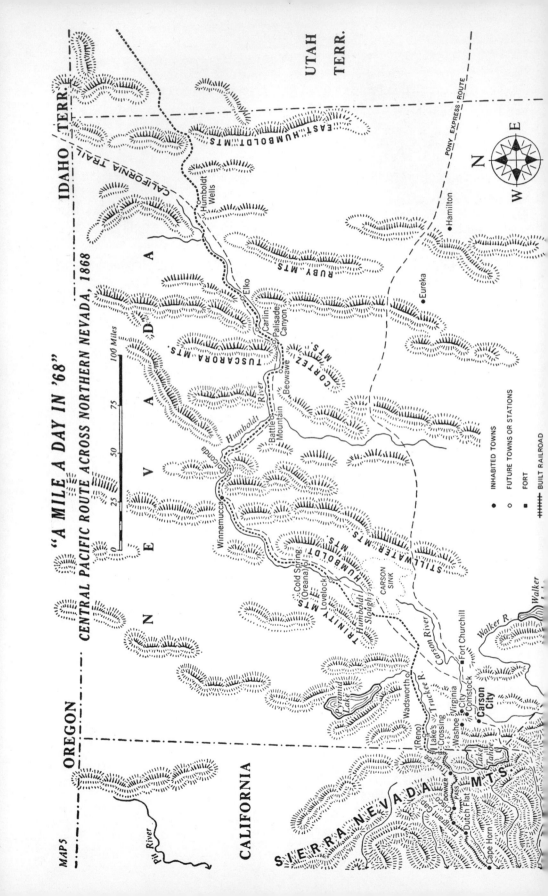

MAP 5

"A MILE A DAY IN '68"

CENTRAL PACIFIC ROUTE ACROSS NORTHERN NEVADA, 1868

OREGON

IDAHO TERR.

UTAH TERR.

N E V A D A

CALIFORNIA

CALIFORNIA TRAIL

PONY EXPRESS ROUTE

EAST HUMBOLDT MTS.

RUBY MTS.

TUSCARORA MTS.

CORTEZ MTS.

STILLWATER MTS.

HUMBOLDT MTS.

TRINITY MTS.

SIERRA NEVADA MTS.

Humboldt Wells

Elko

Carlin

Palisade Canyon

Beowawe

Battle Mountain

Golconda

Humboldt River

Winnemucca

Cold Spring (Oreana)

Lovelock

Humboldt Slough

CARSON SINK

Eureka

Hamilton

Carson River

Fort Churchill

Walker R.

Walker Lake

Walker

Pyramid Lake

Wadsworth

Truckee R.

Lake's Crossing (Reno)

Virginia City

Comstock

Washoe

Carson City

Lake Tahoe

TRUCKEE PASS

DONNER PASS

EMIGRANT GAP

CISCO PASS

Dutch Flat

Cape Horn

Pit River

100 Miles

75 50 25 0

INHABITED TOWNS •

FUTURE TOWNS OR STATIONS ○

FORT ■

BUILT RAILROAD ┼┼┼┼┼

N E W

N

E

S

W

northeasterly tangent across the last of the meadows. On their left rose the squat eight-thousand-foot pile of Virginia Peak with Pyramid Lake beyond and the receding rampart of the Sierras pressing into the sky like a misty blue backdrop. On their right hills rolled in long brown folds up into the Stillwater Range. Ahead there was just shimmering, sun-washed distance.

On the nineteenth of the month end of track poked into Wadsworth, ancient site of a sprawling seasonal village of the nomadic Paiute Indians. Now the place was occupied by another tiny trading post, and by no other permanent work of man. But Charley Crocker designated it a Central Pacific division point; a depot, a water tank, a roundhouse and its appurtenances grew where the Paiutes once had camped. For a brief while the tents of the Chinese host swelled the ancient village to the proportions of a wood and canvas metropolis, and the smoky shufflings of thirty-car supply trains behind double-headed locomotives filled it with clangor and clamor. The Truckee lay a mile behind; the rails had come thirty-five from Reno. The pace was still a great gap short of a mile a day, though it was quickening.

At Wadsworth the construction crew took their last look at trees and growing grass and fertile earth. The work animals cropped the last green forage they would get for many a day. From here on was desert, sere, sun-baked and powder-dry for a hundred northeastward miles to the great bend of the Humboldt River, and then more desert beyond as the location stakes turned in single file eastward through the Humboldt Valley. There would be little else but desert, five hundred miles of it in fact, watered only by scattered, stagnant sinkholes and the scant and undependable Humboldt itself for the whole way across Nevada and western Utah almost to Great Salt Lake. And this was no misnamed grassland like so much of the Great American Desert the Union Pacific had already mastered. This was real, genuine, sand-and-alkali, sagebrush-and-cactus *desert;* parts of it so bad, went the bitter local jest, that "even the jackrabbits carried canteens and haversacks."

The engineers' reports on the advance surveys warned of the difficulties. In all the five hundred miles, the land itself could be counted on for nothing save a few cords of scrub pine and juniper for fuel wood. There was not a coal deposit anywhere on the Central Pacific line. There would be no tree large enough to be sawed into a single plank for building, no stone fit for putting into permanent masonry or foundations, nothing in the way of food for man or work beast. Every tie laid down on the grade would have to be carried from the Sierra forests in the rear, the cost mounting as the distance grew.

But if these problems were new, so too were the forces Charley Crocker led out into the desert this July, and the effort they would make. The change was subtle, not readily apparent. These were the same patient Chinese and hard-bitten Irish, minus the unfortunates disintegrated by nitroglycerin in the Sierra headings or carried away by Sierra snowslides, and the transients who had deserted to chase the will-o'-the-wisp of bonanza. They were all veterans now, skilled in the trades of railroad building and hardened to the work. Having come through the great hardships of the mountains they were not easily to be abashed by other hardships ahead.

Equally as important, in making his cumbersome leap over the Sierra crest and down to the Truckee in the winter of 1866-67, Crocker had done a bit more than transport a giant's load of locomotives, cars, rails and fittings over a virtually impassable barrier. In the process—perhaps not quite realizing it himself—he had begun to shape the kind of task force he needed now. Arduous though the struggle up the western rise of the Sierras had been, the way had led through relatively populous and well-ordered country, with the good base of Sacramento never far behind. Now that was over. In leaving California beyond the Sierra rampart, Crocker faced very much the same two-pronged problem the Union Pacific men had coped with on the Great Plains: a terrain that held nothing of use to him and an ever-lengthening and more difficult supply line through it.

The Casement brothers, railroad builders of long experience, had sized up their situation, made their plans and moved in to get the Union Pacific rolling. Crocker, the amateur, and his indefatigable Jim Strobridge were evolving a very similar effort under the spur of pure necessity.

Two hundred and fifty miles ahead the survey reports promised troublesome going where the Humboldt River plunged between the rugged Cortez Mountains and the Tuscarora Range through Palisade Canyon, and the Central Pacific grade would have to follow. Crocker loaded three thousand Chinese, their white overseers and their tools and provisions into wagons and sent them out on the long haul beyond railhead, with orders to have the grade ready when the striving iron got there. The balance of the force, graders and tracklayers, moved into the desert in their wake.

Farther away still, the mountain ridges north of Great Salt Lake promised potential delays. Mormon grading contractors engaged by Leland Stanford already were at work out of Ogden, but they were handicapped by the lack of tools and materials. Crocker sent those, too, a railroad carload of stuff transshipped by independent wagon freighters over the Overland Stage road south of the lake and into Salt Lake City, thence on northward. The freight bill ran to more than five thousand dollars. A drop in the bucket, for the race was on for real now. The Union Pacific was across the Black Hills, across the Laramie Plains and striking on into its own Red Desert.

It was high time Charley Crocker began to hit his promised mile a day, if he was ever going to. Backed by Strobridge's hard drive and know-how, he was ready.

A reporter from the San Francisco *Alta California* came out to see and to marvel.

Camp equipage, work shops, boarding house, office and in fact the big settlement literally took up its bed and walked [he wrote]. The place that knew it at morning knew it no more at night. It was nearly ten miles off, and where was a busy town of 5,000 inhabitants in the morning was a deserted village site at night, while a smooth, well built, compact road bed for traveling stretched from the morning site to the evening tarrying place.

Such talk represented a startlingly new editorial tack for the paper that had inveighed so scathingly on "Dutch Flat" and "the large-sized elephant" in '63 and '64. But the *Alta* was only swinging with the changing breezes of public opinion. The Great Pacific Railway was going to make it after all! There was news value in the dawning fact, and a great upgushing of local pride. Outside of Sacramento, California had done little enough to further the Central Pacific's progress, and San Francisco had done least of all. But the Central still was a California enterprise, and nothing succeeds like success. The man from the *Alta* would be much at railhead from now on, with busy pencil and great enthusiasm.

He was guilty of some exaggeration, for the rails did not advance any ten miles a day, or anything approaching such a pace. But the force began to bite off two, three, even four and more a day, showing its mettle now that the land gave it a chance. Like the plains of Nebraska, this flat desert offered few obstacles to grading and track-laying. Picks and shovels broke the dry and sterile earth easily; the right of way ran for mile after mile with never a sharp curve, hardly a ridge to be cut through or a sag to be bridged or filled. The desert's hostility was all passive; the sun flaming in brassy summer heat; drearily endless distance; most of all the lack of water.

Succeeding articles in the *Alta California* told of a headquarters train at end of track that was practically a counterpart of the Casements': hulking high cars fitted up as rolling bunkhouses, dining halls, kitchen, office. There was a rolling blacksmith shop and a harness shop to keep tools and gear in shape. Jim Strobridge's private car was described as "a home that would not discredit San Francisco." Mrs. Strobridge still was with Jim. It may be that the woman's touch helped to add an incongruous note of gracious living that softened the rough construction-camp atmosphere.

Iron trains were scheduled so that the first one each day pulled in and was unloaded at sunrise, while the work force breakfasted and was marshaled for the day's planned stint. The empty iron train backed into the clear. The headquarters train followed. Small flatcars were loaded with ties, rails, fastenings, and drawn by horses out to end of track. Ties were put down. The iron gangs laid down the rails while a Chinese distributed spikes, two to each tie; another distributed fishplates; a third the bolts and nuts to fasten them. Two to each side of the track came the spikers, nailing rails to ties. Two more men followed to adjust and tighten the fishplates, the flatcar rolling ahead in the meantime, the next pair of rails clanking down. Emptied at last, the car was tipped off the track to make way for a loaded one. Coolies fetched the seven more ties needed to bring each rail length up to standard specifications and inserted them in place. Other coolies spiked them fast. The boss checked and trued the rails. Last of all came the coolie ballast gang.

It was a system markedly similar to the Casements', and as effective. The race had come down now to crew against crew, man against man. The improved fishplate method of joining rails was available to both sides now. Something over a hundred miles of the Central Pacific's track had been laid with the older chairs; considerably more than four hundred of the Union Pacific's.

The problem of water supply laid a heavy burden on progress, piled up costs and diverted both rolling stock and labor from the main business at hand. Tunnels were gouged into the mountains east of Wadsworth in the effort to develop every possible source. From flowing springs pipe lines were laid to carry the precious liquid to the main line. Water trains hauled it on into the desert, the hauls growing to forty miles and more as railhead crept forward. From there it went onward by tank wagons and six-mule hitches to the graders ahead, the total distance reaching as much as eighty-five miles, the water warm, often contaminated and barely drinkable when it arrived. And it was never under any circumstances plentiful, the boilers of construction train locomotives even greedier than human needs. The white men suffered cramps and dysentery; if they turned in their thirst to the occasional stagnant sinks, as some of the more heedless did, alkali poison doubled them up in agony. The Chinese, whose drink was tea, suffered less and stayed healthy. Tea required the boiling of water, an elementary lesson in hygiene which was nevertheless learned only imperfectly as the work went on.

This was the dreaded Forty-Mile Desert of the early emigrants, the dried-up bed of prehistoric Lake Lahontan; now a baked plain deep in sand, volcanic ash and crusted, gleaming white alkali. Emigrants heading southward from the Humboldt Slough always soaked their wagon wheels, checked tongues and axles, filled their casks with the fetid water of the slough and encouraged their animals to drink all they would. It was possible for whole trains to bog down in sand so deep the wagons had to be abandoned; when other wagons turned out to avoid them, they sometimes bogged down in their turn. Some early chroniclers had described the trail as paved with wreckage, told of the stench of rotting flesh and claimed they counted a dead horse, mule or draft ox every 106 feet. It was claimed that forty-niners had gone astray and perished here in numbers never even counted. Modern-day parties, better equipped, organized and led, fared better. But none spoke lightly of the experience.[2]

Crocker's men, traveling straight northeastward with the location stakes going on before, left no recorded dead behind them, nor any wreckage save the normal debris of their passing.

Westward the Trinity Mountains lifted a long, knobbed backbone along the horizon. To the east, across the desolate alkaline swamps of the Carson Sink, rose the Stillwaters. This Nevada was a washboard of a state, ridged with mountain ranges, the desert running between like the fingers of a great, dry hand. It was a lifeless land, or so it seemed to the laborers who saw few living creatures but lizards, tarantulas and the little, ghostlike desert coyotes that appeared able to subsist on nothing. In spring and fall the blooms and foliage of cactus, yucca, salt bush and seepweed would lay brilliant splashes of yellow and crimson against the stark white of alkali patches. But this was summer, dry and colorless. There was literally nothing to leaven the monotony save the prospect of laying enough rail, eventually, to arrive somewhere beyond such barrenness.

By and large it was the Chinese who made the best of the life. Some of them were new hands, for Charley Crocker still was recruiting—so vigorously that coolies were unceremoniously snatched up at the gangways of ships on the San Francisco wharves, led ashore from river boats and herded into Central Pacific cars on the levee at Sacramento, trundled over the Sierras so fast they hardly glimpsed this strange new world of the Occident till they were deposited at the desert railhead, told off into gangs and put to work. Where they were going and why were twin mysteries that did not actually matter very much. Work they understood. Instructions relayed by their fellow Chinese they knew how to follow. They quickly picked up the necessary smattering of pidgin English. Otherwise they remained a segment of old Canton set down in Nevada, and remarkably unaffected by the change.

Their blue cotton smocks and trousers and their broad, basket hats were ideal for the climate. When the felt-soled slippers of the new arrivals wore out, they purchased American boots at the company commissary, the price checked off against their wages due. The fit seems seldom to have been very good, for it remained a continuing joke among the superior whites that a coolie always insisted on his full money's worth in the form of the biggest boots he could get. But if the result was agony, the new China boy gave never an outward sign. He came of long-suffering and patient stock, well acquainted with pain and hard knocks. And by temperament he was far better fitted than any Irish-American to endure the starkness and monotony of life in the desert.

Pay was regular—far more so here than among the contractors of the Union Pacific—and always in gold and silver coin, the only acceptable medium here in Nevada as it had been in California. It was said that the average coolie saved as much as twenty dollars a month out of his thirty-dollar wage; unless, of course, he lost it all at the eternal fan-tan games. But conversely, the stakes usually ran so high that it was always possible for a lucky gambler to make a big enough killing in a single night to enable him to buy out of his contract, retrace the long journey home to China and live in modest mandarin style for the rest of his life.

This, at least, seems to have been a belief widely held among the white workers. Whether any significant number of Chinese did actually go home to live lives of well-earned ease we do not know. Many of them certainly stayed on long after Central Pacific construction was over. But they left no memoirs that Americans could read, and no white historian was interested enough to record the lowly Chinese's impressions of what they saw and did and experienced. The color line was no less rigid for being largely unwritten, and neither yellow man nor white felt any inclination to step across it.

The bunk, dining and kitchen cars in the headquarters train appear to have been used mostly by clerical workers, overseers and the elite among the Irish-American laborers. The coolies were housed in tents at railhead or in the grading camps beyond, and did their own cooking over open campfires.

None of this bothered them. But the desert did hold terrors that burst in sudden, unexpected trouble.

Even the newest of the China boys from across the sea were painfully Indian-conscious. The veteran coolies, fed on tall and gruesome yarns by the gleeful white men, proved no less so. In California the Indians had long since disappeared, not enough of them left to be even an imaginary menace to anyone. But now all at once, here in the Nevada wilderness, nervous Oriental eyes began to glimpse war paint and feathers behind every sagebrush clump and creosote bush. The weird shapes of Joshua trees shimmering in the heat haze become stealthy red murderers creeping across the middle distance. And grading would stop abruptly, picks and shovels clattering down, blue smocks and basket hats scattering for cover amid panicky twitters of high-pitched Cantonese.

Indians!

The situation had its funny aspect, though nothing that interfered with work could be very funny to Charley Crocker or Jim Strobridge. There were Indians to be sure; small roving bands of Paiutes and Shoshones mainly, Diggers and Snakes in the whites' contemptuous (and erroneous) parlance. They had little in common with the proud and warlike Sioux and Cheyenne who warred with the Union Pacific. These nations already had fought their battles for their ancestral hunting grounds and been bloodily put down by emigrant, miner and cavalryman; "pacified," in the pat term the Army liked to use. They had made no trouble for the Central Pacific survey parties, and there was little reason to expect trouble from them now.

But such assurance was not easily conveyed to the terrified coolies. To them an Indian was an Indian, and it appeared that the stoical Oriental fatalism which had accepted nitroglycerin and crushing snowslide without complaining was not sufficiently all-embracing to shrug off the scalping knife and the torture stake. They demanded protection. Perhaps Charley Crocker was not entirely sure the Indians were harmless either, for he contacted Governor Blasdel of Nevada. The Governor promised to do what he could, and in due time managed to have a small cavalry detachment sent up from Fort Churchill near Carson City. The troopers rode back and forth along the right of way for a while, found nothing in particular to do and soon departed again.[3]

It did not matter by that time, for meanwhile Charley Crocker had worked out a unique solution for his own problem. The Paiute chiefs were sought out and presented with passes good on all passenger trains. Trainmen were instructed to let the common braves and their squaws ride the freights unmolested. In return a solemn pledge of no interference with the railroad or its workers was exacted from the Indians.

Contrary to the usual fate of such treaties in the sorry history of Indian-white relations on the frontier, this one was honored on both sides. The system worked so well with the Paiutes that it was soon extended to the Shoshones, too. So Central Pacific supply trains and drag freights rolled out along the Truckee and on across Nevada with dignified aborigines squatting on the car tops, and peace prevailed.

Paradoxically, the white inhabitants of Nevada proved a more troublesome threat. The great brouhaha over "yellow labor" that had flared up and then smoldered down in California was reborn here. It was even more violent; this was a newer state, life rougher, rawer and closer to frontier elementals. As in California, the despised Chinese was acceptable as cook, laundryman, flunky and handy butt for crude humor. But pigtailed chinks working at white men's jobs? For white men's wages? By God it was an insult, and no bonanza-chasing rowdy with a few tots of redeye whiskey under his belt was going to stand for it! The fact that few indeed of these same stalwarts would themselves even consider swinging a pick on the railroad grades was altogether beside the point.

From the California line all the way across the Truckee meadows the railroad's passage was accompanied by mutterings and mumblings of outrage, with ominous threats of direct action by the bolder troublemakers. Quite possibly only the right of way's comparative remoteness from the wilder mining settlements around the Comstock and along the Carson River prevented serious outbreaks. In all the Nevada diggings it was considered great fun to make John Chinaman dance with the contents of a six-gun kicking up the dust around his frantic feet, or even to raid his encampments in the dead of night, set fire to tents and huts and send the heathen scurrying in highly comic panic. Such incidents actually involving the Central Pacific appear to have been few, and not important enough to be remembered. There was considerably more sound than fury, a great deal more threat than action. But it kept the coolies uneasy and on edge, their bosses worried. Very likely Crocker's appeal to the Nevada Governor was motivated as much by white hostility as the possibility of red. The presence of the Fort Churchill cavalry helped to keep the peace, no doubt.

Despite such problems the Central's progress eastward was uneventful, staid and even sedate compared with the Union Pacific's turbulent westward drive. Charley Crocker's terminal towns were just that: working camps and staging centers, roughly put together, bustling in furious but temporary activity, then left behind by the advancing iron. Some survived to make it as permanent railroad way stations. More faded in quick decay as desert ghost towns. None ever attracted the kind of hungry harpy hordes that rode the Union Pacific's coat tails.

The source simply was not there. The great pioneering push was westward, not eastward. Back of the Central Pacific was no land bursting at the seams and crowding its human overflow out into the wake of the rails. California had gone through its roaring, uninhibited youth in the years following '49, and long ago settled down to sober and responsible statehood. The sin merchants had their citadel in San Francisco's lawless Barbary Coast; the saloonkeepers, easy-money boys, crooked gamblers, the madams and their gaudy girls had far too good a thing going there to fare forth after chancy profits and the rugged life at Central Pacific railhead. And for those afflicted with the itch to travel or the need to get out of town, Virginia City and the fabulous Comstock promised rewards incomparably more glittering than any to be found in the railroad camps, where Crocker's coolies were immune to temptation by either the white man's whiskey or the white man's women, and gambled only at their own games.

The great majority of Nevadans themselves, obsessed with the statewide craze for quick mineral wealth, displayed a remarkable lack of interest in the railroad.

Given the chance, the Central Pacific Irishmen might well have proved themselves as wild and woolly a pack of roughnecks as their brethren in General Jack Casement's army. The potential was there, and enterprising whiskey peddlers tried hard to follow the construction camps. Everywhere, though, they found Nemesis waiting in the person of burly Jim Strobridge, a man with none of Jack Casement's easy tolerance toward sinful pleasures.

"Neither whiskey nor places of dissipation are permitted by the Central Pacific near their lines," the man from the *Alta California* reported. He went on to tell of an inspection trip in the course of which Strobridge "got out to look after some business and returned in a somewhat excited manner. . . .

" 'I have just discovered one of those whiskey mills!' " the *Alta* man quoted him.

Immediately, the account continued, Strobridge called the gang foremen together and ordered them to see that the whiskey mill moved at once, "and if objection was made to destroy the liquor."

Personally, Strobridge appears to have been a sincere temperance man, unyielding and militant in his opposition to John Barleycorn. Possibly, too, company policy took into account the mixed nature of the work force. With a skinful of strong drink, even a Central Pacific Irishman might have been moved to express his superiority over the shuffling coolies as violently as any mining camp bully. In any event, Strobridge's system was unvarying and effective. First the whiskey peddler was warned to move on. If he refused, his tent saloon was summarily pulled down about his ears, his whiskey barrels stove in, his bottles shattered and his precious stock in trade speedily drunk up by the thirsty earth.

"Of course," as the *Alta* man pointed out somewhat stuffily, "the company had no legal right to prevent free American citizens from selling poison . . . but they found it to be to their own interest and took the law into their own hands, and as a result of this their army of workers is enjoying the full fruits of their earnings."

Some of the whiskey peddlers sued, and those with the means and the stomach for long litigation presumably collected damages in the end. But that was the legal department's worry. Lawsuits bothered Jim Strobridge not a particle as long as he kept his camps dry.

In the established towns along the way, where Strobridge's tight control could not prevail, it was a different story. The track-layers and the hoggers, firemen and car hands who kept the iron trains rolling could indulge their natural bents for fun and frolic. The early annals of Winnemucca, a Nevada community attained by railhead later this same year, tell how the arrival of the Central Pacific pay car never failed to touch off a spree, the night loud with song and the sounds of drunken altercation, the morning after revealing its invariable quota of black eyes and broken heads. But the towns along the Central Pacific's route were few and scattered from now on; such opportunities to fall from grace came rarely.

Everywhere on the long supply line the effort swelled toward the gigantic. Iron, five hundred tons of it a day, poured over the Sierras; its passage stained the sky with locomotive exhausts and raised the desert dust in perpetual haze. In New York Collis Huntington outdid his own coup of '66, when he had rounded up the twenty-three ships needed to carry Central Pacific rails around Cape Horn. This year thirty bottoms were at sea, all at the same time, all deep with Central ladings. Former postwar shortages were easing steadily now. The price of rail was down to seventy-five dollars a ton delivered at San Francisco.

Little things went wrong, as they must in such a striving. Delays kept Charley Crocker busy, raging up and down the line in his business car as before. Later he was to recall a typical one for a representative of historian Hubert Bancroft. An iron train pulled in at end of track with a full load of ties, but no rails. While his track gang waited in costly idleness he hurried back to the terminal town (in this instance unidentified), found the iron there where it had no business being and discharged his camp manager, one McQuade, on the spot. The man, a long-time employee of Crocker's, tried to apologize for the oversight.

"McQuade," said Crocker stonily, "this is not an oversight, it is a crime. Now just take your baggage and go. I cannot overlook it."

The erstwhile manager pleaded. He broke down and wept. "But it is very hard on me, for I have been a good, faithful man. . . ."

"I know you have," Crocker told him, "but we must have discipline on this road and I cannot forgive anything of that kind. You must go; send your assistant to me."

He let the man stew for a month and then restored him to his position. And for years afterward, he recalled, McQuade remained in his employ, presumably a better, more careful manager.[4]

The days of summer were waning when, like a long-watched landmark, brown hills lifted up off the desert floor: the first southerly spurs of the

Humboldt Mountains. Skirting them to the westward, the location stakes ran along the edge of a broad, shallow tule marsh where the waters of the Humboldt River spread out and lost themselves in the parched sands. This was the Humboldt Slough, now sere and brown with oncoming fall. Above lay the famed Big Meadow of the California Trail, another old emigrant resting place. Wagon trains usually stopped here to cut hay and fatten stock and draft animals for the arid drag ahead.

The Central Pacific grade had left the Forty-Mile desert behind and now struck out along the easier going of the Humboldt Valley.

An English adventurer by the name of George Lovelock had maintained a small stage station in the Meadow since the early '60's. Like Mr. Lake down at Reno he laid claim to the land, but when the track-layers would have toiled on past he showed a willingness to dicker, and offered terms so advantageous that Crocker made a Central Pacific station of the place, the first permanent one east of Wadsworth. Hustling his railhead forward he set up another at Cold Spring, later to be called Oreana, where clear, icy water bubbled from the ground to afford men and draft animals their first good drink since leaving the Truckee.

Mark Twain, the erstwhile "Josh" of Virgina's City's *Territorial Enterprise*, and before that a whilom prospector in the Nevada wilds, had been immensely unimpressed by the Humboldt River. A man who was bored and lacking anything better to do, he wrote in *Roughing It*, might amuse himself by jumping back and forth across the river until he was tired and thirsty, and then drink it dry. But drinking it, he wrote also, was like drinking lye, "and not weak lye, either." It was true that the Humboldt was not much of a river. Existing only by virtue of the runoff of snow water in the mountains of northeastern Nevada, it was shallow and crookedly meandering, sometimes over broad flats of sand and gravel, sometimes through narrow rock cuts, its lower reaches frequently dry or nearly so. Many of its pools were so heavily alkaline that cream of tartar was advised as an item of wagon train supply, in the belief that this rendered the alkali a little less corrosive to the stomach.

Yet the Humboldt had been an historic highway west since the early years of the century. Tradition claimed that somewhere along its length an unmarked grave held the remains of the first white man to die in Nevada; one known as Paul, member of a party led through the region in the '20's by Peter Skene Ogden of the old Hudson's Bay Fur Company. The river had been called successively the Unknown, the Mary's, the Ogden's, the Paul's before John C. Frémont, the Pathfinder of the '40's, titled it in honor of the German explorer, Alexander Von Humboldt, a name that finally stuck.

The first mountain men had found beaver in it, and willow groves grew in its bends, the wood useless for railroad construction but providing splashes of greenery that were very welcome in a land tinted mainly with the somber grays and browns of barrenness. This still was desert, the river notwithstanding. Volcanic ash flung up by the labors of graders and track hands hung in choking clouds all day. Wagons lumbering forward to supply the advance grading camps sank and stalled hub-deep in sand and gravel drifts.

Right along with railhead went Amos Bowsher's telegraph crew. Poles unloaded by the same supply trains that brought in ties and rails were reloaded into wagons and carried ahead to be distributed at measured intervals along the grade. A gang nailed crossarms fast; another dug holes; right at their heels a third manhandled the poles erect with rope tackles and main strength. A wagon followed with reels of wire, the wire from each in turn spliced to the end of the one that had gone before, fed out over the tailgate, carried up the pole and fastened to the insulators. Keen and jovial rivalry crackled between track-layers and the pole-erecting gang, each determined to stay abreast of the other. These telegraph poles, like the ties, had to come all the way from the tall pine forests of the Sierra slopes. Sometimes the supply failed temporarily, or there were not enough wagons at hand to get them out along the right of way. When that happened, all sorts of makeshifts were pressed into service: empty barrels, piled sagebrush, anything that would keep the wire above the ground for a while—including ties stolen shamelessly from under the noses of Track Boss Minkler and his gang foremen unless they watched their supplies like misers.

The competition was friendly but hard, helping to lighten the monotonous desert grind. Amid the profanity, the insults, the threats of punched noses, there was an *élan* growing here to match that among the swaggering bully boys on the Union Pacific. Even the coolies seemed to share in it, in their own inscrutable fashion understanding at least the demand for speed if not the reason.

The rank and file of each railroad was becoming aware of the other as they groped closer across the great gap of miles. And communications were growing closer, too.

At dusk each evening when the work ended, the wire was brought from the last telegraph pole and connected to the key in the office car. Requisitions for material needed in the next day's work were sent back to the current terminal base, and orders covering the longer-range needs were flashed on to Sacramento, along with the daily figure on track laid. In reply, Sacramento came back with the latest news at home, including any messages from Collis Huntington in New York and other important dispatches received from the East via the Overland Telegraph.

Increasingly, as fall came on and the nights grew bitterly chill with the promise of approaching winter, those Eastern dispatches held disquieting news of the Union Pacific. Excellent though Charley Crocker's progress was —he would make good his mile-a-day promise for sure now, perhaps with miles to spare—the U.P. was doing as well or better.

CHAPTER 23

ROARING TIMES AND IRON MEN

On the Great Plains, '68 began in the midst of a long, hard winter, and spring was long delayed. In spite of that, and while passengers and supplies for the Central Pacific were being forwarded laboriously through Donner Pass by sledge and mud wagon, the Union Pacific kept its trains steaming into Cheyenne. Rails stacked up there. The Casements' big knock-together warehouses bulged with railroad fittings, materials, provisions. Tie contractors had a thousand men busy up on the Black Hills slopes, cutting, not the flimsy cottonwood that had had to do before, but good hard pine and spruce and hemlock. In their camps along the Laramie, Medicine Bow and North Platte rivers huge stocks of ties and bridge timbers accumulated, ready to be floated down to the grade as soon as the thaws of spring should swell the streams.

Cheyenne flourished. A call for labor went out in the East as winter began to wane. Every incoming train brought its contingent of restless Irishmen, some of them fresh out of the steerages of Western Ocean immigrant packets, to join the veterans who whiled away their final weeks of idleness in drinking, gambling, fighting and whoring.

It was North Platte all over again but bigger, more vigorous, surer of its destiny. It was as wild and tough as a Julesburg arisen from the dead. Grenville Dodge called it the gambling capital of the world, noting that "Every known gambling device is in lucrative operation there." Much was made of the dimensions of the Headquarters Saloon—thirty-six by a hundred feet, and enriched by a lavish gilt and gingerbread bar mirror freighted in from the East—as compared with those of the U.S. Post Office: only ten by fifteen, and rough, bare planking at that. There were six bonafide theaters, and at least seventeen "variety halls," which meant, usually, saloon, theater and fancy bagnio combined under a single roof. The Cheyenne *Leader* ran a daily column under a standing head, "LAST NIGHT'S SHOOTINGS," and a local magistrate, Colonel Luke Murrin, was said to levy a ten-dollar fine on any man who drew a gun on another inside the city limits, "whether he hit or missed."

But law enforcement was feeble, hardly existing in more than name only. This was Dakotah Territory. The capital, Yankton, was far away and officials there could back the local authorities with little save moral support. Cheyenne, in fact, had started life in a mass gesture of lawlessness. The first settlers who moved into Dodge's new town site in '67 had scoffed at the Union Pacific's claim to ownership, staked out their own locations where they chose and loudly let it be known they would shoot any railroad land agent who demanded payment. Dodge had countered that by a prompt telegraphic appeal to an old Army friend, General J. D. Stevenson, who happened to be commandant of the new Fort Russell nearby. The Army's standing orders were to aid and abet the railroad in every possible way, so Stevenson simply marched a detachment to the outskirts of Cheyenne, formed a skirmish line and swept through town from one end to the other driving every inhabitant out into the bare plain beyond. There every man's credentials were examined at leisure, and no one was permitted back unless he showed a deed to his property, signed and sealed by a lawful representative of the Union Pacific. It was effective, but it got law and order off to a bad start in the popular mind.

At that, the claim jumpers had very little basis for complaint. Town lots for which the railroad had exacted the sum of $250 were shortly being resold at $2,500 and up as the population soared to ten thousand following the entry of the rails. Even legitimate business ventures were reaping harvests as high as thirty thousand dollars a month as the winter wore on. With pickings as rich as that, few wanted to apply the damper of restraint.

After a while vigilante committees did spring up in an effort to keep crime from getting too blatant. An old log cabin was converted to a one-room jail. When it grew intolerably crowded, a semiofficial mob would release the occupants one at a time, ask each where he wished to go, point him in the indicated direction and send him on his way, frequently with a bull whip or a spray of six-gun slugs snapping at his heels if he loitered. Such methods disposed of the pettier criminals without much trouble. But these first Cheyenne vigilantes seem to have been a remarkably meek and tentative set of town-tamers. Despite an occasional hanging the worst of the real criminal leaders were scarcely interfered with. And the result was that Cheyenne's reputation spread far and wide, a stink in the nostrils of the godly. If Julesburg had billed itself as the wickedest city in America, the depths of Cheyenne's depravity may be judged by the fact that visitors from outside revealed a unanimous and almost compulsive tendency to describe it in terms of the nether regions.

Even the tolerant took it up and made jokes about it. For years there was a story current along the Union Pacific, concerning the conductor whose train was boarded somewhere in western Nebraska by an obstreperous drunk who loudly announced that he "wanted to go to Hell." Unhesitatingly the conductor sold him a ticket to Cheyenne.

More specific and very typical was the comment, apparently made in reference to the Cheyenne populace and the railroad workers indiscriminately, that "Hell must have been raked to furnish them and to Hell must they naturally return after graduating here."

The remark was ascribed to that old transcontinental friend of '65, Editor Samuel Bowles of the Springfield, Massachusetts, *Republican*, who came out on another trip west early in this piping year of '68. This time he expressed satisfaction with the state of progress on the Union Pacific, but frowned on the immoral didos he observed along the line. Bowles was the man, also, who was credited with coining the classic expression, "Hell on Wheels," originally inspired by Cheyenne, probably, but presently accepted as a generic term to characterize the railroad's entire westward march.

Yet under all the tawdry glitter, the evil and the drunken caperings, lived solid, sober citizens who had followed the Union Pacific into town, too. The times and the frontier were inexorably changing; the good was less eye-catching than the bad, but it was present. And it was rugged. On January 5, 1868, with the thermometer standing steady at twenty-three degrees below zero, the *Leader* noted, Cheyenne's first public school building was dedicated. At the time the town was said to have two hundred children of school age. A little later this same spring a Rev. J. W. Cook organized an Episcopalian congregation to give Cheyenne its first church.

The seeker who kept his eyes open could find other signs of a dawning insistence on the niceties of civilized behavior. An editorial in the *Leader,* for example, advised the manager of the Melodeon Theater to "shut down on a certain class of comic songs if he would desire a remunerative business." The advice was taken to heart, too, for soon the Melodeon was advertising that "Ladies may now attend this place of amusement with impunity," while the rival Théâtre Comique announced formally that "On Tuesday and Friday, entertainment designed especially for ladies. No smoking or drinking permitted."

So Cheyenne swaggered, worked, played and went about its affairs lawful and unlawful all through fall and winter and oncoming spring, the biggest, loudest, toughest—and most promising—terminal town the Union Pacific had spawned yet, or would spawn.

Then on the first day of April, '68, a thousand horse and mule teams dug in their hoofs to the jingle and creak of new harness and the cracking of teamsters' whips, and jogged west out of town on the Black Hills approach, with a thousand wagons swaying and groaning beneath the weight of grading camp equipment. Something between five and ten thousand graders and track-layers followed, broke and chastened after their winter-long spree, the exodus forecasting hard times, but saner ones, for the Magic City of the Plains.

The ground still lay snow-covered, too hard to be pierced with a pick. It was broken with blasting powder. From last fall's westward end the grade came alive and crawled forward, dipping through Rock Creek basin, breaching the low folds of the Rattlesnake Hills, thrusting its raw-earth tongue out into the new-green carpet of the Laramie Plains. In action again and glad of it, Jack Casement's iron gangs moved on Sherman Summit, topped it and stood panting in the thin air of a bleak, flat little saddle 8,235 feet above sea level. Here was the topmost point on the whole transcontinental line, even though the Continental Divide itself remained to be crossed.

Swiftly end of track drove down the descending grade for Fort Sanders and points west. At Dale Creek, a little way past the summit, a chasm gaped, wide and deep out of all proportion to the inconsequential stream below. A spidery trestle was cobbled together out of green timber, 700 feet long and a dizzy 130 high; the Union Pacific people claimed at the time that it was the highest railroad bridge in the world. The structure was so limber and spindling it swayed alarmingly in every wind that blew; scarcely had it been finished, in fact, than a full gale blew down out of the north and threatened to take the frail thing apart piecemeal. A U.P. engineer named Hezekiah Bissell saved the day, rushing men out to spike down bracing timbers and rig guy ropes at the risk of their lives. The gale blew itself out and the trestle still was there, but construction trains crawled over it on a four-mile-an-hour slow order, and when the government commissioners came along a while later they flatly refused to accept it at first. Finally they relented to the extent of giving their provisional approval only on condition that a new iron span be erected within a year. But the Dale Creek bridge, having been born in such perilous circumstances, would be a favorite topic of controversy among the railroad's critics for a long time to come.[1]

The late spring was a handicap. Snow lay deep on this high ground and frozen earth was slow in thawing. But a mile a day was old hat to Jack Casement's boys now, shaking out the kinks of idleness and picking up where they had left off four months before. They exchanged brief, hearty badinage with the garrison at Sanders—poor, ignorant sojers, chasin' Injuns for beans, hardtack and a dog's pay—and swept on.

Twenty-three miles beyond Sherman Summit was Laramie, a motley settlement of two hundred people huddled expectantly beside the river in wagon boxes, tents and dugouts even before the Union Pacific land agent arrived on the scene in mid-April. He sold two hundred town lots in the first week; the second saw a building boom in progress. On May 9 (the same day the Central Pacific founded Reno) the Casements' construction train came howling down the grade into town, brake shoes clamped hard on smoking wheels, car hands stationed spraddle-legged on the roof walks. The first revenue train rolled in next day with the main body of madams, gamblers and other live wires from Cheyenne, and the new terminal town set up shop as the self-styled "Gem City of the [Laramie] Plains."

Almost overnight Cheyenne had shrunk from a hot-blooded ten thousand people to a sober fifteen hundred and settled down, as the editor of the *Leader* wrote, "to be a quiet, moral burg." But things were not quite so bad as all that. The Magic City would still have the roundhouse and repair shops of a railroad division point. Within a year the grade of the Denver City connection, the Denver Pacific Railway, would be under construction, and within a very few more all this barren buffalo range would be in the throes of transformation to cattle country.

So far the Union Pacific track-layers were off to a faster start than the Central's, some thirty miles as against only about fifteen. But Grenville Dodge, still trying to divide his time between Congress and the Union Pacific, had had his engineering department on the move long before the first grading outfits pulled out of Cheyenne. He knew the long-haul handicap he had to overcome.

The Central Pacific location survey was complete as far east as Great Salt Lake, and good preliminary lines had been run far east of there. The survey crews of Ives, Buck and Epler had worked in freedom from many of the difficulties that had to be overcome by their opposite numbers on the U.P. In crossing Nevada they had for the most part traversed country already known and mapped by reason of extensive mineral prospecting and the long-established California Trail. Only in western Utah had they encountered terrain that in addition to its roughness was virtually unexplored. Only east of Ogden had they faced any appreciable threat of Indian trouble. And here it appears that they were lucky, for William Epler's small party that penetrated the Wasatch Range in '67 reported no sign of Sioux or Cheyenne. The few surviving company records indicate, too, that the Central's engineers, slow to push surveys eastward out of California in the beginning, had striven for speed from '65 on, with little emphasis on the painstaking reconnaissances carried out by the U.P. under Grenville Dodge. Nevertheless they had done their work with a competence that has gone largely unremarked by most commentators.[2]

Dodge certainly was not underrating them. And on Nassau Street in New York Thomas Durant was looking far ahead, determined to bottle up the Central Pacific Associates in the Nevada desert just as they had cut him off from the California line. Both men were aware also that their own location surveys were in a dangerously fluid state. Hence the program formulated in New York at the start of the year, and the vigorous steps taken to put it into practice.

By the first of February Jacob Blickensderfer, Jr., had his orders as chief engineer of the Utah division: get into the field at the earliest practicable date and have location work under way, if possible, not later than March 1. He pulled his party out of Omaha late in February. Snow in the Wasatch passes covered the tops of the Overland Telegraph poles, but he crossed by sledge and snowshoe and was in Ogden by March 5. James Evans, surveyor of Dodge's own Black Hills line, got the immediately pressing appointment as chief of the Laramie division. His job: to complete the location to the Green River and strike on to meet Blickensderfer's crews working eastward from Salt Lake Valley. The survey parties got their assignments and headed out, well briefed and impressed with the urgency of the situation.

Then in May Dr. Durant himself appeared on the right of way, hurrying out from New York to speed things up. This time he came with the approval of Oliver Ames. All factions agreed, for once, that progress must be spurred to a faster pace even than the one laid down in the previous winter's meetings. Dodge had estimated that the speed-up would mean ten million dollars, at least, in added construction costs. The board's answer had been terse and to the point: do it. Oakes Ames had made the decision for the Credit Mobilier— the sole responsibility his own—with homely New England simplicity:

"Go ahead. The work shall not stop even if it takes the shovel shop."[3]

But controversy followed Thomas Durant as implacably as his own shadow, and no truce could last long where he was involved. One of his first moves, taken on the advice of Silas Seymour, was to shift the division point from Cheyenne, where Grenville Dodge had located it, to Laramie City. And once again Seymour objected to the location line. In a well-meant effort to save heavy grading on the western descent from the Black Hills slopes into the Laramie Plains, he ordered a new line laid out on a roundabout route through the valleys of Rock Creek and the Medicine Bow River, and as usual Durant backed him up. The change did indeed reduce grading and fill by about half, but it lengthened the route by some twenty miles. And since the work was covered by the new Oakes Ames contract calling for payment through this particular section at a rate of $96,000 per mile, the added cost came to $1,920,000.

When news of these goings-on reached Washington, it put an abrupt end to Grenville Dodge's activities as a Congressman. He dropped everything and hastened out to the construction front. Armed with an order from U.P. President Oliver Ames, he confronted Durant at Laramie and bluntly nipped in the bud any possibility that division headquarters would be moved there from Cheyenne. He was too late to remedy Seymour's meddling, though. Grading had been pushed with such rapidity that it was considered best to let the altered line stand rather than waste more time by another change-over.

The short-lived peace between the Ames and Durant factions was over almost before it had begun, the feud only worsened, if anything; and now Dodge and Durant were all-out enemies as well.

To add a somewhat sinister implication to the whole business, President Andrew Johnson had, the previous fall, designated a point just west of Cheyenne as the eastern base of the Rocky Mountains, which meant that all this section would draw the top government bond issue of $48,000 per mile. Inevitably this soon was being rumored as the logical motivation for Silas Seymour's changed location line, and before long charges began to circulate that the Union Pacific route was being lengthened in a cold-blooded plot to milk the public treasury. There still was a hard-core minority of men in Congress who felt that the Acts of '62 and '64 had been too generous, and that an accounting by the railroad was already long overdue. Such charges, therefore, while they could be shrugged off for the time being, would have to be answered one day, and the answering would not be easy.

Dodge remained in the field to do what he could with an accelerated schedule that now called for a location survey completed from the Green River to Great Salt Lake within one month, and to Humboldt Wells in three. It meant four months for a job previously programmed for seven, and a back-breaker at that. By telegraph where it was possible, by messenger as soon as that could be done, he caught the parties in the field and reshuffled their alignment as best he could, to throw every available engineer forward into Utah and beyond. Fortunately, the Laramie-Green River location, much of it already staked before the end of operations the preceding year, had gone ahead rapidly under Evans' hard-driving supervision and now was well along toward completion.

Humboldt Wells was four hundred miles west of the Green River, a long, hard way for just three months' work. But Charley Crocker, this May, still was struggling out along the Truckee, no lightning express by any means, while his army of coolies still pitched snow out of Donner Pass and the seven-mile gap at Donner Lake remained unclosed. The Wells might, *just might*, be wrested from the Central Associates at that.

During May and June and into July, Jack Casement kept his construction train grinding on over the Laramie Plains, riding an average two miles of bright new track each working day. In May, not stopping to wait for anything, he had thrown temporary track in a series of sharp curves around a spur of the Rattlesnake Hills where the Union Pacific's first tunnel was being blasted and dug through a soft sandstone ridge on Mary's Creek, 618 miles out of Omaha. A hundred horse and mule teams were whipping his rail cars out to end of track and hauling supplies to the graders' camps beyond. Swelled by new recruits, his track gangs overflowed the bunk cars and slept in tents rigged on the car tops, or rolled into blankets on the ballast underneath. He still could arm a thousand men at a word; but the Sioux had learned their lesson by now, and let the Casements' headquarters alone.

Laramie City lived the high life of a terminal town for three months. Its vigilantes, learning from Cheyenne's experience, organized fast and were tough from the start. They hanged a shady character known only as "The Kid." His friends rallied for revenge and there was a spirited gun battle in the Belle of the West saloon, several vigilantes killed before the last four outlaws surrendered and were swung aloft in their turns. By that time the Casements had rolled on, and the iron trains from Omaha were hesitating in Laramie for only as long as it took to replenish locomotive tenders and cool car wheels heated by the long Black Hills descent. Laramie, a law-abiding town at last, was very nearly an empty one as well.

Benton was the new railhead town, sprung full-blown out of bleak nothingness at the edge of the Red Desert, seven hundred miles west of Omaha, three hundred east of Great Salt Lake. At its peak Laramie had boasted only five thousand people, and its gay days had been shorter than those of North Platte, Julesburg or Cheyenne. The halcyon time of "Hell on Wheels" was passing, the hangers-on having a harder go of it. Once the rails crossed Sherman Summit, Dodge was to write later, "we moved our bases so rapidly they could not afford to move with us." The sin towns became progressively more squalid as they hustled to keep up.

For all that, Benton had its day. Its natural setting contributed nothing: not a tree, shrub or spear of grass. For as far as the eye could range, remarked one observer, there was only white alkali, gray desert and sere, rusty-ocher hills.[4] But Benton was stage terminus, freight terminus, railroad terminus. It gloried in a population of three thousand, mostly railroaders, mule-skinners, soldiers, human parasites of all the recognized varieties. It had twenty-three saloons and five dance halls. Buildings of new lumber painted to simulate brick or fashionable brownstone were shipped, knocked down, all the way out from Chicago and cost three hundred dollars each, delivered. Six men, it was claimed, erected a business block in a day. Two, armed with hammers and screwdrivers, could have a house standing in three hours. Even allowing for exaggeration, it appears that Casement's track-layers had no monopoly on efficiency or the production-line method.

The town's water was hauled three miles by wagon from the North Platte River, and sold for a dollar a barrel or ten cents a bucket. The streets lay more than ankle-deep in white alkali dust as fine and clinging as flour. But liquor dealers booked 80 percent profits on sales running high into the multiple thousands of dollars—as long as Benton lasted.

It lasted sixty days.

They were full days though, everywhere along the U.P. line. Grenville Dodge was often at his wits' end. Grading, a main item of construction, usually was awarded to the contractors in hundred-mile parcels; on the plains, an average of thirty days' work. But in this desert country and in the mountainous region ahead, grading would inevitably take much longer. So the contracts had to be assigned and the work started several hundred miles in advance of the fast-moving railhead. The situation was complicated, over some stretches, by the delay in finalizing location lines; then in the hurried reorganization of work at the end of April many contractors found themselves caught in the switches. Going forward on an inspection trip late in July, Dodge found some graders idling in their camps for want of essential tools and supplies. Out on the Utah approaches to Great Salt Lake, where a sulky Brigham Young was only lately reconciling himself to doing business with the likes of Grenville Dodge, the Mormon grading crews nevertheless were hard at work. But here, too, the lack of tools was a handicap.

So a call for help had to be flashed back, all the way to Omaha, ultimately. By fortunate foresight great stacks and mounds of supplies had been amassed there in anticipation of the Herculean effort planned for this year. The burden on the U.P.'s motive power and train operating departments grew heavier, but the necessities moved west. Wagon trains groaned on from railhead under a constant pall of desert dust; three hundred rigs coming and going without letup; then four hundred as the tempo was relentlessly stepped up. The total of draft animals in construction and supply services went to more than ten thousand. The total working force—graders and track-layers combined—crowded past the ten thousand figure, for the first time approaching the size of Charley Crocker's Oriental-Caucasian host which coped with difficulties practically identical in its own distant desert ordeal.

In the face of confusion, changed orders and the danger always present in so wild and desolate a land, however, Evans' and Blickensderfer's men staked their location lines with dedicated diligence. The surveys were shaping up as speedily and well as anyone could have expected. There were close calls and hardships, but no stoppages.

F. C. Hodges, assistant to Blickensderfer, was marooned by two solid weeks of snow and rain in the Wasatch Mountains this spring. His party had been furnished with wagons for transport; a mistake, for late in May they mired in deep snow and had to be abandoned. Most of the supply packs were swept away in the fording of a stream raging in spring spate; the rest were lost when the party's last four mules were buried by an avalanche. On foot, exhausted and stripped of provisions, Hodges had to give up and lead his men back to Salt Lake City, a debacle reminiscent of Thomas Bates's in the Red Desert a year earlier. But this was the worst of the surveyors' vicissitudes. There were no dead men, no scalps lost, no parties driven off their lines by Indian attacks. War parties remained a threat all the way to the Green River and beyond, but in climbing the Wasatches, graders and surveyors were nearing the westward limits of the Sioux and Cheyenne range.

Up north in the Powder River country and Montana Territory there was a nervous lull in hostilities. This July an impressive delegation of high Army brass, including General Grant himself, journeyed out to Fort Laramie to make peace talk with Red Cloud's Sioux. The Army capitulated, for once. The treaty that resulted provided for the closing of the Bozeman Trail and the abandonment of the forts that guarded it. So there were fewer braves looking for trouble in raids across the Red Desert and the Bitter Creek basin this summer. But there was a fresh outbreak of terror back on the Nebraska plains.

In April Sioux dog soldiers raided Elm Creek in force and butchered five U.P. section hands. On the same day another war party struck Sidney, a thriving buffalo hunters' headquarters and hide shipping point in western Nebraska, and again the railroad bore the brunt. William Edmondson and Tom Cahoon, a pair of freight conductors off duty, happened to be fishing in Lodgepole Creek a mile from the station. They heard the shooting, climbed the creek bank for a look and were spotted by Sioux outriders. Cahoon went down in the first rush, was promptly scalped and left. Edmondson, armed with a derringer pistol, held the warriors off while he legged it in spurts for the beleaguered station. Its defenders opened the door for him and he dove through, four arrows bristling from his hide. But none of the wounds proved mortal, and he lived to swing many a future highball from the platforms of

U.P. cabooses. So did Tom Cahoon, surviving as miraculously as Plum Creek's Thompson had before him.

Such sallies went on all summer, the proud Sioux fighting a losing battle now but still spurning the Army's brand of reservation peace. In September they matched the exploit of Porcupine and his fellow Cheyenne by wrecking a mixed train west of Ogalalla. The ends of the bent-up rails pierced the locomotive's boiler and loosed a cloud of live steam that scalded the fireman to death. The engineer jumped from the gangway and joined the trainmen and passengers in a defense that held the wreckers off till a relief train arrived.

The cased rifle became a standard item of passenger car equipment west of Kearney; of caboose equipment too, ever since Plum Creek. Many an engineer and fireman climbed into the cab with a Navy model Colt in his waistband. Coaches and cabooses were built with sand packed between the planks of inner and outer sheathing, the better to stop bullets. The famous Lincoln car was a favorite conveyance of officials and government commissioners traveling the line, as much for its boiler-plate armor as for its aura of historic tradition.

But the on-line harassments, serious enough to those who suffered and died in them, could not stop or even seriously hinder the forward stride of grade and railhead. The railroad was setting bigger things in motion this summer than the inevitability of Indian defeat. Developments of national import were building up around it as relentlessly as the steps in a chain reaction. The Central Pacific was coming east with the prosaic single-mindedness of private enterprise in pursuit of profit. But the Union Pacific, having been born of a coupling between political maneuver and public expedience, marched with politics as its companion.

This was a national election year. By U.S. territorial law, the railroad workers had the right to vote in whatever territory they found themselves. And with the construction forces concentrated in the Dakotah Wyoming, it became obvious that the Union Pacific stood in a position to swing the election in all the vast but sparsely settled Dakotah Territory. Local politicos at Yankton saw the possibilities, decided they liked them not and put their heads together. Some sentiment for the creation of a separate Territory of Wyoming already existed, hinting at a way out. Ambitious citizens of Cheyenne, glimpsing the power and the status of a new territorial capital, hurried to climb aboard the bandwagon. In short order the Wyoming Organic Act was drawn up, and approved on July 28. Since parts of Utah and Idaho Territories also went into the new Wyoming, the Union Pacific, simply by the fact of its being, was the instigator of rather far-flung boundary changes.

In July there was another important excursion out to railhead, of a significance far exceeding the lighthearted travels of George Francis Train's clutch of editors in '67, and even the imposing Great Excursion of '66. Chief junketeer this year was no less a celebrity than Ulysses S. Grant, now the Republican nominee for the U.S. Presidency and an odds-on favorite to beat the Democrats' Horatio Seymour, wartime Secessionist-leaning Governor of New York, in November. The Savior of the Union came west by special Union Pacific train from Omaha, attended by a military entourage that included Generals William T. Sherman; Phil Sheridan; August Kautz, who had led the first Negro troops into conquered Richmond in '65; William S. Harney, bluff old veteran of years of early Western campaigning; Frederick T. Dent, Grant's brother-in-law and West Point classmate; and others. No such conflux of illustrious military figures had been gathered for public exhibition in a single group since the war's end.

It was actually the Fort Laramie conference with Red Cloud that brought the group west; it made excellent news copy for the Presidential candidate, who was also the nation's foremost soldier, to come out and settle an Indian war in person. But the Pacific Railroad was good news copy, too, and Ulysses S. Grant had his reasons, besides, for wanting to talk with the U.P. officials. From Laramie the party went down to Fort Sanders and was met by Dr. Durant and Sidney Dillon, Union Pacific director and Credit Mobilier president. Colonel John Gibbon, another of Grant's old comrades in arms, who had been present at Appomattox as brevet commander of the XXIV Army Corps and now commanded at Sanders, greeted the visitors with appropriate military honors, having first prudently thrown out a cavalry cordon to guard against any possible embarrassment by unpacified Indians. The children of the garrison and of families from nearby railroad establishments were paraded, all scrubbed, combed, brushed and lectured on the niceties of good deportment; each received a solemn handshake and pat on the head from the future President, in true campaign style.

There was more behind this trip of Grant's than mere electioneering, however. Grenville Dodge, just then busy putting his grading camps into shape, had been called in from the field by an urgent telegram from Sidney Dillon. And presently, sandwiched in at some time during the round of banquet, regimental ball and other social amenities, a political gambit of another kind was played out to its conclusion.

Dodge's protest at Silas Seymour's meddling with the Black Hills surveys, apparently ignored at the time, had traveled a long way and by devious channels since he had submitted it in January. There is no doubt that it became enmeshed in the now irreconcilable conflict between Durant and the Ames faction on the Union Pacific board. As an influential member of the House of

Representatives, Oakes Ames may have used his position in government to back Dodge's stand and embarrass Durant. In any case, the matter, if kept alive long enough, was bound to find its way into the War Department and the Department of the Interior; the Pacific Railroad was of course a national issue anyway, and Grant, as a nominee for the highest office in the land, would have been wooed assiduously by both Durant and Ames. He was, besides, an old friend of Grenville Dodge, who was in a sense his protégé.

All this makes it clear that Grant was here at Fort Sanders now for a hard and judicious look at the squabble which had for so long threatened to split the Union Pacific high command wide-open.

The showdown took place privately. There were few present in addition to Grant, Dodge, Durant and Sidney Dillon. Dillon, of course, was there as a representative of the Ames brothers. Another Union Pacific director and a government commissioner are mentioned in contemporary accounts. Silas Seymour is not, though his absence was not necessarily significant; as a brother of Grant's Democratic opponent his presence may simply have been considered inappropriate. Whether Sherman took any role in the meeting is uncertain. Accounts of what happened are brief, but hardly briefer than the meeting itself.

Thomas Durant wasted no time in setting the tone with a coldly bitter attack on Dodge. The chief engineer, he charged, had been grossly irresponsible in his recommendations for the railroad's route. Specifically, he blamed Dodge's insistence on the location line north of Great Salt Lake for the loss of Salt Lake City as a station and the whole Brigham Young imbroglio that still was only precariously smoothed over. He further accused him of squandering time and money on needless reconnaissances and preliminary surveys, and of deliberately flouting the advice of his associates in other matters (this last probably referring to the difference over the selection of Cheyenne versus Laramie as a division point). Basically, the bulk of these complaints would seem to be the natural ones of the promoter, zealously seeking business opportunity along the line, as opposed to the engineer concerned only with practical facts of terrain and railroad operation. But it was obvious from Durant's attitude that annoyances had been accumulating until a serious amount of bad blood now existed between the two.

When the vice-president had had his say at last, Grant invited Dodge to speak. The moment must have had its drama. The chief engineer—a short, sturdy, weather-beaten figure in striking contrast to the always dapperly turned-out Durant—made no attempt to answer the accusations in detail. His statement was short, but clipped off straight from the shoulder:

If Durant or anyone else connected with either the company or the United

States government altered his survey lines one more time, he would resign. At least the thing was out in the open now.

When Grant gave his answer, it was equally blunt and forthright:

The government of the United States expected the Pacific Railroad to be completed, and expected the Union Pacific Company to carry out its obligations to that end. And, he added with the succinct bite of military decision, the government of the United States also expected that Grenville Dodge would remain with the railroad till the task was done.

So that was that. Ulysses S. Grant as a political office-seeker had no authority, of course, to make decisions for the Union Pacific Railroad. But nobody was going to be so foolhardy as to flout the wishes of Ulysses S. Grant, the future President of the nation; nobody as astute as Dr. Thomas Durant, certainly. He yielded gracefully, with the debonair poise that never failed him in a tight spot. One is impelled to suspect that he had been fighting with his back to the wall anyway, and knew it; that he must have been aware that Grant was unlikely to act against a respected wartime subordinate; and that this trip of Grant's had been none of his doing in the first place.

The air was cleared, at any rate. There would be no more front-office interference. Grant boarded his special train for a pleasant hundred-mile jaunt out across the Laramie Plains to railhead, where General Jack Casement paid his respects and tough Irish veterans, Union and Johnny Reb alike, lined up to shout themselves hoarse with huzzas for "Old Unconditional Surrender," "Little Phil" and old "Uncle Billy." The special pulled out eastward then, Grant to receive the plaudits of fifteen thousand enthusiastic Omaha Republicans on his way to November and destiny. The track gangs set their faces westward again, into the Red Desert.

Glaring sun glanced in painful splinters off the Russia-iron boiler jackets of the construction locomotives, and heated rails till they burned like fire to the touch. Water from the North Platte was hauled up in tank trains and sent forward by wagon, brackish and foul by the time it arrived at its destination. For a hundred miles ahead there were no adequate supplies. Untreated alkali foamed in locomotive boilers, choking the exhausts to labored sogginess in the tall stacks; it corroded crown sheets, piping and water pumps and ate at human stomachs. Grading camps farthest to the front supplied themselves where and how they could, hauling water from stinking potholes in the red rock or niggardly little trickles in the barren hills.

The Casement Brothers' track-laying contract called for payment at the rate of eight hundred dollars per mile for anything less than two miles a day. When two or more miles a day were laid the rate jumped to twelve hundred per mile.[5] Confident of their own ability and cannily aware of the exigencies

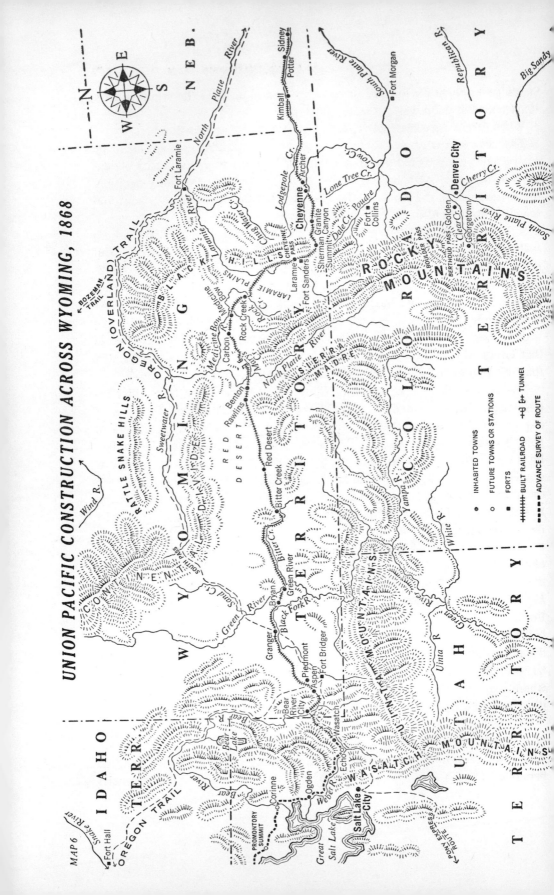

of railroad construction, they had insisted on a clause paying them three thousand dollars for every day lost in idleness because of unfinished grades. It was a rare day that saw them earning under $2,400 now, and out ahead the graders had to hump to stay there.

They did not always manage to. Cursing like the troopers they had been, the track gangs drove their iron into the rear guard of the pick-and-shovel brigades and had to lay off, flinging raucous abuse at their Irish compatriots till pitched battle threatened and General Jack had to call them off. Casement Brothers collected their three thousand dollars a day, but this thing was beyond mere money now. Pride and the driving urge to lay track were at least as important. Then Dodge's reorganized supply service took effect. With a new lease on life the grading crews surged forward. Casement drove his men after them, straining human skill and endurance to the utmost, spiking down three and four miles of track a day.

They put the Continental Divide behind, hardly knowing it. By the end of burning August the rails had spanned the Red Desert and were crawling down off a bleak plateau into the no less desolate Bitter Creek basin. Benton died. A few of its camp followers tagged along to Rawlins, the next desert division point. But the ambitious ones, perceiving the essential futility of so piecemeal a pursuit, by-passed Rawlins entirely and plodded by high-piled wagon, rickety buggy or crowbait mule all the way to the Green River, 140 miles farther on, where a brand-new settlement already waited in unconcealed anticipation.

Former Mayor H. M. Hook of Cheyenne had founded it. To the foresighted, he reasoned, would go the choicest rewards. The military had foiled claim-jumping at Cheyenne, but a man with his own town laid out ahead of time on a spot where the railroad had to pause a while would be sitting squarely in the catbird seat. He led a wagon train across the Red Desert and the Bitter Creek and staked out his community where he found a Union Pacific bridge gang putting in the massive stone piers and abutments of a bridge over the Green. Others followed his lead; two thousand others by September. Land speculators bought up lots. Permanent adobe buildings went up. Storekeepers freighted in their stocks and waited. The gamblers rigged their wheels and tables, amusing themselves with endless games of solitaire while they waited, too. So did the girls of Virgin Alley, growing a little bedraggled now with the ravages of time and travel.

In September the screams of whistles out beyond the fluted sandstone tower of Castle Rock signaled the coming of boom times to Green River City. The iron-slingers clanked down the grade to the river bank, and the city was ready with a good old riproaring welcome. The bridge was ready, too.

End of track whipped across and kept on going; thirteen and a half miles on, before it paused briefly to let the lumbering headquarters cars catch up. Someone named the place Bryan; a poor place, another ramshackle log-and-board-and-canvas shantytown, nothing at all to compare with Green River City which was left, all the same, with its high hopes blasted. Mr. Hook had outguessed nobody but himself.

Jack Casement was headed for Ogden, had notions about being there for the new year and could afford no sympathy for the disappointed he left behind. Now the grim ridges of the Wasatch were piling up across his path, promising fresh obstacles. Fall was here. Winter would be close in its wake.

And still Crocker's infernal coolies were coming eastward at a pace that matched his own, day for day and mile for mile. General Jack knew it well enough. He too had the telegraph wire brought into his office and connected up each evening when the work was done, stayed in constant communication with the rear, had all the news relayed from the Overland Telegraph. His Paddies jeered when he passed the word. One Irishman, they bragged, was the equal of any three Chinamen ever spawned.

Excursionists still flocked west over the Union Pacific, people caught up in the excitement of pioneering and the great trek west. They braved the prairie's heat and dust, the inconvenience of frontier living facilities and the Indian danger. They came, they saw, they went home to tell their friends. Some were tourists pure and simple, and some were old friends of Grenville Dodge, the Casements and other leaders in the construction effort. Many were sportsmen with shiny new Ballard or Sharps rifles, eager to shoot the buffalo, the antelope, the mountain deer, the storied grizzly bear. They poured into Fort Sanders and Laramie, went on to railhead and even to the graders' camps. Among them was a thick sprinkling of journalists. Practically every paper of any importance east of Omaha—the New York *Sun, Tribune, Express, Observer;* the Boston *Journal, Traveller, Transcript;* the Chicago *Tribune* and *Journal of Commerce;* the Philadelphia *Bulletin, Age, Press, Inquirer;* the Baltimore *American;* the Pittsburgh *Chronicle;* the Cincinnati *Commercial;* any number of others—had their correspondents out in Wyoming Territory this summer and fall. Many of their front pages were carrying daily bulletins on the railroad's progress, eagerly watched by homebody citizens over breakfast coffee or in the lamplit evenings after work: "Two and three-quarters miles of track laid yesterday on the Union Pacific Railroad." "Three miles of track laid yesterday . . ."

Few of these papers paid more than the most cursory scraps of attention to the poor, eastward-faring Central. But the Central refused stubbornly to fall by the wayside. Casement's Paddies put on a mighty spurt and laid down six miles of track in a day, sunrise to sunset. It was the best stint yet. Time passed, and the implacable chatter of the telegraph sounder brought fresh news: Crocker's men had laid seven.

"No damned Chinamen can beat me laying rails," said General Jack, or so tradition quotes him.

September was past now, and the greater part of October. End of track was at Granger, a new terminal camp, sixteen miles beyond Bryan, within eight of the Utah line. But it was growing late. The nights held the bitter nip of dying fall. Ice froze in a hard, thick crust on a bucket of water left standing by the steps of the kitchen car, and ahead new snow mantled the steep shoulders of the Wasatch.

Casement entertained friends one night: General J. M. Corse of Iowa, an old wartime companion, and Edward Creighton from Omaha, the man who had strung the wires of the Overland Telegraph. After dinner they sat up late over whiskey and cigars in General Jack's quarters in the office car; quite late, it was said afterward—it was a convivial evening and the talk got a little boastful. Nevertheless Casement had his guests out early next morning, the cold predawn blackness already loud with the clank and grumble of locomotives and the clatter of iron trains being unloaded. It looked like a fine, bracing day, dawn laying its wash of clear, pale gold over the steel-dark eastern sky. The foremen mustered their gangs while the word went around: This was going to be the day that discouraged Crocker and his coolies once and for all!

Under the eyes of Jack Casement and his friends the iron was laid as it never had been laid before. The lorry cars shuttled back and forth behind the horses' flying hoofs. The crash of rails going down made an unceasing clangor across the land. Small mishaps threatened. A construction train locomotive ran out of water and her fire had to be dumped hastily lest the crown sheet burn and her boiler blow sky-high. The Paddies worked on, far into dusk and then full night, with lanterns lighting the way along the grade. When it was over and Captain Clayton bawled "Lay off!" at last, the railroad was longer by some seven and a half or eight miles; subsequent accounts never quite agreed on the exact figure. The telegrapher tapped out his report to the rear, and a statement from John S. Casement with it: The next stint would be longer still, unless Crocker was ready to call quits.

It seemed that Crocker was not. His reply presently came in, arrogantly couched as a public announcement, to whomever it might concern. The Central Pacific, he declared, promised ten miles of track in one working day.

When that message reached New York, Thomas Durant decided that this was in no sense a private fight, and money talked loudest. His wire went to

Charley Crocker direct: he had ten thousand dollars that said Crocker could not do it before witnesses.

From Sacramento, silence for a while. The bluff had been fairly called—if it was a bluff? It appeared so, for Crocker's answer when it came held a hint of temporizing.

He would let the Union Pacific know, he wired curtly.[6]

CHAPTER 24

STRIVE EAST; STRIVE WEST

Weightier matters than track-laying occupied Charley Crocker's mind this fading fall; and more urgent worries than a problematical ten thousand dollars to be won or lost, or even his own very touchy pride. Farther to his rear with every day that passed, the Sierra Nevadas nevertheless remained an ominous factor in the race for Great Salt Lake. Through two successive winters the snows up there had been by-passed, leapfrogged, but never conquered. And since the very start of this make-or-break year of '68 it had been obvious that they could be by-passed no longer. The primitive sledge and mud wagon transport that had proved just sufficient to supply a minimal effort down the Truckee River canyon could never handle the masses of material now being gobbled up in the mighty drive up the Humboldt. Another Sierra blockade could be fatal to the Central Pacific's ambitions.

The defense would have to rest on Arthur Brown's snowsheds.

Back there between Cisco and Donner, the bridge boss had started work so early in the spring that six to eight feet of snow had to be shoveled out to get down to bare earth. Even earlier, every sawmill in Cisco and vicinity was busy turning out the massive timbers needed. Carpenters were recruited at four dollars a day, a princely wage far above the going rate. Common laborers drew $2.50 and $3.00, and they, like the carpenters, were scarce at that. Brown hired where and as he could. He was on his own, for little help could be diverted his way from Jim Strobridge's coolie gangs; the pressure for speed and intense effort was unremitting everywhere. No able-bodied man along the Central right of way had any excuse for languishing in idleness this year, not if he really wanted work.

By summer, in defiance of California's chronic labor shortage, Brown had his work force up to 2,500. He had six construction trains in service distributing timber, spikes, tools and workmen along the mountain grades. They were

hampered by the eternal, irksome necessity of running for sidings to clear
the main line for regular freight and passenger movements and Charley
Crocker's supply trains that shuttled in unceasing smoke and thunder between
the Sacramento levee and the advancing railhead out in Nevada. The operating
department had to stretch itself dangerously thin to keep everything moving.
In the company shops at E Street and Sixth, along the old China Slough in
Sacramento, mechanics worked overtime on hard-driven locomotives. New
ones kept coming around the Horn or across the Isthmus, dispatched by tireless Collis Huntington, but it took time to erect them and break them in.

All summer the sheds arose and took form: great, gloomy galleries bulking
in the deep cuts, crawling out along the steep sidehill slopes like medieval
shield-carapaces moving on the besieged Sierra battlements. The work was
done hurriedly and crudely, no time or effort wasted on fancy finish. It was
strong, though, built to last. Side timbers twelve inches thick by fourteen wide
were set vertically, twenty inches apart and eighteen feet high, covered with
steeply pitched roofs of four-inch planking, the whole structure bolted firmly
to the solid mountain granite. By itself, however, not even such sturdy construction was enough to do the job. It would suffice in the cuts, where drifted
snow was the only problem to be overcome. But out on the worst of the
sidehill locations, in the open, the past winter and the first sheds put up in
'67 had proved that timber alone was incapable of withstanding the titanic
mass of snowslides roaring down unchecked from the crests above. In such
spots great retaining walls of rock had to be built, to serve as dams holding
the snow above the sheds, letting it spill over the top and accumulate till
ultimately the slides would skim harmlessly across the gallery roofs.

This was the theory. The test would come soon enough; too soon, for the
Sierra summer was short and time ran out.

Sawmill capacity proved inadequate. From sawn lumber Arthur Brown had
to turn to rough, hand-hewn tree trunks felled in the forests above Cisco
and on the eastern slopes, and dragged to the tracks by ox team. The difficulties grew greater, the costs also, "because axemen in those days were very
scarce," he recalled later in a statement prepared for the Pacific Railroad
Commission. In all, snowsheds would cover thirty-seven miles of Central
Pacific track, distributed over a stretch beginning below Cisco on the west
and extending past Donner Lake on the east. They would require 65,000,000
board feet of lumber, nine hundred tons of bolts and iron work, something
in excess of two million dollars. But the job would not be finished this year.

The first autumn snows fell. Still construction was pushed, shovel gangs
pressed into action. Brown would carry on as long as any man could, till the
thickening blizzards overwhelmed him. After that, the army of workers out

on the Nevada haul, expending iron and supplies by the fifty-car trainload now and demanding more every day, might be in a pretty bad way.

By November, end of track was 132 miles beyond Wadsworth, at Winnemucca, named for a famed old Paiute chief and the first permanent settlement of importance the Central Pacific had so far hit west of the California line. There was a toll bridge across the Humboldt here, a rude hostelry named the Winnemucca Hotel, and the terminus of a stage line running north into Idaho Territory. The Winnemucca Mining District had been organized in '63, and the mountain that overhung the river and the town was dotted with workings old and new. Coming up along the river, the Central's iron gangs had noticed some thirty miles of unfinished canal beside the right of way. An early settler by the name of Gianacca, an Italian entrepreneur a long way from home, had pressed the project as a short route to a proposed mill city where smelters could be run by water power. But his investors had lost interest when the railroad approached. It was the second instance (Reno had been first) of local Nevadans grasping the significance of a location on the Central's line without urging.

The town had been selected as the next division point after Wadsworth, so the track-layers remained long enough to spike down the necessary sidings and switches before heading up and away through the low saddle below Winnemucca Mountain. Here the Humboldt, which had been followed almost straight northeastward from the slough on the edge of the Forty-Mile Desert, turned in a great bend to skirt the northern foothills of the Stillwater Range, and led the way due east in a series of sweeping loops and bends. Apart from the grinding need for hurry and the incessant, routine annoyances that grew out of men, tools and systems pushed to the limit, this was a time of satisfaction and relative serenity for Crocker and Jim Strobridge.

Progress was steady and good. The incidence of labor troubles and workers' complaints stayed amazingly low, considering the desolation and monotony of this drab land. It began to grow very cold here on this high, dry floor of Nevada, but there was no snow. For the present, the Sierra passage to the rear remained open; the endless procession of supply trains rolled in, day by day; the construction train lumbered forward.

All the while, and in strong contrast, the Union Pacific was coming west in the usual atmosphere of storm and strife—but more than matching Crocker's best. Roaring on from Granger at the tag end of October, the Casements' hard-bitten professionals had scaled the outlying ridges of the Uinta Mountains, founded Piedmont as a terminal camp, left it behind and labored forward and upward another nine miles and a half to Aspen, at milepost 937, elevation 7,540 feet; highest point on the line west of Sherman

Summit. Ahead of them the grade plunged over and down to the Bear River; on its bank stood Bear River City. And here hell broke loose again.

Beartown, as it was more commonly called, had been there as a loggers' camp huddled at the mouth of White Sulphur Creek for a year or more before the graders arrived. The hard cases moved in, all the other riffraff, too; the town swiftly followed the old, familiar "Hell on Wheels" formula. It bloated to a population of two thousand, put up some 140 buildings almost overnight, boomed and bellowed like all the terminal towns that had gone before. But this time there was a difference. Beartown, it appears, took itself somewhat more seriously than the early riptailed roarers from the very beginning. It had a high percentage of sober citizens who saw their town as a legitimate business community with solid and honorable prospects, and did not propose to have those prospects ruined by the lawless element. These good burghers took immediate steps to organize a vigilance committee. And in doing so they were not disposed to recognize any difference between the out-and-out blacklegs on the make and the rough, hard-drinking tie-cutters and graders who represented the railroad.

Beartown also boasted a newspaper, the *Frontier Index,* edited and published by one Leigh Freeman, who had founded his journal at Kearney in '66 and brought it along in the Union Pacific's wake ever since. He had published at Julesburg for a while, and perhaps at Cheyenne; had contributed to Laramie's growing pains and participated in Benton's boom and bust before moving on to Bear River City. Somewhere in this peripatetic career, Freeman had become a militant enthusiast for vigilante justice. He was, moreover, a violently irresponsible editorialist and a bitter, fire-eating, unreconstructed Southerner with a whole headful of pet hates, dogmas and prejudice; in his own peculiar way, he was one more example of the displaced, the misfits and the rootless who had drifted west to the frontier in war's turgid backwash.

Quite naturally, Ulysses S. Grant came in for a lion's share of Freeman's bile as the Presidential campaign hammered down to the wire this November. And quite as naturally, since a majority of the U.P. graders were Union veterans, the *Frontier Index* was muttered over and resented with increasing choler out in the camps west of the Bear River.

Then on November 11, even while Grant was storming to a decisive victory over the Democrats and their Horatio Seymour, the new Bear River City Vigilance Committee struck its first blow for civic reform. Three miscreants were hanged beside the railroad grade and a crowd of other lawbreakers and troublemakers were summarily rounded up and locked in the town's log-cabin jail. It is not known what the hanged men had been charged with, or whether any of them were U.P. graders; but many of those jailed for drunkenness and disorderly conduct undoubtedly were. And if there had been any possibility of avoiding trouble as a consequence of that, Leigh Freeman proceeded to kick the situation wide-open in his next edition. Not only did he applaud the vigilantes' action, but he took cognizance of the election returns in a frenzied outburst of venom that began: "Grant, the whiskey bloated, squaw ravishing adulterer, nigger worshipping mogul is rejoicing over his election to the Presidency . . ."

As it happened, part of the grading for this section was in the hands of a contracting firm known as Cheesborough and Magee. Of the former we know nothing, but Magee has been preserved in Wyoming legend as a 240-pound, redheaded Irishman who customarily expressed disapproval of slow work on the U.P. grades by knocking laggards flat with a pick handle. It was not until two days later that this volatile giant heard of the goings-on in town. But when he did, he lost no time in mustering some two hundred of his toughest men; putting himself at their head he set off on trouble bent.

Beating down the jail door, the rampaging graders set their friends free, then went to work to take Beartown apart. Their first stop was the *Frontier Index*. Freeman, warned at the last moment, managed to slip out, climb aboard a handy mule and gallop out of town to safety. But the rioters wrecked his press and burned the tent in which it was housed. And just about then, the vigilantes began to rally. They numbered only a hundred or so, but they brought their rifles with them, whereas Magee's buckoes were armed, most of them, only with pick handles and Old Colony shovels. Assembling in good order in one of the town's largest buildings, the vigilantes opened fire as the mob approached. A little of that went a long way; soon the graders were in full retreat toward their camp, with the aroused citizens buzzing at their heels.

More than sixty years later a Beartown resident by the name of J. P. Ericson, who claimed to have seen the whole thing from beginning to end, wrote down his recollections of it. Fifty-three of the graders were shot dead that day, he said, their bodies gathered up and unceremoniously dumped into a single hastily dug trench grave.[1] An old man's memory is of course subject to failings. Most Wyoming historians put the number of dead at a more reasonable seventeen or eighteen; still plenty, in all conscience. The affair is still accepted as the bloodiest fight between white men only (as distinguished from Indian warfare) ever to take place in Wyoming Territory.

Thus Beartown was tamed. The significance of the affair lies in the evidence it affords that the railroaders were not always blessed as the bringers of progress and prosperity by plain folk along the right of way.

End of track came in shortly afterward, and did no lingering. As at Green River City, there was a bridge ready; the construction train clanked across the

Bear and went on, climbing again on the long approach to Wasatch Pass. But the railroad had the last word on Beartown after all, and it may very well have been the result of Magee's humiliation, for railroaders were and are a clannish lot, quick to close ranks against the outsider. On December 5 the *Sweetwater Mines,* another newspaper in the region, reported that "people are moving from Bear River City." And the writer went on to explain in a single meaningful sentence: "By refusing to put a switch [i.e., sidings and yard facilities] on its line there the railroad has effectively ruined Bear River City as a business town."

Hence Beartown learned a harsh lesson: it *was* the Union Pacific that brought prosperity, and could take it away as well. Certain graders may have learned restraint, too, though it is to be doubted. Of the rough and tough Magee no more is heard. Presumably he stuck to his grading contracts and his pick-handle discipline thereafter.

In very short order, just sticking to the job was providing enough trouble to suit anyone.

It was snowing now; not hard as yet, but shovel crews had to be deployed ahead of graders and track gangs, diverting precious time and energy. The spectacular bursts of four, five and more miles in a working day were no more. Now the old, standard mile a day was not bad going at all. Some days they were lucky to make that. Here was comeuppance, in a sense; the Union Pacific's turn at the kind of brutal mountain hardship Crocker's coolies had had to suffer in the Sierras. Or rather, a foretaste of it; this was only December, and the worst was yet to come.

The Central Pacific hordes were still racing up the flat valley of the Humboldt at a pace better than good. By late November their railhead had reached the northward bend where the river flowed out of the narrow defile of Palisade Canyon, named for the sheer, wind-sculptured wall of the Cortez Mountains jutting high on the eastern side. No emigrant wagon trains ever had traveled this route, the California Trail forking some way above to pursue alternate courses around it to north and south. But this was where Charley Crocker's outpost force of three thousand coolies had been at work in stark isolation since June. Under the direction of Lewis Clement, as location engineer, the Chinese had wrought a near-miracle. Crossing the river by a temporary wooden bridge, the track gangs and telegraph men found the grade waiting, and pressed ahead. Smoothly and solidly the grade led them through Fifteen-Mile Canyon, through Five-Mile Canyon and on through Twelve-Mile Canyon, eight hundred feet deep and so gloomy and cramped it was said no man or animal ever had traversed it before. This magnificent grading job, done under the most primitive conditions and in almost complete silence and obscurity, stands even today as one of the great engineering feats on the original Central Pacific line.

For impatient Crocker and dour Jim Strobridge, it was sufficient that the grade was there, and no time to indulge in kudos. Issuing from the eastward end of Twelve-Mile Canyon into a little valley pent between the river and the Tuscarora Mountains, the track-layers went to work on the next division point, and Crocker named it Carlin. Here milepost 444 (from Sacramento) was set up. The California line had been put more than three hundred miles behind. It was only December; the year was not yet over. But such rapid progress had not been accomplished without sniping from the rear. The entry into Carlin found the Associates and especially Crocker, fretting over a new problem just then swelling like a boil ready to be lanced.

That sturdy old friend and indomitable ally, the Sacramento *Union*, had unaccountably turned heckler following a change of editors in '64. And this fall the new man, James Anthony, had started printing charges that the Central Pacific track across Nevada had been laid so hurriedly and haphazardly that the road's government commissioners were guilty of inexcusable carelessness, if not worse, in approving it. One twenty-five mile stretch in particular, claimed Anthony, was so bad that passengers took their lives in their hands whenever they rode over it. The *Union* was a paper of great prestige in faraway Washington, D.C., where it maintained an active correspondent, and presently the accusations came to the attention of Secretary of the Interior Orville Hickman Browning, who appointed a special commission to go west for an on-the-spot investigation.

A good while afterward, Charley Crocker reviewed the commission's inspection trip for Hubert Bancroft's researchers. Upon approaching the suspect section of track, he recalled, he filled a tumbler with water and set it on the car floor. Then he sent word forward to the engineer to increase speed to fifty miles an hour. The willing hogger actually hit a little more than that, he said. But only a few drops were splashed from the tumbler.

"Now," declared Crocker, "gentlemen, there is your Sacramento *Union*." Upon which the commissioners laughed and agreed it "was the strongest proof that could be given."[2]

To any railroad historian who stops to consider the limitations of the light rail and rolling stock of the '60's, this yarn of Crocker's has to be pure tall tale. Undoubtedly the gentlemen of the commission were convinced in some more prosaic fashion. But convinced they certainly were. On December 3 their preliminary telegraphic report to Secretary Browning announced that the road was nearly ready for commercial operation to Carlin, that ties were being laid 2,400 to the mile and passenger trains could run safely and smoothly at speeds of fifteen to thirty miles an hour, and that heavy supply trains were being run daily with rails, ties, and fuel. Without qualification they gave it as their opinion that the road was being constructed "in good faith and in a substantial manner, without stint of labor, and the equipment [was] worthy of its character as a great national work. The telegraph line [was] first class."

It was a heartening triumph to spur a garrison finish for the construction year. But Ogden still was three hundred miles away. The Union Pacific still was coming west. U.P. engineers were in Humboldt Wells and a force of U.P. graders had been hard at work there since late summer, to the angry distress of Central observers. Speed, it seemed, only begat the need for more speed. With the days of December running out, Jim Strobridge drove his crews out of Carlin and up through Carlin Canyon, still following the course of the friendly Humboldt.

There was little snow in this arid country, but now it began to be brutally cold. The configuration of the land permitted a clean sweep for north winds blowing down out of Idaho Territory, then penned them against the southerly wall of the Ruby Mountains to lay a paralyzing chill over this whole section of the Humboldt Basin. (Modern weather stations have recorded temperatures as low as fifty degrees below zero here.) Dense, freezing fogs, the dreaded pogonip of the Paiutes, settled down at night in gelid pea soup that lifted only grudgingly under the thin morning sun, and left everything coated with glistening ice crystals. The earth was frozen rock-hard. The grade had to be blasted out with gunpowder, as it had been blasted out of Sierra granite before. But the clods turned up were still solid with frost. When spring came and melted out the moisture, all this grade would settle and sag and cause no end of trouble, as Strobridge well knew. But that problem could be dealt with in its own good time. For the present, track mileage was all that mattered.

Twenty-odd miles upriver from Carlin sprawled Elko, founded some years earlier as a freighting center to serve the Hamilton and Eureka silver districts to the south. The Central Pacific's track-layers arrived there during Christmas week and found the place running wide-open, traders and land sharks reaping a boom-town harvest, streets a-boil with rough humanity, saloons and bawdyhouses busy around the clock; in short, the Central's sole authentic taste of "Hell on Wheels," Union Pacific style.

But very little of it was for the railroaders' benefit. Seventy-five miles south, Nevada's latest big silver bonanza, the White Pine, had roared to a climax this year and Elko was headquarters metropolis for the stampede. As far as Nevada was concerned, the Central Pacific still played second fiddle to the richer promise of mining boom. Tradition claims, nevertheless, that the town had not been dignified as yet with a name that stuck. Charley Crocker is said to have picked Elko, which went down on the Central Pacific's maps and up on the depot the railroad presently built there, and so endured.

Elko marked the end of construction for '68. A thumping 363 miles of main line had been laid, far better than Crocker's promised mile per working day. Back in the Sierras, Arthur Brown's snow galleries covered twenty-three miles, thirteen of them in one unbroken stretch. And that would have to be it for the year. Most of his laborers were manning shovels now, in a faltering effort to keep the job under way, and in the snowbound forests an army of bullwhackers and their plodding spans of oxen could no longer move out the timber needed. Thus far, though, the Sacramento passage remained open. Operating headquarters in Sacramento was announcing with pardonable smugness that no Central Pacific train had suffered delays of more than two hours through the mountains; in comparison with past winters, a victory of resounding import.

This same Christmas week, however, Union Pacific track-layers struggled through falling snow to the crest of the divide between the Bear and Weber rivers and carried their own end of track into Wasatch, a mile and a half high in Utah Territory, 966 miles west of Omaha and sixty-five east of Ogden. For the year, Casement Brothers had put down 425 miles of main line track plus another hundred, more or less, of sidings—handily beating even Charley Crocker's magnificent drive across Nevada.

Central Pacific maps and the engineers' survey data still gave grounds for calculated optimism. Humboldt Wells lay only a little more than fifty miles away. The first weeks of '69 would see the Central Pacific's railhead there, while Wasatch was almost three hundred miles distant. U.P.'s claims to the Wells had gone glimmering, then. And beyond the Wells only the northern spurs of the East Humboldt Range interposed anything in the way of a serious natural obstacle. The Central's survey line circled around them in a long curve and ran northeastward over open, level desert clear to the Promontory Range north of Great Salt Lake. It looked like much easier going than the Union Pacific people would find coming west through Echo and Weber canyons—with three tunnels to blast out en route—and then turning north for their own route around the lake.

Besides, Collis Huntington had left New York toward the end of December on a hurried trip west, for the first face-to-face conference of all the Associates since '63. He would have some things to report, and probably a few ideas; trust Huntington for ideas on how to beat the other fellow. Things were happening back East, maybe things the bickering U.P. high command had been a little slow to grasp.

There might be more ways to win a railroad race than just laying track.

CHAPTER 25

A TEMPEST AT INTERIOR

Somewhere in the Wasatch Mountains as he hastened west by chartered stagecoach from the Union Pacific passenger terminus at Bryan, Collis Huntington met a party of tie-cutters on their way to the U.P. grade. Being a man always alert for any scrap of information on how the opposition was doing, he ordered his driver to stop while he engaged the men in conversation.

"I asked what the price was," he told later. "They said $1.75 each. I asked where they were hauled from, and they said from a certain canyon. They said it took three days to get a load up to the top of the Wasatch Mountains and get back to their work. I asked them what they had a day for their teams, and they said ten dollars.

"This would make the cost of each tie more than six dollars," Huntington pointed out in telling the story. At the time, the Central Pacific was paying about as much for ties transported all the way from the Sierra slopes. No doubt he found it good to know the Union Pacific was doing no better. The story, however, had an even more encouraging sequel.

"I passed back that way in the night in January, and I saw a large fire burning near the Wasatch summit, and I stopped to look at it. They had, I think, from twenty to twenty-five ties burning. They said it was so fearfully cold they could not stand it without having a fire to warm themselves."[1]

Huntington's remembering so slight an incident, and bothering to tell of it later, is illuminating. But if he habitually watched the small costs as sharply as any penny-pinching bookkeeper, his instinct for the big money and his eye for the main chance were far, far keener, and unfailing always. The mind that could take relish in a couple of dozen Union Pacific ties wastefully burning was already deep in an ambitious scheme to discomfit the opposition on a scale so huge it might end the transcontinental race out of hand, if it worked.

Quite routinely, the previous October, a map of the Central Pacific's advance survey from Monument Point all the way to the head of Echo Canyon had been submitted to the Department of the Interior. Secretary Browning had approved it with hardly any delay, though he maintained afterward that he had the sanction of President Andrew Johnson and the Cabinet before doing so. The approval, at any rate, was tantamount to giving the Central Pacific the legal right to build to Echo Summit, or so the Associates assumed.

Browning was somewhat new in his office, having replaced the resigned James Harlan of Iowa, an old and knowledgeable hand at the affairs of the Pacific Railroad, who would very likely have avoided the imbroglio that ensued. Still, if Browning acted in good faith (and there is little reason to suspect he did not), he was guilty of almost incredible naïveté. This was the first time a survey line covering territory to which both companies might justifiably lay claim had come up for official approval. On the face of it, in fact, the Union Pacific appeared to have much the stronger claim. Brigham Young and his Mormon subcontractors already were well along on grading and tunnel work in Weber and Echo canyons, under U.P. contract, and the U.P. railhead at the time was approaching the Utah line while the Central's was far out in Nevada. For an added fact, neither the original enabling Act of '62 nor any of its amendments provided a legal solution to such a situation. Thus Browning's ruling in the Central Pacific's favor—in effect, without giving the Union Pacific an opportunity to file its own claim—was obviously hasty, arbitrary and ill-considered. And to make him look even worse, the Union Pacific people did not hear of what happened for almost two months.

When they did, of course, their cries of anguish were loud enough to be heard in Washington all the way from Nassau Street, New York. Oakes and Oliver Ames at once descended on Browning, and were joined by Grenville Dodge, back at the Capitol to wind up his term as a Congressman from Iowa. Under the pressure of their indignation the bumbling Secretary backed down to the extent of assuring them that his action had *not* bestowed any exclusive privilege on the Central Pacific. All he had meant to do, he insisted, was designate an official route so as to insure that the two railroads would meet *somewhere,* as Congress had intended. But until they did, he declared, both companies had the right to lay track, subject to the usual approval by their government commissioners and acceptance in Washington.

Grenville Dodge wanted to know, probably somewhat testily, if that track had to be laid on the Central's survey line; the Union Pacific's own, he asserted, was much superior. Not at all, the Secretary replied; it was his intention merely to designate an approved route *in general*.[2]

So, finally, the Union Pacific men had subsided, still ruffled over the affair but reassured to the extent that they foresaw no future obstacles placed in their way as a result of it.

As happens all too often with the well-intentioned blunderer, however, Orville Browning had started something that would not easily be stopped. His retreat under the U.P.'s fire, as it was inevitably construed from the Central Pacific side, left the Associates disappointed and a little shaken, but still convinced that they, and they alone, had been awarded a legal priority to build to the head of Echo.

So they insisted for the record, anyway. Actually there were, and are, strong indications that the whole contretemps had been precipitated by a typically bold gambit on the part of Collis Huntington. The extent and thoroughness of the Central Pacific surveys east of Great Salt Lake and beyond were, at best, open to serious doubt. Grenville Dodge questioned them with particular sharpness. He declared that he himself had met and talked with Butler Ives in the Wasatches, and that the Central Pacific man had admitted his company was running a trial survey only. The outspoken chief engineer for the U.P. would shortly go even further. In an affidavit read on the Senate floor in April, and subsequently entered in the *Congressional Globe,* he would state flatly that the Central Pacific map submitted to the Department of the Interior was "fraudulent," and go on to add that it was worthless for practical engineering purposes, having "no topography, no stations, no courses, no angles, no scale—nothing by which any line could be identified by it on the ground."[3]

Fraudulent or not, the map had failed to win the immediate victory the Associates had hoped for. But Orville Browning's approval of it, though now hedged about by his later reservations and hence subject to arguable interpretations, nevertheless constituted an advantage of sorts for the Central Pacific. And the Associates, whether sincere or still clinging to an audacious bluff, were determined not to relinquish that advantage. Collis Huntington had advocated boldly that the Mormon contractors engaged by Leland Stanford be put to work immediately on a grade westward from Echo, as a physical buttress for the Central's claim. For once, he had been voted down by his more cautious colleagues in favor of a wait-and-see policy. At the meeting just concluded, however, it had been decided to augment the contract with Benson, Farr and West by assigning them to grade eastward from Monument Point to Ogden, thus tightening the battle lines in the Salt Lake Valley. And considering what was to happen just a few short months in the future, it is altogether reasonable to suppose that the outlines of a new and even bolder plan were forming in Huntington's tireless brain even as he jounced eastward in his hired stage this first week of January, '69.

With any luck—bad weather holding the Union Pacific snowbound in the Wasatches, for example—things might yet work out favorably. That was to say, if a man was the kind to leave his affairs to luck. Huntington was not. With the inauguration of Ulysses S. Grant in March, a new administration would be installed in Washington. Grant was the good friend of Grenville Dodge and so, perhaps, somewhat too good a friend of the U.P. also. A poor risk, if things came again to a governmental showdown. Better, if need be, to hurry affairs a little, deal with the Johnson administration and Mr. Browning. Huntington thought there might be a way. . . .

CHAPTER 26

WASATCH ODYSSEY

Mr. J. H. Beadle, itinerant correspondent for the Cincinnati *Commercial* and author of one of the countless books on the West ground out by practically every literate venturer beyond the Missouri River during the '60's and '70's, told of breakfasting at the California Hotel at Wasatch this January. Men were nailing the weather-boarding to the outside of the building at the time, he reported, but the temperature inside the room was five degrees below zero, and from his place at table he could inspect the outer landscape through gaping cracks in the walls. For a week, he added, the temperature never lifted higher than three below, but building went on at a furious pace, not stopping night or day. During the town's three-month career as the Union Pacific's terminal it acquired a cemetery with a population of forty-three. Of these, Mr. Beadle also noted, only five died naturally. Three were drunks who fell down in the street and froze to death and two were prostitutes who committed suicide; one inhaled charcoal fumes, the other chloroform.[1]

Everybody had his troubles this winter. In his final report to the U.P. board, Grenville Dodge mentioned plaintively that "Men who went out in the morning with overcoats on, and would have to work with overcoats on all day, were not able to do very large days' works." The simple statement rings, somehow, with the faint but telling pathos of a small discouragement piled atop a heap of vaster ones; the last straw that did not quite break the camel's back, but perhaps came close.

Collis Huntington was not the only front-office man to brave a trip west this winter. Late in December Dr. Thomas Durant was on the scene for the Union Pacific, a circumstance that contributed materially to everyone's complaints of trouble. Durant was not popular along the U.P. right of way, and never had been. He was too much the imperious brass hat from "higher up," groomed and barbered and tailored too elegantly by far, and altogether lacking in the common touch and the bluff qualities of man-to-man leadership possessed by men like Dodge and the Casements and Samuel Reed. And his authority along the grades and at railhead was by this time badly impaired. It is unlikely that the session with U. S. Grant at Fort Sanders in July had been bruited about very generally. But earlier, during the dispute over Durant's proposal to locate the divisional shops at Laramie City instead of Cheyenne, he and Grenville Dodge had engaged in a public altercation on Laramie's main street. Dodge had declared, in the hearing of any number of bystanders, that *he* intended to give the orders, and that those orders, not Durant's, would be the ones obeyed in the Union Pacific construction camps. The Paddies and their bosses had said a hearty "Amen!" to that, and the story had spread far and wide along the line, with deep satisfaction in the discomfiture of the high-handed dude from New York.

So Thomas Durant was scarcely the man to inspire any great upsurge of effort in the midst of a Wasatch winter's hardships. It was not for lack of trying, though.

Sam Reed's letters to his wife complained disgustedly that the vice-president was interfering with everything this winter, slowing the work down far more than he speeded it up. But patient Mrs. Reed had been listening to similar tales of woe ever since '64, the engineer carping constantly of overwork, in one letter threatening to quit, in the next bemoaning the fact that he had not. Despite his undoubted competence, and beneath a disposition pleasant and likable enough on the surface, he comes through by the testimony of his own letters as a confirmed complainer. Jack Casement, more philosophically, hewed to his track-laying and took the attitude that if Durant wanted to throw money away by disorganizing everything on the right of way, that was Durant's own business. Grenville Dodge fretted over pyramiding construction costs, multiplied by Durant's speed-up orders earlier this year and his present insistence that work be pushed at full throttle in the face of an adverse mountain winter.[2]

The fact remains that but for this hard insistence on Durant's part the Union Pacific might very well have lost a fatal amount of ground to the oncoming Central this winter. Then as now, prodding from the front office was not taken in a kindly light by the men out on the line.

The truth was that behind the rugged façade of activity at railhead and down through the canyons toward Great Salt Lake the Union Pacific was a pretty creaky piece of financial machinery, held together by little more than the proverbial spit and baling wire. Oakes Ames's $47,000,000 contract for construction from the one hundredth meridian had ended somewhere east of Piedmont on the Wasatch approaches (the exact point is still a matter of some dispute), and with it Ames was about at the end of his rope. Ames Tool and

Shovel Company had grown and prospered at a prodigious rate during the construction years, was now turning out Old Colony shovels by the thousands of dozens annually. But it was neck-deep in debt, its output mortgaged far into the future. Erstwhile friends, sober financiers who once had sought Oakes Ames's advice, had turned away from him as a wild man for taking on such a stupendously risky contract in the first place. They were congratulating themselves now, saying they had been right all along.

Drained by the ill-advised dividend at the close of '67, and by others afterward, the Credit Mobilier was short of money, forced to hypothecate Union Pacific securities for whatever they would bring for cash to carry on. The condition of the Union Pacific's own treasury was anemic, as indeed it always had been. In the crisis the Ames contract had been replaced by another, a sort of catch-as-catch-can document drawn up to cover construction to the shadowy finish line. Again the Credit Mobilier was the instrument, though for some reason a U.P. tie-cutting contractor named James Davis was persuaded to put his name to it. He would lose money, in the final summing up.

Meanwhile, grading and timber-cutting contractors, and even the Casements, had been paid only in sporadic driblets for months past. Some of the grading firms had dropped by the wayside during the long haul from the Laramie Plains, either unable to stay in business under the circumstances or shunning the more difficult stretches of country as unprofitable even had they been paid regularly. Casement Brothers had taken over where necessary, pushing the grades forward as relentlessly as they did the iron. But pay for workers all along the line was four to six weeks in arrears, train-operating personnel feeling the pinch as well as iron-slingers, graders and axmen. Dodge, the Casements, Sam Reed and other executives pleaded, promised, cajoled and threatened. By such extemporaneous persuasion—and because back wages amounted to stakes too great to walk away and leave, and a man could always get his board, at least, in the construction camps—most of the work forces were held on the jobs. But the mood was growing surly. They would not stick forever.

In point of fact, the situation was not so bad as it looks today. Slow pay, and even bosses who decamped without paying at all, were phenomena not uncommon in the frontier '60's. It was the poor working stiff's usual lot to wait for his payday till his employer's profits were in hand. Similar conditions existed on many, if not most, of the railroads that snaked across the West in the years that followed.

Nevertheless, and in galling contrast, the Associates' Contract and Finance Company was paying its men, Irishmen, coolies and Mormon contractors alike, regularly and in good hard gold and silver on the barrel head.

Characteristically, Dr. Durant ignored all this and continued with his bland assertions that the work must be pushed harder; day and night shifts, and a seven-day work week. The men growled, but he promised double pay for Sundays; promises again, but apparently they helped. In his own way, Durant was no shirker. From end of track west of Wasatch he journeyed down the grade to Tunnelville at the upper end of Echo Canyon. In November the advance guard of Union Pacific Irishmen had reached there and taken over from Mormon crews who had been at work on the 772-foot bore of tunnel No. 2 since July. The takeover had been amicable; the Mormons had simply moved farther down the canyon and now were busy on the grade there under the direction of Bishop John Sharp of the Latter-day Saints, a partner of Brigham Young. "His new neighbors and he are upon very affable terms," the Salt Lake City *Deseret News* had reported shortly afterward, in a communiqué more significant than it may seem at first glance. For there had been no little uneasiness among the God-fearing Mormon people over the effects of this first contact with the profane and dissolute railroaders.

But Dr. Durant did not go down to greet the bishop. Those Mormons had back wages coming, too, in bald violation of the terms of Brigham Young's contract, which specified regular payments covering 80 percent of the work done every month. And Brigham Young was not a man to be put off with glowing talk like an ignorant pick-and-shovel Paddy. Last fall Durant had had to make a personal appearance at Salt Lake City with Grenville Dodge in order to placate the unpaid Saint. He had done it, finally, only by coming up with most of the money then owing, and was not anxious to have to do so again. Instead, he repeated his speed-up orders and his promises to the Irish tunnel grubbers, and turned back to Wasatch, his private Pullman palace car and the long run home.

Thus he and Collis Huntington headed for New York only a few weeks apart, for a last behind-the-scenes grappling in the long transcontinental struggle.

A lonely man was Thomas Clark Durant as his train rattled eastward this January of '69. His was the very special loneliness of the man who dares greatly, for great stakes, plays by no rules save his own and dares trust no human creature but himself. The years of internecine warfare in the Union Pacific's secret councils had left him virtually friendless. His devious, lone-wolf skirmishing with the Ames faction in the Credit Mobilier and on the U.P. board was all uphill now, his position kept barely tenable only by means of a series of delaying actions skillfully and doggedly fought with lawsuits and legal injunctions. He must have realized that; must have realized, too, that the whole sorry scuffle was by this time an open secret on Wall Street and among informed Easterners generally; the Credit Mobilier beginning to be publicly suspect as an instrument of flagrant financial juggling and corruption. In Washington the Congress itself was growing ever more sensitive to the charges and the rumors. Since '67 there had been increasingly querulous demands there for an accounting of the public monies turned over to the builders of the Pacific Railroad. He was aware of that too, of course, and he knew how Congress could worry an issue when political controversy got into the picture. The Pacific Railroad had been a political controversy since before '62. Quite possibly, like a locomotive with steam pressure building up in the boiler, this whole thing would have to blow off sooner or later.

Old hand though he was at railroad enterprise and all the speculative maneuver that went with it, Thomas Durant never had tackled a manipulation as big as this Union Pacific colossus was turning out to be. His back was to the wall now; he was slipping.

To his rear, down the snowy grades from Wasatch to Tunnelville and on beyond, the restless doctor's going fetched great sighs of relief. The sheer physical problems faced by the engineers and the army of graders, iron men, axmen, bridge gangs and wire-stringers were forbidding enough without additional complication. For the men of the Union Pacific, in fact, this was the great time of testing, and all the more critical because it came with the goal almost within reach.

Payment was exacted now for the last-minute rush in which the location surveys had been finalized. There may have been some justice in Durant's charge at Fort Sanders that Grenville Dodge had wasted time in excessive reconnaissance and preliminary survey work. On the other hand, Dodge and his engineers—Evans, Blickensderfer and their subordinates—had done surpassingly well under the circumstances, though the proof was not forthcoming until some thirty years later. Shortly after the turn of the century, track relocations carried out as part of a broad program of improvement and modernization on the Union Pacific were able to shorten the original route by no more than forty-odd miles. And of these, more than thirty were accounted for by restoring the lines changed by Silas Seymour between the Missouri River and Omaha Summit in '64 and on the western descent of the Black Hills in '68. In his old age, Grenville Dodge would note the facts with pardonable satisfaction.[3]

Regardless, in these opening months of '69 location lines so recently completed meant that many preparations which should have been started long in advance had to be carried out now, under the worst of conditions, or left undone altogether. Snowsheds or snow fences might have helped in places, but there had been no time to build them. There had been no time for permanent bridge spans either. Rough timber work had to do instead, and cutting and transporting timber during the throes of a Wasatch winter was no light task, as Collis Huntington had observed.

The tunnel at the head of Echo Canyon, not begun till July, might have proved a more hampering obstacle than it was, had it been necessary to cut through granite like that encountered by the Central's men in the Sierras. But heavy excavations required by long, deep approach cuts at both ends robbed both time and manpower from the grade ahead. And the soft clay rock and sandstone crumbled on exposure to the air, so that every foot had to be timbered as the blasting proceeded.

Whether nitroglycerin was employed in this tunnel has not been definitely established, the contemporary evidence on both sides hazy and inconclusive. But the explosive very definitely was used in tunnels three and four, farther down in Weber Canyon. Very little information ever was given out by Union Pacific authorities, however, as indeed very little ever was said by the Central on the same subject in '66 and '67. From a public relations point of view, if from no other, both companies chose to be as close-mouthed as possible. Even reminiscing a long while later, Grenville Dodge vouchsafed no more than that nitroglycerin was used in "all" Union Pacific tunnels, "greatly expediting the work."[4]

Presumably the ingredients were freighted in and the explosive compounded on the spot, as had been done on the Central, for transporting the finished product any distance by rail and trail would have been unthinkably hazardous. However it was handled, the U.P. blasters appear to have been somewhat luckier, or perhaps more skillful, than the Central's. There were no recorded instances of lives lost by the kind of premature or delayed explosions that obliterated so many of Crocker's coolies two years earlier.

Headings did not meet in tunnel No. 2 until the end of January, and it would be late spring, at best, before track could be laid through. But Jack Casement's iron gangs, working in night-long shifts by lantern light, had arrived at the head of Echo much earlier than that, during January's first week, in fact, and had not paused to wait. Veering aside, they hammered timbers together into a rickety stiltwork, scratched a goat path into the frowning red rock of the canyon wall and laid a perilous eight-mile zigzag of track—a "shoofly" in modern rail-road parlance; they called it "the Z"—to run around the unfinished bore. Now supplies and materials could go forward in more satisfactory quantities to the diggers laboring in the west heading; and tools, the crying need, to the Latter-day Saints at work on the grade all the way out into the Salt Lake Valley.

The track-layers toiled ahead along the narrow banks of Echo Creek, crossing and recrossing the stream a total of thirty-one times in all, fighting their way through snows that fell and drifted, packed down and hardened to lay an icy crust over the frozen grade. Never men to sneer at innovation, Jack and Dan Casement put their heads together and decided on their boldest gamble yet. Ties and rails were laid directly on the snow and ice, without benefit of ballast or the grade beneath.

The expedient was somewhat less than successful, yet not entirely a failure either. Trains did get through, carefully creeping with crews poised to jump for their lives. Sometimes they had to. The *Deseret News* reported accidents that might easily have been disasters but somehow never were: cars derailed and teetering on the edge of perilous drop-offs. Less well authenticated but certainly likely enough was the story of an entire iron train, locomotive to rear end, that took a section of track with it in a long sidewise slide into the creek bed. In such a driving rush to shove the iron forward, everyone worked on the thin edge of trouble.

The standard link and pin coupler had a nasty little penchant for coming apart as slack ran in and out on a moving train. That happened to a sixteen-car construction drag drifting down through Echo Canyon. No one noticed at the time; four loaded flatcars were left behind for a while, and then began to pick up speed on the descending grade. Intent on the track ahead, the hogger was warned by a shout from one of the brakemen, looked rearward and saw the errant flats hurtling down on him like a pursuing fury. He jerked his throttle open and fled before them, whistle bouncing its wildcat squalls back and forth between the canyon walls while track workers ahead hurried to line up switches and clear the right of way. The chase was brief but hair-raising, bucking and rolling around tight curves and over shaky wooden bridges till a construction foreman riding the train thought of tumbling ties off the last car to block the runaways. It worked, and they bounded off the embankment in a glorious, splintery crash. A couple of workmen aboard them who might have tied down the brakes, slept through the whole incident instead, ended up in a deep snowbank and came out of it with nothing more serious than a bad shaking up and the shock of a rough awakening. There was a lot of luck riding the U.P. rails this winter, along with all the hardship.

But these were hard-won miles, and a literal miracle of jerry-building.

By the middle of January, in defiance of hindrances great and small, the first locomotive steamed into Weber Canyon, below Echo, and rolled past milepost 1,000. A tall, lone pine tree stood at the spot. Someone nailed a bit of plank to it, daubed with crude lettering, "1000 MILES," and tree and sign stood for many years afterward as a notable landmark on the transcontinental line.

Now it was only five more miles to tunnel No. 3, 508 feet long, burrowing through a spur of dark limestone and blue quartzite on a three-and-a-half-degree curve. Work on it had been started in September and was still in progress, so another by-passing track had to be laid as the rails plunged on.

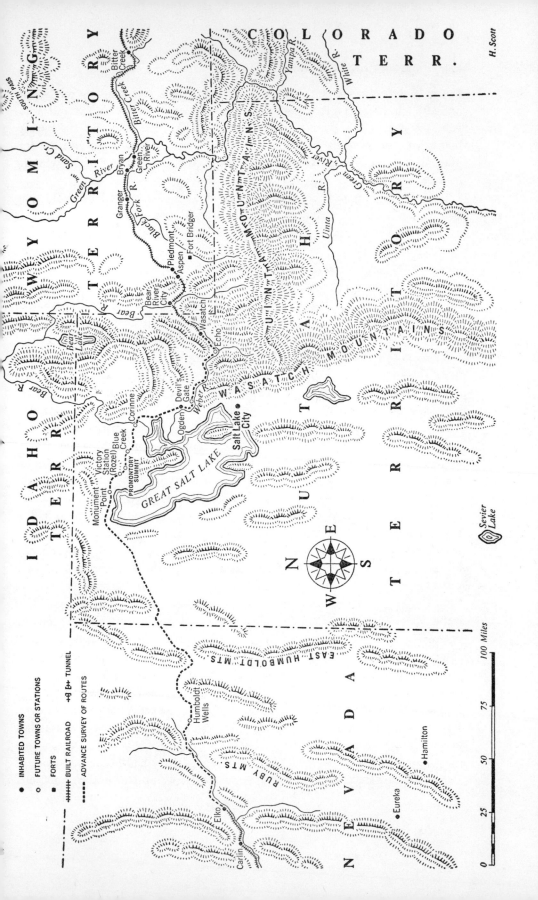

COLORADO TERR.

H. Scott

WYOMING

South Pass

Sand Cr.

Bitter Creek

Green River

Bitter Creek

Bryan

Granger

Green R.

Green River

Black's Fork R.

Piedmont

Aspen

Fort Bridger

Bear River City

Wasatch

Echo

Bear Lake

Bear R

Devil's Gate

Weber R.

Corinne

Ogden

Blue Creek

Victory Station (Rozel)

PROMONTORY SUMMIT

Monument Point

Salt Lake City

GREAT SALT LAKE

IDAHO TERRITORY

UTAH TERRITORY

UINTAH MOUNTAINS

Uinta R.

Green River

Yampa R.

White R.

WASATCH MOUNTAINS

NEVADA TERRITORY

Sevier Lake

N E S W

Humboldt Wells

EAST HUMBOLDT MTS.

RUBY MTS.

Elko

Carlin

Eureka

Hamilton

NEVADA

● INHABITED TOWNS
○ FUTURE TOWNS OR STATIONS
■ FORTS
┼┼┼┼ BUILT RAILROAD
╞═╡ TUNNEL
•••••• ADVANCE SURVEY OF ROUTES

0   25   50   75   100 Miles

But only three-quarters of a mile farther, tunnel No. 4 was nearly ready, this one 297 feet long on a four-degree curve. And less than twenty-five miles beyond lay Ogden, and the shore of Great Salt Lake. Painfully but stubbornly, borne forward on stout Mormon dependability, Irish toughness and the implacable resource of the brothers Casement, the Union Pacific was winning its way through the Wasatch winter.

Thus far the weather had been kind, even taking January's bitter cold snap into account. Snowfall, though hampering, had been much lighter than was usual in this mountain region. The supply line eastward had been kept relatively free of trouble also, in spite of one blizzard that broke early in January, flogged all the western part of Wyoming Territory with snow and gale-force winds and choked train movements to a perilous crawl. Materials continued to come through and even to pile up in dumps at railhead; fortunately, too, for weather is a fickle beast. It was a little late in showing its teeth this winter, but when it did the snarl was far-reaching.

The Central Pacific, which had been basking in a mild winter also, was hit first. Toward the end of the first week in February a mighty storm buried the Sierra crest under tons of snow. For a while, by dint of all-out efforts, double-headed supply trains struggled over the hump and down into the Truckee Valley. But the flow of iron was cut to the bone as the storm raged unabated, and the pace of track-laying east of Elko slowed accordingly. Then a slide carried away a trestle just below Cisco, and in the whole section up over the summit and beyond trains were stranded and snowplows bogged down in the clogging drifts. Iron trains and revenue movements piled up on the western Sierra approaches; vital loading operations on the levee at Sacramento had to stop for want of the empty cars immobilized on the Nevada side. It might have been the brutal frustration of that construction winter of 1866-67 all over again, but Arthur Brown's new snowsheds came through the test brilliantly. Not a one of them collapsed or was seriously damaged; only in the stretches not yet roofed over had the drifts been able to block the line. For four straight days not a wheel turned, but then the railroad was able to dig out and start moving again. The blizzard blew on eastward, and it was the Union Pacific's turn to catch it even worse.

A telegraphic dispatch from Salt Lake City in the Sacramento *Union*'s issue of February 20 remarked that the "most terrific storm for years" was then raging, with mail service from Omaha completely blocked. It appears, however, that the worst of the snow, if not the cold, had leaped far over the Wasatches to vent its fullest fury on the Laramie Plains in eastern Wyoming. At the time the *Union* printed its dispatch, Dan Casement already had headed east out of Echo with a snowplow and shovel crew. Arriving at Rawlins without any undue trouble they found something like two hundred eastbound passengers stranded, with food stocks in the town running low, train crews' discipline beginning to come apart under the strain and nothing moving between there and Laramie, almost a hundred miles away, save snow and the wind that drove it in blinding sheets across the land.

Fighting on eastward, Casement's crew was able to make less than thirty miles during the next four days, bucking drifts as deep as twenty-five feet in some of the cuts. Finally the plow and its locomotives stalled for good, and Dan, every bit as doughty a battler as his more celebrated brother Jack, led his men on afoot. They slept in stations and lineside shanties along the way, cleared a path through the massive drifts as best they could and eventually floundered into Laramie with Dan himself almost dead of exposure and exhaustion. The town was bulging at the seams with several hundred westbound passengers tied up there, the snow still coming down without letup and no prospect of getting a train through. Presently, though, part of the two hundred left behind at Rawlins came tramping in, having elected to walk also. They were weary and somewhat frostbitten but otherwise little the worse for the experience. This was a group of prominent California Republicans on their way to Washington for Ulysses S. Grant's inaugural. But they never made it. March 4 had come and gone by the time they got as far as St. Louis, in a mood to unburden themselves of some pretty sour comment on the Union Pacific Railroad and the vaunted transcontinental route.

The line between Laramie and Rawlins was not opened for three weeks, all told, so that the U.P. suffered a much worse tie-up than the Central. In the interim, however, the materials stockpiled at Wasatch and beyond prevented any drastic work stoppages. Supplies ran very short, and Sam Reed and Grenville Dodge did some tall worrying before the first train from Omaha came slugging up the grade into Utah Territory and whistled "down brakes" for the end of the line, but Jack Casement's track gangs had laid iron down to Devil's Gate before the end of February. The Weber River boils out of its canyon there and flows across open, gently sloping terrain to the shores of Great Salt Lake.

Bad as it was, the storm had come a little too late to be a real catastrophe.

The iron-slingers crossed the Weber one last time, over a mighty trestle knocked together in a week out of 180,000 feet of rough timber—a fact noted with some awe by a Mormon correspondent of the *Deseret News*—and found Brigham Young's good, level grade ready for the dash into Ogden, only ten miles away. Nothing could stop them now. The race was as good as won.

Or so it seemed.

CHAPTER 27

MR. HUNTINGTON IN WASHINGTON

From Sacramento and Salt Lake City the Central Pacific Associates had watched the passing of '68 in a comfortable glow of certainty that everything was going well for them. The splendid progress of track work during the year; official government approval of the route through Echo Canyon; mild weather; the Union Pacific's apparent discomfiture in the Wasatch Mountains —all this contributed toward a pleasant mood in which to spend the holidays. It was quite out of character for the knotty Pacific Railroad enterprise, though. It did not last long, and it ended rudely, in a series of jolting realities.

Out on the survey line stretching northeastward from Elko to Humboldt Wells and from the Wells on toward the Utah border, track-laying progress fell off alarmingly during the opening weeks of the new year. All sorts of sudden difficulties cropped up. The storm that briefly blocked the Sierra passage in February was among the least of them. Charley Crocker's tremendous supply shuttle between Sacramento and the farthest reaches of Nevada was slowed and tangled by mishaps, miscalculations and schedules gone awry. Most of these were probably no more than the kind of thing to be expected in so big an undertaking carried on under the handicaps the Central faced. Basically, the trouble lay in the natural hazards of wind and weather that were inherent in the long sea routes around Cape Horn or via the Isthmus; an old problem to be sure, but magnified to huge proportions now by the accelerated construction pace. And knowing the reasons why was poor compensation for delays that resulted when rail shipments lumbered up to end of track without the ties on which to lay them, or ties came through while desperately needed iron reposed in the cargo hold of some ship still beating up for the Golden Gate against stiff head winds, or any of innumerable other things went wrong to fray the tempers of Crocker and Jim Strobridge.

There was a rash of wrecks on the line, too, as '69 began. The Sierras had other difficulties to put in the way than snows and winter gales. In any season, the long, steep descent from the east portal of Summit Tunnel to the Truckee meadows represented mountain railroading at its roughest. Engineers and undermanned crews of car hands nursing heavy trains downgrade with brakes clubbed down to the smoking point faced the constant peril of runaways or of coupler pins working out of their links, as occurred on that wild incident on the U.P. in Echo Canyon. On grades that plunged 115 feet to the mile through looping curves, though, the happy ending was rare.

The Reno *Crescent* occupied a front-row seat for the show, and its columns told a running story of men killed or injured, locomotives badly damaged and cars shattered as January and February crept by. The *Blue Jay,* a fine, spanking-new passenger engine, plowed into a stalled timber train headed upgrade for Cisco. A construction train parted coming down the mountain; its hogger tried to outrun the loose cars, apparently, but could not; two brakemen died in the crash and several cars were reduced to kindling. Within the week, another runaway train thundered through the sweeping curves along the Truckee River almost to Reno before it could be stopped. Then, while the engineer was on the ground inspecting his locomotive's abused running gear, a following train ran into the rear end and strewed the right of way with the wreckage of a dozen cars and their ladings.

The high incidence of such rear-end collisions suggests that the density of traffic on the line and the shortage of skilled railroad operating personnel were contributing factors to the awesome record. In truth, the Central Pacific was outgrowing its facilities badly during this critical period.

Unlike the U.P., which had started out of Omaha into the barren and sparsely settled Territory of Nebraska, the Central had had, in the populous Sacramento Valley, a good source of local passenger and freight revenue from the very beginning. That business had grown steadily as the rails made contact with Dutch Flat and Cisco and struggled over the Sierra crest and down to the Nevada line. Now, with Reno thriving as the busy connection for the Comstock, and with trackage completed through other mineral districts across the state—Winnemucca, Golconda, the White Pine—revenue service burgeoned in a fine, profitable spate. Theodore Judah had predicted as much in the long-ago promotional years. But not even Judah, nor anyone else, could have foreseen the present frantic construction push and the consequent burden Charley Crocker's supply trains were imposing. Combined with the revenue freight and passenger traffic, that burden strained the locomotive roster unmercifully, put cars at a premium and clogged the rails beyond the safe capacities of dispatching know-how and signal systems of the era. Seasoned railroad old-timers were not to be had.

California still lacked anything comparable to the network of railroads which covered the Eastern United States, and thus afforded no reservoir of experienced engineers, firemen, conductors, brakemen, mechanics, telegraphers, switchmen, dispatchers—all the many and varied skills in the great army of manpower needed to keep a railroad running smoothly. Greenhorns were learning as they went, but learning the hard way in a hard and dangerous school.

Out at railhead the labor shortage was hitting Jim Strobridge especially hard this winter. From the start, bonanza-chasers who hired out solely for a free ticket to Nevada had caused serious annoyance, and it grew worse the farther the rails penetrated toward the mining camps. Now, with Elko on the Central's main line and Chloride Flat, the Eberhardt, Yellow Jacket and other lodes teeming with excited prospectors as part of the big White Pine furor, construction workers were deserting in unprecedented droves. Two thousand new hands were hired and given free transportation out to Humboldt Wells, the company stated later, for every hundred who actually got there and stuck.

No wonder, then, that construction stumbled badly in these crucial opening months of '69, just when the need for a driving finish was so pointed. What touched the Associates with even greater consternation, though, was the unexpected speed with which the Union Pacific had come on through the Wasatch Mountains in the dead of winter. Moreover, the U.P. people were acting, all at once, as though they had no intention of conceding anything to the Central. Now, with eighty-odd miles of grade reaching eastward along their own survey line from Humboldt Wells toward Promontory Summit, they had recalled the contingent of veteran Casement Brothers Irishmen who had put it in, and had them hard at work along with Brigham Young's Mormons on a corresponding grade north of Ogden.

Leland Stanford had remained in and around Salt Lake City as the guardian of his company's interests in the land of the Latter-day Saints and a close watcher of Union Pacific activities ever since his hurried trip out in the summer of '68. With growing nervousness, he reported developments to Sacramento and New York. The bid for Humboldt Wells might well be, probably was, nothing more than a costly bluff, typical in an adversary like Dr. Durant. Collis Huntington had thought so all along. But suddenly it seemed that nothing could be taken for granted any more. Stanford grumbled over the slowness of Charley Crocker's progress in Nevada, and the unusually light snowfall in the Wasatches which had failed to bog the Union Pacific down.[1] Then those worries abruptly became as nothing. About the middle of January, more than a month before Jack Casement's iron-slingers came hammering down to Devil's Gate, Collis Huntington forwarded the most unnerving development yet.

Arriving back in New York City from his trip west, Huntington had found bad news waiting in the form of a report from one Richard Franchot, a former New York Congressman and at present the Central Pacific's chief lobbyist in Washington. Secretary of the Interior Orville Browning had acted again; thrown a real bombshell this time.

The Secretary, obviously confused and irritated by the melee of claims and counterclaims in the wake of his ill-advised approval of the Central's survey from Monument to the head of Echo Canyon, had appointed a special commission to assemble at Salt Lake City, inspect the situation at first hand and recommend the one best survey line between the two approaching railheads. The commission's powers were broad and apparently final. They could approve either company's existing survey or they could reject both in favor of a wholly new line of their own, if they deemed that advisable. In which case, of course, a frightening amount of money already spent on conflicting grades would turn out to have been wasted with no possibility whatever of recompense.

Browning's action was no victory for the Union Pacific, of course; the U.P. would welcome this kind of governmental interference no more happily than the Central. But the Associates stood to lose the most, or so it appeared. They had counted heavily on Orville Browning's previous approval; had accepted it as final (or professed to) and on the basis of it had assumed the whole section in question to be theirs by right of official decision. At the very least, such an attitude had placed them in the advantageous position of dealing from strength in any future arguments on the subject. But now, without warning, Browning had chopped the ground from under their feet. Huntington, having dispatched the unwelcome news west, fired off a long, indignant letter of protest to President Andrew Johnson (who, it appears, did nothing about it) and sat down to do some hard pondering on his next move.

Apparently some little time elapsed before the Western Associates rallied from their shock and began to think in terms of what might be done to retrieve the situation. They had little enough with which to work. The names of the special commission members offered both mild encouragement and the reverse. One, a Lieutenant Colonel Williamson, had been a member of Browning's earlier special commission which reported such unqualified approval of the Central's construction across Nevada in '68. He was, in fact, still in California, and the chances seemed good that he might be disposed to favor the Central in this instance also. The commission's chairman, Major General Gouverneur Warren, was an Army engineer of unquestioned competence, though still suffering under something of a public stigma as the officer whom Little Phil Sheridan had relieved of command under enemy fire during the battle at Five Forks, Virginia, in '65. The public still took its wartime heroes and its wartime goats pretty seriously; there was nothing in Warren's reputation, however, to suggest that he would be anything but a capable and impartial investigator in Utah.

Quite inexplicably, considering Leland Stanford's long stay at Salt Lake City, and the closeness with which he had followed the Union Pacific's progress, the name of the commission's third member, Jacob Blickensderfer, Jr., seems at first to have been accepted with equanimity. Blickensderfer, of course, was the U.P.'s chief engineer on the Utah Division, and as such extremely unlikely to agree to any condemnation of a U.P. survey line run under his own personal supervision.

How so blatantly unsuitable an appointment could have been made in the first place was never explained, by Secretary Browning or anyone else. But as soon as Stanford realized who Blickensderfer was—which was not till some time after the commission had assembled and started work—he wired vehement objections to Collis Huntington, with the suggestion that in all fairness the Central's own assistant chief engineer, Lewis Clement, ought to be named as a fourth commission member. Huntington hastened to Washington to press the point, and Browning agreed readily enough, though there was a protracted delay before Clement received the notification of his appointment.

It did not matter anyway. In the end the whole affair was a great deal of ado about nothing. The commission started out to inspect the terrain in Weber Canyon, was somehow persuaded to break that off and travel west with Leland Stanford for an examination of the entire Central Pacific line, and finally was lost in the shuffle of events that followed so fast and confusedly that hardly anyone could keep up with them or guess what might happen next.

But that was all in the future. For the immediate present, Stanford, Crocker and Hopkins worried in gloom and uneasiness, suspected the worst and saw nothing but woe ahead. And in such an atmosphere, General Jack Casement's track gangs storming down along the Weber River on their way to Ogden loomed large and threatening indeed.

Calmly Huntington wired reassurances. In effect, Crocker and Stanford were advised to hew to the line and leave the problems to him: "Come right on as fast as you can, and leave a good road behind."[2] He had thought things over and made his plans; now was the time for doing.

The timing, in fact, hardly could have been improved. Down on the banks of the Potomac the Johnson administration waited out its last lame-duck days, marking time till Ulysses S. Grant's takeover in a mood of impotence and defeat. It had not been a successful administration. A radical Republican Congress had thrashed Andrew Johnson badly in the savage controversy over his efforts to impose a soft Reconstruction policy on the states of the late Confederacy, and his subsequent campaign to take the issue to the public had proved undignified and ineptly managed. Mutinous Secretary of War Edwin M.

Stanton had added humiliation to injury by barricading himself in his office and successfully defying all attempts to dismiss him, while Grant had betrayed his President shamefully by refusing to embroil himself in the mess, or so Andrew Johnson would believe until the day he died. Finally, the President's slim one-vote acquittal in the impeachment proceedings just last May had been an unsatisfactory sort of vindication, leaving the administration shaken and drained of any capability for real national leadership.

No doubt Collis Huntington, the man who overlooked nothing, found this troubled situation to his liking. He still relied on that much discussed approval of the Central Pacific's survey to the head of Echo. The Cabinet had endorsed Browning's decision there and no one had since reversed it, no matter how far the Secretary himself had backed away under Union Pacific pressure. But Huntington had other arguments to use if need be. He knew, as practically everybody in New York and Washington knew, that the U.P. had come under heavy fire for shoddy and dangerous construction, by critics both inside and outside of Congress. To be sure, the Central, too, had had its critics on the same score—witness the Sacramento *Union's* charges just last year—and the Union Pacific's government commissioners already had officially accepted 940 miles of the line west from Omaha. But that was neither here nor there; the point was, the matter still was open to argument. And no less an authority than Jesse L. Williams, senior member of the U.P.'s board of government directors and a staunch friend of the company besides, had decried the haste with which the grades had been put in and the track laid down.

Huntington probably knew, also, that Williams had recommended to the Union Pacific directorate that a sum of three million dollars be set aside to make necessary improvements in the road, and had in addition advocated Congressional action to permit the withholding of final federal subsidies till it was certain that the Pacific Railroad had been brought up to snuff.[3]

The rising ground swell of rumors charging wholesale fraud and chicanery in the relationship of the Credit Mobilier and the Union Pacific board was all to the good too, from Huntington's point of view. His own personal reputation, and the Central's corporate one, still were excellent on Wall Street and in Washington. Under the circumstances, that might make a very pointed and useful little contrast.

Taken altogether, and in the hands of a man who knew how to use it, here was the material for some very potent persuasion. Huntington was the man. He understood exactly what he wanted; and he possessed, besides, the relentless patience of the honest, homespun Yankee insisting on his rights, coupled with a bland effrontery capable of turning cannon balls at pointblank range. He had come prepared.

Unobtrusively but persistently he went from office to office in the capital, refusing to take no for an answer, smoothly talking his way past underlings and watchdogs. He had confidential chats with Senators William Stewart and James Nye of Nevada, both harsh critics of the Union Pacific and staunch friends of the Central; Michigan's Jacob Howard, chairman of the Senate's influential Pacific Railroad Committee; and several others. He spent enough time with Secretary of the Interior Browning, it appears, to make that vacillating man forget all about his recently appointed special commission. He was closeted for a while with Attorney General James Speed. He had studied the enabling legislation carefully, of course, and undoubtedly his pitch was simple, logical and unvarying.

The Act of '64, amending the Act of '62, clearly stated that government bonds could be released in amounts up to two-thirds of the total in advance of railhead, as soon as a continuous roadbed had been prepared for the track. It is uncertain just how much of the Central's grade east of Monument Point was "complete and continuous" at this time; not all of it, certainly, by a considerable amount. But there was no one in Washington outside of the Union Pacific people themselves—who naturally had been kept in ignorance of what was going on—to dispute any claims Huntington chose to make. The very confusion and lack of any clear picture of the situation out in Utah worked to his advantage. In addition, he could cite the glowing report of Browning's special commission of 1868 as proof that the Central's transcontinental intentions were honest and aboveboard; moreover, it was a self-evident fact that the whole gigantic effort was a costly one, and financing it a serious problem, so that the whole situation could be made to look like the most urgent sort of emergency.

All this was brought to bear, no doubt, though no records survive to tell precisely what Collis Huntington said, what specific arguments he used to buttress a case palpably built on just the right modicum of truth plus subtle deception and a blithe disregard of the Union Pacific's right to be heard, or just how he arrived at his figure of $2,400,000 in federal bonds due. That was the sum he asked, covering the Central Pacific's grade to Ogden from Monument Point. And somehow he wrung an opinion from the Attorney General that his claim was legally sound, and convinced everyone up to and including President Johnson, apparently, that the bonds were rightfully his. Orville Browning wired a peremptory stop-construction order to Grenville Dodge at Salt Lake City. By approval of the Cabinet, Secretary of the Treasury Hugh McCulloch was directed to release the bonds.

"I wanted to get them the day the administration closed," said Huntington ingenuously. Quite clearly, he knew what he was doing.[4]

While all this went on, the once potent Union Pacific lobby was markedly inactive; part of the toll, probably, for the dismal imbroglio into which U.P. affairs had been allowed to fall. Dr. Durant was much too immersed in personal and corporate feuds in New York to spare any attention for the Washington scene. And Oakes Ames, though still in the capital as a Congressman from Massachusetts, also was preoccupied with the stormy inner affairs of the Credit Mobilier, and with the now Herculean effort to keep his personal credit intact under the continuing demands of railroad construction. The upshot: nothing was done until it was too late to do much of anything. Then, getting wind at last of what was about to happen, Ames hurried to use what influence he could on Hugh McCulloch. We must take Huntington's word for that, however. The only story of what transpired next is Huntington's own, dictated in his comfortable elderly years to representatives of the ubiquitous California historian, Hubert H. Bancroft:

"I went to McCullough [McCulloch] and said I, 'Here's a report I want you to have.' He had heard we were working there—meaning among the departments—and he had a talk with Ames. I knew he had agreed not to show me the bonds; but I was determined to have them if I could.

"I got a report from the Attorney General that I was entitled under the law to those bonds. I got one from the Solicitor of the Treasury; he asked for that, I was legally entitled to them. I got two cabinet meetings in one week outside of the regular day. The majority of them voted that I should have the bonds." (All this appears to be Huntington's summation of the earlier activities by means of which he had won his point.)

"Then," he added with the indignity of justice outraged, "he would not let me have them.

"I went there nearly a week. . . . I called at McCullough's office; I sent in my card. McCullough would let me know the next morning. . . . I said, 'Never mind, I will go and see him.' I did not know McCullough. I wanted those $2,400,000 bonds. 'Well,' said he, 'you seem entitled to them.' I answered: 'That is right; give me the reasons, Mr. Secretary, why you won't let me have them?' 'Well,' he said, 'you seem entitled to them under the law.' I said: 'That is all right, give me the bonds.' 'Well,' he replied, 'No, I can't do it.' 'Well,' I said, 'I want your reasons. I have men in New York who are interested with me; when I go back, if I don't have the bonds I want the reasons why. You can see for yourself.' Finally he remarked, 'You do seem entitled to them.' "

The portrait of the bewildered bureaucrat—honestly undecided, heckled toward his wits' end and wanting nothing, undoubtedly, but to be let alone in peace while the rest of his term in office ran out—comes poignantly alive in this exchange. But it was McCulloch's misfortune that he had been flung into the arena with a tiger, and Huntington had no intention of letting him off. He continued to haunt the office daily. On each call he asked again for the bonds; then when he was refused, asked the reasons why. One day he found about twenty others in the office, also waiting to see the Secretary. Badgered beyond endurance, McCulloch exploded, according to Huntington:

" 'Now,' said he, 'if you do not let these gentlemen see me, I will decide this thing against you.' 'Now,' I replied, 'Mr. Secretary, rather than have the Secretary of the United States do so foolish a thing as that, I will sit here for a fortnight.' For half an hour or so I sat down. 'Now,' said he, 'Mr. Jordan (he came up just then), Mr. Huntington is worrying me to death. He says he wants those bonds; what do you think of it?' Jordan said: 'I have given you a written opinion, Mr. Secretary, that he is entitled to the bonds under the law.' 'Well,' said he, 'he shall have the bonds. . . .' "

And so Huntington did, with the helpful boost from the assistant, Jordan. By his own account he found the bonds in his hotel room when he returned there around eight o'clock that same evening. He said he got the full amount due: $2,400,000. But here a discrepancy arises. Most sources indicate that the bonds delivered actually amounted to $2,399,000, and that in claiming the larger sum Huntington was slightly in error. At least one later writer, however, makes the discrepancy much greater with the statement that only $1,333,000 was turned over.[5] Whatever the true sum, Collis Huntington never made any complaints.

The date of his final call on McCulloch was March 3, the Johnson administration's last day in office. It was about as near a thing as near could be.

Five days later, on March 8, the Union Pacific's end of track arrived triumphantly in Ogden. The Casements' construction train steamed in behind, grown to twenty-two cars in length now, their paint faded and their frames sagged in swayback curves from weather and the long miles. The broad, muddy streets of the tiny town first laid out by Brigham Young in '49 boiled with the excitement of a hurriedly organized celebration. "HAIL TO THE HIGHWAY OF NATIONS!" read the legend on a long banner borne aloft by a cheering procession, "UTAH BIDS YOU WELCOME!" The Army had a detachment on hand, complete with the indispensable brass band and a battery of light artillery to bellow in salute. It was by all odds the most rousing reception Jack Casement and the boys had been treated to since Cheyenne, in spite of the dearth of whiskey and fancy girls among these staid Mormon Saints.

Characteristically, the railroaders had a rowdy little fillip of their own to contribute. From his cab, according to legend, the construction-train engineer suddenly announced in stentorian tones that he was going to turn the engine around, and followed up by hauling down hard on the whistle cord and (very probably) opening his cylinder cocks to drench the surroundings in a cloud of warm, wet steam. A sizable number of these long-isolated people never had seen a locomotive before, in all likelihood, and their reaction was all the guffawing railroad men could wish, as dignified Saints in their Sunday best stampeded frantically through a slough bordering the right of way. It was hours, local raconteurs claimed later, before the last frightened child was rounded up by the last anxious mother, and peace settled down on Ogden again.

When the first passenger train duly pulled in some time later, the conductor in charge was Tom Cahoon, the same who had lost his scalp to Sioux raiders at Sidney, Nebraska, the year before. He remained in service on the U.P.'s Ogden Division for many years, ultimately retired in the city, had a street named after him and was remembered with affection by old-timers long into the twentieth century. He always wore his hat at an odd angle, most of them used to recall. They assumed the purpose was to "hide a peculiar bald spot on the back of his head."

With his time as Secretary of the Interior rapidly running out, Orville Browning's stop-construction order had simply been ignored by Grenville Dodge. Four days before the rails reached Ogden, Ulysses S. Grant had taken office as the eighteenth President of the United States, and one of his first official acts was the rescinding of that order. As for the federal bonds now secure in the Central Pacific treasury, there was no way to get them back; they had, after all, been issued legally by accredited representatives of the government. There was no legal way, either, for duplicate bonds to be issued on the U.P. grade beyond Ogden. So Collis Huntington's coup remained unspoiled. And it was no small one. The shrewd Central vice-president had hit the enemy precisely where he could be hurt worst: in the pocketbook.

The Union Pacific had won Ogden, all the same. No amount of politicking in Washington could take that away, though there were men there who still would try.

Meanwhile Charley Crocker, with his and Strobridge's supply and labor difficulties partially ironed out at last, was pushing on across the bleak mud and salt flats of northwest Utah at a roaring four-mile-a-day clip once more. A magnificent effort, but the Central's track-layers were a long way west of the Promontories still. By rounding Great Salt Lake and dashing on west —if they had the strength left to do it—the Union Pacific men still might shut them out.

Many months earlier, during the exploratory surveys of this region, Grenville Dodge and his engineering chiefs had envisioned a bold stroke that, had it proved possible, would have made a far-reaching difference now. Their idea had been simple but ambitious: to leap straight out across the great lake's thirty-mile width from eastern shore to western over a gigantic trestle or a filled-in causeway, or a combination of the two. They were ahead of their time, but considerably more than idle dreamers; for the thing *was* done, over thirty years later and then not by the U.P. but by the Southern Pacific, successor to the Central. The Lucin Cutoff was justly hailed as an epochal feat of railway engineering and construction even in 1902 and '03, when the Southern Pacific did it. In the 1860's, lacking any kind of heavy machinery and with Great Salt Lake in the midst of one of its periodic rises—and hence deeper than it was later, or is today—the project proved far outside the bounds of practicability. Boats were swamped in the endeavor to take soundings, there were some near-drownings, and the idea finally was shelved.

No short cuts, then; no choice for the winter-weary graders and iron men of the Union Pacific but to turn northward out of Ogden and make a race of it for Promontory Summit. The Central Pacific men were as weary as they; there was that consolation. Neither side could afford to think of giving up now, nor think of resting on shovels, picks or spike mauls either.

March turned mild, promising an early spring. And as the passing days brought warmth and sprouting greenery and the calls of birds flying north, the air held an electric tingle of climax, of the end approaching. It was unmistakable: '69 would see the finish, though the how and the where remained in doubt.

CHAPTER 28

YEAR OF CLIMAX

1869 would, in fact, be a year of endings.

In March Lieutenant General William T. Sherman had a letter from Philip H. Sheridan, his second-in-command in the Military District of the Missouri. The winter just past had seen the Army's most determined effort so far to put a stop to the humiliation of repeated Indian raids on the plains settlements. It was an all-out, many-pronged offensive along a front sweeping from western Kansas and Colorado far down through Indian Territory almost to the Texas line, conceived by Sheridan himself and reluctantly approved by a majority of the Federal Peace Commission. Now Sheridan reported complete success. The most troublesome of the Cheyenne and Arapaho war chiefs had taken sound thrashings; all the principal bands of hostiles were now confined to their reservations.

To Sherman, the man who bore the burden of the long and often uphill struggle to pacify the plains tribes, the news was like the last piece of a jigsaw puzzle finally falling into place. Northwestward, the treaty negotiated with Red Cloud's Sioux at Fort Laramie in '68—the one that had blessed the Union Pacific with peace for the drive across Wyoming—still stood. The vast expanse of country east of the Big Horn Mountains and north of the Wind River was granted to the Sioux in perpetuity, and Army forts along the Bozeman Trail remained ungarrisoned in spite of the grumblings of miners greedy to get into the western Montana gold fields. Red Cloud was keeping his side of the bargain, too: letting government mail and peaceful wagon trains go through unmolested. On similar terms Spotted Tail and other chiefs of the Sioux Nations that had harried the U.P. across Nebraska the preceding year were giving up and accepting reservation lands up in Dakotah Territory. Lumped together with Sheridan's successes these were developments that spelled peace and a virtual end of the "Indian problem" on the Great Plains, a thing truly epic in its significance for the future. It would not turn out quite that perfectly in practice. Various provocations would keep the Indian wars going for a decade and more, but only sporadically now; the back of the problem had been broken.

Uncle Billy Sherman would leave the plains for good before '69 was over; be called to Washington by new President Ulysses S. Grant to assume Grant's old rank as General of the Army.

Other figures that had loomed large out here were passing, too. By early spring old Jim Bridger, pioneer fur trapper, trader, blazer of trails and Army scout, was off on his last assignment, with a military column exploring the headwaters of the Yellowstone River up in the remote corner where Wyoming, Montana and Idaho Territories met. The West was giving up its last secrets rapidly now. And in Jim Bridger it was losing the last of the genuine, old-time mountain men; one whose lifetime spanned an amazing amount of history. His were the first white man's eyes known certainly to have looked out over Great Salt Lake, long ago in 1824. He had thought it an arm of the Pacific Ocean then, a striking illustration of the kind of geographic naïveté that seemed incredible in the America of '69.

Even earlier, the Great Plains and the Overland Trail had seen the last of another, more recent pioneer. Squeezed between the oncoming railheads of the U.P. and the Central Pacific, Ben Holladay had sold his famous Overland Stage line—horses, harness, Concord coaches, everything—to Wells, Fargo and Company late in '66. Now he was up in the Pacific Northwest promoting a railroad of his own to run southward down Oregon's Willamette River and link Portland with the new Pacific Railroad. Meanwhile, this March, advertisements in the Cheyenne *Daily Leader* were announcing to commercial travelers that the Union Pacific was "open from the Missouri to the Rocky Mountains, Omaha to Wasatch," and promising that by April there would be "direct connections with Wells, Fargo and Company's daily line of Overland Mail and Express coaches to and from Salt Lake City and all points in Utah, Idaho, Montana and California."

If this was a year of endings, it was one of hopeful beginnings as well. The spring of 1869 saw a frontier lawyer out of Pennsylvania, by name Cyrus K. Holliday, putting down the first rails of another railroad, modestly named the Atchison and Topeka, southwestward across Kansas along the old Santa Fe Trail. And up in Minnesota a hardy group of promoters was striving to interest Eastern financiers in another transcontinental, the Northern Pacific, authorized by the same Congress that had liberalized the subsidy rules for the U.P. and the Central in '64.

1869 was the year that cattlemen out of Texas, no longer content with driving their trail herds north over the hazardous Chisholm and West Pawnee Trails to Abilene or Junction City on the Kansas Pacific Railroad, began to spread farther afield. It had been inevitable that they should. The buffalo, bluestem and grama grasses of the Kansas prairie made rich grazing on which to hold herds for fattening before shipment. The continuing demand for beef from the populous East and the growing industrial centers along the Great Lakes and the Ohio River Valley made it eminently profitable to do so, and the pressure of homesteading dirt farmers moving steadily westward across the Missouri forced the cattlemen inexorably west and north into farther Kansas and Nebraska, and ultimately even beyond, toward the grassy uplands of Colorado, Wyoming and Montana, where the grazing was as good and the great spaces lay wide-open for the first comers. In '69 this movement was only getting under way, but presently the Union Pacific would be carrying its share of beeves eastward out of Ogalalla, Cheyenne and Laramie City. Within a year (by November of 1870) the Denver *Rocky Mountain News* would be telling of a new ranch on the South Platte where a Palo Pinto County Texan named John Hittson would winter five thousand steers and to which, the season following, he planned to drive ten thousand more for fattening.

Ranches of this size constituted the first real, large-scale investment in Great Plains land. The old concept of a Great American Desert was out of date already.

1869 was the year, too, that a raffish Broadway publicity man on the make came west on the lookout for the raw material of which new popular heroes could be built. He came as a natural progression of more serious journalists like Samuel Bowles and Albert Richardson, and the eager writers and sketch artists of periodicals like *Harper's Weekly* and *Leslie's Illustrated Weekly*. Ned Buntline, he called himself, and would be famous as a veritable Homer of the dime novel and the penny dreadful before his career ended. In young Buffalo Bill Cody, the onetime meat hunter for the Kansas Pacific, he found precisely the man he was looking for, and so launched a legend more enduring than he could have imagined. There were many men of Cody's stamp out here: Wild Bill Hickok, the original lightning-draw two-gun man, for one; dashing, dandy Lieutenant Colonel George A. Custer of the famed Seventh Cavalry, for another. In these and others like them—hawk-faced, long-haired, steely-eyed fellows in richly tanned buckskins and sweeping Western hats; bona fide Indian fighters and sharpshooters, but natural poseurs, too—the frontier was already taking on the journalistic semblance of a romantic glamour it never really had in life. In a sense they were symptomatic of the frontier's final extravagant flowering preceding its swift decline; signs, like the shrinking buffalo herds and the Indians' sullen yielding before the white man's superior medicine—and like the march of the Pacific Railroad itself—of an old era giving way to a new.

Leland Stanford, having coaxed Secretary Browning's special commission safely away to Sacramento and managed the appointment of the Central's own Lewis Clement to that body, was back in Salt Lake City by the early part of March. The change of scene and a brief visit at home with Mrs. Stanford and his infant son appear to have lightened his outlook not at all. Everywhere he turned—from Ogden, now left three miles behind by the Casements' track gangs, to Promontory, where U.P. graders already were breaking ground—the Central's president saw signs of trouble ahead.

On the fourteenth of the month, in a long, worried and somewhat contradictory letter to Mark Hopkins, he declared that in his opinion, if the Union Pacific people knew of Collis Huntington's success in collecting subsidy bonds for the unfinished work north of Ogden, they would "call off their graders" immediately. This, it would seem, ought to have been just what the Central Pacific wanted. But in almost the next strokes of his pen Stanford remarked that, "Just now, as we have these bonds, we had better keep quiet."[1]

Why? He did not explain. But he had a host of other things on his mind, and poured them all out in the same letter. "The U.P. have changed their line so as to cross us five times, with unequal grades, between Bear River and the Promontory. They have done this purposely, as there was no necessity for so doing." It was Stanford's theory that the Union Pacific men meant to claim the Central's line for their own, and were counting on a favorable report by the special commission. He had his suspicions on this score, too. "That the thing was set up with Warren and everything understood as to what the U.P. needed, I have no doubt," he wrote, adding that the plot would probably have succeeded "but for the addition of Clem [Clement] to the Commission." He did not think the danger was past though, for he made it clear that he considered the Union Pacific people adversaries who would balk at nothing.

The Central's own grading was going well, he said. But rather than push to a finish just yet, he planned to "keep men scattered along it until our track is close upon them." And his explanation had an ominous ring: "I don't think there will be any attempt to jump our line while it is unfinished and we are working upon it."

This letter was remarkable not only for its revelation of Leland Stanford's state of mind, but even more as an indication of the confusion and chaos now beginning to prevail. The Central president never told what reasons, if any, he had for his suspicions of General Warren. It was gossiped, however, and never denied, that about this same time Cornelius Wendell, one of the Union

Pacific's government commissioners, came out on an inspection trip, took a look at the "Z" that circumvented tunnel No. 2, examined the largely unballasted track snaking down along Echo Creek and the Weber River and coolly suggested $25,000 might be a bargain price for his official approval. Moreover, the sum was paid, so it was said, by Webster Snyder, superintendent of the U.P.'s operations department, who panicked and authorized the payment without waiting to consult any superior. To a worried Leland Stanford, therefore, bribery of a government commission would have seemed by no means out of the question.[2]

Out on the grades, as he foresaw, the impending collision of Eastern and Western rivals threatened to unleash a gargantuan brawl. Far away in Washington the transcontinental race, likely a runaway locomotive, began to defy the ingenuity of politicians in devising a way to set the brakes. In New York the confusion was compounded by a new twist in the Union Pacific's corporate fortunes. And in Utah the Latter-day Saints saw their simple economy and serene way of life all at once turned end over apple cart by the railroads' advent, and abruptly came to realize that progress sometimes has its drawbacks.

Mormon hay for the contractors' draft stock fetched a hundred dollars a ton. Potatoes soared to seven dollars a bushel. Other commodity prices jumped accordingly. Wages for men and boys began at three dollars a day and ranged upward; a man with an ox or mule team could count on at least ten, plus keep for himself and his animals. Both railroads were paying through the nose. But so were the Mormon people, caught in an inflationary bind made all the tighter by the Union Pacific's continuing habit of slow pay, with promises in lieu of cash passed along through Brigham Young to his subcontractors and thence to the men who did the work. This was a hectic and disappointing kind of prosperity, after all the high expectations. And those conservative elders who had feared the impact of the rude railroaders on peaceful, sober Utah saw many of their worst forebodings realized.

By early March the terminal town of Corinne was flourishing around an advance base for the grading crews of the U.P., twenty-eight miles out of Ogden. Corinne: it was a pretty name, and the first Gentile town in the Salt Lake Valley. The Saints eyed it askance, listening to the boastful pitches of promoters. Corinne would have a population of ten thousand within two years; it was "the Chicago of the Rocky Mountains," "the Queen City of the Great Basin"; with the Bear River and Great Salt Lake for waterways, the untapped territories of Montana and Idaho as trade sources and the Pacific Railroad itself as a through connection east and west, it was the proud possessor of a destiny unlimited. Underneath the big talk, though, it was the same old story: just "Hell on Wheels" in one more reincarnation. J. H. Beadle, having observed the rise and decline of Wasatch, trailed along behind the U.P. to edit the Corinne *Reporter* for a while. He told of the town's nineteen saloons and two canvas dance halls, its eighty *nymphs du grade*. Sunday was the big day, he wrote, because most of the graders came in from the camps then. The male citizens prudently made themselves scarce, went hunting or fishing, usually, and the "girls" threw a dance. Dog fights, Mr. Beadle added, were a popular form of outdoor entertainment.[3]

To the scandalized Latter-day Saints it was Sodom and Gomorrah in their midst. "The place is fast becoming civilized, several men having been killed there already," remarked the *Deseret News* with gloomy cynicism. And an editorial advised workers leaving for the grades to instruct their womenfolk in the use of firearms and order them to keep doors bolted and windows closed.

But these Latter-day Saints were a hearty and tough-fibered lot; frontier people in the finest sense of that term, and well able to take care of themselves when the occasion arose. Not long after Brigham Young's first grading crews went to work for the U.P. a *News* reporter who called himself "Anon" made a tour of Echo and Weber canyons and wrote with satisfaction that he had heard profanity used in but one small camp, "and it is not likely to be tolerated there long." But if these good Mormons opened and closed each day's work with hymns and a prayer, it did not detract from the fine, full-blooded gusto with which they went at the job. The opening stanza of their own work song told everybody within earshot how they felt about it:

> . . . *Hurrah, hurrah, the railroad's begun.*
> *Three cheers for the contractor; his name's Brigham Young.*
> *Hurrah, hurrah, we're honest and true,*
> *And if we stick to it, it's bound to go through.*[4]

Now this same spirit was abroad on the grades pushing across the wasteland around the head of Great Salt Lake. Leland Stanford's contractors, Benson, Farr and West, were making the dirt fly. The firm of Sharp and Young had every available man laboring on the U.P. line. As early as the preceding fall the *Deseret News* had told of rough horseplay between the two work forces. Dirt for fill was stolen from one grade or the other in the dead of night, then stolen back the next night. Blasts were set off without warning. Finally the respective foremen arranged a truce, lest the fun become too dangerous.

Strangely, no specific record exists today to tell of the first contact between grading crews of the U.P. and the Central, though as the first real meeting of the two railroads it was in its own way an epic event. Speculation suggests that it took place in Nevada, when the Union Pacific threw its advance contingent out to Humboldt Wells. If not, then these Latter-day Saints of the two Mormon contracting firms must have been the first rivals who actually met and vied with one another. In the competitive rush, apparently no one bothered to note the occasion or to remark upon its historic significance.

Stanford's plan to "keep men scattered" along the Central Pacific's grade seems to have dissolved in the momentum of urgency. Charley Crocker was not the kind for cautious holding back; not with the Union Pacific coming on full tilt. The terrain on the eastward Promontory approach grew difficult; long stretches of mud flats, soggy and treacherous in the thaws of spring, interspersed with hard rock ledges that required heavy blasting. Crocker threw an advance guard of his coolies forward over the crest to work toward the men of Benson, Farr and West. Casement Irishmen strove westward here, in advance of the U.P.'s Mormon contract crews. The antagonists took stock of one another, Irish buckoes and pigtailed Chinese laboring just a short stone's throw apart.

The Paddies reacted with resentment and contempt. More clearly than the Chinese, probably, they understood that one side or the other was working in vain here. And to them the coolies were the interlopers. The heathen Chinee, on his part, remained imperturbable. Whatever he thought of the big, hairy barbarians on the other grade, he kept it to himself, ignored their hoots and catcalls and minded his own business as he had minded it all the long way over the Sierras and across Nevada.

But these Irish were men in whom the war years had ingrained a conviction that life was pretty cheap, and nothing in their experience since, along the U.P. right of way or in the roaring railhead towns, had made it seem any dearer. Their grudges were hair-triggered, their sense of fun robust. And the Chinese's very imperturbability was infuriating. So they would have to be shown. The Irishmen laid a "grave": a charge of blasting powder strategically placed and fused to hurl coolies skyward in a spectacular explosion, and bury others under cascading earth and rock. It happened at least once, and possibly oftener, as Grenville Dodge recalled afterward.

Jim Strobridge protested vigorously. Perhaps the Union Pacific foremen remonstrated with their men; quite as likely, though, they were in on the fun themselves. Strobridge's protests went higher, finally to Grenville Dodge himself. But the gleeful Irishmen were not to be stopped now. They laid another grave.

Then the coolies, saying nothing to anyone, laid a grave of their own. The ensuing blast killed a number of Paddies and injured several more. And that was enough. The Irish had to own up to a new respect for the little yellow men, however grudgingly, and the undeclared war ended as informally as it had begun.[5]

The two grades, though, continued to struggle along in opposite directions.

For a month and more the two railheads were hustled forward in mounting prodigies of effort, the question of a meeting point growing more urgent with every day that passed. But no one had an answer. By the end of March the Union Pacific graders had their advance camp at Blue Creek, eighteen miles past Corinne, only ten from Promontory. Jack Casement kept his iron men coming close behind. They were closer to the summit by a considerable margin than Strobridge's track gangs. But they, and their graders ahead, had much the harder going now. The summit was six hundred feet up, Grenville Dodge stated in his final report, "with scarcely four miles of direct ascent from the east." The survey line looped and curved in a stiff climb of eighty feet to the mile. There were several ravines to be bridged or filled. And Strobridge and Crocker were coming fast on the easier western approach, driving hard to make up for previous delays, working their crews by the light of great sagebrush bonfires through night shifts as well as day. The situation smacked more and more of potential impasse. Yet neither company felt itself able to yield a foot in the bitter-end scramble.

Months earlier Grenville Dodge, for one, had become convinced that this race around the lake could end only in a wasteful and pointless duplication of effort. His opposite number, Chief Engineer Samuel Montague of the Central, was in Utah Territory also and the two frequently came into personal contact. More than once, as Dodge recalled it later, he had broached the subject of a junction point satisfactory to both sides. But Montague had objected that he had no authority to speak for his company. When Dr. Durant came out from New York late in the fall of '68, Dodge had urged him to consider some sort of compromise. There are a few hazy indications that, as a result, some tentative discussions did take place between Durant and Leland Stanford in Salt Lake City. But government bonds to the tune of $32,000 per mile constituted a sharp spur to competition, and it was about this same time that Orville Browning was handing the Central Pacific an apparent priority on the route all the way to the head of Echo. So Stanford could hardly have been in a mood to make concessions. Such talks as were held, then, did not get very far.[6]

Now that was all ancient history, so swiftly were events moving. The Union Pacific held the important advantage in track actually laid down, and was not disposed to bargain it away. To the Central people, anything short of an entry into Ogden was unthinkable. Secretary Browning was out of office now, though; the Grant administration might well be disposed to favor the U.P. over the Central. On the other hand, the Union Pacific people must have known by this time, or were soon to find out, that Collis Huntington had maneuvered them out of any chance for subsidy bonds on their work north of Ogden.[7]

Neither company trusted the other, and with excellent reason. Both had bluffed to the limit, and still were bluffing. The Union Pacific claimed a pre-liminary survey line all the way to the California border while the Associates had graded ten miles east of Ogden, and still claimed their original survey line to a point much farther east. The special commission under General Warren never had been disbanded; though it seemed to be fading rapidly into limbo, its official report still might affect the issue.

Rumors got about. One, current since the previous October, when the *Deseret News* had judged it worth dignifying in print, held that the Union Pacific intended to abandon California to the Central and strike out on a line northwestward to the Snake River and an ultimate Pacific terminus of its own somewhere in Oregon.[8] It was hinted also that powerful San Francisco interests still hostile to the Associates were making overtures to bring the U.P. into California via Beckwourth Pass, which crossed the Sierra Nevada Range some way north of Donner. It is seldom possible to determine how rumors start, but this one suggests an inspired story designed to force the Central's hand. And it was probably not too incredible, in the fevered atmosphere of early '69.

On Capitol Hill in Washington the developments in Utah began to concern Congress acutely as the spring wore on. The public's stake in this Pacific Rail-road was the most important, after all, and the lawmakers did not propose to ignore their prerogatives. The trouble was that Congress never had been able to decide exactly what it wished to do for or about the Pacific Railroad. The original Act of '62 had been a hodgepodge of political expediency, and the amending Acts of '64 and '66 had been thoroughly chewed over by lobbyists and politicians committed either to the Union Pacific on the one side or the Central on the other. Among the many shortcomings of the resulting mass of legislation, one suddenly looked very glaring indeed:

Nowhere was there any legal provision for a meeting of the rails.

Some Congressmen had begun to feel concern about this two years earlier. In February of '67 a House committee had brought the question up, and been answered by Orville Browning that the point of junction was "assumed" to be 78.295 miles east of Salt Lake City, or at a point that would "entitle the two companies to equal amounts of bonds." Like most of the Secretary's thinking on the Pacific Railroad, this assumption was quite wishful, arbitrary and un-realistic. Neither company was interested in "equal amounts of bonds," and even less in a theoretical junction located by mathematical formula. Besides, there was no legal basis whatever for the specious 78.295-mile point. But Browning's pronouncement remained the only official word on the subject, notwithstanding the fact that events had now made it palpably ridiculous.

In the Senate, chief battleground for advantage, both railroads had their vigorous proponents. Nevada's William Stewart was the Central's strongest standard-bearer. J. M. Thayer of Nebraska fought the good fight for the Union Pacific, somewhat cautiously seconded by Ohio's John Sherman. Here again, it looked like an impasse. Unpalatable as it was to everyone, the possibility seemed to loom that the two railheads would plunge right on past each other in their stubborn drives toward . . . well, toward what? The Missouri River? The Pacific Ocean? How far could a thing like this be carried?

Not far, actually. Both companies were tired, the Union Pacific all but finished financially, the Central also feeling the strain badly. Human endurance was reaching its limits, too. For months past Charley Crocker had been complaining of insomnia and apologizing to patient Mrs. Crocker, during his hurried visits in Sacramento, for the surliness of his temper. Samuel Reed's letters home, seldom cheerful throughout the whole period of Union Pacific construction, now read like the installments in one long tale of weariness and woe. Grenville Dodge's letters to Mrs. Dodge revealed a man wallowing in the depths of despondency; he fretted over the monumental costs of construction and—quite uncharacteristically for a man who always had stood staunchly back of his subordinates—cried out against the inefficiency and waste which he claimed had all but wrecked the U.P.'s forward progress.[9]

Then on the New York front the fantastic corporate affairs of the Union Pacific took another turn.

Until now, in spite of all the harsh things said of Thomas Durant by his contemporaries and perpetuated by much loose writing ever since, the worst of Wall Street's piratical elements had been kept out of the company's concerns. But widespread tales of the rich pickings being enjoyed by the Credit Mobilier were too tempting to be ignored forever, and the first buccaneer to react was a flamboyant fat man by the name of James Fisk—the notorious Jim, then thirty-five years old and soaring toward the pinnacle of a dazzling career: an ex-circus hand, ex-tinware peddler, ex-drygoods salesman; more recently broker, speculator, "Barnum of Wall Street" and "Prince of Erie." Already Fisk, in alliance with wily old Uncle Dan'l Drew, had wrested control of the Erie Railroad from the redoubtable Commodore Vanderbilt and the two were milking that unfortunate line for all it was worth. The Union Pacific looked like a bird equally ripe for plucking, and surely Dr. Durant and his cohorts could be foes no more formidable than the fire-breathing Commodore. Or so it appeared to Jim Fisk. Early this same year, in a raider's typical opening move, he had acquired a small block of U.P. stock and then filed suit to force the company into bankruptcy, on the pretext of protecting his rights as a shareholder.

He may have had a legitimate point, for the Union Pacific assuredly was staggering close to ruin. But it was no part of Fisk's plan to let the case be tried on its legal merits. He formed an alliance with Tammany Boss William

Marcy Tweed. And since the corrupt New York courts were firmly under Tweed's thumb it was no trick at all to obtain a judgment declaring the company bankrupt, appointing the boss's son, William Marcy Tweed, Jr., receiver and forbidding any further stockholders' meetings.

All this was a *fait accompli* by early March. On the tenth a stockholders' meeting was broken up by sheriff's deputies before any business could be transacted. And on April 2 New Yorkers could chuckle or shake their heads in disgust, according to their individual bents, over a lively story in the New York *Post*. Young Tweed had led a force of deputies into the Union Pacific offices on Nassau Street and ordered the safe battered open with sledge hammers and chisels. His purpose, Tweed announced piously, was to make sure that no company records or other vital documents had been removed. In the physical melee that followed, however, Dr. Durant and his clerical force somehow managed to scoop up all the safe's most important contents and escape with them into the crowd of bystanders that had gathered. Eventually they were spirited across the state line into New Jersey, out of the New York courts' jurisdiction.

Here, though, was another impasse, this one the Union Pacific's own private problem. In fleeing the clutches of Jim Fisk and Boss Tweed, Durant had tied his own hands. The U.P.'s federal charter specified New York as its headquarters; legally, no stockholders' meeting could take place elsewhere. Yet the re-election of officers and directors was an urgent order of business, and the state of the firm's affairs required action on a large accumulation of other matters.

There was no way out but an appeal to Congress for sanction of another headquarters city, preferably Boston. So once again the hapless Union Pacific had to go adventuring in Washington, though this time neither Dr. Durant nor any of his colleagues was very happy about it. Too many Congressmen were already asking pointed questions about the company's operations, and frowning over the lack of straight answers. As an example, there was John A. Bingham of Ohio. Aroused by Jim Fisk's lawsuit, he had stood up in the House of Representatives on March 10 and proposed a joint Congressional resolution "to protect the interests of the United States in the Union Pacific, and other matters." The Senate had not so far acted on it, but any further airing of this latest contretemps seemed all too likely to be embarrassing.

Subsequent developments very quickly began to bear this out. In neither House nor Senate was there any serious objection to the Boston move. The reputations of Tweed and Fisk were too well known for any Congressman in his right mind to argue in their behalf. But in filing his lawsuit Fisk had charged that the Union Pacific was being systematically looted by the Credit

Mobilier, and here was something into which the Congress could get its teeth.

During a Senate session early in April William Stewart, an uninhibited bonanza lawyer who had fought his way to the top in the stomp-and-gouge politics of Virginia City, took the floor to declare silkily that, regardless of Jim Fisk's personal character, if his accusations contained even a grain of truth, then "Congress had better find out about it." And then he added— giving the first public utterance to a story which had been current in Washington cloakrooms for a long time—that he had heard talk of some "enormous dividends" having been received by certain unnamed Congressional leaders as a result of their financial interests in both the Union Pacific and "this identical Credit Mobilier . . . and I have not heard it denied."[10]

In saying this the Senator from Nevada was flirting with a situation that was perhaps more ticklish than he realized. No one challenged him, however, and he did not press his point. But he had fired the opening gun in a frankly partisan skirmish, and the Senate at once plunged into acrid debate over the conflicting rights of U.P. against Central Pacific, and vice versa, on the distant shores of Great Salt Lake.

Senator Thayer promptly rose to read Grenville Dodge's affidavit claiming the Central's map of their survey to the head of Echo Canyon was fraudulent, and thus brought Ex-Secretary Browning's approval of that survey into the controversy. Jacob Howard of Michigan, chairman of the Senate Committee on the Pacific Railroad and apparently trying hard to be neutral, mentioned the Central's counterclaim that persons unknown had torn up the location stakes and so rendered the map meaningless. Thayer retorted with the suggestion that the circumstances surrounding the payment of government bonds on the unfinished Central Pacific grade from Monument to Echo might bear looking into.

All this was mostly talk, not very meaningful and getting nowhere, till Stewart called for the floor again and launched into a lengthy and intemperate denunciation of the Union Pacific's construction practices. Citing the temporary track laid around tunnel No. 3 in Weber Canyon, he charged that the builders meant to skip much of their tunnel work altogether and declared, therefore, that the company actually had no continuous line to Ogden, "or within many miles of Ogden." He attacked the advance grade into Humboldt Wells, "in my state," as another example of outrageous trickery, and hinted broadly that large sections of U.P. trackage had been approved, and the government subsidies on it collected, without any adequate inspection. And he concluded by reading into the record an angry letter lately published in the Chicago *Tribune,* in which fifty recent Union Pacific passengers aired a wide variety of grievances, stated that there was "general dissatisfaction and demoralization" along the whole western end of the road, named the Dale Creek trestle on the western Black Hills grade as an especially blatant hazard to life and limb and declared that the whole railroad was no more than a potential death trap; "an elongated slaughter house" was the graphic term they used.

This was much the most savage diatribe to which any American railroad had been subjected since the early years of railroading in the nation, when the toll in human lives had indeed been appalling. Yet there had been no disastrous wrecks on the Union Pacific. The Central's accident record was measurably worse, as a matter of fact. Clearly, these letter writers were people with powerful capacities for indignation—or people inspired for a purpose. Many of them, Stewart declared, were known to him personally, another point which might have merited a closer look.

On this bitterly critical note, however, the debate was allowed to end. The session obviously had gone badly for the Union Pacific men.

Even as the Senate debated, however, a way out was opening. Late in March Grenville Dodge had been called to Washington by his old friend and mentor, Ulysses S. Grant. Once again, as on that long-ago spring day in '63, it appeared that Dodge was to be cast in the role of emissary from the President of the United States to the Union Pacific management. He wanted the Pacific Railroad finished, Grant explained frankly; and if the two companies could not get together on a junction point, then the federal government would decide the matter for them. So once more Dodge took a train for New York to inform Dr. Durant that the President meant business.

Durant, Dodge and Collis Huntington arranged a meeting. None of the three ever revealed precisely what they had to say to one another, but the horse-trading was not protracted. Shortly thereafter Huntington was in Washington for a talk with Oakes Ames. On April 9 the Senate convened, primed for further debate preceding action on Mr. Bingham's joint resolution sent up from the House. But Senator Howard immediately rose and requested the floor in order to make an important announcement. The two component companies of the Pacific Railroad, he said, had reached an agreement. He proposed that its wording be written into the resolution. And he proceeded to read:

Resolved: that the common terminus of the Union Pacific and the Central Pacific Railroads shall be at or near Ogden; and the Union Pacific Railroad Company shall build, and the Central Pacific Railroad Company shall pay for and own, the railroad from the terminus aforesaid to Promontory Point, at which point the rails shall meet and connect and form one continuous line.

So it was over, abruptly and somewhat anticlimactically, for these gentlemen of the Senate as for the workers far off in Utah who would not get the word until the next day, by telegraph.

The Senate speedily incorporated the agreement into the joint resolution, and the House concurred. The resolution also named Boston as the place of the next Union Pacific stockholders' meeting and authorized the establishment of U.P. general offices anywhere in the United States. That was not all of it, though. For the two companies and for the hoary old principle of private enterprise permitted to go its way unchecked, the agreement had come just a little late. This whole matter of the Pacific Railroad had been much too controversial for much too long; there had been too much talk of hidden wrongs committed. And the Congress had reacted in three specific, tough-minded provisions:

First, the President of the United States was authorized to appoint a board of five "eminent citizens" to examine both railroads and report on the condition of each, together with an estimate of the expenditures still necessary to make each "first class."

Second, the President was authorized to withhold subsidy bonds and land-grant patents in amounts sufficient to cover such expenditures. And if the amounts of bonds and land grants still due proved insufficient, the President was given the additional authority to collect the necessary sums in the form of both companies' first mortgage bonds, or in any other form he deemed suitable.

Third, the Attorney General was instructed to conduct an investigation for the purpose of determining whether either company had forfeited its federal charter through the perpetration of fraud, payment of illegal dividends or violation of any penal laws by its employees or its agents.

Thus the joint resolution as finally released by Congress delivered a stiff jolt, not only to the suspect Union Pacific, but to the apparently respectable Central Pacific as well. Within it was a plain warning that the American people and their government had not approved of all the things done in the name of the transcontinental railroad; that there would be an accounting, and payment exacted for sins committed. Here, too, were sown the first small seeds of government control over the railroads of the nation.

But this last point was scarcely perceptible in April, 1869. The engineers and executives of both companies were well aware that in the driving haste of the past several months a great deal of construction work had been neglected. This new notion that bonds and land grants should be withheld, or their own securities requisitioned in order to correct the condition, was irksome, but not greatly disturbing. Even the threat of inquiry by the Attorney General, though it might appear ominous on paper, was not—as things would turn out under the easygoing Grant administration—a matter for prolonged concern. The big, overmastering fact was that the long-heralded Pacific Railroad was now finished, or as good as finished.

The public that had waited so eagerly settled down to wait a little longer. Out in Utah Territory the work went on.

Blue Creek camp began to fill with idle U.P. laborers as a reduced grading crew moved up the eastern slope of Promontory Ridge, the track-layers following at a pace suddenly turned leisurely. Some obstacles remained: a trestle three hundred feet long and thirty high still to be built; another five hundred feet long and eighty-seven high; much difficult rock work in the cuts. But the pressure was off, and the Central Pacific would foot the bill. The Central's engineers, who had shunned trestles in favor of more solid and longer-lasting fill on their own grade, did not entirely approve. They were out of it now, though. The days of April ran on, their tempo strangely peaceful.

Then Charley Crocker spoke up. His message, previously telegraphed to Leland Stanford in Salt Lake City and probably to Thomas Durant in New York, was received at the big Casement Brothers headquarters car, and presently passed by excited word of mouth among the workers all along the line.

Tomorrow, said Crocker, the Central Pacific proposed to lay those ten miles of track he had promised last fall.

CHAPTER 29

BIG DAY AT VICTORY

Seeking Charley Crocker during the morning of Tuesday, April 27, the railhead correspondent of San Francisco's *Alta California* found him engaged in "shooting at a cigar box set up on the ground 100 yards distant." The *Alta* man watched in admiration while the big Central Pacific boss "sent a bullet through it five times out of nine, one of the shots passing almost in the center."

The journalist thought it a remarkable exhibition of aplomb, considering the bad tidings just received in camp. A derailed locomotive had blocked the passage of iron trains bringing in the rails and spikes necessary for the great ten-mile endeavor. Crocker's face clouded, the *Alta* man observed, "when he heard that . . . for that day the feat on which he had set his heart was an impossibility. But in a few minutes his merry laugh was ringing out as if nothing to annoy him had recently occurred."

The account buttresses posterity's picture of a bluffly hearty, rough and ready Crocker; a portrait quite accurate as far as it goes. But there was more to the big man than mere bluffness; a great deal more than appeared in carefree pistol practice at a critical moment or a merry laugh when things went wrong. He was coolly calculating, too, a gambler who believed in coppering his bets beforehand if he could. Last fall's boast had been made only after serious discussions with Jim Strobridge, a gruff, outspoken professional whose advice would never be tinctured by any weak desire to please the boss. Strobridge had reckoned that it might be possible to lay ten miles of track in a day, given favorable conditions and no stinting of men or money. The long wait since then had been deliberate on Crocker's part. In finally picking his day he is said to have told his people, in effect, "We'll do it now, when they can't get back at us." This with reference to the fact that the Casements already had the U.P. railhead within ten miles of Promontory. Any record made now would have to stand.

The record was still to be made, though, as the sun rose over the dragon's spine of the Promontory Mountains on Wednesday morning, April 28. Not a Union Pacific man in Utah Territory believed that it could be. But the Central's preparations had been long and thorough; the whole big job planned and organized step by step; picked crews assigned to every task and drilled hard by Strobridge and Track Boss Minkler. Materials had been assembled, the grade made ready.

The camp train had been run into its siding, out of the way. Before sunup the last of five heavy iron trains steamed in and pulled up close. A fleet of wagons stood with teams hitched and drivers on seat boxes, ready to speed rails and fittings forward. The lorry cars were at end of track, wheels and rollers greased.

President Leland Stanford had come on from Salt Lake City for the day. A more or less official Union Pacific delegation was assembled on a ridge of high ground close to the right of way. Jack and Dan Casement were there, as were Samuel Reed, Marshall Hurd and other engineers, possibly including Silas Seymour. Of the presences of Grenville Dodge and Dr. Durant there is some doubt; certain later happenings indicate strongly that neither had been able to make it.[1] A holiday had been declared in the U.P. construction camps, and as many of the Casements' Paddies as could get there jostled and elbowed for front-row positions. There was a small knot of Army officers from the district and probably a good many hangers-on from Corinne and Blue Creek, eager for anything that promised excitement and a possible celebration afterward. Altogether, swelled by the masses of Central Pacific laborers relegated to the status of onlookers for this one day, it was a sizable gallery. And in the midst of it Charley Crocker sat his horse beside the grade, all eyes fixed on him as the sun rose higher and the minutes ticked off toward seven o'clock.

At a word from Minkler the track-layers stepped out, eight men marshaled in two crews of four. These were no blue-smocked Chinese. They were white, and they looked Irish.

Crocker's arm lifted and fell. The hogger of the first iron train locomotive hauled down his whistle cord. All along the train's sixteen flatcars coolies began to toss off bundles of fishplates and kegs of spikes. Others swung sledges to knock out the side stakes and jumped clear as rails cascaded to the ground. The ringing crash of falling iron, wrote the *Alta California* man, went on for some eight minutes. The first lorry car was quickly loaded and pushed the few feet forward to end of track. Blocks were thrust under its wheels. With a clatter and clank the first two rails were laid hold of, run out, dropped on the ties. Mauls clinked on spike heads; bolts grated in fish-plates. The blocks were snatched away. A coolie crew rolled the lorry car ahead.

The day's work began.

The watchers saw nothing fundamentally new. It was the same system first devised by the Casements and their buckoes along the Platte River, taken up by Crocker and Strobridge through the Truckee meadows and beside the bitter Humboldt. A few new tricks had been added. Rails were tacked in place as they went down, fishplates placed and lightly bolted. Spikers followed to drive the tacking spikes home and add the required number of others. Wrench men moved in to tighten up the fishplate bolts. Chinese walked beside the grade, distributing spikes, bolts, nuts and fishplates as needed. A triple file of coolies came on in the rear, one between the rails and one on each side, placing the ballast and tamping it down around the ties.

"I timed the movement twice," wrote the *Alta* man. "The first time 240 feet of rail was laid in one minute and twenty seconds; the second time 240 feet . . . in one minute and fifteen seconds. This," he added, "is about as fast as a leisurely walk." A Chicago *Tribune* correspondent had used the same comparison, "as fast as a man can walk," in describing the Casement gangs at work about a year before. The *Alta* man contributed the additional thought that this pace was "as fast as the early ox team used to travel over the plains."

Other watches were being consulted. It appears that almost every man who owned one timed the operation as the morning wore along. Union Pacific observers later put the pace at 144 feet, or five pairs of rails, a minute; a pair every twelve seconds. Several others agreed that the rate averaged a pair each thirty seconds.

It was fast, in any event; relentless and unremitting. The Chinese lorry-car crew fell out, exhausted, and was replaced by a fresh one. Then as the new track went on lengthening ahead, horses were brought up, two of them hitched single-file to each car and the rails trundled forward at a gallop. The first iron train's lading was used up; the second's; then the third's. The wagons rocked back and forth to the hoarse yelling of teamsters and the cracking of whips while the dust rolled up in clouds. Mounted overseers galloped along the grade shouting orders, censure and encouragement.

Noon came and went.

By half-past one six miles of track were down. It was a foregone conclusion now that the ten miles would be made good, barring accident. Crocker gave the signal to knock off for dinner and the camp train boss, James Campbell, later to be a division superintendent on the Central Pacific, ran his kitchen cars up and served a hot meal to all hands, construction force and audience, estimated at about five thousand in all. Jubilant workers christened the six-mile stake "Victory Station" on the spot (though the name was later changed to Rozel, for reasons unknown) and the regular hour's nooning was taken.

From this point on the grade steepened markedly and began to wind in a succession of curves. About an hour was lost in bending rails. Edwin L. Sabin, who wrote an account of the building of the Pacific Railroad in 1916, quoted a personal letter from Jim Strobridge, still living at that time, stating that working up a sixty-six-foot slope so tired the horses—meaning both lorry car and wagon teams—that they could not run, though changed every two hours. So it was the animals and not the men who faltered in the tough going, for Strobridge also stated that he had a fresh eight-man iron gang ready to go following the midday meal, but the original eight flatly refused to quit, and carried on to the finish.

At seven o'clock the "Knock off!" sounded. Four miles plus a few rail lengths had been put down during the afternoon. It was enough, ten miles in a day—Crocker's boys had done it! Hurrahs rang out and hats sailed into the darkening sky as Jim Campbell climbed into a locomotive cab and slowly rolled out to end of track in a triumphal forty-minute run. "Just to prove that the work had been well done," declared the *Alta* man, and writers who came after him have repeated the statement. As a matter of fact it was standard railroad construction practice to run an engine back and forth over a newly laid stretch of track, as the simplest and most practical method of spreading the rails to the best operable gauge on curves, smoothing out small inequalities in level and alignment and, in general, "setting" the track for use.

Charley Crocker took the bows, of course, though Jim Strobridge probably did the big job of organization and discipline that made the accomplishment possible.[2] And the true heroes of the day were the eight men of the track gang who, incredibly, worked the full twelve-hour trick at top speed and with no rest or relief except the hour's nooning. Their names survive in an old Central Pacific timekeeper's book: Michael Shay, Michael Kennedy, Michael Sullivan, Patrick Joyce, Thomas Dailey, George Wyatt, Edward Kieleen and Fred McNamara, surely as rugged a crew of the sons of Brian Boru and Finn Mac Cool as any that ever drew Casement Brothers wages. There was some consolation in that for the crestfallen Union Pacific Irishmen. At least they had been beaten by their own kind. No Chinese had done it!

In terms of simple arithmetic alone this was a day's work to stand beside the legendary labors of Hercules. Accepting the Central's statement that standard C.P. rails were used, thirty feet long and weighing fifty-six pounds to the yard, the eight men handled, without the help of mechanical contrivances of any kind save the nippers used to grab each rail end, something more than

985,600 pounds deadweight during the eleven hours of working time. It figures out to a bit over *five and a half tons per man per hour*. In the same time book which contains their names there is a notation indicating that each of the eight was paid the equivalent of four days' wages for the stint.

The Union Pacific crowd seem to have felt, to a man, that they could have done as well or better, given the opportunity and the same set of conditions. It is not unlikely that they could have, for Jack Casement was a tough customer when pressed, and his bully boys never had failed to meet any previous challenge. But Charley Crocker had seen to it in advance that they got no chance this time. A possibly apocryphal story persists that angry Dan Casement was all for tearing up some U.P. track and having another go at it, all the same. If so, cooler heads vetoed him. General Jack took it somewhat more philosophically, as Strobridge remembered their exchange:

"General Casement . . . told me that they had laid every rail they could under their system and he owned up beaten. But he said he would beat me on the Northern Pacific. I said, 'Then I'll beat you on the Southern Pacific.' "[3]

The very next year, 1870, a Kansas Pacific track gang hurrying across Colorado Territory toward Denver claimed to have exceeded the Central's record by a few rail lengths. Perhaps they did, though their feat was neither well publicized nor long remembered. And despite all the very considerable improvements in means and methods developed in later years, no one else ever came close.

Riding back to their own headquarters that night the Union Pacific men passed the sprawling cluster of kerosene lights at Promontory camp, where the two grades had been brought together and the first tent saloons were already springing up in anticipation of the gala day of junction. Promontory, last of the terminal towns, among the shabbiest and least prepossessing of them all, but star-touched by the luck of geographic location and Congressional resolution. Crocker and Stanford would be leaving immediately for Sacramento to take care of various details attendant on the meeting of the rails. As for the high brass of the Union Pacific, well . . . who knew?

Dr. Durant was the man to speak for the U.P., it would seem. But about Thomas Durant just then a bit of a mystery was gathering, and shreds of it still cling to this day. Regardless of whether the unpopular U.P. vice-president was or was not on hand for the Central's day of glory, his was soon to be the central figure in an incident no one could have foreseen and no one ever quite explained afterward.

The time element is most puzzling. It would have been somewhat out of character for a man of Durant's active interest in every phase of the U.P.'s rivalry with the Central to have missed being present for Crocker's exploit, even disregarding the widely accepted tradition of the ten-thousand-dollar bet between the two. Yet from the sketchy evidence available today it seems most logical to believe that he never made it; that his celebrated private Pullman palace car was coupled to the rear end of the regular Union Pacific express-passenger train that rolled across western Wyoming Territory on the morning of April 28, or a day or so earlier.

A ragged spatter of rifle fire greeted the train as it pulled into Piedmont. Ties had been piled on the track and a switch opened to make sure it stopped, and a crowd of some three hundred armed men was waiting. The engineer was waved off the main line into a siding. The Durant car was quickly uncoupled. The train was then ordered to proceed, an order backed by gun muzzles so that the crew had no choice but to obey.

Throughout all this, however, the crowd appears to have behaved with reasonable order. They were all graders and tie-cutters, their leaders told Durant, recently laid off with large amounts of back pay still owing. They meant to have their money, and would hold Durant prisoner until it was paid. The next move was his, and the Union Pacific's.

Later accounts of the total sum owing varied all the way from a modest $12,000 to figures of $200,000 and more. Whatever the actual amount, Durant of course did not have the cash at hand to pay off. The men had expected that; he could wire for it, they suggested. According to the San Francisco *Morning Chronicle,* they warned the Piedmont operator that any attempt at trickery—a telegram asking for help, say, instead of for the money—would result in his being hanged immediately from the nearest tree. Apparently neither Durant nor any of his party was threatened with violence. But if anyone tried to rescue them, said the gang leaders, Durant himself would be taken off into the Wasatch Mountains and held on short rations as long as necessary.

So in the end there was nothing for it but an urgent plea to U.P. President Oliver Ames in Boston, and a galling embarrassment that must have been to stiff-necked, lone-wolf Thomas Durant.

Ames, alarmed and excited, more than a little confused also, could think of no better course than a telegram to Grenville Dodge at Salt Lake City, ordering him to take over. Dodge was in little better position than the captive Durant to put his hands on the necessary cash, of course. But it was Ames's notion that the Army could go galloping to the rescue and put everything right. Dodge did fire off an immediate telegram to Fort Bridger, only twenty miles from Piedmont; a somewhat silly tactic under the circumstances, for the message had to be relayed through the Piedmont operator, who simply took it off the wire and handed it to the gang leaders. Back to Dodge went their bristling reply: any further delay in paying up and the whole Union Pacific line would flare in strikes and work stoppages.

It was a cogent threat, and the chief engineer knew it. Every message already sent cast and west—his, Ames's, Durant's—had been listened to by brass-pounders in every little depot along the right of way, and many of them would surely talk. The company's slow pay was a sore point of long standing; most of the men on the payroll had grievances as valid as the Piedmont crowd's. This might be just the spark needed to set off a general conflagration. The only sensible thing to do was surrender.

Dodge did. He telegraphed Oliver Ames and advised that the money would have to be raised somehow and the men at Piedmont paid off.

It was, and they were. And so the first hold-up on the Pacific Railroad was brought to an end. The confusion and the mystery, however, spread some way beyond the bare facts. Not least among the bewildering facets of the incident is the manner of its coverage in the nation's press. Eastern newspapers knew nothing of it until some time later. Then their stories, quite mistakenly, assumed that the affair was responsible for the subsequent delay in the official ceremony at the meeting of the rails. Salt Lake City's *Deseret News,* sitting almost on top of the story, so to speak, and the leading Mormon paper in Utah, printed not a word about it—which has led one modern theorist to speculate somewhat pointlessly that the whole business was a plot among the Latter-day Saints, with Brigham Young himself involved. The San Francisco *Morning Chronicle* ran only a very brief account as part of a general rundown of events preceding the golden spike ceremony, and this did not appear until May 11.

Oddly enough, one of the most complete stories on the affair appeared in a small church journal, *The Friend,* published in faraway Honolulu in the Sandwich Islands. The editor, a Rev. Charles Damon, happened to be traveling eastward via the Union Pacific, and datelined his report at Cheyenne on May 13. He fixed the date of the occurrence only vaguely: "the week before the Golden Spike ceremony." But he also named the whopping sum of $253,000 as the total amount of back wages paid before Durant was released. So great an exaggeration leaves the suspicion that the Reverend had little or no firsthand information, and merely repeated local hearsay.[4]

Much of this press uncertainty undoubtedly was due to the Union Pacific's official silence about the incident. It was altogether too explosive a situation while it was going on, and probably too embarrassing afterward. All the while, though, rumors must have been rife along the U.P. line from Cheyenne to Utah, and the newsmen picked up what they could. Dr. Durant himself never reminisced about the occurrence.

The Piedmont men's boldness had one salutary effect, at least. Prodded by Grenville Dodge, who had absorbed the lesson thoroughly, Oliver Ames took steps to raise some additional cash and presently dispatched a half-million dollars west, to provide Union Pacific employees with a badly needed payday and reassure the company's other creditors with tangible evidence of better times on the way. Somehow, though, Ames seems never to have grasped the full import of what had happened. Afterward he complained in letters to Dodge that he had had to dispose of some of the company's land-grant acreage (presumably at a distress price) in order to obtain the money. But the danger of widespread labor difficulties was averted.

PART FOUR

The Golden Spike; and Afterward

CHAPTER 30

GREAT EXPECTATIONS

Lack of water was a serious problem at Promontory Summit. Partly for this reason, but also because he knew all about the whiskey mills and other fleshpots that flourished at Promontory camp and in the Union Pacific towns beyond, Jim Strobridge pulled the bulk of his work force to the rear while a skeleton crew put down the last four miles of track, all that the record stint of April 28 had left for the Central Pacific to do. By the first of May the job was finished. About the same time Casement Brothers pushed U.P.'s railhead to the summit, though rock still was being blasted out of a cut some way down the eastward slope and carpenters still swarmed over the last of the trestles there. The Union Pacific's main construction camp was pulled back, too, to the edge of Great Salt Lake south of Blue Creek, where springs furnished an adequate supply of fresh water.

Both companies sent crews farther to the rear and put them to work ballasting and repairing the sagging grades left behind in the winter's frantic rush. With the end so close, both were laying men off as well. The Union Pacific, in the tighter financial pinch, did so with an especially free hand. The inevitable dislocations attending the transcontinental's completion had come, and they brought the inevitable trouble.

Idle men trooping into Blue Creek, Corinne and other towns were met by eager gamblers, rotgut peddlers and bawdyhouse runners dedicated to prying loose the last remaining dollars in furious binges of farewell. The Union Pacific, to its credit, made an effort to ship many of the unemployed back East, whence most of them had come. The well-known Salt Lake City photographer, Colonel Charles R. Savage, had been engaged to make the company's official pictorial record of the meeting of the rails. While waiting he roamed the region around railhead; saw drunken men at Blue Creek heaped aboard flat-cars bound for Omaha—"Democrats," they were called derisively; someone had a nice sense of political irony—and listened to tales of twenty-four men killed at the several camps in the past twenty-five days. Never, he confided to his diary, had a harder set of men been brought together. "Verily, men earn their money like horses and spend it like asses," he concluded.

Not all the "Democrats" were removed, however. Bands of discharged laborers wandered about the Utah countryside, carousing, cadging handouts, breaking into Mormon homes to rob and rape. Justice struck swiftly; almost all of the worst criminals were speedily caught, tried and convicted. But the old pioneer concept that a man took care of his own still ran strong and deep. At least two convicted rapists were shot dead by outraged husbands and fathers, whose peers called it justifiable homicide and acquitted them.

Within the railroad towns crime prospered almost unchecked. A traveler by the name of Henry Wolfe alighted from the Overland Stage at the Union Pacific end of track one day in May and was promptly seized by a gang of toughs, hustled into a wagon, carried to Corinne and stripped of "$65 in gold, $7 in greenbacks, his valise which with its contents he valued at $200 and a U.P.R.R. ticket from Junction City to Omaha." The victim obtained a warrant for the miscreants' arrest, but the deputy United States marshal in Corinne demanded a fee of a hundred dollars before serving it. Being penniless and quite unable to come up with such a bribe, Mr. Wolfe had to make his way east as best he could, "without obtaining any assistance or redress, carrying his warrant along with him." Eventually he reached Omaha and told his story to a sympathetic reporter for the *Herald,* from which this account is taken.

The virus of violence reached out to infect even the usually well-behaved Chinese of the Central Pacific. Two of them argued over a fifteen-dollar gambling debt at the Victory Station camp. The argument erupted into blows. The whole coolie crew took sides and fell to with knives, shovels, pick handles in a battle royal that lasted one whole afternoon and left one man dead and so many maimed that Jim Strobridge curtly refused even to estimate their number for a San Francisco *Chronicle* man who reported the story.

Back at the head of Echo Canyon, workers on the U.P.'s unfinished tunnel No. 2 had walked out on strike earlier in April. The payday engineered by Grenville Dodge and Oliver Ames had not yet taken place, and they stayed out in spite of Construction Superintendent Samuel Reed's best efforts at negotiation.

Through this hectic atmosphere the last stages of construction crept slowly forward. Toward the end of the first week in May the Union Pacific had its final cut cleared at last, and iron laid over the last trestle on the Promontory approach. By the seventh the Pacific Railroad was all but finished. The next day, Saturday, May 8, promised celebration.

That was the understanding at Sacramento, where Leland Stanford, Charley Crocker and even the colorless, unassuming Mark Hopkins had been wined, dined and feted as heroes for a week past. All the old animosities were forgotten now. Throughout California and Nevada everybody was climbing aboard the Central Pacific bandwagon. Enthusiasm for the driving of the last spike burned fever-hot in San Francisco, Sacramento and all the towns around and between. The planning of festivities to make the day forever memorable became a public preoccupation.

The first announcement of a ceremony to be held in Sacramento had appeared in the *Union* weeks before. On May 7 the paper printed a proclamation by "Josiah Howell, Grand Marshal," with all the final details.

Things would get off to a rousing start with a "GRAND CHORUS of GUNS, BELLS, STEAM WHISTLES etc., to commence at or about ten o'clock A.M. when signaled that the LAST SPIKE is driven and continue for ten minutes." There would be a parade, of course, ending at Front Street with "an oration by Governor H. M. Haight, poetry recitations, vocal solos, a benediction and singing with the public requested to join in." Preceding editions of the *Union* had carried advertisements by the Central Pacific announcing that people from the surrounding area who wished to come to the city for the gala day would be provided with free transportation via special trains.

A large number of other celebrants, more solvent financially and determined to see the last spike driven in person, already were Promontory-bound. The regular six A.M. passenger train for Elko, Nevada, had pulled out of the Sacramento depot the previous morning, May 6, with a sizable contingent of excursionists aboard. And right behind it Leland Stanford's Presidential Special had whistled off and soon was laying its trail of wood smoke down the long northward tangent across the American River flats; a gleamingly furbished locomotive pulling a special, newly completed commissary car stocked with choice foods, vintage wines and fresh California fruits, and Stanford's own personal palace car with its self-contained kitchen, luxurious dining room and deluxe sleeping accommodations for ten.

On his guest list the Central's president had Silas W. Sanderson, an associate justice of the California Supreme Court; Governor A. P. K. Safford of Arizona Territory; the three federal government commissioners assigned to the Central Pacific: William G. Sherman (a brother of the general), James W. Haines and F. A. Tritle, the latter a distinguished Nevadan soon to take office as that state's governor. There was Edgar Mills, son of the Bank of California's Darius Ogden Mills, who never had helped the railroad, to be sure, but nevertheless remained on good terms with the Associates and was in any case well worth cultivating. There were in addition a Dr. J. D. B. Stillman, San Francisco County coroner and an old friend of Mark Hopkins, and a Dr. W. H. Harkness, editor of a new Sacramento newspaper, the *Press*. Dr. Stillman, who later wrote a very readable and detailed account of the trip and the subsequent ceremony at Promontory, mentioned "others," though in view of the aforesaid accommodations for ten it seems doubtful that the party could have been very much larger.

As noteworthy as this august human lading were the exhibits nested on lustrous satin in the palace car's drawing room. Largest and therefore most prominent was the special "last tie": a standard eight feet long by eight inches wide and six thick, but hewn out of native California laurel, waxed and hand-polished to a rich luster, bound with silver bands and embellished with a handsomely engraved silver plate that announced to the world:

> The Last Tie Laid on the Completion of the Pacific Railroad, May ——, 1869. Directors—L. Stanford, C. P. Huntington, E. B. Crocker, Mark Hopkins, E. H. Miller, A. P. Stanford and Charles Marsh. Officers—Leland Stanford, President; C. P. Huntington, Vice-President; Charles Crocker, Superintendent; Mark Hopkins, Treasurer; E. H. Miller, Secretary.

This tie, a gift from West Stotts, the railroad's chief tie contractor, was flanked by a silver-headed spike maul presented by the Pacific Union Express Company and by the last spike itself, a regulation seven inches long and made, according to a story current around Sacramento at the time, of twenty-dollar gold pieces melted down, at a total cost of $413. A large nugget had been left attached to the spike's head, to be broken off and made up into souvenir watch charms in the form of miniature spikes after the ceremony. Upon the head itself was graven the legend, "The Last Spike," and on its four sides, respectively: the names of the company's officers; "The Pacific Railroad; Ground Broken January 8, 1863; Completed May ——, 1869"; "May God Continue the Unity of Our Country as This Railroad Unites the Two Great Oceans of the World"; and "Presented by David Hewes, San Francisco."

The donor, Hewes, was a wealthy contractor, descendant of a pioneer settler on the Pacific Coast and a close family friend of the Leland Stanfords. Although neither an important contractor to the Central Pacific nor a financial backer, he had been so carried away by enthusiasm at the prospect of the transcontinental's completion that, so he said later, he had done his best to persuade certain mining magnates on the Nevada Comstock to contribute a pair of solid silver "last rails." He had not quite convinced them, however, and Nevada would content herself with a spike of Comstock silver to be sent from Virginia City and delivered to the train at Reno.

Also on exhibit were another golden spike presented by the San Francisco

News Letter and one of silver, gold and iron brought by Governor Safford as Arizona's tribute.

With all these trappings of official dignity and historic purpose, the Presidential Special very nearly came to grief. It happened on the descending eastern slope of the Sierras, the same gantlet where so many mishaps had plagued the operating department during recent months. A crew of Chinese timber-cutters above the track watched the regular passenger train go through and, knowing nothing of the Special following and assuming everything to be clear, resumed their work of skidding logs down to the right of way. A big one got away from them, bounded down the steep cutbank and came to rest with its massive three-foot butt across one rail just minutes before the locomotive swung around a blind curve on the approach to tunnel No. 14.

Dr. Harkness, riding the pilot deck for a daring journalist's-eye view of mountain railroading, jumped clear as the whistle began to blast frantically for brakes. The pilot smashed into the obstruction, buckled and collapsed; the log end scraped down the full length of engine and tender in a series of grinding bumps, splintered away the steps at both ends of Stanford's palace car but luckily failed to derail the train. Dr. Harkness, shaken but not badly hurt, was picked up and helped to his quarters. A hasty inspection revealed the locomotive to be considerably damaged but still able to limp on into Reno, where the train ahead was caught and held for the party by telegraph.

No particular preparations, meanwhile, had gone forward from the Pacific Railroad's eastern end. The very whereabouts of Thomas Durant, Sidney Dillon and other Union Pacific dignitaries during the final days of April and the early ones of May are only sparsely recorded. A letter from Grenville Dodge to his wife places Dillon at Echo and Durant and John Duff, prominent U.P. director from Boston, in Salt Lake City on May 2. Dodge himself, he wrote, had just returned to Devil's Gate from Promontory.[1]

Dillon's presence at Echo is explained, probably, by the strike at tunnel No. 2, since it is known that he stepped in and helped to bring about the settlement there. The fact holds a significant inference of its own: the capable and personable Credit Mobilier president was taking on more and more of the perquisites of the Union Pacific's general manager, Durant being edged relentlessly out of control at last. But Durant had other problems, too. It seems likely that he and Duff were busy mending fences with Bishop John Sharp and other Mormon subcontractors to the U.P., for payments on their grading work had once again slipped about a million dollars into arrears. They did not see Brigham Young, however, as he was away on church and personal business in the south of Utah.

By the fifth of May, as if these were not complications enough, it was raining heavily. Grades along Echo Creek and the Weber River were washed out. The streams, already foaming bank-full with the runoff of melting snows from the high valleys of the Wasatch Mountains, clawed with growing fury at the U.P. trestles. On May 7 the *Deseret News* reported Weber totally blocked, the spans beginning to go: "The bridge at Devil's Gate commenced giving way last night. The 300 feet of trestle work at Strawberry Ford next evinced signs of 'caving.' The first bridge below the Narrows, or Slate Point, next succumbed."

Every available man of the depleted Union Pacific construction force was rounded up and pressed into service. Lumber by the carload was rushed from supply dumps to shore up bents and piers and patch spans that groaned on the point of collapse. "Vice Presidents Durant and Dillon and the Commissioners," the *News* remarked, "are also at the front."

This was the situation on the afternoon of Friday, May 7, when the Central's smartly groomed Schenectady eight-wheeler, *Jupiter,* steamed into Promontory with the two cars of Leland Stanford's Presidential Special in tow. No welcoming committee awaited. There was nothing and nobody, in fact, but stand-by Central Pacific and U.P. telegraph crews huddled in tents beside their respective ends of track, and the thirty-odd tents and plank-and-canvas shacks of Promontory town itself straggling along their single muddy street in a pelting downpour.

A Union Pacific brass-pounder tapped out Stanford's telegram of inquiry to Ogden. It was handed to General Jack Casement, apparently the only one in authority left there. Casement hurried to order out a special train with arrangements for a dinner of state to be served in his own headquarters car. But tomorrow's celebration was off, he told the Central president. It would be Monday at the earliest before any train from the East could get through Weber Canyon.

Glumly Stanford passed the word to Sacramento, and almost immediately received the reply that it was too late to postpone the scheduled festivities there. The city was already filling up; people were accepting the railroad's offer of free transportation in droves. More than a score of special trains had had to be made up—sixty-five cars in all—and most of them were already rolling, some from points as far away as Nevada. The true state of affairs in Utah was beside the point; there was nothing to do but give these people the celebration for which they had come.

So at ten A.M. on Saturday, May 8, precisely on schedule, the "last spike" signal sounded in a booming salute by *Union Boy,* a small brass cannon owned by a local saloonkeeper and first fired on the occasion of the first run of the Central Pacific's first locomotive back in '63. Locomotives and steamboats along the levee let loose with whistle blasts; bells pealed all over town;

the planned parade, a mile long, swung into motion. Governor Haight delivered his address and there was free lunch for all. That evening Charley Crocker was the guest of honor at a state banquet. All the same, the real news from Promontory must have had a dampening effect, for the *Union* in reporting the big day on Monday remarked with some asperity that preparations for the ceremony had been "hastily made, owing to Stanford's doubts on the suitability of Saturday." But, the *Union* added, "Everything was conducted in a pleasant and orderly way and . . . nothing of a public character disgraced the event."

Buried in the same story was one short sentence declaring that "T. D. Judah is justly entitled to the lion's share of praise for the early completion of the railway." Of all the countless words that would be committed to newsprint by the time the last spike really was driven, these were destined to be the only ones honoring the man who had started it all.

For the living, though, the cup of praise ran over. That Sunday the Rev. I. E. Dwinnell, pastor of the Congregational Church of Sacramento, devoted a lengthy and florid sermon to the railroad builders, "striding across the plains, struggling through valleys, pushing hills right and left, laying hands of iron on the icy manes of mountains and springing over; grinding obstructions of rock and earth to powder and tossing them in the air; accompanied by a noisy retinue of tongues and brogues and a wild commotion of nature, and gaining at last such momentum that they shot 200 miles past each other before stopping."

There was much more in the same vein, the whole vast enterprise described step by step before the Rev. Dwinnell concluded by admonishing the builders to rest from their labors on the Sabbath and to "entrust no engine, no car, no brake, no switch, no depot, no construction of trains, no signaling, no grading or repairing of track, to a man whose brain is not always cool and his judgement clear and steady by freedom from strong drink."[2]

Plainly, the Reverend overlooked nothing and knew whereof he spoke. This was scarcely the first statement of American railroading's hoary Rule G, but no one ever put it more explicitly.

The folk at Sacramento were not the only ones who could not wait. In San Francisco the celebrating got under way early on Saturday and carried on and on with a zesty stamina that promised to last as long as it was going to take to get things moving out there where the railheads waited. And in the opposite direction Cheyenne's *Daily Leader,* after informing its readers on Saturday that "the last rail might not be laid sooner than noon of Monday next," cautioned them that "to those who burn all their gunpowder today, there will be nothing but remorse on Monday."

In Utah the Stanford party, having been entertained by Jack Casement on

Friday evening, left the next morning for an excursion via Union Pacific special train to Taylor's Mill, Corinne and other points of interest on the line, the itinerary extending as far past Ogden toward Devil's Gate as the condition of the roadbed permitted. But there is no indication that they were able to contact Dr. Durant, Dillon, Dodge or other Union Pacific officials at this time. By Sunday afternoon the entire party was back aboard the Presidential Special at Promontory. The weather had continued miserable, rain and blustery winds alternating with fog. Stanford had the train backed thirty miles to Monument Point, a spot affording a magnificent view of Great Salt Lake. The steward ventured out with a shotgun and bagged a mess of plover for dinner. So Sunday evening passed.

Unremitting work all this while had made the damaged bridges down Weber Canyon barely passable. The first through train from the East, out of Omaha on May 5 with excursionists and through passengers from Boston, New York, Chicago and intermediate points, crept down Echo and Weber on a prolonged slow order, flagmen walking in front of the locomotive in places to inspect the sodden grade. Through the gathering dusk of Saturday evening it nosed carefully up to the east end of the Devil's Gate trestle. There it stood all night long, the conductor prudently refusing to proceed by dark. Under the supervision of Colonel Leonard H. Eicholtz, the Union Pacific's chief bridge engineer, a new fifty-foot truss span had been thrust out across the boiling river, and seemed to be holding, though a repair crew stood by anxiously. It did hold, but conditions remained so dubious that it would be kept under close surveillance all day Sunday and Monday. Many of the passengers, chilled, hungry and thoroughly disgruntled, abandoned the train and booked passage by stagecoach for Salt Lake City. In spite of the angry questions of the rest, the U.P. operating department refused to give any assurance of arrival times at Ogden or beyond.

Sunday ended, however, with the sun setting redly through breaking clouds, a promise of fair weather on the morrow.

But one small spasm of the six-year rivalry had still to be played out. In spite of the Durant-Huntington agreement and the ratifying resolution of Congress, both companies seem to have clung to certain reservations of their own regarding the somewhat ambiguous wording, "at or near Ogden." Each railroad therefore saw a possible future advantage in establishing a claim to Promontory. That, at any rate, appears to be the sole valid reason for what happened next.

Sometime during Sunday afternoon or evening, apparently, a rumor reached Jack Casement's ear that the Central Pacific people intended to run a work train up to Promontory Summit bright and early next morning, and expand the temporary spur there into a permanent siding. General Jack acted fast: broke out his rail gang and put them aboard an iron train with orders to get to the summit as soon as possible and start laying track by lantern light. They did. By sunrise on Monday they had some 2,500 feet of siding down, switches in and the Union Pacific's right to Promontory, such as it was, nailed down by concrete accomplishment.

The rumor proved true. At the first light of dawn a Central Pacific construction train snorted in from the west, a coolie work crew perched atop the iron cars. Irishmen raised their voices in a sardonic cheer of welcome, getting a little of their own back for the discomfiture at Victory Station. Swinging down off the cars, the Central foremen stared, shrugged and had to concede the point.

"There was some chagrin and joking," Sidney Dillon wrote of the incident, "but no ill feeling."[3]

Thus the great day began.

CHAPTER 31

"DONE"

Old Glory, run up to the top of a telegraph pole overlooking the gap between the railheads, snapped briskly in a biting wind. The sun climbed a sky of scrubbed and cloudless blue, dazzlingly bright after all the days of rain and fog, but it was so cold that scums of ice formed on standing puddles. Hangers-on from Promontory town commenced to gather; they would be out in force, decked in their shabby best, long before the ceremony began. More construction workers kept straggling in from the camps east and west, riding crowbait draft horses.

The setting was stark and desolate. Southward behind Promontory the land rose sharply in a long ridge clad sparsely with scrub cedar, blocking the view of the point thrust out into Great Salt Lake a thousand feet below. To the north the land sloped upward also, so that the track lay in a shallow valley, barren save for the eternal sagebrush and scattered clumps of stunted cedar.

Among early bystanders on the scene was one Alexander Toponce, a beef contractor to Benson, Farr and West, the Central Pacific's Mormon grading firm. Mr. Toponce would recall this day in a volume of reminiscences written down many years later, not always accurately but with much salty detail some of the more dignified commentators would miss.

Everybody, he remembered, "tried to have a hand in the work. I took a shovel from an Irishman and threw a shovel full of dirt on the ties just to tell about it afterward."[1]

Presently *Jupiter* whistled down the line and steamed up with the Stanford Presidential Special, now augmented by cars carrying the first excursionists from California and Nevada. Additions to the official Central Pacific party included Chief Engineer Montague and Consulting Engineer George Gray, Jim Strobridge and a few others. Collis Huntington, that hard-shelled scorner of pomp and ostentation, had made no plans to come out from New York. Mark Hopkins appears to have been in San Francisco at this time, and Charley

Crocker, of course, had elected to remain in Sacramento, claiming prior business commitments. Of the Union Pacific Special and of U.P. officialdom there was no sign.

The sun climbed higher, beginning to beam down with some heat. The crowd shifted and murmured restlessly. It was ten o'clock before a distant whistle announced the U.P.'s coming. The Special pulled in with a rush behind a brand-new Rogers eight-wheeler, No. 119, to touch off a burst of cheers and a flurry of whistled salutes.

The difference between the two locomotives was at once striking. No. 119 was a coal-burner, one of the Union Pacific's first, and her tall, straight stack stood in marked contrast to the ponderous balloon stack looming atop *Jupiter*'s smokebox; her U.P. livery of dark green and black looked somber in comparison with the Central's use of vivid scarlet to pick out driver spokes, pilot and cab panels. But both had plenty of bright brasswork to flash bravely from domes and boiler fittings. A Union Pacific news release of the day described its train as "the most elegant in equipment with the largest number of passengers" ever to travel over the line. Most published accounts of the ceremony which followed mentioned lavish displays of flags and bunting on both engines, though none of the day's photographs show a scrap of decoration. There were some avid souvenir collectors on hand there at Promontory, and perhaps they stripped it all away before the picture-taking began.

From Dr. Durant's official car the Union Pacific party alighted: Durant himself impeccably turned out in a black velvet coat and flowing tie; Sidney Dillon smiling, courtly and handsome with his magnificent white sideburns; portly, silver-haired John Duff; General Dodge; Silas Seymour; the Casement brothers; Engineers Samuel Reed, James Evans and Marshall Hurd. The Rev. John Todd, Congregationalist minister from Pittsfield, Massachusetts, was present as Duff's guest, and would deliver the prayer of benediction. Quite inexplicably, considering their great stake in the Union Pacific, neither Oakes nor Oliver Ames had made the trip.

Also on the train, Alexander Toponce would recall, were "a lot of newspaper men, and plenty of the best brands of champaign."

The cheers redoubled as the Union Pacific people walked forward and shook hands all around with the Central Pacific party. This was a crowd that had come to cheer, and they did cheer, while a second U.P. special train made up at Ogden steamed in and stopped behind the first. It quickly disgorged four companies of the U.S. 21st Infantry under the command of Major Milton Cogswell, the regimental band from Fort Douglas at Salt Lake City, and a large deputation of Utah luminaries. There was Loren Farr, Mayor of Ogden and a partner in Benson, Farr and West, Central Pacific grading contractors.

Bishop John Sharp, subcontractor for the Union Pacific, was present as the official representative of the Latter-day Saints, conveying Brigham Young's regrets at not being able to attend. Also aboard this train were Utah Governor-designate Charles Durkee, a Gentile, and several lesser lights from Ogden and Salt Lake City. One of these, a Mrs. Ryan identified only as the wife of the U.P. station agent at Ogden, was destined along with Mrs. Strobridge, "the heroine of the Central Pacific," to share a minor niche in history. They were the only *ladies* there to witness the meeting of the rails, though Promontory and Corinne probably contributed primped and painted female contingents of their own.[2]

The Ogden train also brought the city's Tenth Ward Band, resplendent in new uniforms and equipped with shiny new instruments recently imported from England at a cost, it was said, of twelve hundred dollars. Whatever else this ceremony might lack, it obviously was not going to lack music. There was also, according to the observant Mr. Toponce, "a small but efficient supply of Valley Tan." The ceremony would not lack refreshment either!

Briskly Major Cogswell formed his troopers into a double file along the south side of the track, pressing the jostling crowd back so as to leave a cleared space around the last rail's length of bare grade and ties. A small deal table had been set up here, bearing a telegraph key connected with the wires east and west. Here W. N. Shilling, the Western Union operator from Ogden, seated himself in readiness. But now the delay ran on, endlessly it seemed. The sun rode higher, the empty plain and the gray-brown ridges north and south shimmered in its glare. The two bands played on and the locomotives whistled intermittently while the crowd waited in impatience.

Little if any thought had been devoted to a definite program in advance, everyone concerned having been too deeply involved in the details of final construction work, the emergency in Weber Canyon and the problems of simply arranging affairs so as to be present. So from this point on the big day was on its own. Grenville Dodge and Edgar Mills retired to one side and hastily began to haggle over an order of procedure while the official parties grouped themselves in the clear space. Mrs. Strobridge, Mrs. Ryan and a few children present were ushered forward to choice spots in the front row. Some observers later spoke of a small boy who shinnied up a telegraph pole and stayed there for a fine bird's-eye view throughout the proceedings. Amos Bowsher, Central Pacific telegraph superintendent, mounted the pole to which the wires from Shilling's key had been carried and stood by in case of trouble there. So he too enjoyed a good look. Not many did, it appears.

There were some twenty or more correspondents present. In addition to the California journalists who had followed the Central Pacific, reporters had been sent by the New York *Herald,* New York *Tribune,* Omaha *Herald,* Boston *Transcript,* Springfield *Republican,* Chicago *Tribune* and the Associated Press, besides a number of smaller fry. J. H. Beadle, the roving scribe from Cincinnati by way of Wasatch and Corinne, complained afterward that many of the newspapermen were shoved so far back into the crowd that they saw and heard very little of what went on.

The sun stood almost at noon when Grenville Dodge at last stepped forward and lifted a hand for silence. Construction Superintendents Strobridge of the Central Pacific and Reed of the U.P. walked down to the Stanford car and returned with the silver-bound laurel tie borne between them. While a buzz and a craning of necks ran among the onlookers they stooped and placed it in position on the grade. The two last rails were brought up: one by four Chinese in clean blue smocks, shepherded by the Central's H. H. Minkler; the other by four Irish track hands under a Union Pacific foreman named Guilford. Colonel Savage meanwhile had set up his camera near the track and was fussing with final adjustments. From somewhere in the crowd a raucous voice bawled: "Now's the time, Charley. Take a shot!"

It nearly broke things up. To the coolies, hazed by white bullies all the way across Nevada, the word "shot" connoted an experience invariably unpleasant if not fatal. Jerking their heads up in alarm, they saw the glassy demon-eye of the camera fixed on them, promptly dropped the rail and bolted, with the crowd hooting and howling in delight. According to the story—an interjection of slapstick seeming almost too good to be true, but vouched for by several eyewitnesses—it took some time to run the Chinese down and bring them back into the ceremony.

While all this went on, telegraph offices from both directions had been pestering Shilling with impatient queries. Now, as the rails were placed in position and spiked fast to all but the laurel tie (Union Pacific men doing the job on the right-hand rail, looking east, and Central men working along the left-hand one) he dispatched his first message of the day:

"To everybody. Keep quiet. When the last spike is driven at Promontory Point we will say, 'Done.' Don't break the circuit, but watch for the signals of the blows of the hammer." Almost at once, seeing Dodge beckon to the Rev. Dr. Todd, he followed with another: "Almost ready. Hats off; prayer is being offered."

This was bulletined in Washington, D.C., at 2:27 P.M., Eastern time. Western Union's President James Gamble had ordered top priority for the news from Promontory, so that all Shilling's messages were read almost immediately by crowds gathered in front of telegraph offices in virtually every town and city in the United States.

Dr. Todd's prayer ended: ". . . that this mighty enterprise may be unto us as the Atlantic of Thy strength and the Pacific of Thy love. . . . Amen."

There was very nearly an awkward blunder then. But someone remembered in time that Bishop Sharp should, as a courtesy to him and the Mormon Church, be asked for a benediction, too. He was, and briefly complied.

"We have got done praying," Shilling sent, "the spike is about to be presented."

At Chicago there had been some earlier trouble with the circuit. The operator there replied, "We understand. All are ready in the East."

A procession of dignitaries now brought the various ceremonial spikes forward and handed them to either Leland Stanford or Dr. Durant, each of whom knelt as he received a spike and placed it in a hole previously bored in the last tie. The procedure was rapid, the presentation remarks notably brief.

Commissioner Tritle offered Nevada's spike of Comstock silver: "To the iron of the East and the gold of the West, Nevada adds her link of silver to span the continent and weld the oceans."

Governor Stafford, for Arizona Territory: "Ribbed in iron, clad in silver and crowned with gold, Arizona presents her offering to the enterprise that has banded the continent and welded the oceans."

Afterward there was some discussion among observers as to whether both gentlemen had not actually said, or meant to say, "wed the oceans" instead of "weld."

Idaho and Montana Territories were represented by other spikes of silver and gold. Last to step up was Dr. Harkness of Sacramento, apparently quite recovered from the bruises sustained in the near-wreck of the Presidential Special on the way out. He presented California's two golden spikes: "From her bosom was taken the first soil, so let hers be the last tie and the last spike."

Leland Stanford, frequently inclined to be heavily pedantic in his public orations, took only a few minutes for his acceptance speech. Passing lightly over the many obstacles overcome in bringing the great work to completion, he expressed hope for friendship and cooperation between the two railroads in the future, and foresaw a day when not one but three tracks would be needed to handle the flow of freight and passengers across the nation's breadth.

Grenville Dodge responded for the Union Pacific: "Gentlemen, the great Benton proposed that someday a giant statue of Columbus be erected on the highest peak of the Rocky Mountains, pointing westward, denoting this as the great route across the continent. You have made that prophecy today a fact. This is the way to India."

It was the old concept of the Northwest Passage again, and in voicing it the general put words to the thought in a majority of his listeners' minds that day. But old Thomas Hart Benton was an odd personage for Dodge to be citing.

The Senator from Missouri had indeed suggested a colossal image of Christopher Columbus, but his most strenuous advocacy of a way westward had centered around a mighty transcontinental wagon road; he had come in somewhat late as a Pacific Railroad man, and then had campaigned for the old Buffalo Trail and against the Central Route which was basically the one U.P. and Central Pacific had followed.

But such small nuances meant nothing to this shaggy crowd of enthusiasts. They cheered Dodge lustily; cheered Stanford; cheered Union Pacific, Central Pacific, the Stars and Stripes. . . . It might have gone on indefinitely had not a Mr. Coe, representing the Pacific Union Express Company, advanced to hand over the silver-headed spike maul. Wires from the telegraph key had been attached to it. Shilling clicked off the word to stand by:

"All ready now; the spike will soon be driven. The signal will be three dots for the commencement of the blows."

There was another delay, though, while a succession of guests were invited to tap home all but the last golden spike, and gingerly did so, someone providing an ordinary sledge for the purpose. Then Stanford stood alone, hefting the silver maul, obviously nervous and bothered by the dangling wires. It was a solemn moment, variously likened afterward to the signing of the Declaration of Independence, the landing of the Pilgrims on Plymouth Rock and the surrender at Appomattox.

Stanford swung, missed the spike and hit the rail.

"What a howl went up! Irish, Chinese, Mexicans, and everybody yelled with delight. 'He missed it. Yee!' The engineers blew the whistles and rang their bells. Then Stanford tried it again and tapped the spike."

Thus Alexander Toponce remembered it. But Shilling simply snapped out his three dots as the maul crashed on the rail, and instantly flashed the single word: "Done."

Later it was said that there was a panicky moment's difficulty with the hookup in Western Union's Omaha office before an alert operator relayed the word to Chicago.

In Washington the first of the three dots released a magnetic ball rigged to a pole atop the Capitol dome, and as it fell a great, glad shout went up from a watching multitude. The time there was exactly 2:47 P.M. At the War Department General William T. Sherman and some other government officials gathered around an Army telegraph installation and so received the word at first hand. The New York *Tribune* reported that President Grant had planned to join them but was detained in a meeting at the Department of State.

New York City fired a hundred-gun salute while the choir at Trinity Church chanted the *Te Deum*, with "Old Hundred" pealed out on the chimes in the bell tower upon its conclusion. The Liberty Bell was rung in Philadelphia.

Lusty Chicago hastily decorated itself in patriotic bunting, staged a parade four miles long, applauded an oration by Vice-President Schuyler Colfax at a banquet that evening and made merry far into the night. Omaha blasted out another hundred-gun salute and staged another parade.

San Francisco, which had been celebrating hard for two days past, paused briefly to hearken as Stanford's blow touched off the first of 220 cannon shots at Fort Point and set the fire bell in City Hall tower to pealing. Then, fortified with the assurance that it was official now, celebrants carried on with their zeal revitalized. Sacramento fired its own cannon again, blew its whistles and rang its bells as it had on Saturday.

At Salt Lake City Gentiles and Latter-day Saints mingled as one people in the great Tabernacle. Ogden had been too impatient to wait. Fifteen minutes before Shilling's three dots the guns had started booming from the courthouse, city hall and Arsenal Hill. Places of business closed their doors and a crowd of seven thousand jammed the new Tabernacle to listen to speeches and a special concert by Huntington's Martial Band, opening with "Mill May" and closing, on a very proper note of optimistic prophecy, with "Hard Times Come Again No More."

Earlier in the day, in the quiet Massachusetts town of Greenfield, a widow had drawn her blinds to sit alone in the stillness of her darkened parlor. As the great news broke in a burst of whistles and church bells she arose, left the house and walked to the cemetery where her husband had lain for six years now. By an eerie coincidence, Anna Pierce and Theodore Dehone Judah had exchanged the vows of man and wife on another May 10, twenty-two years past. What Anna's thoughts were this day, only she knew. She wrote a friend, many years later, that her husband seemed very close to her again.[3]

Here and there other women mourned, no doubt. The Pacific Railroad had been a great widow-maker. No one knew, or ever paused to total up, the full roster of its dead: shuffled off in Indian attacks, wrecks, boiler explosions, cave-ins, avalanches, freezing cold, sunstroke and heat exhaustion, snake bite, alkali water, bad whiskey, disease and terminal-town brawls.

But this was not a day for mourning.

At Promontory an embarrassed Leland Stanford proffered the silver-headed maul to Dr. Thomas Durant and suggested he take his turn at the last spike. "Then," said Alexander Toponce, "Durant . . . took up the sledge and he missed the spike the first time. Then everybody slapped everybody else again and yelled, 'He missed it too, yow!' "

Who actually did drive the golden spike remains a question. Many published accounts state that the two chief engineers finished the job, Samuel Montague striking the first blow, Grenville Dodge the second, and so on. Others award the honor to Jim Strobridge and Samuel Reed. According to still others, it was

General Jack Casement who stepped in and pounded the spike home. In any event, the ceremony seems to have wound up in an undignified scuffle of pushing, hauling and hammering, everyone who could lay hands on a maul and get close enough tapping away at the several gold and silver spikes while the crowd shouted "fit to bust."

Despite such loose ends, though, and the general air of catch-as-catch-can throughout, the proceedings had been remarkably brief, simple and in good taste for an era distinguished for the length and pomposity of its public rites. From Shilling's first message on the prayer being offered to his climactic "Done," only twenty minutes elapsed.

Some concluding gesture was indicated, however. The two locomotives were now uncoupled from their trains and, festooned from smokeboxes to tenders with enthusiasts clinging to every possible hand- and foothold, chuffed slowly ahead till their pilots gently touched above the last tie. While Dodge and Montague took their places in the foreground and clasped hands for the camera, the two enginemen—George Booth in charge of *Jupiter* and Sam Bradford at 119's throttle—climbed from their cabs and made their ways forward to the respective pilot decks, each clutching a bottle of champagne. Now each man leaned out and smashed his bottle on the other pilot. As the sparkling wine foamed down over the laurel tie and the last spikes, they stood erect and shook hands. Both locomotives were then backed off and coupled to their trains again. *Jupiter* backed down a little farther, making room for 119 to pull her train forward till it passed over the point where the rails met. The Union Pacific engine then retired to let *Jupiter* follow suit.

In this way the first two trains rolled across the transcontinental junction.

It was a more or less impromptu afterthought, with few of the nabobs there to see. Durant already had invited the U.P. and Central Pacific parties to join him in the privacy of his palace car for a reading of the congratulatory telegrams now beginning to clatter in from East and West. A formal wire to President Ulysses S. Grant was composed and dispatched, with a copy going also to the Associated Press in New York:

> PROMONTORY SUMMIT, UTAH, May 10
> The last rail is laid. The last spike is driven. The Pacific Railroad is completed. The point of junction is 1,086 miles west of the Missouri River, and 690 miles east of Sacramento City.
>
> LELAND STANFORD
> *Central Pacific Railroad*
> T. C. DURANT
> SIDNEY DILLON
> JOHN DUFF
> *Union Pacific Railroad*

This amenity attended to, the combined party repaired to Leland Stanford's car for the inevitable round of toasts preceding a lavish luncheon.

Out at the junction point, meanwhile, a joint U.P. and Central work crew pushed through the crowd to draw the precious silver and gold spikes, take up the laurel tie and put in the regulation tie, spikes, bolts and fishplates. No sooner was it done, however, than the souvenir hunters attacked. The new tie was whittled to splinters and carried off; even the two last rails disappeared. The crew replaced them, and put down a total of six "last ties" before its job was done.

By late afternoon it was all over. The Presidential Special and the two Union Pacific trains departed. The crowd dispersed. The hangers-on and most of the workmen, at loose ends now, wandered into Promontory to kill time till the town's own celebration that evening: a torchlight procession, banquet and "grand ball" for which the Central Pacific would later pay the bill—three thousand dollars all told.

David Hewes's golden spike and the silver maul are preserved today at Leland Stanford University, Palo Alto, California. The last tie dropped out of sight for many years, then eventually turned up again, dusty with neglect, in a storeroom at the Southern Pacific's Sacramento shops. It was cleaned up and given a place of honor in the company's board room at San Francisco, where it perished in the great earthquake and fire of 1906.

The crowd present for the ceremony had not been large. Sidney Dillon put it at five or six hundred, "mainly contractors, employees and surveyors," and Grenville Dodge's estimate was about the same.[4]

"It was a very hilarious occasion," wrote Alexander Toponce. "Some of the participants got 'sloppy,' and these were not all Irish and Chinese by any means." And in a sort of poor man's valedictory to the historic day he concluded: "I do not remember what any of the speakers said now, but I do remember that there was a great abundance of champaign."

CHAPTER 32

THE ROAD TO INDIA

On May 11 the Cheyenne *Daily Leader*—incidentally scooping the New York newspapers by a full day—carried a one-sentence telegraphic dispatch from Sacramento: "The first invoice of Japanese tea was shipped today by the Pacific Railroad for St. Louis, inaugurating the overland trade with China."

Aside from its obvious geographical confusion, the very brevity of the item conveys the matter-of-fact quality of an expected development: transcontinental rails fulfilling their manifest destiny, and right on schedule, too. Whether or not it would prove quite the portent it seemed was for the future to determine. For the present the end of the great work brought abrupt changes of far more pressing immediacy to many people. Not all of them were pleasant.

During the run home from Promontory Dr. Thomas Clark Durant found time for some frank facing up to facts. For him the personal satisfaction inherent in the driving of the last spike had been badly flawed. Some accounts of the day mention that he had suffered from a blinding headache throughout the ceremony. If so, it was strangely symbolic of his accumulation of woes. The deplorable episode at Piedmont on the way out had rubbed some of the bloom off the big occasion in advance. The wrangling in the Senate in April had left scars on the Union Pacific's already battered reputation, and hung up some clear warnings as well. His personal grip on company management had been slipping steadily for a long time; his main interest, anyway, had always centered around railroad promotion and construction rather than operation. With the enterprise completed now, the embattled vice-president must have perceived the end of the line at hand.

He submitted his letter of resignation in New York on May 24. In it he contrived to say all the proper things, without a hint of the bitterness of controversy that had marked his whole tenure. He gave the necessity of devoting himself to his private affairs as the reason for his action; declined in advance any election to the Union Pacific board of directors; expressed his faith in "the continued good management of the company"; and added, no doubt with studied meaning, that "I still maintain my interest as the largest stockholder."

He was the first of the Union Pacific's prime movers to go. His passing evoked no great comment in the press and no regrets at all among his uneasy colleagues, who now embarked on the mundane task of making the U.P. a paying business proposition.

Across the West the realization of the long Pacific Railroad dream struck with a somewhat inexplicable suddenness. Many were quite unprepared to cope with it. Wells, Fargo and Company, who had counted on at least six more years of through Overland Stage operation when they bought Ben Holladay out in '66, were caught short after less than three. They had to sell off some fifty thousand dollars' worth of surplus coaches, horses and gear at no more than a third of their original cost. In California and Nevada some of the first impacts of the railroad's completion were nearly disastrous, as merchants found high-priced inventories of goods brought west via the Isthmus of Panama or by overland wagon freight ruinously hard to unload in the face of new railroad freight rates.

It was no wonder, for the reduction in costs was revolutionary. Right up to '69 the rates on wagon freight beyond the Missouri River had averaged about $1.80 per hundred pounds per hundred miles, which meant that a shipment of that weight traveling between Independence, Missouri, and the Pacific littoral over the Oregon and California Trails, or the Overland Stage road, or the old Santa Fe Trail across the Southwestern territories, had its cost inflated by up to fifty dollars or more in freight charges alone. By '66 and afterward the Union Pacific had been carrying U.S. government material, mainly Army supplies, at only eighty cents per hundred pounds per hundred miles. But little commercial freight—very little indeed for transcontinental destinations—could be handled during construction days. The rates immediately set up by both U.P. and Central Pacific as commercial carriers in '69, however, permitted the shipment of one hundred pounds all the way from Chicago to San Francisco for just $7.50 by first-class freight, $6.20 by second-class, and $5.20 third-class.

An estimated seven thousand teamsters and bullwhackers employed on the overland haul lost their jobs almost overnight. And this was only the beginning. While the records are not entirely clear, the last big wagon train bound west over the California Trail was said to have passed the first eastbound Central Pacific freight train somewhere between Great Salt Lake and the Humboldt River within a day or two after May 10. Travel over the Oregon Trail persisted for a considerably longer period. Inside of two years, though, it dwindled to a comparative trickle. So ended the first phase in America's great westward migration. A new era was under way.

But the full, vast scope of it would take time to unfold and even more time to understand. First, this epic year of 1869, the American public, unconcerned with individuals' economic readjustments or the deeper implications of change, rushed to see and ride upon its new iron colossus.

On the same May 11 that saw the first invoice of Japanese tea shipped from Sacramento, the first transcontinental excursion arrived at Promontory. It had traveled by way of the New York Central and Hudson River and the Lake Shore and Michigan Southern Railroads from New York to Chicago; thence by the Chicago and Northwestern to Council Bluffs; then by ferry across the Missouri River to Omaha and so set out at last on the Union Pacific. It was a pioneer commercial excursion, and the pioneers experienced their full share of hardship and disillusionment. One of them, a W. L. Humason of Hartford, Connecticut, wrote it all down in a little volume with the splendidly Victorian title: *From the Atlantic Surf to the Golden Gate, or, First Trip on the Great Pacific Railroad.* Apparently the disillusionment commenced shortly after leaving Omaha.

"The eating houses at the stations," wrote Humason, ". . . seemed to partake of the nature of the country, consisting of miserable shanties with tables dirty and waiters not only dirty but saucy." Among the gastronomic indignities inflicted on the excursionists he mentioned "biscuits made without soda but [with] plenty alkali"; butter "too venerable to be approached"; and knives and forks filthy with "incrustations dark and deep." Meals cost from $1.00 to $1.25 —"a pretty steep price to pay for fried ham and potatoes."

Much of the brutal crudity of life in the roaring railhead towns still lingered. At one station, unidentified but presumably somewhere in Wyoming Territory, the travelers alighted from their train and were at once engulfed in a crowd armed like brigands with rifles, shotguns and horse pistols. This, they were told, was a vigilance committee. "They had hung a man the day before from a telegraph pole for committing a fiendish outrage upon the only respectable woman in the place," Mr. Humason wrote.

Reaching Wasatch, the excursionists cowered in their berths through most of a wild and sleepless night that was climaxed by a fatal gunfight right beneath their sleeping car windows. Delayed by the hazards of flood-threatened Weber Canyon, the party missed the ceremony at Promontory and had to settle instead for a side trip to Salt Lake City and a sermon preached in the Great Tabernacle. Finally arriving at Ogden to resume their trip, they had no choice but to wait until midnight for a train which, when it did at last pull in, carried no sleeping cars for them. "We took seats and reached Promontory about day-light," Humason reported. "We were at the end of the Union Pacific Railroad. Our further journeys were to be over the Central Pacific."

The Central was no improvement. "Owing to a quarrel or misunderstanding between the superintendents of these two roads, we found we could make no connection and could not leave the place until evening." Sorely tried patience collapsed at this latest blow, and "there was some tall talking which fell un-pleasantly upon the ears of Mr. Marsh, a Central Pacific director who had come to Ogden to meet us and had done all in his power to remedy the matter." But Mr. Marsh's good offices did not help much. Union Pacific trainmen rudely ordered the excursionists out of their cars, "They had carried us to the end of their road," Humason noted mournfully, "and they had nothing more to do with us only to discharge us." So out into the cheerless dawn went the hapless party, and found no depot, no shelter of any kind nor any other com-forts, "nothing but sand, alkali and sage brush." They languished miserably in the hot sun all day. Then when the Central Pacific train eventually appeared, they discovered to their chagrin that it carried no sleeping cars either.

In fact, the Central did not own any. Construction had been rushed to a finish so abruptly, it was explained, that the operating department had been caught unprepared. Some sleeping cars were on order, the weary travelers were informed, but would not be delivered before July.

"I went forward into the baggage car," Humason wrote, "rolled up into my blankets, cast my lot among the mail bags and slept soundly until morning. I awoke covered and choked with dust."

The train labored up the eastern Sierra grades and over the summit through a late-season snowstorm that turned to drenching rain on the western descent. At Colfax the tourists were held in a siding for a train bearing the first con-tingent of eastbound transcontinental passengers. (These, five hundred in number, arrived at Omaha aboard a Union Pacific train running in two sections on May 16.) Rain was still falling when the party arrived in Sacramento and alighted for the last time, grimy and heavy-eyed, to board a Sacramento River steamboat for San Francisco. Altogether, it was a rueful little saga Mr. Humason would record when he reached home, a pretty far cry from what the excursionists had expected when they left New York to see the golden spike driven. Just a few years earlier the same trip via Ben Holladay's Overland Stage would have been a good deal slower and not quite so safe, but scarcely less trying. Their experience had been an eye-opener in more ways than one.

Plainly, the trip had been premature. It took something more than a mere joining of "last rails" to make an operating railroad, and neither the U.P. nor the Central Pacific was as yet prepared to furnish the creature comforts or the attention to passengers' well-being required by even the tolerant standards of the '60's. But time and tide waited not. There was pressing demand. Homesick Californians had waited long for a cheap, fast way to visit the "folks back home." Easterners' imaginations took fire at the notion of an America spanned by the longest, highest railroad in the world. The ticket rush was on.

Both the Union Pacific and the Central inaugurated regular transcontinental passenger service on May 15. Trains left daily from Sacramento and Omaha, running on schedules that totaled five days between the two cities. Connections eastward out of Omaha made it six between Sacramento and Chicago and just under seven and a half between Sacramento and New York. An additional twelve hours were required by the steamer trip made necessary if San Francisco was either the starting point or the destination. It usually was. By September of '69 the Central Pacific owned and operated twenty-seven steamboats and a score of cargo barges for this river passage. The company's receipts for this month hit an unprecedented peak of $609,787.90, of which the largest single item, more than $300,000, was passenger revenue. Including the Sacramento River connection, first-class fare between Atlantic and Pacific coasts came to $173, with an added tariff of two dollars per day and two dollars per night for sleeping car accommodations. But by September, also, the Associates had their subsidiary Western Pacific Railroad completed from Sacramento through Melrose to Oakland, leaving just a short ferry trip across the bay to San Francisco.

(Conversely, though, the Union Pacific had not yet bridged the Missouri River at Omaha, despite urgent plans to do so ever since '66. The work had been held up, first by a long disagreement among engineers as to the best location, then by lack of funds, finally by arguments on a sharing of the costs by the railroad and the cities of Omaha and Council Bluffs. The bridge was not built, in fact, until 1872.)

Early in June the first of the Central Pacific's Silver Palace sleeping cars was received from the builders, Jackson and Sharp of Wilmington, Delaware. A reporter from the Sacramento *Union* was on hand to examine it, and his story in the issue of June 4 rhapsodized at great length on the fine walnut and bird's-eye maple woodwork, the many mirrors set into the walls, the upholstery of red silk plush and the seats arranged in such a manner that "two of them, when the occasion arises, form a luxurious berth wide enough to accommodate two." Seats were trimmed with "lavish silver mountings"; the car boasted Brussels carpeting throughout, "a washroom conveniently fitted up" and even such ultimate touches as "small lamps for the convenience of passengers desirous of reading while lying in their berths." Comprising a bedroom and drawing room in addition to the convertible berths, the car had a capacity of forty-six persons, and was so much wider than standard passenger cars, the reporter commented, that "in passing through the snow sheds of the mountains [it] rubbed the timbers occasionally." It seems a shame that Mr. Humason and his fellow excursionists could not know what they had missed!

This kind of rococo magnificence, matched on the Union Pacific by the finest sleeping car creations Mr. George M. Pullman could turn out, pushed the grand tour on the Great Pacific Railroad to the height of fashion all through the '70's. It became the thing to do, *de rigueur*. Traveling Americans and globe-trotters from all over the world came, rode, saw, experienced—and having done so, sat down and put it all on paper. Or it seemed so, anyway. Guidebooks at once sprang up as profitable publishers' items. Samuel Bowles hurried into print with *The Pacific Railroad—Open; How to Go; What to See*. Crofutt's *Trans-continental Tourists' Guide* was kept up to date with semi-annual editions. There were Lester's *The Atlantic to the Pacific, What to See and How to See It;* Alfred Hart's *The Traveler's Own Book;* a sizable library of others.

"The Union Pacific and overland excursion had become too common," that earlier, hardier traveler along the U.P. trail, J. H. Beadle, wrote to the Cincinnati *Commercial* as early as August of '69. And he added with something of the old pro's disdain that "everybody who could sling ink became correspondents."

Certainly the old, rough, frontier aspects of a trip across the West seemed to vanish as if by magic. The new adventure smacked much more of the ways of polite society. "Let no man make this continental trip without his wife," advised one travel agent, a member of a group of them who went as guests of the U.P. and the Central Pacific in the fall of '69. "Some of us in thoughtlessness or otherwise left ours at home. It was an oversight, a mistake. . . . The journey is too vast and the scenery is too varied to be enjoyed without such genial influences."

Right along with the information on points of interest and things to do, in fact, many of the guidebooks included some stern little lectures on proper transcontinental deportment. This, for example, indicating that the "genial influences" were not without their faults: "It is not customary, it is not polite, it is not right or just for a lady to occupy one whole seat with her flounces and herself and another with her satchel, parasol, big box, little box, bandbox and bundle."

Another blended the practical with the polite and admonished the tourist: "In packing your little lunch basket, avoid tongue by all means, for it will not keep over a day or two, and its fumes in a sleeping car are anything but like those from 'Araby the blest.' "

The sleeping car was by no means fully accepted in the America of the '70's. According to the stricter mores of the time there were strong connotations of immorality about the whole idea of bedding down two to a berth in a public conveyance, and ministers frequently preached against the sinful practice quite as vehemently as they did against the operation of trains on the Sabbath. But one guidebook author flatly advised his readers that "Prejudices against the sleeping cars must be conquered at the start. They are a necessity of our long American travel."

Then as now, tipping was a subject of some concern to the neophyte traveler. "Fee your porter always," he was instructed, "—a moderate allowance of twenty-five cents per day, for each day's travel."

By May of 1870 those who insisted on the very last word in "luxury, comfort and seclusion" could make their transcontinental tour aboard the Pacific Hotel Train—called the Atlantic Hotel Train eastbound—which ran but once a week and made the phenomenal time of only eighty-one hours between Omaha and Oakland. According to Alfred Hart in *The Traveler's Own Book*, the Train consisted exclusively of drawing room, sleeping and dining cars, so that passengers had "no need to step from the train during the journey of 2,000 miles." This was a tremendous innovation for the times. As a matter of fact, the cars were all Central Pacific Silver Palace sleepers with special kitchen compartments built in (an arrangement which incidentally provided a handy source of hot water for the washrooms also) and berths fitted with removable tables for dining as well. But apparently such a crack flier was a little ahead of its time, for the service lasted only a few months during 1870. It was discontinued at the instigation of the Central Pacific, and thereafter no interchange of passenger equipment between the two roads took place for many years.

The regular daily passenger trains carried both sleeping cars and second-class coaches, which seem also to have doubled as smoking cars for gentlemen traveling first-class. Within the first year of operation the over-all fare from New York to San Francisco was reduced to $150 first-class, $109 second-class and $65 third-class, or "emigrant." Not even the most impecunious tourist, though, was advised to travel emigrant, for the coaches were old, dirty and decrepit, usually moved only as parts of freight consists and took an average of seventeen to twenty days to cross the continent.

Though George M. Pullman had placed his first dining car, the *Delmonico,* named for the celebrated New York restaurateur, in service on the Chicago and Alton in '68, the innovation was generally shunned on the Pacific Railroad in favor of the old system of eating stations along the line. Prices remained about the same as those of which Mr. Humason had complained, but the wealth of comments in the travel books indicate that both food and service had improved rapidly. Many places became famous for their individual specialties. North Platte was known for its generous servings: "They give you all you can possibly eat there." Sidney, Nebraska, was praised for its antelope steaks and roasts; and here too the portions were far from niggardly, to judge by a breakfast described by an English commentator named W. F. Rae:

"There were given us eight little dishes apiece, containing hot beefsteak, two slices of cold roast antelope, a bit of cold chicken, ham and poached eggs, a couple of boiled potatoes, two sticks of sweet corn, stewed tomatoes and four thin buckwheat 'hot cakes' laid one on top of the other." The Union Pacific schedule allowed thirty minutes for meal stops; all too short a time, Mr. Rae thought, for the consumption of such a mass of nourishment.[1]

Cheyenne's dining room was noted for the impressive array of big-game heads displayed on its walls. At Sherman Summit, wrote Alfred Hart, lived a character known as "Uncle John," from whom "the finest trout, ready-cooked and delicious, can always be secured." And at Laramie a Mrs. Maxwell kept "a magnificent collection of exquisitely stuffed Rocky Mountain animals and birds for sale." The souvenir trade had sprung up early.

The flavor of slow change, of old things stubbornly lingering along the U.P. right of way, is apparent in some of the trackside features called to the tourists' attention by Mr. Hart. He was impressed by the fine farms to be seen in the thickly populated German settlements of eastern Nebraska; an old sod fort erected "against the flaming arrow and deadly bullet of the red man" at Willow Island on the Platte River; an especially notable example of a prairie dog village near Potter, Nebraska; and the "vast herds of elk and antelope often seen" on the Laramie Plains. But the once dominant buffalo was seldom mentioned by the travel writers. Already the hide hunters had decimated and scattered the herds along the railroad line.

There was small reason for the alert and forewarned tourist to miss any of the sights, for even on the long prairie tangents train speeds averaged only a leisurely twenty-two miles an hour. The day of the ballast-scorching fast mail and the famous Overland Limited was still to come.

From Ogden there were in 1870 four excursion trains weekly for Salt Lake City over Brigham Young's Utah Central Railroad. The energetic Saint had broken ground for it within a week of the golden spike ceremony at Promontory, making good use of construction equipment and other surplus material turned over by the Union Pacific in partial payment of the sum owing on his grading contracts.

Of Corinne, evidently still pursuing its wicked ways, *The Traveler's Own Book* said merely that it "can not be mistaken for a Mormon town—the tourist can tell why and also can easily judge of the changes which would take place

. . . if the loaves and the fishes should fall into Gentile hands for distribution." Few observers had anything good to say of Promontory either, though the Englishman, Rae, reported one gallant little custom of the gambling sharks who plied their trade during the brief service stops there. Having stripped the unwary greenhorn, he wrote, they were wont to give him back a gold piece so that he need not go hungry during the remainder of his trip. At Elko, Nevada, the traveler was advised to change his paper money into gold and silver coin, which would from this point westward "be a better friend than greenbacks." The massive timbering of the Sierra snowsheds was much admired. And for many years all westbound Central Pacific passenger trains were stopped on the beetling granite shoulder of Cape Horn a few miles below Gold Run so that tourists could descend from the cars for a full appreciation of the awe-inspiring view out over the American River. There was a dramatic flair about even the arrival at journey's end. The same travel agent who advised all men to bring their wives along wrote of boarding the ferry at Oakland after nightfall: "The lights of San Francisco five miles across the bay presented a beautiful sight, the city being built on a side hill giving at one view the gas lights of numerous streets."

That the transcontinental tour grew sensationally popular is attested by the figures. The Central Pacific handled thirty thousand through passengers for the year 1869. In 1870 the Union Pacific recorded 142,623, the huge majority of them through also. But local, short-haul business made a sorry contrast.

A young veteran of Shiloh traveled west to Columbus, Nebraska, in 1870. James H. Kyner was his name, and in putting his impressions on paper some years later he recalled nothing very satisfactory about his first ride on the Union Pacific. Omaha, he wrote, was in the throes of a depression brought on by the end of railroad construction work. He paid for his ticket at the exorbitant rate of ten cents per mile, and rode in an ancient, worn-out "sowbelly" coach with seats hard and uncomfortable and windows so tiny—only ten inches by twelve—"one had to stretch one's neck considerably to look through them at all." He summed up the ninety-mile trip to Columbus as "a constant teetering upon my seat, swaying from side to side and jolting back when the track was climbing one of those gentle prairie swells, jerking forward when the car, over the top, coasted and rattled down upon the cars ahead."[2]

The fact was that much of the rolling stock of both the U.P. and the Central Pacific had been beaten to a sad state of disrepair in the grueling construction effort. And it was not illogical to relegate old locomotives and cars to short-haul service. But it was also true that the managements of both roads (the Union Pacific in particular) could see scant prospects for profit in local traffic. Consequently they neglected it badly, while still setting freight rates so high that merchants in Fremont, Nebraska, for example, complained they found deliveries from Omaha, only forty miles away, much cheaper by wagon than by rail.[3]

Writing in 1891 from a much enlightened viewpoint, Sidney Dillon declared that those who saw the junction made at Promontory "connected it with the development of transcontinental communication, and trade with China and Japan, rather than with internal development."[4] And Leland Stanford testified before the U.S. Pacific Railway Commission in 1883 that, "We were very much disappointed with regard to the business with Asia."

This disappointment might have been less had Stanford and his fellow railroad builders been more alert to events elsewhere in the world. For the ten years preceding '69 the celebrated French engineer, Ferdinand de Lesseps, had been digging away at a canal across the Isthmus of Suez between the Mediterranean and Red Seas. Henry M. Stanley, the same newspaper correspondent who had catalogued the sins of North Platte and Julesburg on the U.P. line, and observed Jack Casement's iron-slingers at their best in '67, was in Egypt a year later. He watched twenty thousand Arabs and Europeans at work on the canal and began dispatching stories to the New York *Herald* declaring that the Great Pacific Railroad was coming to completion ten years too late. But the entrepreneurs of the Union Pacific and the Central, preparing just then to wade into their final, bare-knuckle scrimmage for advantage, had had neither time nor attention to spare for a ditch being grubbed out of a sandy waste half the earth away.

On November 17, 1869, the Suez Canal was formally opened with an elaborate international fanfare. Situated virtually at the crossroads of the immemorial trade routes between Western civilization and the ancient cultures of the Orient, slashing some seven thousand miles off the old sea passage around the Cape of Good Hope, the canal killed at one stroke any possible advantage the businessmen of Europe might have found in an American overland short cut. To that extent the Pacific Railroad had been founded and built upon a gigantic misconception.

Such errors in judgment might have proved fatal to the entrepreneurs. That they did not was due only to the incalculable potential of America herself. The transcontinental traffic exceeded even the rosiest expectations almost immediately; in spite of neglect, local business developed more slowly but just as surely.

With the swift decline of the Oregon Trail, the railroad became the chosen way to the whole Pacific littoral, northern California the great funnel through which both goods and people flowed. For the Golden State it meant a flourishing of all kinds of local enterprise, a rapid step-up in population growth, the promise of new Eastern markets for an expanding agricultural effort, ultimately the rise of a vigorous new economy built on a far broader base than the gold that had been the mainstay since the days of '49.

Nevada prospered immediately and well. The mining tools and heavy machinery which had formed an essential part of the old trans-Sierra wagon freight—after coming west via the long Cape Horn voyage or across the Isthmus—now sped directly out from the East by rail, faster and at lower cost. Hence, among other results, low-grade ores suddenly became profitable; there was a busier delving into old diggings once thought exhausted; smelters and reducing mills could be erected in hitherto impracticable localities. At Battle Mountain, a new mining district opened in northern Nevada on the Central Pacific in 1870, copper ore began to be dug out and shipped east for smelting. Here was the start of something as economically exciting, for the long run, as the West's gold and silver past; baser metals coming into their own at last.

Locked in the earth of Nevada, Montana, Idaho and Utah were vast treasures of copper, lead, iron and zinc. They were untapped, lacking only the key of cheap mass transportation. The locomotive and the iron rail supplied it. The working of the Wyoming coal beds first verified by the Union Pacific's geologist, Van Lennep, burgeoned toward industrial importance under the railroad's own swelling demands for fuel.

These changes came with a swiftness remarkable by comparison with the creeping pace of Western conquest through the decades that had gone before. They hastened, and were in turn hastened by, the irresistible tide of Western settlement.

On May 10, 1869, even as the last spike was being driven at Promontory Summit, the U.S. Department of the Interior doubled the price of public lands along the Pacific Railroad in the Platte River Valley. At an average pre-'69 figure of $1.25 an acre most of these lands had gone begging. At the new price there was a steady demand for them from '69 on; and this held true as well, of course, for the Union Pacific's land-grant acreages which alternated with the government sections along the right of way. And because it did, a big, blatant new chapter in the history of the West was opened.

By itself the overflow population of the American East was nowhere near enough to fill the vastness beyond the wide Missouri. It took the millions of Europe's restless, downtrodden and persecuted to do it. And with a modicum of encouragement Europe's millions came. Quite early in the 1850's the Illinois Central had been the first of the Western land-grant railroads to go in for large-scale promotion of its real estate, and its efforts had been highly successful. George Francis Train had grasped the idea and even embellished it, with his ambitious Credit Foncier and his grandiose schemes for Rocky

Mountain spas and such. But Train had not lasted long, being booted out by Dr. Durant in '68 in favor of the Union Pacific's own land sales company. By the time the railroad was completed this company had its agents busy by the hundreds in Eastern and Midwestern cities and towns. Gaudy posters and glowing prose promised fertile lands, salubrious climate and opportunity unlimited for farmer, mechanic and artisan alike. Soon the agents numbered in the thousands, many of them working out of offices set up in populous centers across the Atlantic. The Central Pacific joined in; to all intents and purposes, in fact, both companies operated as one in the promotion of their land-grant holdings, and the organization grew fantastically efficient.

By means of arrangements with most of the major transatlantic shipping lines the poor, bedazzled and non-English-speaking immigrant was provided with a cheap through ticket all the way from his point of departure in the homeland to his chosen destination along the railroad, where local land agents working on commissions of 3 to 5 percent took him in hand and did not let him go until he was signed and sealed as a bona fide new colonist. All too often he ended as a bitterly disappointed one. The promises were largely misrepresentations, the whole operation frantically high-pressured and conditions aboard the early emigrant trains frequently scandalous: cars ill kept and poorly ventilated; people crowded in like animals; trainmen heedless, more often than not, of even the simplest of company regulations for the passengers' welfare.

Yet in the final analysis both the new settler and the railroad that brought him west got what they wanted, the one the independence and the better life he had dreamed of—though he faced years of grinding labor before he wrung them from the prairie soil—and the other the growing population and the prosperous countryside which alone could make the business of transportation pay. The nation benefited most of all as a new mid-American melting pot wrought its changes where once had been only barren emptiness.

Meanwhile a curious thing happened. Coincidentally with the Pacific Railroad's completion the rain belt began to move westward from the Missouri River at a rate of some eight miles a year, thus markedly increasing the Great Plains' crop-bearing potential. Strangely, it bore out a typical nineteenth-century scientific prophecy made by a Professor Agassiz who visited Colorado Territory in 1867 and predicted an increase in rainfall, which "would come by the disturbance of the electric currents, caused by the building of the Pacific Railroads and settlement of the country."[5]

In its ultimate high tide this pell-mell flood of European settlers covered the entire West, reached well into the early twentieth century and was carried forward by other railroads in addition to the U.P. and the Central Pacific.

Nothing wrought by the first transcontinental railroad, in fact, was more far-reaching in terms of eventual results than the impetus it gave to the spanning of the West by still other strands of iron.

The Kansas Pacific finally pounded home its own last spike at Denver in August of 1870. Earlier that year the Denver Pacific came snaking down the South Platte from Cheyenne, so that the once neglected Queen City all at once had two separate rail links with the East. (The Union Pacific absorbed them both in 1880.) By '71 the little Atchison and Topeka had its railhead in a scruffy buffalo hunters' camp town called Dodge City in southwestern Kansas. Later it struggled on across Colorado, New Mexico and Arizona Territories and at last, as the Atchison, Topeka and Santa Fe, achieved Los Angeles and a transcontinental destiny of its own. The Northern Pacific laid its first rail in Minnesota in 1870. In time it carried on along the old Northern Route of the '53 surveys and arrived at tidewater in the Pacific Northwest. So did the Great Northern, which in '69 was scarcely even a gleam in the one eye of a shaggy young Red River steamboat operator by the name of James J. Hill. Meanwhile the Central Pacific Associates, long since known as the Big Four and committed irrevocably as railroad barons, were turning their attention to a branch line into southern California, the Southern Pacific. By '77 they pushed it into Arizona Territory and presently, carrying on, met Jay Gould's Texas and Pacific to complete a continuous line between Los Angeles and New Orleans.

Well within the generation following the War Between the States, then, the nation was possessed of not one but five great transcontinental railroad systems. It would be specious to claim that the Union Pacific and the Central made the other four possible. But they *were* first, and in attaining union at Promontory they did much more than prove the thing could be done. In the doing, quite incidentally but nonetheless importantly, they set up the most all-inclusive training school for railroad engineers, technicians and skilled labor the world till then had known.

The Central Pacific, always a comparatively taut and businesslike concern, kept the elite core of its organization—men like Strobridge, Montague, Clement and others—for the jobs of improvement and expansion that needed doing after '69. But the U.P., neither so sound financially nor so sure of where it intended to go from Promontory, scattered its trained men with a prodigal hand. Jack and Dan Casement, whose construction train and track-laying system were in themselves valuable new contributions to the techniques of railroad building and maintenance, backtracked from Utah to put down the final iron on the Denver Pacific, later went on to build long and successful careers as railroad contractors. Colonel Leonard Eicholtz, U.P. bridge engineer, went to the Denver Pacific, too, as chief engineer. Samuel Reed, capable and energetic superintendent of construction, helped to drive the Canadian Pacific Railroad, the Dominion's first transcontinental, to completion in a like capacity. Grenville Dodge left the Union Pacific presently, went on to the Texas Pacific and lived out the balance of a long and distinguished life as a builder of that and other Western railroads. Scores of lesser men who had served their apprenticeships as rodmen, chainmen and transit men with U.P. and Central survey crews graduated to better jobs and other accomplishments elsewhere. And thousands of the U.P.'s "Democrats" laid off and shipped out of Blue Creek and Corinne in '69 later moved on to keep the liquor flowing, the dirt flying and the spike mauls clattering on the Kansas Pacific, the Northern Pacific, the Atchison and Topeka and the various short lines and branches that presently were wriggling like blacksnakes through the prairie grass.

It is virtually certain that the railroad boomer was born and flourished toward his apogee among these fiddle-footed U.P. veterans. The derivation of the word "boomer" is indefinite. In some contexts it referred to the itinerant worker at any trade. But the railroad boomer eventually emerged as the true aristocrat of the breed, and until World War I thinned his ranks and the great depression of the 1930's wiped him out for good, no section of the United States went untouched in his rovings. To the end, though, the long, far-running iron of the Western roads was his favored range; it was most appropriate, somehow, as the setting for the restlessness that was a legacy of the old, wild construction days.

Other repercussions of those days continued even as the Great Pacific Railroad settled into the transition from epic historical event to a workaday role in the nation's commerce. There had been too much controversy, too many rumors of financial jugglings and political thimble-rigging to let sleeping dogs lie.

As early as 1866 Congress had begun to show signs that its patience was not inexhaustible. In that year the House Committee on the Pacific Railway had asked to be relieved of its duties, on the grounds that it did not believe any further pecuniary obligations ought to be assumed by the government in behalf of the Union Pacific Railroad. Hostility had shown up in various resolutions introduced in both houses throughout '67 and '68, calling for accountings of the federal bonds issued to the Union Pacific. And in '68 a bill to regulate fares and freight rates on both the U.P. and the Central Pacific had passed the House, though it died in committee in the Senate. The joint resolution of '69 which ended the race at last was simply one more official expression of Congressional impatience with the situation. The threatening provisions of the resolution still hung over the heads of both companies' managements in the years after '69.

They did not seem particularly onerous, however. The job was done, after all, and both railroads had been given essentially what they wanted. True, Congress did intervene to examine the terms of the agreement between Collis Huntington, Thomas Durant and Oakes Ames whereby the Union Pacific track-age between Ogden and Promontory was sold to the Central for four million dollars. Considering the price excessive, Congress scaled it down to three million—paid mostly in bonds, which cut it still further, to $2,698,620 actual cash value—and thus took away any profit the U.P. might have wrung from the final drive to the finish line. True, too, President Grant lost no time in naming the commission of "five eminent citizens" to examine both roads and estimate the expenditures still necessary in order to make each "first class," as spelled out in the resolution.

But it proved a good commission, headed by Samuel M. Felton, a respected engineer and president of the Philadelphia, Wilmington and Baltimore Rail-road; and the report it brought in was unexpectedly favorable. The locations of both railroad lines were declared logical and admirably free of errors. On both roads the weaknesses in construction were found to be remarkably few, con-sidering the speed with which much of the work had been done and the obstacles overcome. The Union Pacific's much-maligned iron trestle over Dale Creek in the Black Hills received a clean bill of health. And in con-clusion the commission estimated that the Central Pacific would need to spend only some $576,650 on improvements, the U.P. about $1,586,100. Both figures were modest; excessively so, it developed later.

The Secretary of the Interior immediately ordered the withholding of one-half the land-grant patents still due each railroad until such time as the improve-ments were made. But both companies already held immense acreages of the choicest land along their rights of way, so were in no great hurry. Not until 1874 did the Union Pacific finally apply for another inspection of the line look-ing toward release of the patents. In the five-year interim the U.P. had spent $2,215,975 and the Central Pacific $4,338,387 in excess of the amounts the Felton commission had indicated. And so the great work ended with the Pacific Railroad, at last, declared first class.[6]

In the fall of 1879 the young Scotsman Robert Louis Stevenson, ill with tuberculosis and low in funds, traveled across America by emigrant train. For a bed he had to make do with a board and three straw cushions purchased from a profiteering Union Pacific employee at Council Bluffs. His daily ablutions were made precariously in a tin basin on the open coach platform, with "one elbow crooked about the railing." He endured the brutal arrogance of conductors; uncertain meal schedules; endless delays in isolated sidings; "an empty sky, an empty earth" of the Nebraska prairie; the "sterile canyons" of the mountains; but nevertheless ended the journey with his writer's imagination fired by the vast magnitude of the enterprise that had made it all possible.

He reflected on "pigtailed Chinese pirates [working] side by side with border ruffians and broken men from Europe . . . and then when I go on to remember," he wrote, "that all this epical turmoil was conducted by gentlemen in frock coats, and with a view to nothing more extraordinary than a fortune and a subsequent visit to Paris, it seems to me, I own, as if this railway were the one typical achievement of the age in which we live, as if it brought together into one plot all the ends of the world and all the degrees of social rank."

And he wondered: "If it be romance, if it be contrast, if it be heroism that we require, what was Troy town to this?"[7]

EPILOGUE

*Recriminations; Scandal;
the Public Betrayed?*

CHAPTER 33

SPECTACLE ON THE POTOMAC

Savior of the Union or not, Ulysses S. Grant had had his troubles as its President. Before his first year in office was over an audacious attempt by Jay Gould and freebooting Jim Fisk to corner the national gold market culminated in the infamous Black Friday of September 24, '69, shook public confidence badly and sparked rumors of scandal in high places. Grant was perfectly innocent, but the affair laid a cloud over the young administration all the same. And as his first term ran its course, one political gaucherie after another offered disturbing evidence that military genius did not necessarily carry over into the management of civilian government.

Largely as a result of this, the election year of 1872 found the reform elements of the incumbent Republican Party actively feuding with the hard-nosed machine politicians who had stepped into the vacuum created by the President's ineptness. It was not a healthy situation, and it was complicated by the increasing restlessness of the states of the defeated Confederacy, still chafing under the harsh terms of Reconstruction, and by a Democratic Party mustering for a determined assault on the electoral votes it had missed in '68.

In May the distinguished reform Senator Charles Sumner of Massachusetts and Missouri's crusading Carl Schurz led a group of dissidents into a convention of what they called the Liberal Republican Party, bent on nominating a Presidential candidate behind whom the Democratic Party organization might rally also to form a coalition. Their choice was Horace Greeley, editor of the New York *Tribune;* and an incredibly poor choice it was, for Greeley had been not only an ardent wartime Abolitionist but a lifelong campaigner against Democratic candidates. Even so the Democrats, crossing off old scores in their zeal to unseat the greater enemy, promptly nominated him, too. Thus all the elements existed—entrenched machine leadership on the one side; a fierce reform movement on the other; deep political cleavage besides; and a resurgence of war's old bitternesses—for the most violent kind of clash.

The campaign was fought out in a mutual savagery of mud-slinging, scandal-mongering and vicious political lampoon. When finally it was over in November, Grant was still President, by an electoral margin even greater than he had amassed in '68, and he carried most of the Republican slate with him. But the election returns had settled almost nothing. In their wake they left unhealed wounds and unresolved differences, and the debris of one angry little tempest in particular defied covering up.

Among the skeletons exhumed from Washington closets during hostilities was the old inference first voiced by Nevada's Senator Stewart during the Pacific Railroad debates in April of '69 that "certain Congressional leaders" had acquired financial interests in the Union Pacific and the Credit Mobilier, and had collected "enormous dividends" therefrom. Stewart had named no names, but in the heat of the '72 campaign no hard-running office seeker was bound by any such delicacy and neither were the newspapers. Representative James Brooks of New York was the first to hear himself charged with complicity in the affair. Then opponents brought New Hampshire Senator James W. Patterson's name into it. And that was only the beginning.

Internal disaffection still had the Credit Mobilier in a turmoil, with Oakes Ames and Colonel Henry S. McComb, Dr. Durant's onetime henchman on the board of directors, at loggerheads in the old struggle for control. In a mammoth lapse of discretion they allowed their differences to drift into lawsuit, and in a Pennsylvania court McComb introduced a list of names in evidence. Some of them were big enough to be sensationally newsworthy. There were James G. Blaine of Maine, powerful and respected Speaker of the House of Representatives; House members James A. Garfield and Rutherford B. Hayes of Ohio; John Logan of Illinois; Schuyler Colfax, Grant's first-term Vice President and former House Speaker; and several other, lesser Congressional lights. Every one of them, according to McComb, was a Credit Mobilier stockholder, brought in at the insistence of Oakes Ames.

With that, the lid shot sky-high. The election campaign was just rising to its climax when, on September 4, the New York *Sun* headlined the revelation as "THE KING OF FRAUDS: How the Credit Mobilier Bought Its Way Into Congress."

Every one of the accused Congressmen who happened to be up for reelection dismissed the charges as political smears, and in the furor none of their opponents produced any substantiating evidence; it was a dirty election on both sides, and the *Sun*'s handling of the allegations does not appear to have affected it materially. But the Credit Mobilier's past unsavory reputation, the dark hints of fraud surrounding the Union Pacific's corporate struggles in '68 and '69 and the growing public impression of Wall Street as a den of high financial iniquity, reinforced by the recent Black Friday unpleasantness—all these made too fertile a field for the radical reform press to ignore. The kettle went on boiling and in the end the *Sun* had the *cause célèbre* it had been looking for, the Grant administration had the makings of a full-fledged scandal on its hands, and Congress was caught in a dilemma of ethics that could be resolved by nothing less than an official inquiry.

Before the end of the year a House Investigating Committee headed by Representative Luke Polland of Vermont was calling witnesses and taking testimony. The question of conflict of interest in Congress was a touchy one, however, and in an effort to hold the scandal to manageable proportions Chairman Polland at first conducted his hearings behind closed doors. Unfortunately, secrecy only thickened the atmosphere of passionate partisan turmoil, and soon such luridly garbled reports of the committee's findings were being bruited about that it was deemed advisable to switch to public hearings. The harm had been done, though, and now unbiased truth was going to be very hard to come by.

It would not have been easy in any case. Dr. Thomas Durant was an early witness. He came down from New York in November, answered questions with cordiality and seeming frankness and coolly thrust a knife between Oakes Ames's ribs by reading a prepared statement. The Ames crowd, he pointed out, had come into the Union Pacific enterprise only "by virtue of their character as contractors and their interests in the Credit Mobilier. . . . The claim of patriotism and of far-seeing, intelligent and honest policy put forward in their behalf is ridiculous."[1] So the keynote was sounded for much of the testimony to follow: bad blood and recrimination, making the truth more elusive still.

The thing had its wry, comic aspects. In the beginning Congressmen vied with one another in their eagerness to take the stand and deny, with varying degrees of vehemence, that they ever had had anything whatever to do with the Union Pacific or the Credit Mobilier. Oakes Ames, however, proved an embarrassingly honest witness. It was quite true, he stated, that he had made stock in the Credit Mobilier available to some of his fellow lawmakers. But he denied that his motives had been anything more than the praiseworthy impulse to share a good investment with his friends. In no case, he declared, had he either asked or expected any legislative favors in return.

It was brought out that all this had taken place in 1868. At a Credit Mobilier board meeting early that year Ames had requested that a block of stock be reserved for Congressmen to whom he had already promised shares. Colonel McComb and others had objected, the amount of stock available for sale being limited and they having commitments of their own to make good. But

Ames had insisted and at length prevailed. Some Congressmen had then taken the stock, others had not. Since the Credit Mobilier had paid its first dividend late in '67, however, there was an upsurge of interest in it, with many requests for delivery of the promised shares.

Faced with Ames's story, both Representative Brooks and Senator Patterson hastily reversed their own previous testimony and conceded that they had, indeed, purchased the stock, but only, as Ames had said, as legitimate investments, with no hint of bribery or other wrongdoing involved. Brooks, however, was a government-appointed director of the Union Pacific, prohibited by law from stock ownership in the enterprise. Thus, though the Credit Mobilier was not, legally, a part of the U.P., there was a particularly pointed question of ethics in his case. Ames's testimony also established that Congressmen William Allison of Iowa and William D. Kelley of Pennsylvania had purchased Credit Mobilier stock. There was evidence that Garfield of Ohio had done so also, in spite of his denials. Speaker Blaine, Hayes, John Logan of Illinois and others, however, stoutly maintained that they never had owned a penny's worth of the stock, and no one was able to prove otherwise. Efforts were made to cast suspicion on Grenville Dodge's part in the affair, not only because of the one hundred shares in the Credit Mobilier held in his wife's name, but also because he had been a Congressman at the time. But no one was able to prove his complicity either.

Schuyler Colfax did not come off so well. He too insisted on his complete innocence, even pleading personal poverty as proof that he could not have reaped any illegitimate profits from anything. But in his case investigators of the committee produced a canceled check made out to "S. C. or bearer" which had been cashed by Colfax with the sergeant at arms of the Senate and deposited in the First National Bank of Washington on June 22, 1868. The amount was twelve hundred dollars, and there was evidence to show that it represented the dividend on twenty shares of Credit Mobilier stock. This was a very generous return on a modest investment, certainly, though hardly the "enormous dividends" the scandalmongers had inferred. But the Vice President of the United States had been caught in an apparent lie, which was bad enough in itself. And the whole thing centered attention on another allegation: that the Congressmen all had been allowed to buy their shares at less than par value, and had not even been required to pay for them until after the issuance of the first dividend.

The testimony of Colonel McComb, an obviously vindictive man with no love for Oakes Ames, was even more damaging. The much discussed list of names, the colonel stated, was actually Ames's; he (McComb) had merely jotted it down in the course of a personal conference with that gentleman.

He had been so vigorously opposed to making any shares available to Congressmen, McComb further stated, that Ames had later written him a letter defending the action. He produced the letter for the committee's inspection. And in it was a sentence which undeniably could be construed as damning. "I have so disposed of the stock," Ames had written, "as to enhance the general strength and influence of the Company for whose welfare your solicitude is not less than my own."[2]

This did not really say very much to an objective reader, perhaps. But there were very few objective readers among the angry masses now following the investigation. The key word was "influence," when applied to Congress, a word with sinister implications to be sure. The press, led by the New York *Sun,* had treated the entire affair in an emotional and irresponsible manner from the start; the public was becoming aroused to the point of demanding a scapegoat; and whatever chance there might once have been for a reasoned and dispassionate conclusion was fading rapidly away.

By this time, in fact, public concern already had leaped far beyond the limited matter of an alleged attempt to bribe Congressmen and into the longer-standing and more meaty question of whether the government and the taxpayer had been victimized by the Union Pacific promoters. Earlier—another manifestation of Congress's long preoccupation with an accounting of the federal subsidy bonds paid out for Pacific Railroad construction—a separate House committee had been set up under the chairmanship of J. W. Wilson of Indiana to examine the possibility of fraud and illegal practices in general. And some of its initial findings had hinted at gross irregularities. Now that the Polland Committee's revelations were bringing the nation to a boil, the Wilson Committee began to intensify its own activities. In view of the gossip and the innuendo that had gone on so long, a thorough investigation was undoubtedly overdue. The timing, though, was unfortunate; two inquiries running concurrently tended to overlap and add to the confusion. And where Mr. Polland tried, at least, to hold his hearings to an attitude of judicial detachment, Chairman Wilson appears to have yielded to the general hysteria and let his degenerate very quickly into a sort of Roman holiday on the Potomac.

To give the committee its due, it had a knotty tangle to unravel. And its investigation was not helped by the fact that, whatever their larger shortcomings, the managers of the Union Pacific and the Credit Mobilier had been miserably careless bookkeepers. Government accountants assigned to examine the records of both organizations complained of omissions and inadequacies. Called to the witness chair, representatives of the Ames and Durant factions filled the gaps with nothing more affirmative than harsh opinions of one another. Dr. Durant had started it in his appearance before the Polland Committee. Oliver Ames, testifying before the Wilson Committee early in '73, spoke his mind on Thomas Durant.

"We examined every bill that is there in the details to the full amount of $435,000," he said, referring to funds expended during 1864. "The charge was that Dr. Durant, instead of spending this money as he alleged he had spent it, for the purpose of getting a charter and for doing all things necessary, had put the money in his own pocket."[3]

Regardless of its accuracy, which no one could assess in the absence of tangible evidence, this kind of testimony painted a sordid picture of thieves falling out, a seamy and undignified spectacle for a nation that had so recently exulted in pride over its transcontinental railroad. Viewed in this light, the paucity of records seemed doubly incriminating.

Many details of the alleged Boomer and Williams contracts by which U.P. construction had been pushed west of the one hundredth meridian after the expiration of the original Hoxie contract were never clarified. There were few verifiable cost figures; hardly anything to go on but Dr. Durant's statement that approximately 153 miles of this section had cost not more than $27,500 per mile. It appeared that fifty-eight miles of it had been paid for more than once, however. At least, the Union Pacific board had proposed in a resolution dated January 5, 1867, to "consider the Hoxie contract extended to the point already completed, namely, 305 miles west from Omaha . . . and to settle with the Credit Mobilier at $50,000 per mile for the additional 58 miles." In explanation it was claimed that the Credit Mobilier had carried on for that distance in the expectation of getting a contract, hence had the payment coming. But the resolution had never been carried out because of Dr. Durant's objection, though later it had been included in the Ames contract, and there paid for at the rate of $42,000 per mile. But in that case, what of the $27,500 per mile? Had it been the Credit Mobilier's actual cost for those fifty-eight miles? Or had it indeed gone into Durant's pocket at some earlier date?

Confusion? There was more. By the date of the Oakes Ames contract—August 16, 1867—138 miles of the road west of the one hundredth meridian had been completed, and accepted by the U.P.'s government commissioners, at a cost of about $27,000 per mile. Again, though, this figure was Durant's only. The Union Pacific books did not show it. And by the time the contract was ratified by all U.P. stockholders (not just a simple majority, this being a safeguard insisted upon by Ames because of the factional strife which already existed on the board), 238 miles of the construction covered by it had been completed. Thus Oakes Ames—in reality the Credit Mobilier—reaped an instant profit of between two and a half and three million dollars before so much as a tap of work had been done to earn it. It could scarcely be considered a coincidence, therefore, that on December 12, not more than two months after the ratification, the Credit Mobilier had declared its first dividend: $2,244,000 in Union Pacific first mortgage bonds and an equal amount in U.P. stock, with a total combined cash value at the time of about $2,580,600.

Sifting through such evidence, the Wilson Committee eventually reached its conclusions as to the total expenditures made by the Union Pacific under the three major construction contracts:

Hoxie Contract	$12,974,416.24
Ames Contract	57,140,102.94
Davis Contract	23,431,768.10
Total	$93,546,287.28

Fixing the contractors' actual costs proved a much tougher problem. Here contested items and conflicts in testimony combined to make a bookkeeper's nightmare. Yet it was precisely these cost figures which were the crux of the whole investigation. Somewhat arbitrarily, it appears, the committee eventually reached its conclusions:

Hoxie Contract	$ 7,806,183.33
Ames Contract	27,285,141.99
Davis Contract	15,629,633.62
Total	$50,720,958.94

Here then was a total profit of $42,825,328.34, all of it divided among the shareholders of the Credit Mobilier, assignee of all three contracts. The committee added another $1,104,000 as its best estimate of the overpayment involved in the aforesaid fifty-eight miles and came up with an over-all $43,929,328.34—a profit of more than 86 percent; scandalous to be sure! Unfortunately for the truth, many a contemporary sensation-monger was satisfied to stop there, and too much careless writing since has boosted the figure to a good round 90 percent or more.

As a matter of fact, it could not have approached even the 86 percent figure. The Union Pacific records available showed that of the total payments made under the Ames and Davis contracts almost four millions were in the form of company first mortgage bonds accepted at par value but worth at the time no more than ninety cents on the dollar; nearly six millions in income bonds worth sixty cents on the dollar; and twenty-four millions in U.P. stock worth, on an average, about thirty cents on the dollar. The books showed cash payments to the Credit Mobilier of some $2,346,195 only. Similarly, more than a million dollars on the Hoxie contract had been paid in first mortgage bonds worth about eighty-five cents, and over five millions in stock at about thirty cents. By this reckoning the total profit shrank to $23,374,914.81, or approximately 48 percent of costs.

Furthermore, Credit Mobilier officers claimed additional costs which did not appear in the records. First mortgage bonds had been given away in large numbers, they said, as bonuses to encourage lagging stock sales, and more than five million dollars (par value) of stock had been sold to meet expenses at only $4.50 a share, because that was all it would bring. These losses, they maintained, brought their true cash profit down to only $8,141,903.70, plus the current (1873) value of Credit Mobilier stock itself, which, though difficult to appraise, was put at two million dollars. So, according to their own figures, the building of the Union Pacific Railroad had yielded a quite reasonable profit of about 12 percent.

The Wilson Committee summarily rejected the Credit Mobilier figures and announced its official conclusion: a vast fraud had been perpetrated. The company protested in return that the committee was totally lacking in any understanding of the situation and the unusual problems it had involved. The public, in effect, was left to take its choice. And in the fevered political climate of the day that choice was inevitable: the Credit Mobilier would go down in popular history as a greedy corporate monster guzzling astronomical gains from the public treasury.

Other scandals were to come before the unfortunate Grant administration ended. Not until the Teapot Dome affair in the 1920's, though, would the American people be shaken by so violent a storm of mass outrage as ensued now. It rocked the nation to its heels; tarred all "Wall Street" with guilt by association; helped bring on the disastrous financial panic that broke later in '73; ushered in an era of muck-raking journalism that ran rampant for years; and laid the foundations of a public distrust of and resentment against the railroads that have not completely died to this day.

The justice of it all remains dubious.

That the letter of federal law as embodied in the Pacific Railroad Acts of 1862, '64 and '66 was broken in various ways there was, and is, no doubt. Some of Dr. Durant's early financial manipulations by which more than 85 percent of Union Pacific stock wound up under Credit Mobilier control were clearly illegal, since the law set specific limits to the amount of shares any one owner could hold. Examined in detail, many of the relationships between the two companies had been fraudulent; as when, for example, the Credit Mobilier would accept the Union Pacific's check for services rendered, then turn the same check back in payment for U.P. securities and enter the whole thing as a "cash transaction" as required by law, though, in fact, the cash to back the check may never have been on deposit. No one could deny that there had been greed for profit, shameful waste and individual selfishness to the detriment of the construction effort—along with some plain bad judgment and honest error. But the true magnitude of the "enormous dividends" garnered by the participants in the Credit Mobilier was something else again. Somewhere under the welter of fuzzy bookkeeping, accusations, denials and conflicting interpretations the facts lay buried. To a considerable extent, they still do. In later years apologists for the Credit Mobilier arose, but the mass audience no longer was listening. That the dividends, whether large or small, consisted almost entirely of Union Pacific securities—which could have no real potential value unless and until the enterprise was successfully carried through—has not generally been emphasized.

Federal subsidy bonds issued to the Union Pacific amounted to an aggregate of $27,236,512, not much more than half the figure accepted by the Wilson Committee itself as the total of legitimate construction costs. And these bonds were not gifts, but thirty-year, 6 percent loans. The land grant awards were very generous, certainly: almost twenty-four million acres to the U.P. and the Central Pacific together. Over a period extending many years into the future, most of it would eventually be sold at an average price of five dollars an acre. But the great bulk of it had been practically valueless until the railroad came. Any "vast fraud" against the government or the people of the United States would seem to have been extremely well hidden.

In spite of its conclusions, the Wilson Committee was unable to recommend valid legal action against anyone. Not a single individual ever was prosecuted. But politics demanded a victim, and it was Oakes Ames who was on the spot, target not only for the specific Polland Committee charge of "selling to members of Congress shares of the Capital stock of the Credit Mobilier of America, with intent to bribe said members," but for all the inferential indictments being aired in the larger investigation and in the press as well.

Ames knew it. On February 25 he took the House floor to read a long, articulate and well-reasoned statement in his own defense.[4] It might well have served as a defense for everyone else involved in the Union Pacific undertaking. In it he reminded his judges and his accusers that every reputable railroad capitalist in America had refused to touch the Pacific Railroad endeavor prior to passage of the amending Act of '64, and denounced two provisions of that Act itself as "well-nigh fatal blows." One, he said, was the authorization for the Kansas Pacific to make its connection with the Union Pacific at any point west of the one hundredth meridian, which thus provided the U.P. with an aggressive rival for some 516 miles west of the Missouri River. The other was the privilege granted the Central Pacific to build 150 miles west of the California-Nevada border (later changed to an unlimited distance by the Act of '66). By setting up the extravagant race across the continent, he charged, these provisions contributed to construction costs far in excess of all original estimates.[5]

Pointing out with some accuracy that constructing companies on the order of the Credit Mobilier had been the accepted medium of railroad building for twenty years past, Ames declared that profits of 20 to 30 percent for such firms were not considered out of line, and that "upon the construction of the Union Pacific Railroad, estimating it with reference to the magnitude of the work and the risk incurred, no man could reasonably object to a profit of fifty percent."

Denying the charge of bribery, he stated that at the time the stock was sold to members of Congress it "was not anticipated that any further legislation would be needed or asked for." This, however, was not quite true, and hence the weakest spot in his entire defense. In December of '67 Congressman Washburn of Wisconsin had introduced a bill in the House that would have given Congress the power to set passenger and freight rates on both the U.P. and the Central Pacific. The bill had died in committee, and there was plenty of suspicion that Congressional holdings of Credit Mobilier stock had helped to kill it. As for the allegation that the Congressmen had obtained their shares at sub-par prices, he said, Credit Mobilier stock never had been offered for sale on the open market, so had no fixed market price.

Finally—and plainly striving for a rebuttal to the trend of opinion so obviously taking shape in the Wilson Committee hearings—Ames cited official reports from various governmental departments for the six-year period ending in 1872 to show that the savings made possible by the Union Pacific Railroad in the costs of mail service, military transport and other functions would, by the time the subsidy bonds came to maturity, exceed the total of principal and interest due by some six million dollars. The government could not lose, in other words, even if the loan were never to be repaid.[6]

The nation was growing, marching forward. Nothing would stop it, Ames warned, but Congress' own lack of foresight. And on that note of ringing challenge he left the floor.

It was a good try, but quite futile. Every man in the House must have realized that the Polland Committee's verdict was already as good as reached, and that it would be a harsh one. It was: a recommendation that Oakes Ames and James Brooks be expelled from the House, and that the Senate take like action in the case of James Patterson. It was as stiff a punishment as even the rabble-rousers could have expected, and harsh indeed considering the inconclusive nature of the evidence. Most members of the House appear to have thought it unnecessarily so, for when Speaker James Blaine himself led a movement to have the recommendation softened to one of censure for all three men, he faced little opposition. To Ames though, who undoubtedly had been indiscreet at best, but whose good character and dedication to principle never before had been questioned, it still meant incredible disgrace to stand, as he did on February 28, and hear the resolution read out that "the House absolutely condemns the conduct of Oakes Ames. . . ."

There were cries of whitewash from the liberal press. As late as July 2 the New York *Sun* continued to harp on the subject in an editorial asserting,

The record shows that two of the most prominent Republicans of Ohio, GARFIELD and BINGHAM, were connected with the Credit Mobilier . . . [and] entered into the conspiracy which was mainly manipulated by Speaker BLAINE to defeat even the mild report of the committee of investigation.

To Oakes Ames it no longer mattered. Broken in heart and health by the ordeal, he had died of a stroke at his home in North Easton, Massachusetts, on May 8. As an estate for his son Oliver he left the Ames Tool and Shovel Company burdened by debts aggregating several millions of dollars taken on to further the construction of the Union Pacific Railroad, a fact which seems to dispose effectively of all charges that the chief financier of the enterprise had taken any tainted profits from it. For a man who claimed to have become involved in the first place to, as Abe Lincoln put it, "become the remembered man of [his] generation," he had been singularly unlucky.

Notwithstanding the *Sun*'s efforts to keep the embers of controversy hot, and though the Wilson Committee continued in session for some while afterward, the great Credit Mobilier scandal was over.

The *Sun* tried hard to manufacture a sequel out of Central Pacific material. On July 19 it snatched at its readers' attention with a screaming front-page headline:

THE ACME OF FRAUD
The Credit Mobilier Outdone—The
Central Pacific Ring
$211,299,328.17 Gobbled!

In a long story datelined Washington, D.C., the paper traced the beginnings of the Central Pacific company, taking pains to emphasize that in 1863, while stock amounting to some $1,364,000 was subscribed and $863,140 paid in, something more than $1,060,000 was spent on construction and a total indebtedness of $1,045,000 was assumed. The similarity of the latter two figures, according to the writer, "suggests no, or little, private capital expended by the road."

At the end of construction, the story went on, the four Associates and

Secretary Charles Marsh owned, between them, practically all of the Central's $100,000,000 in capital stock, and extensive holdings of valuable land-grant real estate besides. They had also, in 1870, managed to procure an act by the California state legislature permitting the Central to be amalgamated with the Oregon Railroad Company, the San Francisco, Oakland and Alameda Railroad and the San Joaquin Valley Railroad. On June 23, 1870, the Central had absorbed its subsidiary, the Western Pacific; the following October it had absorbed the San Francisco and San Jose Railroad Company and the Santa Clara and Pajaro Valley Railroad Company. Shortly afterward the Southern Pacific and the California Southern Railroad companies had been gathered in.

Despite this striking evidence of growth as a railroad colossus, the Central Pacific's few independent stockholders never had received a penny of return on their investment. Two of these, Samuel Brennan and Orville D. Lambard— determined, said the *Sun,* "to find something through the courts that might be divided"—had brought suit in equity for the profits on their combined 421 shares. "Knowing great disclosures would come," the paper added, the Associates settled the case out of court by buying up the plaintiffs' stock for a half-million dollars, or more than $1,187 per share. Then, however, the supervisors of Placer County, California, who had previously allowed the Associates to buy back the county's 2,500 shares for $250,000, sued in equity to recover the profits that never had been paid, basing their case on the contention that "sale of the stock conveyed none of the prior rights of stockholders."

The plaintiffs' estimate of $211,299,328.17 in total profits was the sum "gobbled," according to the *Sun*'s headline, by Huntington, Stanford, *et al.*

It made an interesting story, factually correct; and the inference of unconscionable greed on the part of the Associates was plain enough. The Wilson Committee, still convened, took cognizance of it by summoning Collis Huntington down from New York City and putting him in the witness chair on July 28.

But Collis Huntington was far too cagey a customer to be trapped by any Congressional committee. He made a superficial show of earnest cooperation, though his memory proved astonishingly poor and his grasp of Central Pacific affairs seemed suspiciously incomplete. To question after question— the whole proceedings reported verbatim in the columns of the *Sun*—he responded with a casual "I don't remember," varied occasionally with an apologetic "Hopkins handled that." The Associates' Contract and Finance Company might have been as fertile a field of exploration as the Credit Mobilier; the committee obviously suspected so. But it was not possible to subpoena the books of that organization. All records, said Huntington blandly, had been destroyed by an unfortunate fire in the company's offices some time before.

The committee dismissed him. Perhaps it was simply discouraged, for it made no effort to call Stanford, Hopkins or Crocker from California. And not even the *Sun* could make a case out of surmise and assumption alone. So the bombshell fizzled out, though some of the stink of suspicion lingered on.

CHAPTER 34

AND IN CONCLUSION . . .

Official Washington's concern with its Great Pacific Railroad did not end for a long time. The matter of interest payments on the 6 percent subsidy bonds grew into a long-drawn and deeply involved contention as the years passed. Legalistic arguments over the actual date of the transcontinental's completion as a "first class road" complicated the issue, and so did differing interpretations of the wording and intent of the first enabling Act of '62. Consequently the U.S. Pacific Railway Commission went on digging into U.P. and Central Pacific affairs in intermittent hearings right up to the dawn of the twentieth century, when the thing was finally settled by compromise, to everyone's relief if no one's complete satisfaction.

Meanwhile, railroad and nation grew and prospered.

The Central Pacific's Big Four all lived to build for themselves the conventional gingerbread palaces of the very rich on San Francisco's Nob Hill. Even Collis Huntington, who never was more than an occasional California resident after 1863, did so. And all—such neophyte railroad dabblers in the beginning—stayed railroad moguls to the end.

Mark Hopkins was the first to go, dying as quietly and unobtrusively as he had lived in 1878. Charley Crocker, having recuperated from his gigantic labors as ramrod of the construction effort by selling out to his fellows and taking a leisurely trip around the world, returned to find that the Panic of '73 had left the other Associates unable to meet their notes for his stock. He thereupon took it back and plunged into railroad building anew as the Big Four steadily expanded their Pacific Coast empire. His death came in 1888, appropriately enough, in his private palace car.

Leland Stanford went on to added prestige and pleasant distinction as a United States Senator; endowed Leland Stanford University as a memorial to the only son whose untimely death was the great tragedy of his life; and through it all remained the Central Pacific's president until 1891, when Collis Huntington unceremoniously ousted him. The two, it developed, had not gotten on well personally since '63, though neither had ever let it affect their mutual interest in the building of the Central Pacific or its growth as an instrument of power and affluence. The ouster was a heavy blow to Stanford, and lavish expenditures on behalf of the university had somewhat depleted his huge fortune. He died shortly afterward, not altogether a happy man.

Huntington lasted the longest and climbed the highest of all. He rose to become one of the biggest railroad magnates of his day, a shrewdly cynical buyer of legislative privilege and ruthless crusher of opposition. Left a widower late in life, he married a young and attractive second wife, acquired an art collection and in his declining years mellowed sufficiently to endow a very few modest charities. He lived to see the new century in, dying quite suddenly at his summer home in Maine in 1900, a perfect embodiment of the crusty, self-made tycoon of American legend and tradition.[1]

Of the Union Pacific men, Sidney Dillon came out of the Credit Mobilier furor unscathed. He served as the U.P.'s president from 1874 to '84 and again from '90 to '92 before stepping up to the chairmanship of the board of directors, which he held for the rest of his life. Grenville Dodge continued as a railroad builder and executive for many years. He spent some time abroad, studying European railroad engineering methods as a special emissary of President Grant; later held the presidencies of the Denver, Texas and Gulf and the Missouri, Kansas and Texas Railroads; was several times elected a Union Pacific director; and toward the end of his long career was retained as a consultant by the Russian government in the planning of the Trans-Siberian Railway. He once calculated that he had surveyed sixty thousand miles of railroad line during his professional lifetime. He died in his eighty-fourth year at Council Bluffs in 1916. Perhaps inspired by memories of the angry clashes with Silas Seymour and Dr. Thomas Durant in the long-ago days of the U.P.'s westward faring, he had written a strangely moving little clause into his will:

As my life has been a busy one, and I have engaged in many enterprises and held many military, civil and official positions, and persons in high official and civil positions have given me their confidence, there may be in my large correspondence private and other matters that would, if made public, give some person pain; and I therefore direct that not a word or line written by me that would reflect upon anyone or give anyone the right to complain shall ever be published or made public in any way.

Dr. Thomas Durant, stormy petrel of the transcontinental enterprise, reaped a great fortune from his Union Pacific stock holdings. With part of it he engaged in one last flier into railroad speculation, as builder of the Adirondack

Railroad in New York State. The Panic of '73 hurt him badly, however, and he was never again active on the railroad scene. He died in quiet retirement in 1885.

In many ways he remains a great enigma. Through the years since the driving of the last spike he has tended to come down as the villain of the story, the archconspirator around whom most of the shadier aspects of the Credit Mobilier scandal have gravitated. Possibly it has been too easy for the casual historian to put him in the role, since he never bothered to defend his conduct publicly while the great undertaking went on, and left no memoirs afterward. Devious he was, beyond any question; a man driven hard by ambition, secretive and unscrupulous. Yet he was still, more than any other individual, the essential catalyst that transformed Union Pacific from an inert and impracticable mass of legislative good intentions into the living human effort that punched its iron out across the Great American Desert to destiny at Promontory.

Like all the rest—Union Pacific and Central Pacific alike—who joined him and opposed him and in the end, one way or another, gave their brains and brawn and substance to the enterprise, he was scarcely all hero nor yet all rascal, but something in between. They all stood a little larger than life, not only the products but the shapers too of the times in which they lived.

NOTES

Chapter 1. WASHINGTON, 1860

1. These two railroads were the forerunners of the present Missouri Pacific and St. Louis and San Francisco lines. In spite of their corporate titles, neither ever reached the Pacific Coast. In addition, the St. Louis and Iron Mountain, a short line running southward to Ironton, Missouri, should be mentioned here, though it does not appear to have had any Pacific Railroad aspirations.

2. *The Education of Henry Adams.*

3. The present Colón, originally named for a member of the great shipping firm of Howland and Aspinwall, which was among the first to advocate an Isthmian railroad.

4. *A Practical Plan for Building the Pacific Railroad,* by T. D. Judah, Civil Engineer, San Francisco.

5. *Theodore D. Judah,* by John C. Burch.

6. *Report of Theodore D. Judah, accredited agent Pacific Railroad Convention, Upon His Operations in the Atlantic States,* August, 1860. The source of the funds Judah spent so generously in his long promotion of the Pacific Railroad is not entirely clear, since his own personal means were obviously limited. Mrs. Judah's parents in Massachusetts were well-to-do, however, and it is possible that he borrowed from them.

7. Anna F. Judah Papers.

Chapter 2. MR. JUDAH'S RAILROAD

1. *A Practical Plan for Building the Pacific Railroad.*

2. Anna F. Judah Papers.

3. Huntington Autobiographical Notes.

4. Anna F. Judah Papers.

5. This line followed the Pit River down into the upper Sacramento Valley. By modern engineering standards it is considered impracticable for a railroad route.

Chapter 3. "WE HAVE DRAWN THE ELEPHANT"

1. In fact, all of these connections were subsequently made, though under different corporate names and not until some time after the first transcontinental railroad had been completed.

2. The telegram has also been credited to Collis P. Huntington, and as the

senior officer of the company he may in fact have been the sender. On the other hand, so little is known of Huntington's Washington activities in behalf of the bill that the claim appears doubtful.

3. At the time, apparently, there was some slight objection to this disposal of land to the Union Pacific, on the ground that some of it was Indian territory and therefore not the federal government's to give away. But in 1862 such an objection was highly idealistic and could scarcely have constituted any serious obstacle.

Chapter 4. THE NATURE OF THE BEAST

1. Like the Pacific Railroad Act itself, the Homestead Act had been held up for many years by the free soil versus slavery impasse in Congress, and for the same reasons.

2. In this discussion of steam locomotive types, the modern Whyte system of classification has been followed. The system provides a numerical designation for each locomotive type by grouping all wheels according to their purpose: leading truck, drivers and trailing truck. Thus the "eight-wheeler" or "American," with a four-wheeled leading truck, four drivers and no trailing truck, emerges as the 4-4-0. The "ten-wheeler," with a four-wheeled leading truck, six drivers and no trailing truck, becomes the 4-6-0. And so on. In fact, though, the trailing truck had not yet been introduced as a feature of locomotive design in the 1860's.

Chapter 5. FOUR STRONG MEN

1. There was a strong Southern element in California, and this, coupled with its remoteness, had led to serious fears in the North that the state might secede. At least one contemporary authority, Alexander K. McClure, a prominent Pennsylvania Republican leader, later credited the strong and forthright Pacific Railroad plank in the Republican platform, as compared with the weaker and more ambiguous stand taken by the divided Democrats, with winning California in the national election of 1860.

2. Crocker Autobiographical Notes.

3. The Central Pacific shops were erected here, nevertheless. But as late as 1880, according to a *History of Sacramento County* published in that year, ". . . there was a good deal of fever and ague in the shops last summer, its prevalence is attributed to the filling in of the slough and the consequent agitation of its stagnant waters."

4. Frederick F. Low, who succeeded Stanford as Governor of California, commented on this vigor and single-mindedness in his reminiscences, *Reflections of a California Governor*. The tone of some of Low's remarks also infers that the ability shown by Stanford as Governor came as something of a surprise to many of his own party members.

5. Huntington Autobiographical Notes.

6. The correspondent was letting his enthusiasm run away with him in one respect. Nevada did not become a state until 1864. But territories were frequently referred to, by their own inhabitants at least, as states.

7. *Twenty-Eight Years in Wall Street,* by Henry Clews.

8. Huntington Autobiographical Notes.

9. There is no record of any Central Pacific shipment falling into the hands of Confederate commerce raiders. But at least one consignment of locomotives appears to have been seized on a War Department priority while still under construction.

10. Gideon Welles, Lincoln's Secretary of the Navy, described the incident in his famous diary. He did not give the names of the California delegation, however, and thus left some doubt as to whether or not Collis Huntington was a member of it. Following the delegation's visit, according to Welles, President Lincoln asked his Cabinet to vote on the proposed gauge. It was Welles's "recollection" that the vote favored a gauge of four feet, eight and one-half inches, and he professed some amazement that the President nevertheless issued his decree in favor of the five-foot gauge. It was dated January 21, 1864. Congress reacted promptly and unfavorably, a bill designating the four-foot, eight-and-one-half-inch gauge being introduced in the Senate on February 2. It was opposed only by Senators from Kansas and California and passed by a vote of 26 to 9. The House passed it without debate on March 2. Lincoln then signed it without delay. The inference seems plain that the President had no strong convictions in the matter but was simply amenable, as always, to any suggestion which promised to hurry the railroad's construction.

11. Anna F. Judah Papers.

Chapter 6. CHICAGO, '62

1. Albert D. Richardson, famed roving correspondent for the New York *Tribune,* was one contemporary journalist who made no secret of being impressed by Thomas Durant. Writing in 1866, he commented on the financier's blooded horses, "the envy of Central Park," and his entertainments aboard his yacht in the Hudson River. But he pointed out that Durant was a hard worker, too: "Sometimes he was hardly in bed for a week. . . . Narcotics and stimulants were avoided that he might keep his brain clear." And Richardson concluded with: "I fancy there were times when he could not have told whether the next turn of the wheel would leave him worth a few millions or a few millions worse than nothing."

2. Durant himself described his procedure in testimony given before the Polland Committee of the U.S. House of Representatives late in 1872.

Chapter 7. A GROUND-BREAKING ON THE MISSOURI

1. *How We Built the Union Pacific Railroad,* by Grenville M. Dodge.
2. *Ibid.*
3. *Ibid.*

Chapter 8. TROUBLES AND A TURNING POINT

1. Crocker Autobiographical Notes.
2. Huntington Autobiographical Notes.
3. *Ibid.*

4. The New York *Sun,* July 28, 1873, reporting on Huntington's testimony before the Wilson Committee of the U.S. House of Representatives.

5. Huntington Autobiographical Notes.

Chapter 9. THE MONEY MEN

1. Omaha's concern seems to have stemmed from the fact that on several occasions during this general period Durant apparently considered, or pretended to consider, another starting point for the Union Pacific at Bellevue, some way south of Omaha. In all probability Durant was simply trying the common railroad promoter's gambit of playing off one community against another in order to obtain the maximum benefits in local concessions.

2. Dey was vindicated in the end, though some forty years too late. The Union Pacific right of way was restored to his original line as part of an extensive program of improvement and rehabilitation undertaken in 1900.

3. The present Laramie Mountains in southeastern Wyoming.

4. *How We Built the Union Pacific Railroad.*

5. The process was named for its inventor, an Englishman by the name of Burnet.

6. *The Ames Family of Easton, Massachusetts,* by Winthrop Ames.

7. The statement was made by Henry B. Blackwell, speaking at the dedication of an Oakes Ames memorial in 1881. Considering that the United States of the 1850's and '60's was an agricultural nation and that barter was the common means of exchange in frontier areas, it was probably no exaggeration.

Chapter 10. THE CLIMBING MILES

1. The Fisk here was Harvey Fisk, a native of Vermont, and not the more celebrated Jim of Erie Railroad and Black Friday fame.

2. Huntington Autobiographical Notes.

3. *Chronicles of the Builders of the Commonwealth,* by Hubert Howe Bancroft.

4. *Beyond the Mississippi,* by Albert D. Richardson.

5. These changes do not necessarily reflect on Judah's skill in running the original survey. It was not uncommon for the specific line locations to vary from such originals. And the bulk of Judah's early survey work had of course been directed toward proving that a feasible route existed, with less emphasis on locating the best practicable line.

6. Not to be confused with the present Western Pacific Railroad.

Chapter 11. HIGHBALL ON THE PLAINS

1. The Casement firm included a third brother, who does not, however, appear to have been an active figure in the Union Pacific endeavor.

2. *How We Built the Union Pacific Railroad.*

Chapter 12. GENERAL DODGE'S ARMY

1. Such special hunts seem to have been the only ones staged by the Union Pacific, and there are no records to indicate that they ever were offered on a com-

mercial basis. This was in marked contrast to the practice on the rival Kansas Pacific, which a little later on did a good passenger business in special sportsmen's trains, usually run from Kansas City out to Sheridan Station in Colorado Territory. Contemporary illustrations showing buffalo being slaughtered from these trains have sometimes been identified with the Union Pacific, probably due to confusion arising from the Kansas Pacific's early title of Union Pacific, Eastern Division.

Chapter 13. MERIDIAN 100

1. *How We Built the Union Pacific Railroad.*
2. *Ibid.*
3. Actually, of course, the old Leavenworth, Pawnee and Western had dropped out of the race almost immediately, being superseded by Samuel Hallet and Company. But the element of rivalry remained.

Chapter 14. THE WHEELS ROLL WEST

1. *Building the Pacific Railway,* by Edwin L. Sabin. Mr. Sabin did not specify the source of his information. But the possibility is suggested that this *Pioneer on Wheels* may have been confused with, or was an early version of, Leigh Freeman's *Frontier Index,* which figured somewhat more prominently in the Union Pacific story later on. Freeman is known to have started his paper at Kearney and to have followed the U.P. from town to town, though the earliest issue of the *Index* now extant is dated at Fort Sanders, Dakotah Territory, March 6, 1868.

Chapter 15. CAPE HORN PASSAGE

1. The Wilder reminiscences were among original source material assembled in the 1920's by Erle Heath, editor of the *Southern Pacific Bulletin* and published under the title, *Trail to Rail.*
2. By something of a coincidence, the town was named for John J. Cisco, Assistant United States Treasurer and Union Pacific treasurer.
3. *Chronicles of the Builders of the Commonwealth.*
4. Like most folk songs, this one has been handed down in a host of different versions. The lines here are quoted as being particularly appropriate to the Central Pacific. But other variations of the same song undoubtedly were sung along the Union Pacific grades, too, and on many another American railroad as well.
5. It was not adopted, nationwide, until 1883.
6. Huntington Autobiographical Notes.
7. *Ibid.*

Chapter 16. TIME OF TRIAL

1. *Chronicles of the Builders of the Commonwealth.*
2. Development of the fulminate of mercury detonating cap, patented by the Swedish chemist Alfred Nobel in 1864, was the first step toward making nitro-glycerin a safe and reliable explosive. Obviously, however, the fulminate of mercury cap was not available to the Central Pacific builders in '66.

3. According to *Trail to Rail,* a Hollywood motion picture company endeavored to duplicate this feat during the 1920's by transporting a single small locomotive by trail over the Sierra crest. Though possessed of several advantages not available to Crocker and his men—including modern steel cables, block and tackle of the latest improved type and a large Southern Pacific locomotive to supply plenty of steam power—they gave up the effort as too arduous after only some five hundred yards.

Chapter 17. WAR PATHS AND SURVEY STAKES

1. The letter is quoted in Grenville Dodge's unfinished personal memoirs in the Council Bluffs, Iowa, Public Library.
2. Contemporary letters from Samuel Reed and Grenville Dodge to their wives make this abundantly clear.

Chapter 18. "THUNDER ALL ALONG THE SKY"

1. The present Lexington, Nebraska.
2. *The Fighting Cheyennes,* by George Bird Grinnell.
3. According to Porcupine, the Cheyenne brave, another trainman ran forward to the wrecked locomotive and was killed by the Indians. But there are no records indicating that anyone but the engineer and fireman died. Porcupine's story also makes it apparent that he confused the surviving members of the train crew with men from the following train.
4. *My Early Travels and Adventures in America and Asia,* by Henry M. Stanley.

Chapter 19. SIERRA SUMMIT

1. Huntington Autobiographical Notes.
2. *Trail to Rail.*
3. Huntington Autobiographical Notes.

Chapter 21. MOSTLY BRIGHAM YOUNG

1. *Three Thousand Miles Through the Rocky Mountains,* by Alexander K. McClure.
2. *How We Built the Union Pacific Railroad.*
3. *Ibid.*
4. However, in an article written for *Scribner's Magazine* in August, 1892, and titled "Historic Moments: Driving the Last Spike of the Union Pacific," Sidney Dillon confessed that issuing this dividend was imprudent, "so that in a short time we were in greater distress than ever for money." And he added that the fact the dividend point had been reached "brought the harpies down on us from outside and led to dissension among ourselves." Even though made long afterward, both statements are significant in view of the situation within the Credit Mobilier at this time.

Chapter 22. THE TRUCKEE TO THE HUMBOLDT

1. *The New West, or, California in 1867-1868,* by Charles Loring Brace.
2. In his personal reminiscences long afterward, Construction Superintendent Jim Strobridge recalled that he saw no signs of the fabled wreckage, nor any skeletons, during the Central Pacific's desert passage, and inferred that the early accounts of the perils along this trail were greatly exaggerated. Strobridge is quoted to this effect by Robert L. Fulton in *The Epic of the Overland.*
3. Here again Strobridge, as quoted by Fulton, disagrees. He claimed that the Army's proffered protection was rejected, on his advice. But on this point at least, Strobridge's memory appears unreliable.
4. Crocker Autobiographical Notes. But Crocker's story of this incident leaves some confusion as to time. He infers that it took place in 1867, as he says just a few pages farther on, ". . . the next year, 1868 . . ." Earlier in the manuscript, however, he states very positively that McQuade's fall from grace occurred at a time when four miles of track a day were being laid. The Central Pacific did not hit any such a pace prior to '68. Since the autobiographical notes were not dictated till some twenty years afterward, it seems most likely that Crocker was a little careless and that the correct year was '68.

Chapter 23. ROARING TIMES AND IRON MEN

1. Hezekiah Bissell later recorded the incident of the Dale Creek trestle's near-destruction in his personal journal, still preserved in the Wyoming State Archives.
2. The collection of Central Pacific memorabilia at Leland Stanford University, Palo Alto, California, includes several letters from Samuel Montague to his assistant engineers. They spell out this emphasis on speed very clearly.
3. *The Ames Family of Easton, Massachusetts.*
4. J. H. Beadle, *The Undeveloped West, or, Five Years in the Territories.*
5. It appears that the Casements passed part of this extra premium along to their iron gangs in the form of incentive pay, each man receiving double wages for every day in which two miles or more of track were laid. There are indications that similar incentives were in force on the Central Pacific, too, as the rivalry grew keener.
6. Documentary evidence on the bet between Durant and Crocker is lacking. It seems particularly strange that Crocker never mentioned it in his autobiographical notes. On the other hand, the story of the bet has been so universally accepted as a part of the Pacific Railroad tradition that it cannot be ignored. It seems completely in keeping, too, with the known, aggressive characters of both men.

Chapter 24. STRIVE EAST; STRIVE WEST

1. Mr. Ericson's story was recalled in an article in the Salt Lake *Tribune* in June, 1961, on which parts of the present account are based.
2. Crocker Autobiographical Notes.

Chapter 25. A TEMPEST AT INTERIOR

1. Huntington Autobiographical Notes.

2. The circumstances suggest that Secretary Browning was taking the most diplomatic way out of an embarrassing corner here. He had a point, nevertheless, in that the routes of both railroads already had deviated quite radically from original expectations—notably in the lines north instead of south of Great Salt Lake, and in the Union Pacific's by-passing of both Denver and South Pass.

3. *The Congressional Globe,* April 5, 1869.

Chapter 26. WASATCH ODYSSEY

1. *The Undeveloped West.*

2. Not even subsequent developments changed Dodge's mind on this score, as his later writings and statements make perfectly clear.

3. *How We Built the Union Pacific Railroad.*

4. *Ibid.*

Chapter 27. MR. HUNTINGTON IN WASHINGTON

1. From the Stanford University's collection of Leland Stanford letters.

2. Huntington Autobiographical Notes.

3. This was a suggestion which later culminated in actual legislation, as will be seen. But taken in the aggregate, the many contemporary comments on the quality or lack thereof of the Union Pacific roadbed and track are contradictory and confusing. Some travelers denounced it in the most emphatic and unrestrained words; others praised it quite as wholeheartedly. Among the latter was Senator Cornelius Cole of California, a devout friend of the Central Pacific, who certainly had no ulterior motive in approving anything about the rival U.P.

4. Huntington Autobiographical Notes.

5. Edwin L. Sabin, *Building the Pacific Railway.*

Chapter 28. YEAR OF CLIMAX

1. From the collection of Huntington-Hopkins letters in the Hopkins Transportation Library, Stanford University.

2. The Central Pacific people had had their own experiences with the necessary bribery of government personnel, too, apparently. In his autobiographical notes, Charley Crocker complained bitterly that various official palms always had to be greased in order to secure prompt delivery of federal subsidy bonds as they came due.

3. *The Undeveloped West.*

4. This is only a part of one stanza of the "Canon Song," which was printed in its entirety in the Salt Lake *Deseret News* of July 31, 1868.

5. Grenville Dodge was the only Pacific Railroad protagonist to mention this incident, and he did so only very briefly in *How We Built the Union Pacific Rail-*

road, many years later. But at least one contemporary magazine, *Harper's Weekly,* took cognizance of the occurrence by printing an artist's conception of the explosion of one of the "graves."

6. Such Durant-Stanford discussions as took place are only vaguely hinted at, mainly by Dodge in *How We Built the Union Pacific Railroad* and in his unfinished memoirs.

7. Precisely how and when the Union Pacific people got the bad news remains uncertain.

8. This rumored line was remarkably similar to the U.P. subsidiary, the Oregon Short Line, later built from Granger, Wyoming, to Huntington, Oregon, for a connection into Portland. In fact, Grenville Dodge himself declared (in *How We Built the Union Pacific Railroad*) that the "true line" for a transcontinental railroad was up the Platte River to its forks and thence northwestward to the Columbia River for a route to Pacific tidewater at Portland. The inference is that this was known to the engineers even at the time the Union Pacific survey was made. But, Dodge added, the line to San Francisco took precedence from a commercial standpoint. In the 1860's this was undoubtedly the case.

9. Grenville Dodge Letter Books, Public Library, Council Bluffs, Iowa.

10. *The Congressional Globe,* April 5, 1869.

Chapter 29. BIG DAY AT VICTORY

1. Strangely, none of the correspondents who covered the event for California newspapers seem to have mentioned any of the Union Pacific men present by name. But Durant, at least, was a prominent enough figure to have been mentioned, had he been there. Or so it would seem.

2. In their subsequent reminiscences both men, not unnaturally, give the impression of claiming the chief credit. But on the face of it Strobridge, the professional, seems the likelier candidate.

3. Quoted by Robert L. Fulton in *The Epic of the Overland.* But in this instance Strobridge's memory must be questioned, inasmuch as work on the Northern Pacific had not been started in '69, nor had the Associates as yet taken over the Southern Pacific and begun its expansion, as they did later. Purely as idle badinage, however, some sort of similar exchange probably did take place.

4. In *Building the Pacific Railway,* many years later, Edwin L. Sabin reported the personal story of one W. H. Hampton of Colorado, who claimed to have been a member of the gang. His share of the back wages owing, he said, was $478 earned by cutting ties. This, apparently, was the only firsthand account of the affair ever written. But even Hampton's story is confusing, for he sets the date of Durant's detention as May 11, on the return trip eastward *after* the ceremony at Promontory. This is so wholly at variance with every other account as to be virtually impossible.

Chapter 30. GREAT EXPECTATIONS

1. Grenville Dodge Letter Books.
2. The full text of the Rev. Dwinnel's sermon appears in *Trail to Rail.*
3. "Historic Moments: Driving the Last Spike of the Union Pacific."

Chapter 31. "DONE"

1. *Reminiscences of Alexander Toponce, Pioneer.*

2. Information on the number of women present, and their identities, is both scanty and confusing. There is some evidence that both Mrs. John Duff and Mrs. Thomas Durant accompanied their husbands west, though neither appears to have been at the golden spike ceremony. Samuel B. Reed is known to have suggested that Mrs. Reed come out for it, and her purported likeness appears in artist Thomas Hill's celebrated painting of the occasion, as does that of a Miss Earl who is not otherwise identified. But Hill's painting, done on commission for Leland Stanford, is notoriously contrary to fact, since it pictures several people known to have been absent—including Collis Huntington, Charley Crocker, Oakes and Oliver Ames and even Theodore D. Judah, who had been dead since '63!

3. Anna F. Judah Papers.

4. Dillon's estimate was made in "Historic Moments: Driving the Last Spike of the Union Pacific." Dodge made his in *How We Built the Union Pacific Railroad.*

Chapter 32. THE ROAD TO INDIA

1. *Westward by Rail: The New Route to the Far East,* by W. F. Rae.

2. *End of Track,* by James H. Kyner. As a grading contractor, Mr. Kyner later helped build two Union Pacific branch lines, and worked on several other Western railroads as well.

3. *A Congressional History of Railways in the United States, 1850-1887,* by Lewis Henry Haney.

4. "The West and the Railroads," by Sidney Dillon, an article written for the *North American Review.*

5. Colonel Henry Inman, in *The Great Salt Lake Trail,* quotes Grenville Dodge as authority for this statement. Professor Agassiz is not otherwise identified, but was presumably Louis Agassiz, the eminent zoologist and geologist of Harvard University.

6. This delay in awarding "first class" status led to a great deal of later controversy over the legal date of the transcontinental railroad's completion, which in turn affected the interpretation of some of the provisions of the enabling Act of '62—most specifically, those relating to the payment of interest on the government subsidy bonds.

7. *The Emigrant Train,* by Robert Louis Stevenson.

Chapter 33. SPECTACLE ON THE POTOMAC

1. *The Credit Mobilier of America,* by J. B. Crawford.

2. *Ibid.*

3. *Ibid.*

4. *The Defense of Oakes Ames.*

5. The breakdown of all federal subsidy bonds issued under the Acts of '62 and '64 is as follows:

Union Pacific	$27,236,512
Kansas Pacific	6,303,000
Central Branch, Union Pacific	
(Omaha to the 100th Meridian)	1,600,000
Sioux City and Pacific	1,628,320
Central Pacific	25,885,120
Western Pacific	1,970,560
Total	$64,623,512

The actual total cost of these components of the first transcontinental is not so easily arrived at. Many of the early guidebooks estimated the cost of the Pacific Railroad as $181,000,000; the figure may have come close to the truth.

6. Some of the figures cited by Ames did, indeed, constitute striking examples of the tangible benefits brought by the Union Pacific. Official statements by the U.S. Postmaster General put the savings in mail transportation charges by rail as against those by stagecoach at $643,579.55 for the six-year period ending June 30, 1872. But this figure covered only equal amounts of mail handled by both carriers. Since the railroad actually had handled a volume six times as great as the stage lines, the true saving worked out to $3,861,477.30. And this took no account of the far faster service provided by rail.

Official War Department figures indicated a total saving on military transport for the same period of $6,507,282.85.

No official figures were available on the savings in transportation of Indian goods, Navy Department material and personnel, or coin and currency; but Ames estimated them, probably conservatively, at not less than $2,500,000.

Chapter 34. AND IN CONCLUSION . . .

1. Huntington's own correspondence provides ample evidence of his down-to-earth attitude toward both Congress and his business rivals in the years following '69. His letters frequently included instructions (not always obeyed, though) that the recipient destroy them after reading. Much of this correspondence is preserved today in the libraries of Leland Stanford University.

BIBLIOGRAPHY

BOOKS AND PUBLISHED ARTICLES

Adams, Charles Francis, Jr.: "The Pacific Railroad Ring." Article in *North American Review*, January, 1869.

Adams, Henry: *The Education of Henry Adams*. New York, 1918.

Alexander, E. P.: *Iron Horses*. New York, 1941.

Ames, Oakes: *The Defense of Oakes Ames*. Printed text of statement given before the United States House of Representatives, February 25, 1873.

Ames, Winthrop: *The Ames Family of Easton, Massachusetts*. Privately printed, 1948.

Bancroft, Hubert Howe: *Chronicles of the Builders of the Commonwealth*, vols. VI and VII. San Francisco, 1890.

Beadle, J. H.: *The Undeveloped West, or, five Years in the Territories*. Philadelphia, 1873.

Bell, William A.: *New Tracks in North America*. London, 1869.

Botkin, B. A., and Harlow, Alvin F., editors: *A Treasury of Railroad Folklore*. New York, 1953.

Bowles, Samuel: *Across the Continent*. New York, 1866.

————: *Our New West*. Hartford, Connecticut, 1869.

————: *The Pacific Railroad—Open; How to Go; What to See*. Boston, 1869.

Brace, Charles Loring: *The New West, or, California in 1867-1868*. New York, 1869.

Burch, John C.: *Theodore D. Judah*. San Francisco, 1877.

Clews, Henry: *Twenty-Eight Years in Wall Street*. New York, 1887.

Collins, Frederick L.: *Money Town*. New York, 1946.

Coutant, C. G.: *The History of Wyoming*. Laramie, 1899.

Crawford, J. B.: *The Credit Mobilier of America*. Boston, 1880.

Cutler, Carl C.: *Greyhounds of the Sea*. New York, 1930.

Davis, John P.: *The Union Pacific Railway; a Study in Railway Politics, History and Economics*. Chicago, 1894.

Dictionary of American Biography. New York, 1928.

Dillon, Sidney: "The West and the Railroads." Article in *North American Review*, April, 1891.

————: "Historic Moments: Driving the Last Spike of the Union Pacific." Article in *Scribner's Magazine*, August, 1892.

Dodge, Grenville Mellon: *How We Built the Union Pacific Railroad, and Other Railway Papers and Addresses*. Washington, D.C., 1910.

Dulles, Foster Rhea: *The United States Since 1865*. Ann Arbor, Michigan, 1959.

Fulton, Robert Lardin: *The Epic of the Overland*. San Francisco, 1925.

Galloway, John Debo: *The First Transcontinental Railroad*. New York, 1950.

Grinnell, George Bird: *The Fighting Cheyennes*. Norman, Oklahoma, 1956.

Griswold, Wesley S.: *A Work of Giants*. New York, 1962.

Gross, H. H.: "The Land Grant Legend." Articles in *Railroad Magazine*, August through December, 1951.

Hafen, LeRoy R., and Rister, Carl Coke: *Western America*. New York, 1941.

Haney, Lewis Henry: *A Congressional History of Railways in the United States, 1850-1887*. University of Wisconsin Bulletin 342, Economic and Political Series, vol. 6.

Harlow, Alvin F.: *The Road of the Century*. New York, 1947.

Hart, Alfred A.: *The Traveler's Own Book*. New York, 1870.

Heath, Erle: *Trail to Rail*. Photostatic copies of installments in Southern Pacific *Bulletin* furnished by Southern Pacific Public Relations Department.

History of Sacramento County, California. Oakland, California, 1880. (Reproduction published Berkeley, California, 1960.)

Holbrook, Stewart H.: *The story of American Railroads*. New York, 1947.

Howard, Robert West: *The Great Iron Trail*. New York, 1962.

Humason, W. L.: *From the Atlantic Surf to the Golden Gate, or, First Trip on the Great Pacific Railroad*. Hartford, Connecticut, 1869.

Inman, Col. Henry, and Cody, Col. William F. (Buffalo Bill): *The Great Salt Lake Trail*. Topeka, Kansas, 1899.

Josephson, Matthew: *The Robber Barons*. New York, 1934.

Kraus, Michael: *The United States to 1865*. Ann Arbor, Michigan, 1959.

Kyner, James H., as told to Hawthorne Daniel: *End of Track*. Lincoln, Nebraska, 1960.

Leech, Margaret: *Reveille in Washington, 1860-1865*. New York, 1941.

Lewis, Oscar: *The Big Four*. New York, 1938.

Low, Frederick F.: *Reflections of a California Governor*, edited, with preface and notes, by Robert H. Becker. Sacramento, California, 1959.

McClure, Col. Alexander F.: *Three Thousand Miles Through the Rocky Mountains*. Philadelphia, 1869.

Nevada Writers' Project of the Works Progress Administration: *Nevada—A Guide to the Silver State*. Portland, Oregon, 1940.

North, Major Frank J.: *The Journal of an Indian Fighter*. 1869 diary of Major North, published in *Nebraska History*, June, 1958.

Olson, James C.: *History of Nebraska*. Lincoln, 1955.

Perkins, J. R.: *Trails, Rails and War—The Life of General G. M. Dodge*. Indianapolis, Indiana, 1929.

Rae, W. F.: *Westward by Rail: The New Route to the Far East*. New York, 1871.

Richardson, Albert D.: *Beyond the Mississippi*. Hartford, Connecticut, 1867.

———: *Garnered Sheaves from the Writings of Albert D. Richardson*, collected and arranged by his wife. Hartford, 1880.

Russell, A. J.: *The Great West Illustrated in a Series of Photographic Views Across the Continent; taken along the line of the Union Pacific Railroad west from Omaha, Nebraska*. Union Pacific Railroad Co., New York, 1869.

Sabin, Edwin L.: *Building the Pacific Railway*. Philadelphia, 1919.

Salt Lake *Tribune*: Feature story on Bear River City riot published in June, 1961. Photostatic copy of clipping furnished by Department of Public Relations, Union Pacific Railroad Co.

Sandoz, Mari: *The Buffalo Hunters*. New York, 1954.

Savage, James W., and Bell, John T.: *History of the City of Omaha, Nebraska*. New York, 1894.

Seymour, Silas: *Incidents of a Trip Through the Great Platte Valley to the Rocky Mountains and Laramie Plains in the Fall of 1866*. New York, 1867.

Silcox, L. K.: *Safety in Early American Railway Operation, 1853-1871*. Princeton, New Jersey, 1936.

Stanley, Henry M.: *My Early Travels and Adventures in America and Asia*. New York, 1895.

————: *The Autobiography of Sir Henry Morton Stanley*. Boston, 1909.

Starr, John W.: *Lincoln and the Railroads*. New York, 1930.

Stillman, Dr. J. D. B.: "The Last Tie." Article in the *Overland Monthly*, July, 1869.

Stone, Irving: Men to Match My Mountains. New York, 1956.

Toponce, Mrs. Kate: *Reminiscences of Alexander Toponce, Pioneer*. Privately printed, Ogden, Utah, 1923.

Union Pacific Railroad Company: *The Great Union Pacific Railroad Excursion to the Hundredth Meridian: From New York to Platte City. Incidents of the Excursion—Character of the Country—Statistics of the Road—Its Progress and Trade*. Chicago, 1867.

Utah Writers' Project of the Works Progress Administration: *A Guide to Utah*. New York, 1941.

Wibberly, Leonard Patrick O'Connor: "The Coming of the Green." Excerpts from book, *American Heritage Magazine*, August, 1958.

Writers' Program of the Works Progress Administration in the State of Oregon: *Oregon, End of the Trail*. Portland, Oregon, 1941.

Wyoming Writers' Project of the Works Progress Administration: *Wyoming— A Guide to its History, Highways and People*. New York, 1941.

DOCUMENTS, MANUSCRIPTS AND LETTERS

Anna F. Judah Papers: A collection of letters written by Mrs. Judah to Bancroft researchers Amos Catlin and David R. Sessions, about 1889. The Bancroft Library, University of California, Berkeley, California.

Bishop, Francis A.: *A Report of the Chief Engineer on the Survey and Cost of Construction of the San Francisco and Washoe Railroad of California: Crossing the Sierra Nevada Mountains from Placerville to the Eastern Boundary of California, on the Line of Business from San Francisco to the Silver Mines of Nevada*. San Francisco, 1865.

Credit Mobilier Investigation: Report No. 77, House of Representatives, 42nd Congress, Third Session, 1873. National Archives.

Crocker Autobiographical Notes: A personal dictation by Charles Crocker, recorded by an unidentified researcher for Hubert Howe Bancroft. Thought to have been done during 1888. The Bancroft Library.

Fisk, Harvey (Fisk and Hatch): *Communications with the Pacific: an account of the Central Pacific Railroad of California; the character of the work; its progress, resources, earnings and future prospects, and the advantages of its first mortgage bonds.* New York, October, 1867.

————: *Railroad Communications Across the Continent.* New York, May, 1868.

Grenville M. Dodge Transcribed Letter Books. Public Library, Council Bluffs, Iowa.

Hopkins-Huntington Letters: Collection at Hopkins Transportation Library, Leland Stanford University, Palo Alto, California.

Huntington Autobiographical Notes: A personal dictation by Collis P. Huntington, recorded for Hubert Howe Bancroft by David R. Sessions, probably about 1889. The Bancroft Library.

Judah, Theodore D.: *A Practical Plan for Building the Pacific Railroad.* Washington, D.C., 1859.

————: *Report of Theodore D. Judah, accredited agent Pacific Railroad Convention, Upon His Operations in the Atlantic States.* San Francisco, August, 1860.

————: *Report of the Chief Engineer of the Central Pacific Railroad Company of California, on his Operations in the Atlantic States.* Sacramento, 1862.

————: Papers: Notebook, data on Sierra Nevada surveys, cost figures, etc. The Bancroft Library.

Leland Stanford Letters: Stanford University Collection.

Report of United States Pacific Railway Commission, 1887. National Archives.

Samuel B. Reed Transcribed Letters: Union Pacific Historical Museum, Omaha, Nebraska.

Samuel S. Montague Letters: Hopkins Transportation Library.

CONTEMPORARY NEWSPAPERS, 1862-1873

Cheyenne *Daily Leader*
Chicago *Tribune*
Congressional Globe (Washington, D.C.; predecessor of the present *Journal of Congress*)
Corinne (Utah) *Weekly Reporter*
Denver *Rocky Mountain News*
New York *Post*
New York *Sun*
New York *Tribune*
Omaha *Weekly Herald*
Placerville (California) *Mountain Democrat*
Reno *Evening Crescent*
Sacramento *Daily Union*
Salt Lake City *Deseret News*
San Francisco *Alta California*
San Francisco *Morning Chronicle*
The Friend (Honolulu, the Sandwich Islands)
The Frontier Index

INDEX

ABOUT THE AUTHOR

James McCague was born in Chicago, and comes by his interest in railroading naturally. His father was a locomotive engineer on the old Lake Shore and Michigan Southern, later the western division of the New York Central, and there was also a liberal sprinkling of engineers, conductors and brakemen among other relatives.

Mr. McCague helped put himself through Northwestern University by working as caller and roundhouse clerk for the New York Central. He worked as a feature writer for the *Brooklyn Eagle,* served as a specialist in anti-submarine warfare with the U.S. Navy during World War II, and then settled in Joliet, Illinois, from 1945 to 1960, where he held positions in sales promotion and publicity while he began to write fiction.

Now living with his wife and two sons in Sarasota, Florida, Mr. McCague devotes himself full-time to writing. He is the author of four novels, including two with —not surprisingly—a railroad background, *The Big Ivy* and *Fiddle Hill.*

Format by Anne Hallowell
Set in Linotype Times Roman
Composed, printed and bound by The Haddon Craftsmen, Inc.
HARPER & ROW, PUBLISHERS, INCORPORATED

UNION PACIFIC RAILROAD.

NEW YORK AND SAN FRANCISCO

1,000,000 Acres of Choice Farming Land an